11th Edition

Your Rights in the Workplace

Attorney Sachi Barreiro

ELEVENTH EDITION	JULY 2018
Editor	SACHI BARREIRO
Cover design	SUSAN PUTNEY
Proofreading	IRENE BARNARD
Index	UNGER INDEXING
Printing	BANG PRINTING

ISBN: 978-1-4133-2541-6 (pbk)
ISBN: 978-1-4133-2542-3 (ebook)

ISSN: 2152-6508 (print)
ISSN: 2371-9982 (online)

This book covers only United States law, unless it specifically states otherwise.

Please note

We believe accurate, plain-English legal information should help you solve many of your own legal problems. But this text is not a substitute for personalized advice from a knowledgeable lawyer. If you want the help of a trained professional—and we'll always point out situations in which we think that's a good idea—consult an attorney licensed to practice in your state.

Acknowledgments

Many people—both outside and inside Nolo—gave their time, expertise, and wise counsel to help make this tome possible initially.

Subsequent editions have been made possible by the many workers since then who have shared their stories, their pains, and gains.

My heartfelt thanks to all.

About the Author

Sachi Barreiro is a legal editor at Nolo specializing in employment law and workers' compensation law. Before joining Nolo, Sachi was in private practice as an employment lawyer, advising businesses on their legal obligations to employees and litigating a variety of employment matters. Prior to that, she gained valuable litigation experience representing plaintiffs in personal injury lawsuits. She is also the coauthor of *The Manager's Legal Handbook* and *The Essential Guide to Federal Employment Laws*.

Table of Contents

Appendix

Your Rights in the Workplace

Maybe you're just curious. Or maybe you're the cautious type who likes to think ahead and prevent a wrong before it happens. More likely, though, you're reading this book because you already have a work-related problem that you need help with, such as:

- You weren't hired for a job and you have good reason to suspect it was because of your race or your disability.
- Your employer promoted a less-qualified person to fill a position you were promised.
- You want to know your legal rights if you consistently work overtime, you want to take leave to care for a sick parent, or you are called to serve on a jury.
- You have just been laid off and you're wondering if you have the right to get your job back, to get unemployment payments, or to get severance pay.
- You want help evaluating a new job you've been offered. Or you want to find out your legal rights as a jobseeker.

This book will help you understand the legal rights that apply to your situation. It explains federal workplace laws, such as those guaranteeing your rights to be paid fairly and on time and to work free from discrimination. It also explains the many state laws that affect your workplace rights, which are often more generous to employees than federal law. Several cities have their own laws as well; however, they are too numerous to include in this book. Contact your local government to learn about these laws, especially if you live in a large metropolitan area. You are entitled to the protections of whichever law is the most beneficial to you.

This book explains the laws that apply to private employers. Many of these laws also apply to government employees. However, there are several areas where government employees have different rights than private employees; these laws are not covered by this book.

While some might prefer to read this book cover to cover, we have also designed it so that you can flip to a particular chapter and quickly find the answer to your questions. For situations that are fact-specific or complex, we also point out where it would be wise to consult with a lawyer.

Also, be aware that there are many public and private agencies, groups, and organizations that specialize in workplace issues, and many of them provide free— or low-cost—counseling, support, or referrals. You will find information on these organizations peppered throughout the book and in a comprehensive listing in the appendix.

Analyzing Your Options

If you think your employer is breaking the law, it's natural to feel angry and want to sue. However, in most cases, immediately running to the courthouse is a bad idea. Although lawsuits are necessary in some cases, they can be costly and time-consuming. And, in some cases, the law actually requires you to notify your employer of a problem or take other action before filing a lawsuit. The better course of action is to know your rights, try to work it out with your employer, gather documentation, and then consult with a lawyer about taking legal action.

Talking It Over With Your Employer

Don't overlook the obvious: First, try talking over your workplace problem with your employer. An intelligent discussion can resolve many wrongs, or at least get your differences out on the table. Most companies want to stay within the law and avoid legal tangles. So, the odds are that your problem is the result of an oversight, a misunderstanding, or a lack of legal knowledge.

Here are a few tips on how to present your concerns to your employer or former employer.

Know your rights. The more you know about your legal rights in the workplace—to be paid fairly and on time, to do your job free from discrimination and retaliation, to work in a safe and healthy place—the more confident you will be in presenting your problem. This book offers a wealth of information about the basic laws of the workplace, and tells you where to turn if you

need more specific information to clarify your rights.

Also, the book contains a number of charts summarizing state laws on various workplace rights, including specific penalties that may be imposed on employers that violate them. It's probably not worth it to sue your employer over a violation of a law requiring paid time off for voting or for a single miscalculation of overtime pay. But knowing whether a particular transgression can be punished with a fine, a criminal conviction, or an order to rehire you is the kind of information that can make your employer take your complaint more seriously in the bargaining process.

Stick to the facts. Keeping your legal rights firmly in mind, write a brief summary of what has gone wrong and your recommendation for resolving the problem. It often helps to have someone who is more objective than you are, such as a friend or family member, review the facts of your workplace problem with you and discuss possible approaches to resolving it.

Check the facts again. The human memory is not nearly as accurate as we like to think it is, particularly when it comes to remembering numbers and dates. Before you approach your employer with a complaint about your pay, check to be sure your math is correct. If your beef is about a discriminatory remark, do your best to quote it verbatim. Review all of your written records to make sure you haven't overlooked a past event or pivotal memo.

Don't be overly emotional. Recognize that dealing with a workplace problem can be stressful. After all, if you are like most workers, you spend about half of your waking hours on the job. Or you may be out of work and having a hard time finding a new job. Acknowledge that these pressures of time and money can make it more difficult to deal with a workplace problem. Then vow to proceed as calmly and rationally as possible.

Stay on the job if possible. If your job is on shaky ground, try not to jeopardize it further by losing your temper and getting fired as a result. A calm presentation of a complaint is always better than an emotional confrontation. Remember the common wisdom that it is easier to find a new job while you still have your old one. At the very least, it's easier to blaze a new career trail if you leave no muddy tracks behind you. And, in some cases, you won't be eligible for unemployment if you're fired or quit your job.

Be discreet. Discussions of workplace problems are often very personal and should take place privately, not in front of clients, customers, or coworkers. Employment problems can be divisive not only for those involved, but for an entire workplace. You don't want to be accused of poisoning the workplace for your own gain. Ask for an appointment to discuss your complaint privately with your supervisor or another appropriate manager. If you give that person a chance to resolve your problem rationally and privately, he or she will be more apt

to see things your way. However, if your workplace complaint affects your coworkers, you have every right to discuss the issue with them and work together to try to get changes made.

Documenting the Problem

Most employers now embrace the workplace mantra reinforced by thousands of court cases: Document, document, document. If your good working situation has gone bad— or you have recently been fired—you, too, must heed the call. Make a written record of everything that happened, with dates and other important facts. You will have little ground to stand on if you don't have any evidence of your employer's wrongdoing.

A little bit of workplace paranoia may later prove to be a healthy thing. Even if everything seems fine now, take the extra time to create a paper trail. Collect in one place all documents you receive on the job: initial work agreements, employee handbooks, management memos, performance reviews. To be safe, keep your file at home, away from the office.

If you have what seems to be a valid complaint, it is crucial to gather evidence to bolster your claim. From the start, beware of deadlines for filing specific types of legal claims. The deadlines may range from a few weeks to a few years but will likely signal that you have to act quickly.

CAUTION

Don't take confidential papers.
While it's true that you are in the best position to gather evidence while you are still working, be wary of what you take in hand. Confidential information, such as evidence of the company's finances and other documents that the employer has clearly indicated should not be disclosed, are off limits. If you take these kinds of documents out of the workplace, that may actually become a legal ground for the company to fire you, or for a court to limit or deny your remedies for wrongful treatment you suffered while on the job.

There are several kinds of evidence you should collect as soon as possible.

Company policies. Statements of company policy, either written or verbal, including job descriptions, work rules, employee handbooks, notices, or anything else that either indicates or implies that the company is treating workers unfairly may be the most meaningful evidence you can amass. A straightforward company policy can also help bolster your case or complaint if you can show that the policy promised something the company didn't deliver.

Written statements by management. Statements by supervisors, personnel directors, or other managers about you or your work are also important. Save any written statements and emails, noting when and from whom you received them. If you have not received any written reasons for a job decision you feel is discriminatory or otherwise wrongful, make a written request for a statement of the company's reasons.

Performance reviews. Keep copies of your annual performance reviews and any positive feedback from customers, clients, or coworkers. If you think your employer has fired you for a discriminatory reason, evidence of your excellent performance record will be very helpful.

We're All in This Together

Coworkers might be reluctant to help you with your workplace complaint, whether by giving statements of their own experiences or by backing up your story of what has occurred. You might run into the same common reaction: "I don't want to get involved."

People might be afraid they'll lose their jobs or suffer in some other way if they pitch in. You may be able to persuade them to help you by reassuring them that the same law that prohibits the initial wrongful treatment also specifically prohibits the company or union from retaliating against anyone who helps in an investigation of your claim.

However, if your attempts to coax coworkers are unsuccessful, respect their rights to remain mum; proceed with whatever other good evidence you can garner.

Verbal comments. In many cases, employers and their managers do not write down their reasons for making an employment decision. In such cases, you may still be able to document your claim with evidence of verbal statements by supervisors or others concerning unwritten company policy or undocumented reasons for a particular action involving your job.

Make accurate notes of what was said as soon as you can after the statement is made. Also note the time and place the statement was made, who else was present, and the conversation surrounding it. If others heard the statement, try to get them to write down their recollections and have them sign that statement. Or have them sign your written version of the statement, indicating that it accurately reflects what they heard.

Considering Legal Action

Wipe the dollar signs from your eyes. While it's true that some workers have won multi-million dollar judgments against their employers, it's also true that such judgments are very few and far between. There are several things to think about before you decide to launch a no-holds-barred legal challenge to your firing or wrongful workplace treatment.

Evaluate your motives. First, answer one question honestly: What do you expect to gain by a lawsuit? Are you angry, seeking some revenge? Do you hope to teach your former employer a lesson? Do you just want to make your former employer squirm? None of these provides a strong basis on which to construct a lawsuit. If an apology, a letter of recommendation, or a clearing of your work record would make you feel whole again, negotiate first for those things.

You will need good documentation. As this book stresses again and again, the success of your claim or lawsuit is likely to depend upon how well you can document the circumstances surrounding your workplace problem. If your employer claims you were fired because of incompetence, for example, make sure you can show otherwise by producing favorable written performance reviews issued shortly before you were fired.

Before you discuss your case with a lawyer, look closely at your documentation and try to separate the aspects of your problem that you can prove from those you merely suspect. If you cannot produce any independent verification of your workplace problem, you will be in the untenable position of convincing a judge or jury to believe your word alone.

Taking action will require time and effort. You can save yourself some time and possibly some grief by using this book to objectively analyze your job loss or problem. If possible, do it before you begin talking with a lawyer about handling your case. Once again, the keys to most successful wrongful discharge lawsuits are good documentation and organized preparation, both of which must come from you.

Be mindful of the expense. Depending on the lawyer's practices and the type of legal claim you have, you might need to pay an hourly fee or a retainer up front. In other cases, lawyers work on a contingency fee basis, which means that they take a percentage of your compensation if you win. In these cases, lawyers are very selective about which cases to take on because they only get paid if they win. Employment lawyers often provide initial consultations for free, or at a relatively low cost, so they can review your case and give you an honest assessment of the likelihood of winning.

(See "Hiring a Lawyer," in Chapter 17, for more on this topic.)

Consider other legal options. Filing a lawsuit is not your only option for getting compensation. You can also file an administrative complaint with a federal or state agency for certain types of workplace violations, such as discrimination or harassment, wage and hour violations, and more. These proceedings can be shorter and more manageable to navigate. However, you might want to consult with a lawyer before initiating an administrative claim to make sure you're on the right track.

Get Updates and More Online

When there are important changes to the information in this book, we'll post updates online, on a page dedicated to this book:

www.nolo.com/back-of-book/YRW.html

Wages and Hours

The French writer Voltaire once pointed out that work spares us from three great evils: boredom, vice, and need. Most of us can tolerate a little boredom, and some may even enjoy a small helping of vice. But need is something we would all rather avoid. Although most people would prefer their jobs to be fun and fulfilling, what they likely want most is to be paid—fairly and on time—so that they can enjoy the other aspects of their lives.

The Fair Labor Standards Act

The most important and most far-reaching law guaranteeing a worker's right to be paid fairly is the federal Fair Labor Standards Act, or FLSA. (29 U.S.C. §§ 201 and following.) The FLSA:
- defines the 40-hour workweek
- establishes the federal minimum wage
- sets requirements for overtime, and
- places restrictions on child labor.

Basically, the FLSA establishes minimums for fair pay and hours, and it is one of the laws most often violated by employers. An employer must also comply with other local, state, or federal workplace laws that set higher standards. So, in addition to determining whether you are being paid properly under the FLSA, you may need to check whether the other laws discussed in this chapter also apply to your situation.

The FLSA was passed in 1938 after the Great Depression, when many employers took advantage of the tight labor market to subject workers to horrible conditions and impossible hours. One of the most complex laws of the workplace, the FLSA has been amended many times. It is full of exceptions and exemptions. Most of the revisions and interpretations have expanded the law's coverage by, for example:
- requiring that male and female workers receive equal pay for work that requires substantially equal skill, effort, and responsibility
- including in its protections state and local hospitals and educational institutions
- covering most federal employees and employees of states, political subdivisions, and interstate agencies
- setting out strict standards for determining, paying, and accruing compensatory or comp time—time given off work instead of cash payments—and
- establishing specific requirements for how and when employers must pay for overtime work.

Who Is Covered

The FLSA applies only to employers whose annual sales total $500,000 or more or who are engaged in interstate commerce.

You might think that this would restrict the FLSA to covering only employees in large companies, but, in reality, the law covers nearly all workplaces. This is because the courts have interpreted the term interstate commerce very broadly. For example, courts have ruled that companies that regularly use the U.S. mail to send or receive letters to and from other states are engaged in interstate commerce. Even the fact that employees use company telephones or computers to place or accept interstate business calls or take orders has subjected an employer to the FLSA.

Who Is Exempt

A few employers, including small farms—those that use relatively little outside paid labor—are explicitly exempt from the FLSA.

In addition, some employees are exempt from FLSA requirements, such as pay for overtime and minimum wages, even though their employers are covered. For example, many airline employees are exempt from the FLSA's overtime provisions. And most companions for the elderly are exempt from both minimum wage and overtime provisions.

Exemption and partial exemption from the FLSA cuts both ways. For employees who are exempt, the often-surprising downside is that they are generally not entitled to wage extras, such as overtime and compensatory time. The upside is that, at least theoretically, exempt employees are paid a salary that is handsome enough to compensate them for the extra duties and responsibilities they have taken on as part of their jobs.

A common mistake by employers is to treat any employee who receives a salary, or any employee with a certain job title, as exempt. However, neither alone is grounds for treating an employee as exempt from the overtime rules. Whether an employee is exempt is a fact-specific analysis that depends on the employee's job duties and authority to make decisions, among other things. If you're not receiving overtime pay and you don't think you fit within any of the exemption categories listed below, consult with an employment lawyer.

Executive, Administrative, and Professional Workers

Sometimes called the "white collar" exemptions, these are the most confusing and most often mistakenly applied categories of exempt workers.

Above all, bear in mind that you are not automatically exempt from the FLSA solely because you receive a salary; the work you do must be of a certain type as well.

The Department of Labor has provided some additional guidance on what type of work these employees must perform to qualify as exempt.

Executive exemption. The requirements for an exempt executive worker are most rigorous. He or she must:

- have a primary job duty of managing the business or a department within the business
- customarily and regularly direct the work of two or more full-time employees or their equivalent
- have the authority to hire or fire employees, or provide recommendations on hiring, firing, promotion, or other

changes in employment status that are given particular weight, and

- be paid on a salary basis earning at least $455 per week (meaning the employee receives this same amount regardless of the quantity or quality of the employee's work).

Employees who own at least 20% of the business and are "actively engaged" in its management are also exempt.

Administrative exemption. An administrative employee generally must:

- primarily perform office or nonmanual work directly related to the management or general business operations of the employer or its customers
- primarily use his or her own discretion and independent judgment with regard to matters of significance, and
- be paid on a salary basis earning at least $455 per week (meaning the employee receives this same amount regardless of the quantity or quality of the employee's work).

Examples of tasks directly related to "management and general business operations" include working in tax, finance, accounting, budgeting, auditing, insurance, quality control, purchasing, procurement, advertising, public relations, research, safety and health, human resources, legal and regulatory compliance, and more. Tasks related to manufacturing or selling the company's products or services, for example, do not qualify as administrative.

Professional exemption. Two types of professional exemptions exist. Both have the salary basis requirement, meaning that the employee must earn the same predetermined amount each week or pay period, and it must be at least $455 per week. The following additional requirements apply:

- **Learned professional.** The employee must primarily perform work requiring advanced knowledge: work that is predominately intellectual and requires the consistent exercise of discretion and judgment. The advanced knowledge must be acquired through a prolonged course of specialized instruction in a field of science or learning, such as law, medicine, technology, accounting, actuarial computation, engineering, architecture, teaching, pharmacy, and various types of physical, chemical, and biological sciences.
- **Creative professional.** The employee must primarily perform work requiring invention, imagination, originality, or talent in a recognized creative field, such as music, acting, and graphic arts. For example, actors, musicians, composers, painters, novelists, and cartoonists might meet this exemption.

Teachers also qualify as exempt if their primary duty is teaching or instruction and imparting knowledge in an educational establishment. However the salary basis requirement does not apply to teachers, nor does it apply to doctors or lawyers.

Minimum Salary Level for Exemptions Might Increase

In 2016, the Department of Labor (DOL) passed a final rule to increase the minimum salary requirement for the white-collar exemptions from $455 per week to $913 per week and the highly compensated employee salary requirement from $100,000 to $134,004. However, after a series of legal challenges, the final rule was invalidated by a federal court—in part, because the proposed increases were too high. The DOL has since issued a Request for Information on issues relating to the salary basis test. This is often the first step in rulemaking by the DOL, and it might signal its intention to pass a new rule with more modest increases to the salary requirements. Legal updates will be published on this book's online companion page; see Chapter 1 for details.

Highly compensated employees. Employees who perform office or nonmanual work and are paid total annual compensation of $100,000 or more—which must include at least $455 per week paid on a salary or fee basis—are exempt from the FLSA if they regularly perform at least one of the duties of an exempt executive, administrative, or professional employee as described above.

Outside Salespeople

An outside salesperson is exempt from FLSA coverage if he or she:

- customarily and regularly works away from the employer's place of business, and
- primarily makes sales or obtains orders or contracts for services or facilities.

Outside sales do not include those made by mail, by telephone, or over the Internet. The salary basis requirement does not apply to this exemption.

Computer Employees

This exemption applies to computer systems analysts, computer programmers, software engineers, and other similarly skilled workers in the computer field who are compensated either on a salary basis of at least $455 per week or at an hourly rate of at least $27.63 an hour.

If you work in such circles, you may well know who you are. But the law specifically requires that an exempt computer specialist's primary work duties must involve:

- applying systems analysis techniques and procedures, including consulting with users to determine hardware, software, or system functional specifications
- designing, developing, documenting, analyzing, creating, testing, or modifying computer systems or programs, including prototypes, based on and related to user or system design specifications
- designing, documenting, testing, creating, or modifying computer programs related to machine operating systems, or
- a combination of these duties, requiring the same level of skill.

Independent Contractors Are Not Covered By the FLSA

The FLSA covers only employees, not independent contractors. However, whether someone is a true independent contractor is determined by law, not by the person's job title or how the employer has classified the worker. An independent contractor is someone who is in business for himself or herself: the contractor usually works for more than one business, decides how and when to perform the work, invests in material and equipment, and stands to suffer a profit or loss. An employee, on the other hand, is typically financially dependent on the employer, uses the employer's facilities and equipment, and follows the employer's instructions on how to complete the work.

Courts generally look to the following factors when determining whether someone is an independent contractor:

- the degree to which the employer has the right to control how the work is performed
- the worker's opportunity to receive a profit or loss
- whether the worker invests in equipment, facilities, or materials
- whether the work being performed requires a specialized skill
- whether the work being performed is integral to the employer's business (for example, to its products or services), and
- the permanency of the working relationship.

Independent contractor misclassification is a common tactic used by some employers to avoid paying minimum wage, overtime, benefits, workers' comp, and more. In recent years, the DOL and other government agencies have cracked down on this illegal practice.

Miscellaneous Workers

Several other types of workers are exempt from the minimum wage and overtime pay provisions of the FLSA. The most common include:

- employees of certain seasonal amusement or recreational businesses
- employees of local newspapers having a circulation of less than 4,000
- seamen or women on foreign vessels
- newspaper delivery workers
- workers on small farms
- casual babysitters, and

- in-home domestic workers who primarily provide companionship to those who are unable to care for themselves. (Most domestic workers are covered by the FLSA.)

Pay Docking

One of the benefits of being an exempt employee is that you receive a steady salary, no matter how many hours you put in each week or the quantity of work that you produce. As long as you perform any work during a week, you are entitled to your full weekly pay. This means your employer cannot dock your pay if you miss a few hours of work here and there. Your employer can't have it both ways by claiming the exemption and not paying you overtime, but then docking your pay for tardiness or the occasional doctor's appointment.

When an employer improperly docks an exempt employee's pay, it can lose the exemption not only for that particular employee but also all other employees in the same job classification. This can result in the employer owing large amounts in unpaid overtime. The FLSA carves out a handful of exceptions, though, where an employer can lawfully dock an exempt employee's pay:

- for absences of one or more full days for personal reasons (other than sickness or disability)
- for absences of one or more full days due to sickness or disability, but only if the deduction is made according to a paid sick or disability leave policy established by the employer
- for unpaid disciplinary suspensions of one or more full days imposed in good faith for breaking workplace rules
- to offset amounts the employee receives in jury or witness fees from the state
- for penalties imposed in good faith for breaking major safety rules
- for leave taken under the FMLA, and
- for time spent not working during the employee's first or last week of employment.

Rights Under the FLSA

The FLSA guarantees a number of rights, primarily aimed at ensuring that workers get paid fairly for the time they work. (See "Enforcing Your Right to Be Paid Fairly" and "Filing a Wage Complaint or Lawsuit," below, for an explanation of how to take action for FLSA violations.)

Minimum Wage

Employers must pay all covered employees not less than the minimum wage: currently, $7.25 an hour.

Many states and cities have established a minimum wage that is higher than the federal one—you are entitled to the highest applicable rate. Employers not covered by the FLSA, such as small farm owners, might still be required to pay workers the state minimum wage. (See "State Minimum Wage Laws for Tipped and Regular Employees," at the end of this chapter.)

The FLSA does not require any specific system of paying the minimum wage, so employers may base pay on time at work, on piece rates, or according to some other measurement. In all cases, however, an employee's pay divided by the hours worked during the pay period must equal or exceed the minimum wage.

Many employers either become confused by the nuances and exceptions in the wage and hour law or they bend the rules to suit their own pocketbooks. Whatever the situation, you would do well to double-check your employer's math. A few simple rules distilled from the law may help.

- **Hourly.** Hourly employees must be paid minimum wage for all hours worked. Your employer cannot take an average or pay you less than minimum wage for some hours worked and more for others.
- **Fixed rate or salary.** Employees paid at a fixed rate can check their wages by dividing the amount they are paid in a pay period by the number of hours worked. The resulting average must be at least minimum wage.
- **Commissions and piece rates.** Your total pay divided by the number of hours you worked must average at least the minimum hourly wage rate.

Form of Pay

Under the FLSA, the pay you receive must be in the form of cash or something that can be readily converted into cash or other legal forms of compensation, such as food and lodging. Your employer cannot, for example, pay you with a coupon or token that can be spent only at a store run by the employer. Employee discounts granted by employers do not count toward the minimum wage requirement.

Pay for Time Off

Neither the minimum wage section nor any other part of the FLSA requires employers to pay employees for time off, such as vacation, holidays, or sick days. Although most employers provide full-time workers some paid time off each year, the FLSA covers payment only for time on the job.

However, some state laws mandate that employees get paid time off for sick leave, jury duty, and voting, as explained later in this chapter, and for family and medical leave (see "State Family and Medical Leave Laws" in Chapter 4). And many state laws provide that if employers offer paid vacation days or PTO, employees are entitled to be paid for the unused portion when they quit or are fired.

Tips

Under the FLSA, when employees regularly earn at least $30 per month in tips, their employers may pay them less than minimum wage, as long as they make enough in tips to earn at least the federal minimum wage ($7.25). The FLSA requires employers to pay tipped employees a minimum wage of $2.13 per hour. However, an employer may count up to $5.12 of the employee's tips towards its minimum wage obligations. This is called taking a "tip credit." If an employee does not make at least $5.12 in tips for each hour worked, the employer must make up the difference. Many states have different rules for tip credits, and some don't allow them at all. (See "State Minimum Wage Laws for Tipped and Regular Employees," at the end of this chapter.)

> **EXAMPLE:** Alfonso is a waiter and earns $10 per hour in tips. The restaurant's owner, Dennis, may count up to $5.12

of those tips as a tip credit towards the minimum wage under federal law. This means Dennis must still pay Alfonso an hourly wage of $2.13 per hour, with Alfonso making a total of $12.13 per hour.

During the two weeks or so following a negative review from a local food critic, business slows to a crawl and Alfonso's tips dip to $2 per hour. Dennis must increase Alfonso's hourly wage. Dennis may take a tip credit of $2, but he must pay Alfonso $5.25 per hour, so that Alfonso is making at least the federal minimum wage.

Commissions

When people are paid commissions for sales, those commissions may take the place of wages. However, if the commissions do not equal the minimum wage, the FLSA requires the employer to make up the difference.

EXAMPLE: Julia, a salesperson in an electronics store, is paid a percentage of the dollar volume of the sales she completes. During one slow week, she averaged only $2 in commissions per hour. Under the FLSA, her employer must pay her an additional amount for

To Whom Do Tips Belong?

Until recently, a Department of Labor regulation made it clear that tips were the property of the employee, not the employer. The regulation, passed in 2011, stated that employers could not take tips away from employees, except as part of a valid tip pool arrangement. According the regulation, employers could not take part in the tip pool, nor could employees who did not customarily receive tips—such as cooks, dishwashers, and other "back of the house" staff.

Two federal appeals courts disagreed as to whether the DOL had the authority to issue this regulation. And, in 2017, new leadership at the DOL announced its plans to rescind the regulation and remove the restrictions on tip pooling for employers that pay at least the federal minimum wage and do not claim a tip credit. In other words, as long as employees are paid the full minimum wage for each hour worked, employers would be free to do what they want with tips under federal law.

The proposed regulation was met with opposition from employee rights advocates who argued that the new law would allow employers to pocket tips for themselves. As a compromise, in March of 2018, the FLSA was amended to prohibit employers from taking any portion of an employee's tips or allowing managers or supervisors to participate in a tip pool. Employers are, however, allowed to include back of the house employees in a tip pool—as long as the employer does not take a tip credit.

each hour she worked through the first 40 hours of that week to equal the minimum wage, and more for any overtime hours.

Mandatory Service Charges

What about those mandatory service charges often tacked on to bills for large tables of diners, private parties, and catered events? Under federal law and in most states, this isn't considered a tip. Even if the customer thinks that money is going to you and doesn't leave anything extra on the table, your employer can keep any money designated as a "service charge." The law generally considers this part of the contract between the patron and the establishment, rather than a voluntary acknowledgment of good service by an employee. Many employers give at least part of these service charges to employees, but that's the employer's choice—employees have no legal right to that money.

Some states have different rules, however, intended to make sure customers know what they're paying for. For example, New York's highest court recently found that companies have to give all mandatory service charges to their employees unless they make it clear to customers that the company is keeping the money. And, the state of Washington requires companies to tell customers—on menus and receipts—what portion of a mandatory service charge goes to the employee who served the customer.

Pay Interval Laws: When Should You Be Paid?

How often you must be paid is typically addressed by state wage and hour laws. The federal FLSA states only that the pay period must be no longer than once a month. However, state laws often require employers to pay employees at least every two weeks or twice a month.

State payday laws can be complicated. They may apply only to certain employers or certain types of work, for example. If you have questions about how frequently you must be paid, contact your state labor department. (See the appendix for more information.) You can also find a brief summary of state payday laws at the federal Department of Labor's website, www.dol.gov; search for "State Payday Requirements."

Equal Pay for Equal Work

Men and women who do the same job or jobs that require equal skill and responsibility must be compensated with equal wages and benefits under a 1963 amendment to the FLSA called the Equal Pay Act. (29 U.S.C. § 206(d).) Be aware, however, that some payment schemes that may look discriminatory at first glance do not actually violate the Equal Pay Act. The Act allows disparate payments to men and women if they are based on:

- seniority systems
- merit systems
- systems measuring earnings by quantity or quality of production, such as a piece goods arrangement, or
- any factor other than sex (for example, unequal starting salaries based on differences in experience levels).

Although the Equal Pay Act basically covers the same employers and employees as the rest of the FLSA, there is one important difference: The Equal Pay Act also protects against discriminatory pay arrangements for executive, administrative, and professional employees, including administrators and teachers in elementary and secondary schools.

(Because the Equal Pay Act is enforced along with other antidiscrimination laws by the Equal Employment Opportunity Commission, illegal wage discrimination based on gender is discussed in further detail in Chapter 7 under "Illegal Discrimination.")

Pay for Overtime

The FLSA does not limit the number of hours an employee may work in a week, unless the employee is a minor. (See "Restrictions on Child Labor," below.) But it does require that any covered employee who works more than 40 hours in one week must be paid at least one and one-half times his or her regular rate for every hour worked in excess of 40.

The math is simple if you are paid a single hourly rate.

EXAMPLE: Raymond works for a software shipping company at the wage of $8 per hour. When he works 50 hours in one week filling back orders in preparation for a national exhibition, Raymond must be paid $12 per hour for the last ten hours he worked that week.

Jody, who is vice president of the software shipping company and Raymond's boss, also worked 50 hours the same week. Because Jody qualifies under the executive exemption under the FLSA (see "Who Is Exempt," above), she is not entitled to overtime pay.

There is no legal requirement under the FLSA that workers must receive overtime pay simply because they worked more than eight hours in one day (although a few states require it). Nor is there anything that requires a worker to be paid on the spot for overtime. Under the FLSA, an employer is allowed to calculate and pay overtime by the week, which can be any 168-hour period made up of seven consecutive 24-hour periods.

It is custom, not law, that determines that a workweek begins on Monday. However, the FLSA merely requires consistency. An employer cannot manipulate the start of the workweek to avoid paying overtime, for example.

Also, because of the nature of the work involved, common sense—and the law— both dictate that some jobs are exempt from the overtime pay requirements of the FLSA.

The most common of these jobs include:

- commissioned employees of retail or service establishments
- some auto, truck, trailer, farm implement, boat, or aircraft workers
- railroad and air carrier employees, taxi drivers, certain employees of motor carriers, seamen and -women on American vessels, and local delivery employees
- announcers, news editors, and chief engineers of small nonmetropolitan broadcasting stations
- domestic service workers who live in their employers' residences
- employees of motion picture theaters, and
- farmworkers.

And, finally, some employees may be partially exempt from the Act's overtime pay requirements. The most common of this hybrid type is an employee who works in a hospital or residential care establishment who agrees to work a 14-day work period. However, these employees must be paid overtime for all hours worked over eight in a day or 80 in the 14-day work period, whichever is the greater number of overtime hours.

In addition to the FLSA overtime provisions, a number of state laws also define how and when overtime must be paid. Some states measure overtime on a daily, rather than weekly, basis. In these states, workers who put in more than eight hours a day are generally entitled to overtime, even if they work a total of 40 or fewer hours in a week. See "State Overtime Rules," at the end of this chapter, for a summary of state overtime rules for private employers. Note that if the federal and state law conflict, your employer must obey the law that is more generous to you).

Regular Rate of Pay

To know how much you're owed in overtime, you will need to know your regular rate of pay. Whether you work for hourly wages, commissions, or a piece rate, your regular rate of pay includes your base pay plus any other compensation—such as shift premiums, hazardous duty premiums, cost of living allowances, and the fair value of food and lodging that your employer routinely provides.

The FLSA carves out only a handful of exceptions that are not included in the regular rate of pay. Here are some examples:

- contributions made by an employer to employee benefit plans, such as health insurance, retirement plans, or disability insurance
- reimbursements for business expenses
- premium payments for working weekends or holidays
- gifts made on special occasions
- payments for occasional periods of absence due to vacation, illness, or holiday, and
- discretionary bonuses.

The regular rate of pay is calculated by adding up all of the compensation paid to an employee in a workweek and dividing it by the number of hours the employee worked. If you are paid an annual salary, you can divide your salary by 52 to get your weekly base compensation.

> **EXAMPLE:** Mei is a Q&A tester who earns a salary of $40,000 per year and works 40 hours per week. Her weekly salary is $769.23 ($40,000 ÷ 52 weeks), and her regular rate of pay is $19.23 ($769.23 ÷ 40 hours).

Piece Rates and Commissions

People who work on piece rates and commissions instead of by the clock have a more complicated task in calculating their rates of pay.

For piece rate workers, the regular wage rate may be calculated by dividing their total weekly earnings by the number of hours worked in the week. Employees are entitled to an additional one-half times the regular rate of pay for each hour worked over 40, plus the full piece work earnings.

> **EXAMPLE:** Steven works as a hair stylist at a salon and is paid on a piece-rate basis for every haircut or color. He works 50 hours and earns $800 for the week. His regular rate of pay is $16 per hour ($800 ÷ 50). For his last ten hours, he should have been paid at an overtime rate of $24 ($16 x 1.5). This means Steven's employer owes him an extra $8 per hour for those last ten hours, or $80.

Some states have different methods of calculating the overtime rate or additional protections for piece-rate workers. For example, in California, piece-rate workers must also be compensated for the non-productive time they spend at work (such as a hairstylist who sweeps floors and answers calls in between clients).

For employees who receive commissions, the regular rate is calculated in a similar manner. All of the employee's earnings for the week, including any hourly pay and all commissions, are totaled and then divided by the number of hours worked in the week. Any overtime hours must be compensated at 1.5 times the regular hourly rate. If you have questions about whether your employer is complying with the wage laws on piece rates and commissions, call or visit the nearest office of the Labor Department's Wage and Hour Division; see the appendix for contact details.

Jobs Involving Tips

If you regularly work for tips, the tips you receive are not counted as part of your regular rate of pay when calculating overtime pay. Your overtime rate is based on the hourly wage paid to you by your employer. However, special rules apply when your employer takes a tip credit. In that case, your overtime rate must be calculated based on the applicable minimum wage. Your employer may still take the regular tip credit on overtime hours, though.

EXAMPLE: Lisa works as a waitress in a state where the applicable minimum wage is $7.25. Because Lisa earns a substantial amount in tips, her employer takes advantage of the maximum tip credit of $5.12 and pays the minimum hourly wage of $2.13 for tipped employees. One week, Lisa works 45 hours. Her overtime rate is 1.5 times the minimum wage of $7.25, which is $10.88. Her employer may take the maximum tip credit of $5.12 for those hours, which means she must receive $5.76 for each of those last five hours.

As explained above, mandatory service charges are not tips. If an employer passes on any portion of a mandatory service charge to the employee, it must be added to the employee's regular wages for purposes of calculating the regular rate of pay.

Split Payscales

If your job involves different types of work for which you are paid different hourly rates, your regular rate of pay is determined by dividing your total earnings for the week by the number of hours you worked in the week.

EXAMPLE: Matt works for a company that manages a large apartment complex. He is paid $8 per hour for landscaping work and $10 per hour for administrative work. During one week

in the spring, Matt works 30 hours with the landscaping crew and 20 hours of administrative work. His earnings for the week for landscaping work are $240 (30 x $8) and his earnings for administrative work are $200 (20 x $10), for a total of $440. This amount is divided by the total hours worked, 50, for a regular rate of $8.80. He would be entitled to an extra 50% of his regular rate for the last 10 overtime hours, which is $4.40 x 10.

Alternatively, you and employer can agree before the work is performed that the overtime rate will be based on the regular rate of pay for the type of work performed during the overtime hours. In the example above, if Matt's ten hours of overtime were for administrative work, his overtime rate would be $15.

Multiple Employers

No matter how many jobs you hold, the overtime pay rules apply to each of your employers individually. If in one week you work 30 hours for one employer and 30 additional hours for another, for example, neither one owes you overtime pay.

However, if your work for two companies overlaps or you interface with two companies for the same job, they might be considered "joint employers." In that case, you are entitled to overtime based on your collective hours.

Compensatory Time

Most workers are familiar with compensatory or comp time: allowing employees to take time off from work instead of being paid overtime. What comes as a shock to many is that the practice is illegal in most situations. Under the FLSA, only state or government agencies may legally allow their employees time off in place of wages—and even then, it's only allowed if certain conditions are met. (29 U.S.C § 207(o).) In the private sector, compensatory time is not allowed. Employees who are eligible for overtime must be paid 1.5 times their regular rate for all overtime hours.

Alternative Arrangements

Employees who value their time off over their money may feel frustrated with the letter of the law preventing them from taking comp time. If you are in this boat, you might have a few options for getting an arrangement that feels like comp time but is still within the letter of the law.

You may be allowed to take time off by rearranging your work schedule. This is legal if both of the following are true:

- The time off is given within the same pay period as the overtime work.
- You are given an hour and a half of time off for each hour of overtime worked.

One way is to subtract the time during a single workweek.

EXAMPLE: Josh, an editorial assistant at a publishing company, normally works eight hours a day, Monday through Friday. One week, Josh and some of the editors need to meet a deadline on a book due at the printer. So, that week, Josh works ten hours a day, Monday through Thursday. The publishing company gives Josh Friday off and pays him for a 40-hour week at his regular rate of pay. This is legal because Josh hasn't worked any overtime as defined by the FLSA; only the hours over 40 hours a week count as overtime hours. (This arrangement would not be legal in the few states with a daily overtime requirement, however.)

But you are not confined to an hour-for-hour trade. You can also take time-and-a-half pay in one week, then reduce your hours the next week so that your paycheck remains constant.

EXAMPLE: Maria works at Wholey Soles, a shop that specializes in handmade shoes, and earns $900 during each two-week pay period. Because she needs to prepare an inventory of shoes to have on hand during a street fair, the shop's owner wants Maria to work longer hours one week. However, the owner doesn't want to increase her paycheck, and Maria does not want to habitually work long hours. She works 50 hours the week before the fair and receives overtime pay but takes 15 hours off the next week (ten hours of overtime x 1.5 = 15 hours). Since Maria is paid every two weeks, Wholey Soles may properly reduce her hours the second week to keep her paycheck at the $900 level.

Restrictions on Child Labor

Minors under 18 years old may not work in any jobs that are considered to be hazardous, including those involving mining, wrecking and demolition, logging, and roofing. The Secretary of Labor defines what jobs are deemed hazardous and, therefore, out-of-bounds for young workers. To find out which jobs are currently considered hazardous for the purposes of the FLSA, call the local office of the U.S. Labor Department's Wage and Hour Division; see the appendix for contact details.

Children who are 16 or 17 can work unlimited hours in any nonhazardous job. Children who are 14 or 15 may work in certain nonhazardous jobs, but there are restrictions on when and how long they can work:

- They may work no more than three hours on a school day and no more than 18 hours per week while school is in session.
- They may work no more than eight hours per day and no more than 40 per week while school is not in session.

- During the period that starts with the day after Labor Day and ends at midnight May 31, their workday may not begin earlier than 7 a.m. or end later than 7 p.m.
- From June 1 through Labor Day, their workday may not begin earlier than 7 a.m., but it can end as late as 9 p.m.

In general, children who are younger than 14 are not permitted to work. However, some industries have obtained special exemptions from the legal restrictions on child labor. For example, youths of any age may deliver newspapers, babysit on a casual basis, or perform in television, movie, or theatrical productions.

The farming industry has been fighting the child labor restrictions as well as the rest of the FLSA ever since the law was first proposed in the 1930s, so less-strict rules apply to child farmworkers. For example, children as young as 12 may work on their parents' farms. And workers as young as ten years old may work for up to eight weeks as hand harvest laborers as long as their employers have obtained a special waiver from the U.S. Labor Department.

Many states also have restrictions on child labor. A number of them are more restrictive than the federal law. For example, some require more frequent meal or rest breaks for younger workers. Check with your state labor department for specific laws that may apply to your situation. (See the appendix for contact details.)

Are Unpaid Internships Legal?

Many employers create unpaid internships, offering work experience to recent college graduates or students on summer break. Some employers might view this as a win-win situation: The workers get valuable on-the-job training and they get free labor. This is particularly common and effective in fields that are competitive and glamorous, or while the country is going through an economic slump.

But not all unpaid internships are legal under federal law. Although government agencies and nonprofits are generally allowed to have unpaid internships, the FLSA restricts unpaid internships at for-profit companies. For several years, the Department of Labor used a stringent six-factored test for unpaid internships. Among other things, the test required that the employer gain no immediate benefit from the internship. Because interns usually do at least some work that benefits the company, most internships failed this test.

Since then, multiple federal appeals courts have rejected the DOL's six-factored test and set forth a new, more flexible test for determining the validity of unpaid internships. In January of 2018, the Department of Labor followed suit, adopting the "primary beneficiary" test. This test looks at all of the circumstances and weighs seven main factors to determine whether the internship is primarily for the benefit of the intern, including the extent to which:

- It's clear to the intern and the employer that there is no expectation of compensation for the work.
- The internship provides training that is similar to what would be provided in an educational environment, including clinical or other hands-on training provided by schools.
- The internship is tied to the intern's schoolwork or the intern receives school credit for the internship.
- The internship accommodates the intern's academic commitments by following the academic calendar.
- The internship lasts only for the period of time in which the intern is receiving beneficial learning.
- The intern's work complements—rather than displaces—the work of paid employees, while also providing significant educational benefits to the intern.
- The employer and intern understand that there is no entitlement to a job at the end of the internship.

This list is not exhaustive, and the DOL or the courts may consider other relevant factors. Some states might have different rules for unpaid internships, as well.

Calculating Work Hours

When a work pay period begins and ends is determined by a law called the Portal-to-Portal Pay Act. (29 U.S.C. § 251.) This amendment to the FLSA and several other workplace laws requires that an employee must be paid for any time spent that is controlled by, and that benefits, the employer.

Work time for which you must be paid includes all the time you must be on duty or at the workplace. However, the courts have ruled that on-the-job time does not include the time employees spend washing themselves or changing clothes before or after work, unless a workplace requires specialized protective gear or other garb that is impractical to don off the premises; nor does it include time spent in a regular commute to the workplace.

In other recent legal challenges, some courts have ruled simply that employees must be paid for prework and postwork activities that are "integral and indispensable" to their principal activities, rather than "de minimis."

Those terms as defined:

- **Integral and indispensable activities** are performed as part of employees' regular work in the ordinary course of business, regardless of whether they occur before or after the workday.
- **De minimis activities** are those that take a few seconds or minutes beyond the scheduled workday to perform and that are difficult to account for administratively.

When It's Unclear Whether You're Coming or Going

Questions about whether a worker is considered to be on the job while enroute to it or from it are also relevant for workers' compensation purposes. For example, a worker who gets in a car crash on the way home from work might claim the employer should foot the bill for medical costs and property damages.

Courts and employers usually invoke the "coming and going" rule, which generally holds that an employee is "not acting within the scope of employment" when commuting to or from the workplace.

There are, however, specific exceptions to this rule. Employees will typically still be eligible for workers' comp if the employer:

- was getting some benefit from the trip, such as new clients or business contacts
- was paying the employee for the travel time and travel expenses, such as gasoline and tolls, and
- had requested that the employee run a special errand on the way to or from work—such as picking up supplies or dropping off a bank deposit.

See Chapter 12 for more on workers' compensation laws.

Employers are not allowed to circumvent the Portal-to-Portal Pay Act by simply "allowing" you to work on what is depicted as your own time. Employers must pay for all time that employees are "suffered or permitted" to work. So even if you work voluntarily or without being asked—for example to finish a project after your shift has ended—you must be paid for that time.

For ease of accounting, employers are allowed to round time records to the nearest quarter of an hour. But the rounding practice must average out over time so that employees are not being underpaid for their work. For example, if an employer always rounds down, that would likely be illegal.

In calculating on-the-job time, most concerns focus on how to deal with specific situations, such as travel time, time spent at seminars, meal and coffee breaks, waiting periods, on-call periods, and sleeping on the job.

Travel Time

The time you spend commuting between your home and the place you normally work is not considered to be on-the-job time for which you must be paid. But it may be payable time if the commute is actually part of the job.

If you are a lumberjack, for example, and you have to check in at your employer's office, pick up a chainsaw, and then drive ten miles to reach the cutting site for a particular day, your workday legally begins when you check in at the office. Likewise, a housecleaner who has to travel during the day between customers' houses must also be paid for that time.

Traveling to another city is treated differently:

- **Special day-trips.** If an employee travels from home to another city for a special one-day assignment and comes home the same day, the travel time must be paid. But the employer can deduct the employee's normal commute time. For example, if it took the employee three hours round-trip to travel to the other city, and the employee's normal commute to the office is a one-hour round-trip, the employer would need to pay for two hours of travel time.

- **Overnight trips.** For overnight trips, all travel that occurs during the employee's normal working hours must be paid. This is true even if the travel occurs on a day that the employee normally doesn't work, such as a Saturday or Sunday.

EXAMPLE: Diego works for an advertising company in San Francisco with regular hours of 8:00 a.m. to 5:00 p.m., Monday through Friday. The company sends a team to Los Angeles to work with a large client for an upcoming ad campaign. Diego leaves Friday morning, traveling from 6:00 a.m. to 10:00 a.m. Diego and his team work with the client all of Friday and most of Saturday. They travel back home on Saturday from 2:00 p.m. to 6:00 p.m. What hours must Diego be compensated for?

The travel time on Friday from 8:00 a.m. to 10:00 a.m. must be paid, because it occurs during Diego's normal work hours. The travel time from 2:00 p.m. and 5:00 p.m. on Saturday must also be paid because they fall during his normal work hours. Diego must also be paid for any time he actually spent working during the trip.

Lectures, Meetings, and Training Seminars

Generally, if your employer requires you to attend a lecture, meeting, or training seminar, you must be paid for that time, including travel time if the meeting is away from the worksite.

The specific exception to this rule is that you need not be paid if all of the following are true:

- You attend the event outside of regular working hours.
- Attendance is voluntary.
- The instruction session isn't related to your job.
- You do not perform any work during the instruction session.

Meal and Break Periods

Contrary to the laws of gastronomy, federal law does not require that you be provided any breaks to rest or eat meals.

However, if your employer chooses to provide breaks throughout the day, federal law does require that some of them be paid. Your employer generally does not have to pay you for meal breaks of 30 minutes or more, as long as you are relieved of work duties during that time. Technically, however, if your employer either requires that you work while eating—or allows you to do so—you must be paid for time spent during meals. Also, you must be paid for break periods that are 20 minutes or less.

A number of states require that employers provide meal breaks or rest breaks once the employee has worked a certain number of hours. To find your state's rules, see the "State Meal and Rest Breaks" chart at the end of this chapter.

Breaks for Nursing Mothers

As a relatively new requirement added to the FLSA in 2010, employers must provide employees with break time for expressing breastmilk. The law calls for a "reasonable" amount of break time for this purpose, as needed throughout the day, for up to one year after the birth of the child. Nursing employees must also be given a private location—other than a bathroom—that is not within view of coworkers or the public. An employer with fewer than 50 employees is not required to provide these breaks if it would cause undue hardship: significant difficulty or expense in relation to its size, resources, nature, or structure. These breaks do not need to be paid. Some states have additional requirements; see "State Meal and Rest Breaks" at the end of this chapter.

Waiting Periods

Time periods when employees are not actually working but are required to stay on the employer's premises or at some other designated spot while waiting for work assignments are covered as part of payable time. For example, a driver for a private ambulance service who is required to sit in the ambulance garage waiting for calls must be paid for the waiting time.

On-Call Periods

A growing number of employers are paying on-call premiums—or sleeper pay—to workers who agree to be available to be reached outside regular work time and respond by phone or computer within a certain period.

If your employer requires you to be on call but does not require you to stay on the company's premises, then the following two rules generally apply:

- On-call time that you are allowed to control and use for your own enjoyment or benefit is not counted as payable time.
- On-call time over which you have little or no control and which you cannot use

for your own enjoyment or benefit is payable time.

Questions of pay for on-call hours have become stickier—and more common—as cellphones make employees more accessible thn ever and more workplaces have flexible arrangements that let employees work outside of the office.

In cases of close calls as to whether on-call time is work time that must be compensated, courts will often perform a balancing act, weighing, among other things:

- whether the worker is constrained to stay in a particular geographic area while on call
- the frequency of the calls received
- the length of time the employee has to respond when called, and
- whether the employee is limited in how he or she may use the on-call time.

EXAMPLE 1: Jack works in an office, 9 a.m. to 5 p.m., Monday through Friday, as a client services representative for a funeral director. His employer also requires him to be on call on Saturday mornings in case a business question arises. Jack can spend his free time any way he wants. All his employer requires him to do is to call the office as soon as is convenient after he receives calls, which are infrequent. Jack's on-call time is not payable time.

EXAMPLE 2: Elizabeth is a rape crisis counselor with a social service agency. The agency that employs her must constantly have someone with her expertise available. During weekends when Elizabeth is the on-call counselor, she is allowed to stay at home but must remain near her telephone at all times. Elizabeth generally receives three to five calls during a 24-hour period, most of which she handles through counseling sessions on the telephone, each of which lasts between 30 to 70 minutes. She cannot leave her apartment except in response to a rape report, and she cannot drink any alcohol. Because Elizabeth's on-call time is not hers to control and enjoy, it is payable time.

Unless there's an employment contract that states otherwise, employers are generally allowed to pay a different hourly rate for on-call time than they do for regular work time, and many do. The employer need only make sure that the employees are paid at least minimum wage.

EXAMPLE: A hospital emergency room has a policy of paying medical technicians a high hourly rate when they are actually working on a patient and just the minimum wage when they are merely racking up on-call time on the hospital's premises. If such a technician were to record 20 hours active time and 20 hours on-call time in one week, the FLSA requires only that he or she receive the minimum wage for the 20 on-call hours.

The courts have generally approved such split-rate pay plans for the purposes of both the minimum wage and overtime requirements if there are marked differences in the types of work performed and the employer has clearly informed employees that different wages are paid for different types of work. (See the discussion of "Split Payscales," above.)

Sleep Time

If you are required to be on duty at your place of employment for less than 24 hours at a time, that time must be paid, even if you are allowed to sleep during your shift of duty. If you are required to be at work for more than 24 hours at a time—for example, if you work as a live-in housekeeper—you and your employer may agree to exclude up to eight hours per day from your payable time as sleep and meal periods.

However, if the conditions are such that you cannot get at least five hours of sleep during your eight-hour sleep-and-eat period, or if you end up working during that period, then those eight hours revert to being payable time.

EXAMPLE: Bill works on an offshore oil rig for two days at a time. At the start of each shift, the boat takes him out to the platform, and does not come back for him until two days later. Bill and his employer have an agreement that requires that Bill gets an unpaid eight-hour sleep period each day, so his payable time for each 48-hour period he spends on the platform totals 32 hours. During one of Bill's shifts, a storm caused so much trouble that he had to keep working through the night. That reduced one of his sleep periods to only two hours. Bill must be paid for the entire sleep period that was cut short, so his payable time at the end of that shift would be 40 hours, or 32 + 8 hours payable sleep time.

Vacation and Sick Leave

Vacation and sick leave are highly sought-after benefits by employees. And while many employers offer one or both as a benefit of employment, federal law doesn't require either. No state requires vacation time either, but some do have rules that employers must follow if they choose to provide vacation or paid time off (PTO). For example, in some states, it's illegal for employers to adopt "use-it-or-lose-it" policies, in which unused vacation or PTO expires at the end of the year. And several states require employers to pay out accrued but unused vacation or PTO when an employee leaves the company.

Paid sick leave, on the other hand, has been gaining steam across the country. To date, around nine states and the District of Columbia have paid sick leave laws, as do many cities around the country. These laws require employers to provide a small amount of paid sick leave—up to five days in some states—to employees for their own illness, to care for an ill family member, or for reasons relating to domestic violence.

To learn about the rules in your area, contact your state labor department or visit its website for more information (see the appendix for details). If you need time off for a more serious illness or medical issue, you might be eligible for family and medical leave; see Chapter 4 to learn more.

Time Off Work for Civic Duties

In most states, employees have the right to take time off to serve on a jury or vote (if they cannot make it to the polls due to work commitments).

Time Off for Jury Duty

Some employers doggedly resist the idea of allowing employees time off from work, and apply subtle or not-so-subtle pressure on them to do what they can to squirm out of jury service. Recognizing this, many state laws prohibit employers from firing employees called to serve on juries or trying to intimidate employees into not serving on juries.

A number of state laws impose obligations on employees before they can claim legal protections. In California, for example, workers on jury duty are protected from discrimination only if they give employers advance notice of the jury summons. In Tennessee, you must show the summons to your employer the day after you receive it.

A few states have gone through gyrations in an attempt to reach a balance between the court systems that sorely need jurors to serve and the reality of workplaces that need to remain productive. Illinois, for example, protects night shift employees, who cannot be required to work nights and do jury duty during the day. And Michigan specifies that the number of hours of jury duty plus work time must not exceed employees' regular number of working hours for that day.

Unless employee handbooks or other published policies state otherwise, employees are not generally entitled to be paid by their employers for time off work spent responding to a summons or serving on a jury. (Many states pay a small daily fee to jurors for their service, though.)

However, a number of states are exceptions to this rule. In Colorado, for example, employers must pay workers—including those who are part time and temporary—up to $50

daily for their first three days of jury services. (See "State Laws on Jury Duty," at the end of this chapter, to learn the rules in your state.)

The rules are also different for exempt employees. As we mentioned earlier in the chapter, employees who are exempt from overtime and other requirements of the FLSA must receive the same weekly salary regardless of how much they work. This means exempt employees who respond to a jury summons are entitled to their usual pay, unless they perform no work during the entire week. For example, if the employee is selected to serve on a jury and is out for two full weeks without doing any work, the employee is not entitled to be paid.

Time Off for Voting

Some state laws set out a specific amount of time that employees must be allowed off from work to cast their ballots. In some states, the time off must be paid. Some states require employers to provide leave only if the employee won't have enough time before or after work, when the polls are open, to vote. And most state laws prohibit employers from disciplining or firing employees who take time off work to vote.

Finally, some states impose requirements on employees who want to claim protection under the voter laws, requiring them to show proof that they actually cast a ballot before they can claim the time off. In nearly half the states, employees must give employers advance notice that they intend to take time off work to vote. For information on your state's laws, see the chart "State Laws on Taking Time Off to Vote," at the end of this chapter.

Time Off for Military Duty

A federal law, the Uniformed Services Employment and Reemployment Rights Act (USERRA), provides job-protected time off to employees who serve in the United States military. Employees may take up to five years of unpaid leave for these purposes and must be reinstated after their service, as long as they are not dishonorably discharged. To take advantage of this law, employees must provide their employers with notice of the need for leave and must return to work within a set period of time after their service ends. USERRA also prohibits employers from firing these employees without cause for a certain period of time after they return.

Most states have similar laws requiring time off for employees serving in the state militia or National Guard. Some provide rights beyond those provided by USERRA, such as a set number of days off for training each year.

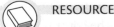

RESOURCE

Specialized government help available. The U.S. Department of Justice, in partnership with other federal agencies, provides additional information and assistance to military members and veterans at www.justice.gov/servicemembers.

Payroll Withholding and Deductions

Since the end of the Depression in the 1930s, the right and responsibility of employers to withhold a portion of your pay has become a virtually undisputed part of American culture. The laws that created the income tax and Social Security programs, for which funds are withheld, typically authorize payroll withholding to finance those programs.

But a growing number of additional deductions are now also authorized.

What Can Be Deducted or Withheld

In addition to Social Security and local, state, and federal taxes, an employer may also make several other deductions from minimum wages: costs of meals, housing and transportation, loans, debts owed the employer, child support and alimony, payroll savings plans, and insurance premiums. As in most other workplace laws, there are exceptions to these rules. And there are often limitations on how much may be withheld or deducted from a paycheck.

Meals, Housing, and Transportation

Employers may legally deduct from an employees' paychecks the "reasonable cost" or "fair value" of meals, housing, fuel, and transportation to and from work. This is true even if it would result in the employee receiving less than minimum wage.

But to deduct any of these amounts from a paycheck, an employer must show all of the following:

- The accommodations are regularly provided by the employer or similar employers.
- The employee voluntarily accepts the accommodations.
- The accommodations are primarily for the benefit of the employee.
- The accommodations aren't provided in violation of federal, state, or local law.
- The employer kept accurate records of the costs of providing the accommodations.

The employer may only deduct whichever is less: the actual cost or the fair value of the accommodations.

Court Judgments

If you lose a lawsuit and a money judgment is entered against you, the successful person or entity can go to court and obtain a wage garnishment if you fail to pay. If your employer receives notice of a wage garnishment, it must:

- notify you of the garnishment
- begin withholding part of your wages
- send the garnished money to your creditor, and
- give you information on how you can protest the garnishment.

Unless you owe child support, back taxes, or student loans (covered below), your creditors must get a court order to garnish your wages. For example, if you defaulted on a private loan or stopped paying your credit card bill, your creditors can't just start garnishing your wages. They must first sue you, win, and get a court order requiring you to pay what you owe.

Federal law places limits on how much judgment creditors can take from your paycheck. They can garnish up to 25% of your disposable earnings (what's left after mandatory deductions) or the amount by which your weekly wages exceed 30 times the minimum wage, whichever is lower. Some states set a lower percentage limit for how much of your wages can be garnished. (To learn the law in your state, select it from the list at Nolo's Wage Garnishments & Attachments page, www.nolo.com/legal-encyclopedia/wage-garnishments-attachments.)

You may not be fired or otherwise retaliated against because your wages have been garnished to pay a single debt. Once you have more garnishments, however, less protection is available. Under federal law, you are not protected from retaliation if more than one creditor has garnished your wages or if the same creditor has garnished your wages for two or more debts. Some states offer protection for multiple garnishments, though.

If you want to protest a wage garnishment, you must file papers with the court to get a hearing date. At the hearing, you can present evidence showing that you need more of your paycheck to pay your expenses or that you qualify for an exemption. The judge can terminate the garnishment or leave it in place.

Child Support and Alimony

Since 1988, all new or modified child support orders include an automatic wage withholding order. (If child support and alimony are combined into one family support payment, the wage withholding order applies to the whole amount owed; however, orders involving only alimony don't result in automatic wage withholding.)

Once the court orders you to pay child support, the court or the child's other parent sends a copy of the order to your employer, who will withhold the ordered amount from your paycheck and send it to the other parent. If you are required to maintain health insurance coverage for your child, the payment for that will be deducted from your paycheck as well.

A lot more of your money can be taken to pay child support. Up to 50% of your disposable earnings may be garnished to pay child support if you are currently supporting a spouse or a child who isn't the subject of the order. If you aren't supporting a spouse or another child, up to 60% of your earnings may be taken. An additional 5% may be taken if you are more than 12 weeks overdue.

You may not be fired, disciplined, or otherwise retaliated against because your pay is subject to a wage withholding order to pay child support.

Student Loans

The U.S. Department of Education—or any agency trying to collect a student loan on its behalf—can garnish up to 15% of your pay if you are in default on a student loan. No lawsuit or court order is required for this type of garnishment; if you are in default, your wages can be withheld.

At least 30 days before the garnishment is set to begin, you must be notified in writing of:

- how much you owe
- how to get a copy of records relating to the loan
- how to enter into a voluntary repayment schedule, and
- how to request a hearing on the proposed garnishment.

Back Taxes

If you owe money to the IRS, the agency can take a big chunk of your wages, and it doesn't have to get a court order first. The amount you get to keep depends on how many dependents you have and your standard deduction amount. Your employer will pay you a fairly low minimum amount each week and give the rest to the IRS. However, the IRS generally works with tax-payers to create payment plans—so if you stay in communication with the IRS, it might not come to that.

If the IRS wants your money, it must send a wage levy notice to your employer, who is required to give you a copy. The notice includes an exemption claim form, which you should complete and return.

State and local tax agencies also have the right to take some of your wages. In many states, however, the law limits how much the taxing authority can take. Contact your state labor department for information on your state's law.

Restrictions on Deductions or Withholdings

As a general rule, the FLSA prohibits employers from making deductions from employee paychecks if it would reduce the employee's pay below minimum wage. (One exception is for deductions of meals and lodging; see "Meals, Housing, and Transportation," above.) For example, employers cannot deduct the costs of uniforms, cash shortages, and property damage when the employee earns minimum wage. However, federal law allows these deductions when the employee would still earn at least minimum wage for each hour worked.

Some states put further restrictions on paycheck deductions. Some common items that are off-limits for an employer to deduct include the cost of:

- company uniforms
- tools and other equipment
- broken merchandise, and
- cash register shortages and losses due to theft.

If you believe you were paid unfairly, you should first discuss it with your employer. It's possible that the issue is the result of a misunderstanding, either by your employer or by you. If that doesn't resolve the issue, or if your employer dismisses your concerns, you have other options for enforcing your rights.

Filing a Wage Complaint or Lawsuit

If your complaint involves what you believe is a violation of the FLSA—for example, a failure to pay the federal minimum wage or overtime—you can file a wage complaint with the Wage and Hour Division of the U.S. Department of Labor. You can call the Division or visit one of its local offices to file a complaint. (See the appendix for details.) A staff member at the Division will take down your information and fill out a complaint form. Or, you can ask for a complaint form to fill out yourself, if you wish. You might be asked to provide supporting documentation, such as copies of your paystubs.

You will have a chance to review the complaint form before it is officially submitted. Make sure that the complaint form and all attached documents are correct and as complete as possible.

If you are assigned to a staff person who seems particularly unsympathetic or unhelpful, calmly and politely ask to speak with someone else. Also, keep in mind that a huge dollop of patience is required. The process—from filing a complaint through investigation and the final outcome—typically takes from one to three years.

Once your complaint has been put together, U.S. Labor Department investigators will take over the job of gathering additional data that should either prove or disprove your complaint.

If the thought of reporting your employer to the authorities makes you apprehensive, take some comfort in knowing that Labor Department investigators must keep the identities of those who file such complaints confidential. If it's necessary to reveal your identity to pursue your claim, the Labor Department will get your permission first. Also, it is illegal for an employer to fire or otherwise discriminate against an employee for filing a complaint under the FLSA or for participating in a legal proceeding related to its enforcement.

If the Department of Labor determines that your employer violated the law, it has the authority to collect unpaid wages on your behalf. The Department can also collect a sum called "liquidated damages": an amount equal to your unpaid wages. For example, if your employer owes you $5,000 in unpaid overtime, you can receive another $5,000 in liquidated damages.

Although the Department has the power to sue your employer in court on your behalf, these actions are rare. Instead, the Department will usually try to handle the matter administratively, by setting up and supervising a plan for your employer to pay back wages to you and anyone else injured by the violations. The Department can also assess civil penalties to be paid to the government or even recommend criminal prosecution.

Instead of filing a wage claim, you may file a lawsuit in court under the FLSA to recover your unpaid wages and liquidated damages. Because this is a much more complicated procedure, you will likely need to hire an employment lawyer. This option makes sense if you have a significant amount in unpaid wages or you have coworkers with similar claims, for example. (To learn more about hiring a lawyer, including the cost, see Chapter 17.)

The deadline, or "statute of limitations," for filing a lawsuit under the FLSA is typically two years from the violation. The deadline is extended to three years in certain cases; however, it's best to consult with a lawyer as soon as possible. The same is true of filing a wage claim: It's best to file well before the two-year deadline, so the Department of Labor has enough time to investigate and try to help you resolve the issue.

Violations of State and Local Laws

The laws of each state and municipality specify which branch of government is responsible for enforcing state and local wage and hour laws, and what remedies—criminal, civil, or both—are available. In most states, you can file a wage claim with the state department of labor to collect unpaid wages and penalties. The department can help you with violations of state minimum wage or overtime rules, unauthorized deductions from pay, and unpaid vacation, for example.

Some states place a maximum on the amount in controversy—for example, in North Dakota, the department does not accept wage claims from employees seeking more than $15,000. The deadline for filing a state wage claim might also be shorter, such as one year from the date of the violation. And, not all states allow anonymous complaints; so be sure to ask whether your identity will be revealed to your employer. You can also sue your employer in court for violations of state wage and hour laws. A lawyer can help you figure out which claims to file and the relevant deadlines.

State Overtime Rules

The overtime rules summarized here are not applicable to all employers or all employees. Occupations that generally are not subject to overtime laws include health care and attendant care, emergency medical personnel, seasonal workers, agricultural labor, camp counselors, nonprofits exempt under the FLSA, salespeople working on a commission, transit drivers, babysitters, other household workers, and many others. For more information, contact your state's department of labor and be sure to check its website, where most states have posted their overtime rules. (See appendix for contact details.)

Alabama

No state overtime rules that differ from FLSA.

Alaska

Alaska Stat. §§ 23.10.060 and following

Time and a half after x hours per DAY: 8

Time and a half after x hours per WEEK: 40

Employment overtime laws apply to: Employers of 4 or more employees; commerce or manufacturing businesses.

Notes: Voluntary flexible work hour plan of 10-hour day, 40-hour week, with premium pay after 10 hours is permitted.

Arizona

No state overtime rules that differ from FLSA.

Arkansas

Ark. Code Ann. §§ 11-4-211, 11-4-203

Time and a half after x hours per WEEK: 40

Employment overtime laws apply to: Employers of 4 or more employees.

Notes: Employees in retail and service establishments who spend up to 40% of their time on nonexempt work must be paid at least twice the state's minimum wage ($572 per week).

California

Cal. Lab. Code §§ 500 to 511; Cal. Lab. Code § 513; Cal. Lab. Code § 860; Cal. Code Regs. tit. 8, §§ 11010 and following

Time and a half after x hours per DAY: Eight; after 12 hours, double time. Agricultural employees only: after 10 hours per day (From 2019 to 2022, this will gradually decrease to 8 hours per day.)

Time and a half after x hours per WEEK: 40; On 7th day: time and a half for the first 8 hours; after 8 hours, double time. Agricultural employees only: after 60 hours per week (from 2019 to 2022, this will gradually decrease to 40 hours per week).

Notes: Employee may make written request to work makeup time for hours taken off for personal obligations. As long as total hours don't exceed 11 in a day or 40 in a week, employer won't owe daily overtime. Employer may not encourage or solicit employees to request make-up time. Employees may, by majority vote in a secret ballot election, opt for an alternative workweek of four 10-hour workdays, in which case the employer will not owe overtime.

Colorado

7 Colo. Code Regs. § 1103-1:4

Time and a half after x hours per DAY: 12 hours in one workday or 12 consecutive hours

Time and a half after x hours per WEEK: 40

Employment overtime laws apply to: Employees in retail and service, commercial support service, food and beverage, health and medical industries.

Connecticut

Conn. Gen. Stat. Ann. §§ 31-76b, 31-76c, Conn. Admin. Code § 31-62-E1

Time and a half after x hours per WEEK: 40. On 7th consecutive workday, time and a half for all hours worked.

State Overtime Rules (continued)

Notes: In restaurants and hotels, time-and-a-half pay required for the 7th consecutive day of work or for hours that exceed 40 per week.

Delaware

No state overtime rules that differ from FLSA.

District of Columbia

D.C. Code Ann. § 32-1003(c); D.C. Mun. Regs. tit. 7, § 906

Time and a half after x hours per WEEK: 40

Notes: Employees must be paid one hour minimum wage for each day a split shift is worked, but not if the employee lives on the premises.

Florida

No state overtime rules that differ from FLSA.

Georgia

No state overtime rules that differ from FLSA.

Hawaii

Haw. Rev. Stat. §§ 387-1; 387-3

Time and a half after x hours per WEEK: 40. Dairy, sugarcane, and seasonal agricultural work: 48 hours per week.

Notes: No employer shall employ any employee in split shifts unless all of the shifts within a period of twenty-four hours fall within a period of fourteen consecutive hours, except in case of extraordinary emergency.

Idaho

No state overtime rules that differ from FLSA.

Illinois

820 Ill. Comp. Stat. §§ 105/3(d), 105/4a

Time and a half after x hours per WEEK: 40

Employment overtime laws apply to: Employers with 4 or more employees (and all employers

with respect to domestic workers).

Notes: Collective bargaining agreement ratified by Illinois Labor Relations Board may provide for different overtime provisions.

Indiana

Ind. Code Ann. § 22-2-2-4(k)

Time and a half after x hours per WEEK: 40

Notes: Collective bargaining agreements ratified by the NLRB may have different overtime provisions. Domestic service work is not excluded from overtime laws.

Iowa

No state overtime rules that differ from FLSA.

Kansas

Kan. Stat. Ann. § 44-1204

Time and a half after x hours per WEEK: 46

Kentucky

Ky. Rev. Stat. Ann. §§ 337.050, 337.285; 803 Ky. Admin. Regs. § 1:060

Time and a half after x hours per WEEK: 40

Louisiana

No state overtime rules that differ from FLSA.

Maine

Me. Rev. Stat. Ann. tit. 26, § 664(3)

Time and a half after x hours per WEEK: 40

Maryland

Md. Code Ann., [Lab. & Empl.] § 3-420

Time and a half after x hours per WEEK: 40; 48 hours for bowling alleys and residential employees caring for the sick, aged, intellectually disabled, or mentally ill in institutions other than hospitals; 60 hours for agricultural work that is exempt from the overtime provisions of the federal act.

State Overtime Rules (continued)

Massachusetts

Mass. Gen. Laws ch. 151, § 1A

Time and a half after x hours per WEEK: 40. Time and a half for work on Sunday and certain holidays (for retail employees).

Employment overtime laws apply to: All employers for 40 hours a week; employers with more than 7 employees for Sunday and holiday overtime.

Michigan

Mich. Comp. Laws §§ 408.412 and 408.414a

Time and a half after x hours per WEEK: 40

Employment overtime laws apply to: Employers of 2 or more employees.

Minnesota

Minn. Stat. Ann. § 177.25

Time and a half after x hours per WEEK: 48

Mississippi

No state overtime rules that differ from FLSA.

Missouri

Mo. Rev. Stat. §§ 290.500 and 290.505

Time and a half after x hours per WEEK: 40; 52 hours for seasonal amusement or recreation businesses.

Montana

Mont. Code Ann. §§ 39-3-405 and 39-3-406

Time and a half after x hours per WEEK: 40; 48 hours for students working seasonal jobs at amusement or recreational areas.

Nebraska

No state overtime rules that differ from FLSA.

Nevada

Nev. Rev. Stat. Ann. § 608.018

Time and a half after x hours per DAY: Eight, if (1) employee receives health benefits from employer and employee's regular rate of pay is less than 1.5 times the minimum wage, or (2) employee does not receive health benefits from employer and employee's rate of pay is less than $12.375 per hour.

Time and a half after x hours per WEEK: 40

Notes: Employer and employee may agree to flextime schedule of four 10-hour days. A live-in domestic worker and employer may agree in writing to exempt the domestic worker from the requirements of subsections 1 and 2.

New Hampshire

N.H. Rev. Stat. Ann. § 279:21(VIII)

Time and a half after x hours per WEEK: 40

New Jersey

N.J. Stat. Ann. §§ 34.11-56a4 and 34.11-56a4.1

Time and a half after x hours per WEEK: 40

New Mexico

N.M. Stat. Ann. § 50-4-22(d)

Time and a half after x hours per WEEK: 40

New York

N.Y. Lab. Law §§ 160(3), 161; N.Y. Comp. Codes R. & Regs. tit. 12, § 142-2.2

Time and a half after x hours per WEEK: 40 for nonresidential workers; 44 for residential workers.

Notes: In some industries, employees must be given 24 consecutive hours off per week. See N.Y. Lab. Law § 161.

North Carolina

N.C. Gen. Stat. §§ 95-25.14, 95-25.4

Time and a half after x hours per WEEK: 40

North Dakota

N.D. Admin. Code § 46-02-07-02(4)

Time and a half after x hours per WEEK: 40; 50 hours per week, cabdrivers.

State Overtime Rules (continued)

Ohio

Ohio Rev. Code Ann. § 4111.03

Time and a half after x hours per WEEK: 40

Employment overtime laws apply to: Employers who gross more than $150,000 a year.

Oklahoma

No state overtime rules that differ from FLSA.

Oregon

Ore. Rev. Stat. §§ 652.020, 653.261, 653.265

Time and a half after x hours per WEEK: 40

Notes: Employees in manufacturing establishments are entitled to time-and-half based on a daily rate (more than 10 hours per day) or a weekly rate (more than 40 hours per week), whichever results in greater wages. Live-in domestic workers must receive time-and-a-half for hours in excess of 44 per workweek.

Pennsylvania

Pa. Cons. Stat. Ann. § 333.104(c); 34 Pa. Code § 231.41

Time and a half after x hours per WEEK: 40

Rhode Island

R.I. Gen. Laws §§ 28-12-4.1 and following, 5-23-2(d)

Time and a half after x hours per WEEK: 40

Notes: Time and a half for Sunday and holiday work is required for most retail businesses (these hours are not included in calculating weekly overtime).

South Carolina

No state overtime rules that differ from FLSA.

South Dakota

No state overtime rules that differ from FLSA.

Tennessee

No state overtime rules that differ from FLSA.

Texas

No state overtime rules that differ from FLSA.

Utah

No state overtime rules that differ from FLSA.

Vermont

Vt. Stat. Ann. tit. 21, §§ 382, 384(b); Vt. Code R. § 24 090 003

Time and a half after x hours per WEEK: 40

Employment overtime laws apply to: Employers of 2 or more employees; doesn't apply to retail or service establishments, hotels, motels, or restaurants (among other industries).

Virginia

No state overtime rules that differ from FLSA.

Washington

Wash. Rev. Code Ann. § 49.46.130

Time and a half after x hours per WEEK: 40

West Virginia

W.Va. Code §§ 21-5c-1(e), 21-5c-3

Time and a half after x hours per WEEK: 40

Employment overtime laws apply to: Employers of 6 or more employees at one location.

Wisconsin

Wis. Stat. Ann. §§ 103.01, 103.02, 103.03; Wis. Admin. Code DWD §§ 274.01, 274.03, 274.04

Time and a half after x hours per WEEK: 40

Employment overtime laws apply to: Manufacturing, mechanical, or retail businesses; beauty parlors, laundries, restaurants, hotels; telephone, express, shipping, and transportation companies.

Wyoming

No state overtime rules that differ from FLSA.

State Meal and Rest Breaks

Note: Certain states are not listed in this chart because they do not have laws or regulations on rest and meal breaks for adults employed in the private sector. Many states also exclude professional, administrative, and executive employees from these rules.

Other exceptions may apply: For example, many states have special break rules for specific occupations or industries, which are beyond the scope of this chart. Check the statute or check with your state department of labor if you need more information. (See appendix for contact list.)

Alabama

Ala. Code § 22-1-13

Breast-feeding: No employment-specific laws. However, breast-feeding is allowed in any public or private location where the mother's presence is authorized.

Arkansas

Ark. Stat. Ann. § 11-5-116

Applies to: All employers.

Breast-feeding: Reasonable unpaid breaks to express breast milk; if possible, break time to run concurrently with other breaks.

California

Cal. Lab. Code §§ 512, 1030; Cal. Code Regs. tit. 8, §§ 11010–11170

Applies to: Employers in most industries.

Exceptions: Motion picture and other occupations. See wage orders, Cal. Code Regs. tit. 8, §§ 11010 to 11160, for additional exceptions.

Meal Break: 30 minutes, unpaid, after 5 hours, except employer and employee can agree to waive meal period if employee works 6 hours or less. Second 30-minute unpaid meal period when employee works more than 10 hours a day, except employer and employee can agree to waive the

second meal period if the employee works 12 hours or less and took the first meal period. On-duty paid meal period permitted when nature of work prevents relief from all duties and parties agree in writing.

Rest Break: Paid 10-minute rest period for each 4 hours worked or major fraction thereof; as practicable, in the middle of the work period; not required for employees whose total daily work time is less than 3½ hours.

Breast-feeding: Reasonable unpaid breaks to express breast milk; if possible, break time to run concurrently with other breaks.

Colorado

C.R.S.A. § 8-13.5-101 through § 8-13.5-104; Colo. Code Regs. tit. 7 §§ 1103-1:7 and 1:8

Applies to: Retail and service, food and beverage, commercial support service, and health and medical industries.

Exceptions: Numerous exceptions are listed in the regulation.

Meal Break: 30 minutes, unpaid, after 5 hours of work. On-duty paid meal period permitted when nature of work prevents break from all duties.

Rest Break: Paid 10-minute rest period for each 4 hours or major fraction worked; if practical, in the middle of the work period.

Breast-feeding: Reasonable unpaid time and private space to express breast milk for up to two years after child's birth.

Connecticut

Conn. Gen. Stat. Ann. §§ 31-40w, 31-51ii

Applies to: All employers, except as noted.

Exceptions: Employers who pay for rest breaks as described below, those with a written agreement providing other break rules, and those granted an exemption for reasons listed in statute.

State Meal and Rest Breaks (continued)

Meal Break: 30 minutes, unpaid, after first 2 hours of work and before last 2 hours for employees who work 7½ or more consecutive hours.

Rest Break: As alternative to meal break, a total of 30 minutes paid in each 7½-hour work period.

Breast-feeding: Employee may use meal or rest breaks for breast-feeding or expressing breast milk. Reasonable efforts to provide private space.

Delaware
Del. Code Ann. tit. 19 § 707

Applies to: All employers, except as noted.

Exceptions: Employers with alternative written agreement and those granted exemptions specified in statute. Law does not apply to teachers.

Meal Break: 30 minutes, unpaid, after first 2 hours and before the last 2 hours, for employees who work 7½ consecutive hours or more.

Breast-feeding: Reasonable accommodations for limitations of a person related to pregnancy, childbirth, or a related condition may include break time and appropriate facilities for expressing breast milk.

District of Columbia
D.C. Code Ann. §§ 2-1402.82, 32-1231.01 – 32-1231.03

Applies to: All employers.

Breast-feeding: Reasonable unpaid time to express breast milk; runs concurrently with other paid or unpaid breaks provided by employer. Employer must make reasonable efforts to provide a private, sanitary location (other than a toilet stall) for expressing breast milk. Employer must provide reasonable accommodations to nursing mothers, unless it would cause an undue hardship.

Florida

Breast-feeding: No employment-specific laws. However, breast-feeding is allowed in any public or private location where the mother's presence is authorized (Fla. Stat. §§ 800.02, 800.03, 800.04).

Georgia
Ga. Code Ann. § 34-1-6

Applies to: All employers.

Breast-feeding: Reasonable unpaid break time to express breast milk. Employer is not required to provide break time if unduly disruptive to workplace operations. Breast-feeding is allowed in any public or private location where the mother's presence is authorized.

Hawaii
Haw. Rev. Stat. §§ 378-2, 378-91 to 93

Applies to: All employers.

Breast-feeding: Reasonable break time to express milk for nursing child for one year after birth each time the employee has a need to express breast milk, in a location, other than a bathroom, that is sanitary, shielded from view and free from intrusion. Employers with fewer than 20 employees exempt if requirements impose undue hardship.

Illinois
820 Ill. Comp. Stat. §§ 140/3, 260/10

Applies to: All employers.

Exceptions: Employees whose meal periods are established by collective bargaining agreement.

Employees who monitor individuals with developmental disabilities or mental illness, or both, and who are required to be on call during an entire 8-hour work period; these employees must be allowed to eat a meal while working.

Meal Break: 20 minutes, no later than 5 hours after the beginning of the shift, for employees who work 7½ or more continuous hours. Hotel room attendants are entitled to a 30-minute meal break if they work at least 7 hours.

State Meal and Rest Breaks (continued)

Rest Break: In addition to meal break, hotel room attendants must receive two paid 15-minute rest breaks, if they work at least 7 hours.

Breast-feeding: Reasonable unpaid break time to express breast milk and reasonable efforts to provide a room or other location, other than a toilet stall, where an employee can express her milk in privacy.

Indiana

Ind. Code § 22-2-14-2

Applies to: Employers with 25 or more employees.

Breast-feeding: Employer must make reasonable efforts to provide a private space, other than a restroom, for an employee to express breast milk and if possible provide a refrigerator for storing breast milk that has been expressed (employee can provide her own).

Kansas

Kan. Admin. Reg. 49-30-3

Applies to: Employees not covered under FLSA.

Meal Break: Not required, but if less than 30 minutes is given, break must be paid.

Breast-feeding: No employment-specific laws. However, breast-feeding is allowed in any public or private location where the mother's presence is authorized.

Kentucky

Ky. Rev. Stat. Ann. §§ 337.355, 337.365; 803 KAR 1:065

Applies to: All employers, except as noted.

Exceptions: Written agreement providing different meal period; employers subject to Federal Railway Labor Act.

Meal Break: Reasonable off-duty period close to the middle of the shift; cannot be required to take it before the third or after the fifth hour of work. Coffee breaks and snack time do not count

toward the meal break.

Rest Break: Paid 10-minute rest period for each 4-hour work period; rest period must be in addition to regularly scheduled meal period.

Breast-feeding: No employment-specific laws. However, breast-feeding is allowed in any public or private location where the mother's presence is authorized.

Maine

Me. Rev. Stat. Ann. tit. 26, § 601

Applies to: All employers, except those with fewer than 3 employees on duty who are able to take frequent breaks during the workday.

Exceptions: Collective bargaining or other written agreement between employer and employee may provide for different breaks.

Meal Break: 30 minutes after 6 consecutive hours of work, except in cases of emergency. Time may be unpaid if employee is completely relieved of duty.

Breast-feeding: Adequate unpaid time to express breast milk, or employee may use rest or meal time, for up to 3 years following childbirth.

Maryland

Md. Code Ann., Lab. & Empl. § 3-710

Applies to: Retail establishments with 50 or more retail employees.

Exceptions: Employees who work in an office or who work at a single location with 5 or fewer employees are not covered.

Meal Break: 30 minutes, unpaid, after 6 consecutive hours of work.

Rest Break: 15 minutes, unpaid, when working 4 to 6 consecutive hours. (This may be waived if the employee works less than 6 hours). Employees working 8 or more consecutive hours must

State Meal and Rest Breaks (continued)

receive a 15-minute unpaid break for every additional 4 consecutive hours after a meal break.

Breast-feeding: No employment-specific laws. However, breast-feeding is allowed in any public or private location where the mother's presence is authorized.

Massachusetts

Mass. Gen. Laws 149 §§ 100, 101; Mass. Gen. Laws 151B § 4

Applies to: All employers, except as noted.

Exceptions: Excludes iron works, glass works, paper mills, letterpresses, print works, and bleaching or dyeing works. Attorney general may exempt businesses that require continuous operation if it won't affect worker safety. Collective bargaining agreement may also provide for different breaks.

Meal Break: 30 minutes, if work is for more than 6 hours.

Breast-feeding: Employers with 6 or more employees must provide breaks for breast-feeding as a reasonable accommodation, unless it would cause undue hardship.

Minnesota

Minn. Stat. Ann. §§ 177.253, 177.254, 181.939

Applies to: All employers.

Exceptions: Excludes certain agricultural and seasonal employees. A collective bargaining agreement may provide for different rest and meal breaks.

Meal Break: Sufficient unpaid time for employees who work 8 consecutive hours or more.

Rest Break: Paid adequate rest period within each 4 consecutive hours of work to utilize nearest convenient restroom.

Breast-feeding: Reasonable unpaid break time to express milk.

Mississippi

Miss. Ann. Code § 71-1-55

Breast-feeding: Employee may use meal or rest break for expressing breast milk.

Missouri

Breast-feeding: No employment-specific laws. However, breast-feeding is allowed in any public or private location where the mother's presence is authorized.

Montana

Breast-feeding: No employment-specific laws. However, breast-feeding is allowed in any public or private location where the mother's presence is authorized.

Nebraska

Neb. Rev. Stat. §§ 48-212, 48–1102

Applies to: Meal break provisions: assembly plant, workshop, or mechanical establishment. Breast-feeding provisions: employers with 15 or more employees.

Exceptions: Other written agreement between employer and employees.

Meal Break: 30 minutes off premises for each 8-hour shift.

Breast-feeding: Employers with 15 or more employees must provide reasonable accommodation to nursing mothers, unless it would cause an undue hardship. Accommodation may include breaks and an appropriate location for breast-feeding or expressing breast milk.

Nevada

Nev. Rev. Stat. Ann. § 608.019, AB 113, § 5

Applies to: Employers with two or more employees.

State Meal and Rest Breaks (continued)

Exceptions: Employees covered by collective bargaining agreement; exemptions for business necessity.

Meal Break: 30 minutes for 8 continuous hours of work.

Rest Break: Paid 10-minute rest period for each 4 hours or major fraction worked; as practicable, in middle of the work period; not required for employees whose total daily work time is less than 3½ hours.

Breast-feeding: Reasonable unpaid breaks to allow an employee to express breast milk for a child under one year of age. (Applies to: All employers. Exceptions: Employers with fewer than 50 employees, if complying would cause an undue hardship.)

New Hampshire

N.H. Rev. Stat. Ann. § 275:30-a

Applies to: All employers.

Meal Break: 30 minutes after 5 consecutive hours, unless the employer allows the employee to eat while working and it is feasible for the employee to do so.

Breast-feeding: No employment-specific laws. However, restricting or limiting the right of a mother to breast-feed her child is discriminatory.

New Jersey

N.J. Stat. Ann. § 10:5-12

Applies to: All employers.

Breast-feeding: Employer must provide reasonable break time and a suitable private location, other than a toilet stall, unless it would cause undue hardship on the employer.

New Mexico

N.M. Stat. Ann. § 28-20-2

Breast-feeding: Flexible unpaid breaks to use breast pump in the workplace.

New York

N.Y. Lab. Law §§ 162, 206-c

Applies to: Factories, workshops, manufacturing facilities, mercantile (retail and wholesale) establishments.

Meal Break: Factory employees, 60 minutes between 11 a.m. and 2 p.m.; mercantile employees, 30 minutes between 11 a.m. and 2 p.m. If a shift starts before 11 a.m. and ends after 7 p.m., every employee gets an additional 20 minutes between 5 p.m. and 7 p.m. If a shift starts between 1 p.m. and 6 a.m., a factory employee gets 60 minutes, and a mercantile employee gets 45 minutes, in the middle of the shift. Labor commissioner may permit a shorter meal break; the permit must be in writing and posted conspicuously in the main entrance of the workplace.

Breast-feeding: Reasonable unpaid break time to express breast milk for up to three years after child's birth.

North Carolina

Breast-feeding: No employment-specific laws. However, breast-feeding is allowed in any public or private location where the mother's presence is authorized.

North Dakota

N.D. Admin. Code § 46-02-07-02

Applies to: Applicable when two or more employees are on duty.

Exceptions: Waiver by employee or other provision in collective bargaining agreement.

Meal Break: 30 minutes for each shift over 5 hours; unpaid if employee is completely relieved of duties.

Breast-feeding: No employment-specific laws. However, breast-feeding is allowed in any public or private location where the mother's presence is authorized.

State Meal and Rest Breaks (continued)

Oklahoma

Okla. Stat. Ann. tit. 40, § 435

Breast-feeding: Reasonable unpaid breaks to breast-feed or express breast milk.

Oregon

Ore. Rev. Stat. 653.077;
Ore. Admin. R. §§ 839-020-0050, 839-020-0051

Applies to: All employers except as noted.

Exceptions: Agricultural workers and employees covered by a collective bargaining agreement.

Meal Break: 30 minutes for employees who work at least six hours, unpaid if relieved of all duties; paid time to eat if employee cannot be relieved of duty; a shorter paid break (but no less than 20 minutes), if employer can show that it is industry practice or custom. If shift of 7 hours or less, meal break must occur between hours 2 and 5; if shift longer than 7 hours, meal break must be between hours 3 and 6.

Rest Break: Paid 10-minute rest period for each 4 hours or major fraction worked; if practical, in the middle of the work period.

Rest period must be in addition to usual meal break and taken separately; can't be added to meal period or deducted from beginning or end of shift to reduce length of total work period.

Rest period is not required for certain solo adult employees serving the public, although they must be allowed to use restroom.

Breast-feeding: Employers with 25 or more employees must provide a 30-minute unpaid break for every 4 hours worked to express breast milk, for up to 18 months after child's birth.

Pennsylvania

43 Pa. Cons. Stat. Ann. § 1301.207

Applies to: Employers of seasonal farmworkers.

Meal Break: Seasonal farmworkers are entitled to a 30-minute meal or rest break if they work at least 5 hours.

Breast-feeding: No employment-specific laws. However, breast-feeding is allowed in any public or private location where the mother's presence is authorized.

Rhode Island

R.I. Gen. Laws §§ 23-13.2-1, 28-3-8, 28-3-14, 28-5-7.4

Applies to: Meal break provisions: employers with 5 or more employees. Breast-feeding provisions: employers with 4 or more employees.

Exceptions: Employers of health care facility or employers with fewer than 3 employees on any shift.

Meal Break: 20 minutes, unpaid, within a 6-hour shift or 30 minutes, unpaid, within an 8-hour shift.

Breast-feeding: Reasonable unpaid break time to breast-feed infant or express breast milk. Employers with 4 or more employees must provide reasonable accommodations to nursing mothers, which may include break time and private space for expressing breast milk, other than a restroom.

South Carolina

Breast-feeding: No employment-specific laws. However, breast-feeding is allowed in any public or private location where the mother's presence is authorized.

South Dakota

Breast-feeding: No employment-specific laws. However, breast-feeding is allowed in any public or private location where the mother's presence is authorized if the mother is in compliance with all other laws.

State Meal and Rest Breaks (continued)

Tennessee

Tenn. Code Ann. §§ 50-1-305, 50-2-103(h)

Applies to: Employers with 5 or more employees.

Meal Break: 30 minutes unpaid for employees scheduled to work 6 consecutive hours or more, unless workplace environment provides ample opportunity for appropriate meal break. Tipped employees who work in food or beverage service may waive right to meal break if employee requests waiver, knowingly and voluntarily, in writing, and employer consents. Employer may not coerce employee into waiving right to meal break. Employer must post waiver policy that includes a form stating the employee's right to a break, how long the waiver will last, and how the employee or employer may rescind the waiver.

Breast-feeding: Reasonable unpaid break time to express breast milk.

Texas

Breast-feeding: No employment-specific laws. However, breast-feeding is allowed in any public or private location where the mother's presence is authorized.

Utah

Utah Code Ann. § 34A-5-106

Applies to: Employers with 15 or more employees.

Meal Break: Employers must provide breaks for expressing breast milk as a reasonable accommodation, unless it would cause undue hardship.

Vermont

Vt. Stat. Ann. tit. 21 §§ 304, 305

Applies to: All employers.

Meal Break: Employees must be given a "reasonable opportunity" to eat and use toilet facilities during work periods.

Rest Break: Employees must be given reasonable opportunities to eat and use toilet facilities during work periods.

Breast-feeding: Reasonable time to express breast milk for up to three years after the child's birth. Breaks can be paid or unpaid. Employer not required to provide breaks if it would substantially disrupt its operations.

Virginia

Breast-feeding: No employment-specific laws. However, breast-feeding is allowed in any public or private location where the mother's presence is authorized.

Washington

Wash. Admin. Code §§ 296-126-092, 296-131-020

Applies to: All employers except as noted.

Exceptions: Newspaper vendor or carrier, domestic or casual labor around private residence, sheltered workshop; separate provisions for agricultural labor.

Meal Break: 30-minute break, if work period is more than 5 consecutive hours, not less than 2 hours or more than 5 hours from beginning of shift. This time is paid if employee is on duty or is required to be at a site for employer's benefit. Employees who work 3 or more hours longer than regular workday are entitled to an additional half hour, before or during overtime. Agricultural employees: 30 minutes if working more than 5 hours; additional 30 minutes if working 11 or more hours in a day.

Rest Break: Paid 10-minute rest break for each 4-hour work period, scheduled as near as possible to midpoint of each work period. Employee cannot be required to work more than 3 hours without a rest break.

State Meal and Rest Breaks (continued)

Scheduled rest breaks not required where nature of work allows employee to take intermittent rest breaks equivalent to required standard.

West Virginia

W.Va. Code § 21-3-10a

Applies to: All employers.

Meal Break: At least 20-minute break for each 6 consecutive hours worked, unless employees are allowed to take breaks as needed or to eat lunch while working.

Rest Break: Rest breaks of 20 minutes or less must be counted as paid work time.

Wisconsin

Wis. Admin. Code § DWD 274.02; Wis. Stat. Ann. § 103.935

Applies to: All employers.

Meal Break: For most workers, 30-minute meal period is recommended but not required. Meal period should be close to usual meal time or near middle of shift. Shifts of more than 6 hours without a meal break should be avoided. If employee is not free to leave the workplace or relieved of all duties for at least 30 minutes, meal period is considered paid time.

For migrant workers employed exclusively in agricultural labor, 30-minute meal period required after 6 continuous hours of work, unless the shift can be completed in an additional hour.

Rest Break: For migrant workers not employed exclusively in agricultural labor, rest period of at least 10 minutes within each 5 hours of continuous employment.

Breast-feeding: No employment-specific laws. However, breast-feeding is allowed in any public or private location where the mother's presence is authorized.

State Minimum Wage Laws for Tipped and Regular Employees

The chart below gives the basic state minimum wage laws. Depending on the occupation, the size of the employer's business, or the conditions of employment, the minimum wage may vary from the one listed here. Minimum wage rates in a number of states change from year to year; to be sure of your state's current minimum, contact your state department of labor or check its website, where most states have posted the minimum wage requirements. (See the appendix for contact information.) Also, some local governments set a higher minimum wage, unless the state prohibits it—contact your city or county government for more information.

"Maximum Tip Credit" is the highest amount of tips that an employer can subtract from the employee's hourly wage. "Minimum Cash Wage" is the lowest hourly wage that an employer can pay a tipped employee. The employee's minimum cash wage plus hourly tips must equal at least the state minimum wage.

State and Statute	Notes	Basic Minimum Hourly Rate (*=tied to federal rate)	Maximum Tip Credit	Minimum Cash Wage for Tipped Employee	Minimum Tips to Qualify as a Tipped Employee (monthly unless noted otherwise)
United States 29 U.S.C. § 203; 29 U.S.C. § 206		$7.25	$5.12	$2.13	More than $30
Alabama	No minimum wage law				
Alaska Alaska Stat. § 23.10.065	Adjusts annually for inflation, posted at http://labor.alaska.gov/lss/whact.htm	$9.84	No tip credit	$9.84	N/A
Arizona Ariz. Rev. Stat. § 23-363	Adjusts annually for inflation, posted at www.azica.gov/labor-minimum-wage-main-page; does not apply to small businesses (those with gross revenue of less than $500,000 that are exempt from federal minimum wage laws)	$10.50 ($11 on January 1, 2019)	$3.00	$7.50 ($8 on January 1, 2019)	
Arkansas Ark. Code Ann. §§ 11-4-210 and 11-4-212	Applies to employers with 4 or more employees	$8.50	$5.87 (increases as minimum wage increases)	$2.63	Not specified

State Minimum Wage Laws for Tipped and Regular Employees (continued)				
State and Statute	Notes	Basic Minimum Hourly Rate (*=tied to federal rate)	Maximum Tip Credit	Minimum Cash Wage for Tipped Employee	Minimum Tips to Qualify as a Tipped Employee (monthly unless noted otherwise)
California *Cal. Lab. Code § 1182.12*		Employers with 25 or fewer employees: $10.50 (in 2018), and $11 (in 2019). Employers with 26 or more employees: $11 (in 2018), and $12 (in 2019).	No tip credit	Same as for non-tipped employees	N/A
Colorado *Colo. Const. Art. 18, § 15; 7 Colo. Code Regs. § 1103-1:3*	Adjusted annually for inflation, posted at www.coworkforce.com	$10.20 (2018); and $11.10 (in 2019)	$3.02	$7.18; and $8.08 (in 2019)	More than $30
Connecticut *Conn. Gen. Stat. Ann. §§ 31-58(j), 31-60; Conn. Admin. Code § 31-61-E2*		$10.10	36.8% for wait staff in hotel and restaurant industries; 18.5% for bartenders	$6.38 for wait staff in hotel and restaurant industries; $8.23 for bartenders (increases as minimum wage increases)	$10 per week (full-time employees); $2 per day (part-time employees)
Delaware *Del. Code Ann. tit. 19, § 902(a)*		$8.25	$6.02	$2.23	More than $30
District of Columbia *D.C. Code Ann. § 32-1003*		$12.50 ($13.25 on July 1, 2018; $14.00 on July 1, 2019)	$9.17 (increases as minimum wage increases)	$3.33 ($3.89 on July 1, 2018; $4.45 on July 1, 2019)	Not specified
Florida *Fla. Const., Art. X § 24; Fla. Stat. Ann. § 448.110*	Adjusted annually, posted at www.floridajobs.org	$8.25	$3.02	$5.23	More than $30

State Minimum Wage Laws for Tipped and Regular Employees (continued)

State and Statute	Notes	Basic Minimum Hourly Rate (*=tied to federal rate)	Maximum Tip Credit	Minimum Cash Wage for Tipped Employee	Minimum Tips to Qualify as a Tipped Employee (monthly unless noted otherwise)
Georgia *Ga. Code Ann. § 34-4-3*	Applies to employers with 6 or more employees and more than $40,000 per year in sales	$5.15 if not covered by Federal Regulations, otherwise Federal Minimum Wage.	Minimum wage does not apply to tipped employees	N/A	N/A
Hawaii *Haw. Rev. Stat. §§ 387-1 to 387-2*		$10.10 (2018)	75¢ in 2016 and beyond, but only if the employee makes at least $7 more than minimum wage with tips	$9.35 (2018)	More than $20
Idaho *Idaho Code §§ 44-1502; 44-1503*		$7.25	$3.90	$3.35	More than $30
Illinois *820 Ill. Comp. Stat. § 105/4; Ill. Admin. Code tit. 56, § 210.110*	Applies to employers with 4 or more employees (and all employers with respect to domestic workers)	$8.25	40%	$4.95	At least $20
Indiana *Ind. Code Ann. § 22-2-2-4*	Applies to employers with 2 or more employees	$7.25*	$5.12	$2.13	Not specified
Iowa *Iowa Code § 91D.1*	In first 90 calendar days of employment, minimum wage is $6.35	$7.25	40%	$4.35	At least $30
Kansas *Kan. Stat. Ann. § 44-1203*	Applies to employers not covered by the FLSA	$7.25	$5.12	$2.13	Not specified
Kentucky *Ky. Rev. Stat. Ann. § 337.275*		$7.25*	$5.12	$2.13	More than $30
Louisiana	No state minimum wage law				

State Minimum Wage Laws for Tipped and Regular Employees (continued)					
State and Statute	Notes	Basic Minimum Hourly Rate (*=tied to federal rate)	Maximum Tip Credit	Minimum Cash Wage for Tipped Employee	Minimum Tips to Qualify as a Tipped Employee (monthly unless noted otherwise)
Maine *Me. Rev. Stat. Ann. tit. 26, §§ 663(8), 664*	Indexed annual increases begin on 1/1/2021.	$10.00 (2018); $11.00 (2019)	50%	$6.00; $7.00 (2019)	More than $30
Maryland *Md. Code Ann., [Lab. & Empl.] §§ 3-413, 3-419*		$9.25 ($10.10 on July 1, 2018)	$5.62 (increases as minimum wage increases)	$3.63	More than $30
Massachusetts *Mass. Gen. Laws ch. 151, § 1; Mass. Regs. Code tit. 454, § 27.03*		$11.00	$7.25	$3.75	More than $20
Michigan *Mich. Comp. Laws §§ 408.412 to 408.424*	Applies to employers with 2 or more employees. Beginning 4/1/2019, the minimum wage will be adjusted annually according to the consumer price index.	$9.25 (2018)	$5.52 (increases as minimum wage increases)	38% of the minimum wage, which is $3.52 (round up) in 2018	Not specified
Minnesota *Minn. Stat. Ann. § 177.24*	Indexed annual increases began on 1/1/2018.	$9.65 for large employers; $7.87 for small employers (businesses with annual gross volume of sales of less than $500,000)	No tip credit	Same as for non-tipped employees	N/A
Mississippi	No state minimum wage law				
Missouri *Mo. Rev. Stat. §§ 290.502, 290.512*	Doesn't apply to retail or service business with gross annual sales of less than $500,000. Adjusted annually based on cost of living; posted at https:// labor.mo.gov/DLS/ MinimumWage.	$7.85	50%	$3.93	Not specified

State Minimum Wage Laws for Tipped and Regular Employees (continued)					
State and Statute	Notes	Basic Minimum Hourly Rate (*=tied to federal rate)	Maximum Tip Credit	Minimum Cash Wage for Tipped Employee	Minimum Tips to Qualify as a Tipped Employee (monthly unless noted otherwise)
Montana *Mont. Code Ann. §§ 39-3-404, 39-3-409; Mont. Admin. R. 24.16.1508 & following*	Adjusted annually; posted at http://erd.dli.mt.gov/labor-standards/wage-and-hour-payment-act/minimum-wage-history	$8.30 ($4.00 for businesses with gross annual sales of $110,000 or less)	No tip credit	$8.30	N/A
Nebraska *Neb. Rev. Stat. § 48-1203*	Applies to employers with 4 or more employees	$9.00	$6.87	$2.13	Not specified
Nevada *Nev. Rev. Stat. Ann. §§ 608.100, 608.160, 608.250; Nev. Admin. Code 608.100; Nev. Const. Art. 15 § 16*	Adjusted annually, posted at labor.nv.gov	$7.25 if employer provides health benefits; $8.25 if no health benefits provided	No tip credit	$7.25 (with health benefits); $8.25 (without health benefits)	N/A
New Hampshire *N.H. Rev. Stat. Ann. § 279:21*		$7.25*	55%	45%	More than $30
New Jersey *N.J. Stat. Ann. § 34:11-56a4*	Adjusted annually based on consumer price index; posted at http://lwd.dol.state.nj.us/labor	$8.60*	$6.47	$2.13 (suggested, not required)	Not specified
New Mexico *N.M. Stat. Ann. § 50-4-22*		$7.50	$5.37	$2.13	More than $30
New York *N.Y. Lab. Law § 652*	Indexed Annual Increases from 12/31/2018 to $12.50 by 12/31/2020. Beginning 1/1/2021, the rate will be adjusted annually for inflation until it reaches $15 an hour).	$10.40; $11.10 on December 31, 2018	Depends on occupation. See https://labor.ny.gov/formsdocs/factsheets/pdfs/p717.pdf	Depends on occupation	Depends on occupation
North Carolina *N.C. Gen. Stat. §§ 95-25.2(14), 95-25.3*		$7.25	$5.12	$2.13	More than $20

State Minimum Wage Laws for Tipped and Regular Employees (continued)

State and Statute	Notes	Basic Minimum Hourly Rate (*=tied to federal rate)	Maximum Tip Credit	Minimum Cash Wage for Tipped Employee	Minimum Tips to Qualify as a Tipped Employee (monthly unless noted otherwise)
North Dakota *N.D. Cent. Code § 34-06-22; N.D. Admin. Code R. 46-02-07-01 to -03*		$7.25	33% of minimum wage	$4.86	More than $30
Ohio *Ohio Rev. Code Ann. § 4111.02; Ohio Const. art. II § 34a*	Adjusted annually, posted at www.com.ohio.gov/dico	$8.30 ($7.25 for employers with gross income under $305,000).	50%	$4.15	More than $30
Oklahoma *Okla. Stat. Ann. tit. 40, §§ 197.2, 197.4, 197.16*	Applies to employers that are not covered by the FLSA and that have more than 10 full-time employees or more than $100,000 in gross annual sales	$7.25	50% of minimum wage for tips, food, and lodging combined	$3.63	Not specified
Oregon *Ore. Rev. Stat. §§ 653.025, 653.035(3)*	Adjusted annually; posted at www.boli.state.or.us	$10.25 ($10.75 on July 1, 2018; $11.25 on July 1, 2019)	No tip credit	$10.25 ($10.75 on July 1, 2018; $11.25 on July 1, 2019)	N/A
Pennsylvania *43 Pa. Cons. Stat. Ann. §§ 333.103 and 333.104; 34 Pa. Code § 231.1 and 231.101*		$7.25*	$4.42	$2.83	More than $30
Rhode Island *R.I. Gen. Laws §§ 28-12-3 & 28-12-5*		$10.10 ($10.50 on Jan 1, 2019)	$6.21	$3.89	Not specified
South Carolina	No state minimum wage law				
South Dakota *S.D. Codified Laws Ann. §§ 60-11-3 to -3.1*	Adjusted annually based on cost of living; posted at http://dlr.sd.gov/employment_laws/minimum_wage.aspx	$8.85	50%	$4.33	More than $35

State Minimum Wage Laws for Tipped and Regular Employees (continued)

State and Statute	Notes	Basic Minimum Hourly Rate (*=tied to federal rate)	Maximum Tip Credit	Minimum Cash Wage for Tipped Employee	Minimum Tips to Qualify as a Tipped Employee (monthly unless noted otherwise)
Tennessee	No state minimum wage law				
Texas *Tex. Lab. Code Ann. §§ 62.051 & 62.052*		$7.25	$5.12	$2.13	More than $20
Utah *Utah Code Ann. § 34-40-102; Utah Admin. R. 610-1*		$7.25	$5.12	$2.13	More than $30
Vermont *Vt. Stat. Ann. tit. 21, § 384(a); Vt. Code R. 24 090 003*	Applies to employers with 2 or more employees; annual indexing begins 1/1/2019, posted at www.vtlmi.info	$10.50 (2018)	50% for employees of hotels, motels, restaurants, and tourist places	$5.25 (increases as minimum wage increases)	More than $120
Virginia *Va. Code Ann. §§ 40.1-28.9 and 28.10*	Applies to employees not covered by FLSA	$7.25	Tips actually received	Minimum wage less tips actually received	Not specified
Washington *Wash. Rev. Code Ann. § 49.46.020; Wash. Admin. Code § 296-126-022*	Adjusted annually; posted at www.lni.wa.gov	$11.50; $12.00 (January 1, 2019)	No tip credit	$11.00 ($11.50 on January 1, 2018; $12.00 on January 1, 2019)	N/A
West Virginia *W.Va. Code §§ 21-5C-1, 21-5C-2, 21-5C-4*	Applies to employers with 6 or more employees at one location who are not covered by the FLSA	$8.75	70% of minimum wage	$2.62 (increases as minimum wage increases)	Not specified
Wisconsin *Wis. Admin. Code DWD § 272.03*		$7.25	$4.92	$2.33	Not specified
Wyoming *Wyo. Stat. § 27-4-202*		$5.15 if federal regulations do not apply.	$3.02	$2.13	More than $30

State Laws on Jury Duty

Alabama

Ala. Code §§ 12-16-8 to 12-16-8.1

Paid leave: Full-time employees are entitled to usual pay.

Notice employee must give: Must show supervisor jury summons the next working day; must return to work the next scheduled hour after discharge from jury duty.

Employer penalty for firing or penalizing employee: Liable for actual and punitive damages.

Note: Employers with 5 or fewer full-time employees: Court must postpone an employee's jury service if another employee is already serving as a juror.

Alaska

Alaska Stat. § 09.20.037

Unpaid leave: Yes.

Additional employee protections: Employee may not be threatened, coerced, or penalized.

Employer penalty for firing or penalizing employee: Liable for lost wages and damages; may be required to reinstate the fired employee.

Arizona

Ariz. Rev. Stat. § 21-236

Unpaid leave: Yes.

Additional employee protections: Employee may not lose vacation rights, seniority, or precedence. Employer may not require employee to use annual, sick, or vacation hours.

Employer penalty for firing or penalizing employee: Class 3 misdemeanor, punishable by a fine of up to $500 or up to 30 days' imprisonment.

Note: Employers with 5 or fewer full-time employees: Court must postpone an employee's jury service if another employee is already serving as a juror.

Note: Employers with 5 or fewer full-time employees: Court must postpone an employee's jury service if another employee is already serving as a juror.

Arkansas

Ark. Code Ann. § 16-31-106

Unpaid leave: Yes.

Additional employee protections: Absence may not affect sick leave and vacation rights.

Notice employee must give: Reasonable notice.

Employer penalty for firing or penalizing employee: Class A misdemeanor, punishable by a fine of up to $2,500.

California

Cal. Lab. Code §§ 230, 230.1

Unpaid leave: Employee may use vacation, personal leave, or comp time.

Notice employee must give: Reasonable notice.

Employer penalty for firing or penalizing employee: Employer must reinstate employee with back pay and lost wages and benefits. Willful violation is a misdemeanor.

Colorado

Colo. Rev. Stat. §§ 13-71-126, 13-71-133 to 13-71-134, 18-1.3-501

Paid leave: All employees (including part-time and temporary who were scheduled to work for the 3 months preceding jury service): regular wages up to $50 per day for first 3 days of jury duty. Must pay within 30 days of jury service.

Additional employee protections: Employer may not make any demands on employee that will interfere with effective performance of jury duty.

Employer penalty for firing or penalizing employee: Class 2 misdemeanor, punishable by a fine of $250 to $1,000 or 3 to 12 months'

State Laws on Jury Duty (continued)

imprisonment, or both. May be liable to employee for triple damages and attorneys' fees.

Connecticut

Conn. Gen. Stat. Ann. §§ 51-247 and 51-247a

Paid leave: Full-time employees: regular wages for the first 5 days of jury duty; after 5 days, state pays up to $50 per day.

Additional employee protections: Once employee serves 8 hours of jury duty, employer may not require employee to work more hours on the same day.

Employer penalty for firing or penalizing employee: Criminal contempt: punishable by a fine of up to $500 or up to 30 days' imprisonment, or both. Liable for up to 10 weeks' lost wages for discharging employee. If employer fails to pay the employee as required, may be liable for treble damages and attorneys' fees.

Delaware

Del. Code Ann. tit. 10, §§ 4514, 4515

Unpaid leave: State pays $20 per diem for travel, parking, other out-of-pocket expenses. State pays certain other expenses if jury is sequestered.

Employer penalty for firing or penalizing employee: Criminal contempt: punishable by a fine of up to $500 or up to 6 months' imprisonment, or both. Liable to discharged employee for lost wages and attorneys' fees and may be required to reinstate the fired employee.

District of Columbia

D.C. Code Ann. §§ 11-1913, 15-718

Paid leave: Full-time employees: regular wages for the first 5 days of jury duty, less jury fee from state. State attendance fee: $30, if not paid full regular wages by employer. State travel allowance: $2 per day.

Employer penalty for firing or penalizing employee: Criminal contempt: punishable by a fine of up to $300 or up to 30 days' imprisonment, or both, for a first offense; up to $5,000 or up to 180 days' imprisonment, or both, for any subsequent offense. Liable to discharged employee for lost wages and attorneys' fees and may be required to reinstate the fired employee.

Florida

Fla. Stat. Ann. §§ 40.24, 40.271

Unpaid leave: Yes. State pays $15 per day for first three days of service if juror does not receive regular wages those days. State pays $30 per day for the fourth and subsequent days.

Additional employee protections: Employee may not be threatened with dismissal.

Employer penalty for firing or penalizing employee: Threatening employee is contempt of court. May be liable to discharged employee for compensatory and punitive damages and attorneys' fees.

Georgia

Ga. Code Ann. § 34-1-3

Paid leave: According to Opinion of the Attorney General Number 89-55, issued in 1989, employers must pay an employee's wages while on jury duty, minus any funds the employee receives for jury service.

Additional employee protections: Employee may not be discharged, penalized, or threatened with discharge or penalty for responding to a subpoena or making a required court appearance.

Notice employee must give: Reasonable notice.

Employer penalty for firing or penalizing employee: Liable for actual damages and reasonable attorneys' fees.

State Laws on Jury Duty (continued)

Hawaii

Haw. Rev. Stat. § 612-25

Unpaid leave: Yes.

Employer penalty for firing or penalizing employee: Petty misdemeanor: punishable by a fine of up to $1,000 or up to 30 days' imprisonment. May be liable to discharged employee for up to 6 weeks' lost wages, reasonable attorneys' fees, and may be required to reinstate the fired employee.

Idaho

Idaho Code § 2-218

Unpaid leave: Yes.

Employer penalty for firing or penalizing employee: Criminal contempt: punishable by a fine of up to $300. Liable to discharged employee for triple lost wages and reasonable attorneys' fees. May be ordered to reinstate the fired employee.

Illinois

705 Ill. Comp. Stat. § 310/10.1

Unpaid leave: Yes.

Additional employee protections: A regular night shift employee may not be required to work if serving on a jury during the day. May not lose any seniority or benefits.

Notice employee must give: Must give employer a copy of the summons within 10 days of issuance.

Employer penalty for firing or penalizing employee: Employer will be charged with civil or criminal contempt, or both; liable to employee for lost wages and benefits; may be ordered to reinstate employee.

Indiana

Ind. Code Ann. §§ 34-28-4-1, 35-44.1-2-11

Unpaid leave: Yes.

Additional employee protections: Employee may not be deprived of benefits or threatened with the loss of them.

Employer penalty for firing or penalizing employee: Class B misdemeanor: punishable by up to 180 days' imprisonment; may also be fined up to $1,000. Liable to discharged employee for lost wages and attorneys' fees and may be required to reinstate the fired employee.

Iowa

Iowa Code § 607A.45

Unpaid leave: Yes.

Additional employee protections: Employer may not threaten or coerce employee based on jury notice or jury duty.

Employer penalty for firing or penalizing employee: Contempt of court. Liable to discharged employee for up to 6 weeks' lost wages and attorneys' fees and may be required to reinstate the fired employee.

Kansas

Kan. Stat. Ann. § 43-173

Unpaid leave: Yes.

Additional employee protections: Employee may not lose seniority or benefits. (Basic and additional protections apply to permanent employees only.)

Employer penalty for firing or penalizing employee: Liable for lost wages and benefits, damages, and attorneys' fees and may be required to reinstate the fired employee.

Kentucky

Ky. Rev. Stat. Ann. §§ 29A.160, 29A.990

Unpaid leave: Yes.

State Laws on Jury Duty (continued)

Additional employee protections: Employer may not threaten or coerce employee based on jury notice or jury duty.

Employer penalty for firing or penalizing employee: Class B misdemeanor: punishable by up to 89 days' imprisonment or fine of up to $250, or both. Liable to discharged employee for lost wages and attorneys' fees. Must reinstate employee with full seniority and benefits.

Louisiana

La. Rev. Stat. Ann. § 23:965

Paid leave: Regular employee entitled to one day full compensation for jury service. May not lose any sick, vacation, or personal leave or other benefit.

Additional employee protections: Employer may not create any policy or rule that would discharge employee for jury service.

Notice employee must give: Reasonable notice.

Employer penalty for firing or penalizing employee: For each discharged employee: fine of $100 to $1,000; must reinstate employee with full benefits. For not granting paid leave: fine of $100 to $500; must pay full day's lost wages.

Maine

Me. Rev. Stat. Ann. tit. 14, § 1218

Unpaid leave: Yes.

Additional employee protections: Employee may not lose or be threatened with loss of employment or health insurance coverage.

Employer penalty for firing or penalizing employee: Class E crime: punishable by up to 6 months in the county jail or a fine of up to $1,000. Liable for up to 6 weeks' lost wages, benefits, and attorneys' fees. Employer may be ordered to reinstate the employee.

Maryland

Md. Code Ann., [Cts. & Jud. Proc.] §§ 8-501, 8-502

Unpaid leave: Yes.

Additional employee protections: Employer cannot threaten or coerce an employee. An employee may not be required to use annual, sick, or vacation leave. An employee who spends at least 4 hours on jury service (including travel time) may not be required to work a shift that begins on or after 5 p.m. that day or before 3 a.m. the following day.

Employer penalty for firing or penalizing employee: Employer penalty for violating these provisions is a fine up to $1,000.

Massachusetts

Mass. Gen. Laws ch. 234A, §§ 48 and following

Paid leave: All employees (including part-time and temporary who were scheduled to work for the 3 months preceding jury service): regular wages for first 3 days of jury duty. If paid leave is an "extreme financial hardship" for employer, state will pay. After first 3 days, state will pay $50 per day.

Michigan

Mich. Comp. Laws § 600.1348

Unpaid leave: Yes.

Additional employee protections: Employee may not be threatened or disciplined; may not be required to work in addition to jury service, if extra hours would mean working overtime or beyond normal quitting time.

Employer penalty for firing or penalizing employee: Misdemeanor, punishable by a fine of up to $500 or up to 90 days' imprisonment, or both. Employer may also be punished for contempt of court, with a fine of up to $7,500 or up to 93 days' imprisonment, or both.

State Laws on Jury Duty (continued)

Minnesota

Minn. Stat. Ann. § 593.50

Unpaid leave: Yes.

Additional employee protections: Employer may not threaten or coerce employee.

Employer penalty for firing or penalizing employee: Criminal contempt: punishable by a fine of up to $700 or up to 6 months' imprisonment, or both. Also liable to employee for up to 6 weeks' lost wages and attorneys' fees and may be required to reinstate the fired employee.

Mississippi

Miss. Code Ann. §§ 13-5-23, 13-5-35

Unpaid leave: Yes.

Additional employee protections: Employee may not be intimidated or threatened. Employee may not be required to use annual, sick, or vacation leave for jury service.

Notice employee must give: Reasonable notice is required.

Employer penalty for firing or penalizing employee: If found guilty of interference with the administration of justice: at least one month in the county jail or up to 2 years in the state penitentiary, or a fine of up to $500, or both. May also be found guilty of contempt of court, punishable by a fine of up to $1,000 or up to 6 months' imprisonment, or both.

Note: Employers with 5 or fewer full-time employees: Court must postpone an employee's jury service if another employee is already serving as a juror.

Missouri

Mo. Rev. Stat. § 494.460

Unpaid leave: Yes.

Additional employee protections: Employer may not take or threaten to take any adverse action. Employee may not be required to use annual, sick, vacation, or personal leave.

Employer penalty for firing or penalizing employee: Employer may be liable for lost wages, damages, and attorneys' fees and may be required to reinstate the fired employee.

Montana

Mont. Admin. R. 24.16.2520

Paid leave: No paid leave laws regarding private employers.

Nebraska

Neb. Rev. Stat. § 25-1640

Paid leave: Normal wages minus any compensation (other than expenses) from the court.

Additional employee protections: Employee may not lose pay, sick leave, or vacation or be penalized in any way; may not be required to work evening or night shift.

Notice employee must give: Reasonable notice.

Employer penalty for firing or penalizing employee: Class IV misdemeanor, punishable by a fine of up to $500.

Nevada

Nev. Rev. Stat. Ann. §§ 6.190, 193.140

Unpaid leave: Yes.

Additional employee protections: Employer may not recommend or threaten termination; may not dissuade or attempt to dissuade employee from serving as a juror, and cannot require the employee to work within 8 hours before jury duty or if employee's duty lasts four hours or more (including travel time to and from the court), between 5 p.m. that day and 3 a.m. the next day. Cannot be required to take paid leave.

State Laws on Jury Duty (continued)

Notice employee must give: At least three days' notice.

Employer penalty for firing or penalizing employee: Terminating or threatening to terminate is a gross misdemeanor, punishable by a fine of up to $2,000 or up to 364 days' imprisonment, or both; in addition, employer may be liable for lost wages, damages equal to lost wages, and punitive damages to $50,000 and must reinstate employee. Dissuading or attempting to dissuade is a misdemeanor, punishable by a fine of up to $1,000 or up to 6 months in the county jail, or both.

New Hampshire
N.H. Rev. Stat. Ann. § 500-A:14

Unpaid leave: Yes.

Additional employee protections: Employer cannot threaten or coerce employee.

Employer penalty for firing or penalizing employee: Employer may be found guilty of contempt of court; also liable to employee for lost wages and attorneys' fees and may be required to reinstate the fired employee.

New Jersey
N.J. Stat. Ann. § 2B:20-17

Unpaid leave: Yes.

Additional employee protections: Employer cannot threaten or coerce employee.

Employer penalty for firing or penalizing employee: Employer may be found guilty of a disorderly persons offense, punishable by a fine of up to $1,000 or up to 6 months' imprisonment, or both. May also be liable to employee for economic damages and attorneys' fees and may be ordered to reinstate the fired employee.

New Mexico
N.M. Stat. Ann. §§ 38-5-10.1, 38-5-18 to 38-5-19

Unpaid leave: Yes.

Additional employee protections: Employer cannot threaten or coerce employee. An employee may not be required to use annual, sick, or vacation leave.

Employer penalty for firing or penalizing employee: Petty misdemeanor, punishable by a fine of up to $500 or up to 6 months in the county jail, or both.

Note: Court must postpone an employee's jury service if the employer has five or fewer full-time employees and another employee has already been summoned to appear during the same period, or if the employee is the only person performing essential services that the employer cannot function without.

New York
N.Y. Jud. Ct. Acts Law § 519

Unpaid leave: Yes.

Paid leave: Employers with more than 10 employees must pay first $40 of wages for the first 3 days of jury duty.

Notice employee must give: Must notify employer prior to beginning jury duty.

Employer penalty for firing or penalizing employee: May be found guilty of criminal contempt of court, punishable by a fine of up to $1,000 or up to 30 days in the county jail, or both.

North Carolina
N.C. Gen. Stat. § 9-32

Unpaid leave: Yes.

Additional employee protections: Employee may not be demoted.

Employer penalty for firing or penalizing employee: Liable to discharged employee for reasonable damages; must reinstate employee to former position.

State Laws on Jury Duty (continued)

North Dakota

N.D. Cent. Code § 27-09.1-17

Unpaid leave: Yes.

Additional employee protections: Employee may not be laid off, penalized, or coerced because of jury duty, responding to a summons or subpoena, serving as a witness, or testifying in court.

Employer penalty for firing or penalizing employee: Class B misdemeanor, punishable by a fine of up to $1,500 or up to 30 days' imprisonment, or both. Liable to employee for up to 6 weeks' lost wages and attorneys' fees, and may be required to reinstate the fired employee.

Ohio

Ohio Rev. Code Ann. §§ 2313.15, 2313.19, 2313.99

Unpaid leave: Yes.

Additional employee protections: An employee may not be required to use annual, sick, or vacation leave.

Notice employee must give: Reasonable notice. Absence must be for actual jury service.

Employer penalty for firing or penalizing employee: May be found guilty of contempt of court, punishable by a fine of up to $250 or 30 days' imprisonment, or both, for first offense.

Note: Employers with 25 or fewer full-time employees: Court must postpone an employee's jury service if another employee served within thirty days prior.

Oklahoma

Okla. Stat. Ann. tit. 38, §§ 34, 35

Unpaid leave: Yes.

Additional employee protections: Employee can't be subject to any adverse employment action, and can't be required to use annual, sick, or vacation leave.

Notice employee must give: Reasonable notice.

Employer penalty for firing or penalizing employee: Misdemeanor, punishable by a fine of up to $5,000. Liable to discharged employee for actual and exemplary damages; actual damages include past and future lost wages, mental anguish, and costs of finding suitable employment.

Oregon

Ore. Rev. Stat. § 10.090

Unpaid leave: Yes (or according to employer's policy).

Additional employee protections: Employee may not be threatened, intimidated, or coerced, and can't be required to use annual, sick, or vacation leave. Employers with 10 or more employees that provide health, disability, life, or other insurance benefits must continue coverage during jury service at the election of the employee.

Employer penalty for firing or penalizing employee: Court may order reinstatement with or without back pay, and a $720 civil penalty.

Pennsylvania

42 Pa. Cons. Stat. Ann. § 4563; 18 Pa. Cons. Stat. Ann. § 4957

Unpaid leave: Yes (applies to retail or service industry employers with 15 or more employees and to manufacturers with 40 or more employees).

Additional employee protections: Employee may not be threatened or coerced, or lose seniority or benefits. (Any employee who would not be eligible for unpaid leave will be automatically excused from jury duty.)

Employer penalty for firing or penalizing employee: Liable to employee for lost benefits, wages, and attorneys' fees; may be required to reinstate the fired employee.

State Laws on Jury Duty (continued)

Rhode Island

R.I. Gen. Laws § 9-9-28

Unpaid leave: Yes.

Additional employee protections: Employee may not lose wage increases, promotions, length of service, or other benefit.

Employer penalty for firing or penalizing employee: Misdemeanor punishable by a fine of up to $1,000 or up to one year's imprisonment, or both.

South Carolina

S.C. Code Ann. § 41-1-70

Unpaid leave: Yes.

Employer penalty for firing or penalizing employee: For discharging employee, liable for one year's salary; for demoting employee, liable for one year's difference between former and lower salary.

South Dakota

S.D. Codified Laws Ann. §§ 16-13-41.1, 16-13-41.2

Unpaid leave: Yes.

Additional employee protections: Employee may not lose job status, pay, or seniority.

Employer penalty for firing or penalizing employee: Class 2 misdemeanor, punishable by a fine of up to $500 or up to 30 days in the county jail, or both.

Tennessee

Tenn. Code Ann. § 22-4-106

Paid leave: Regular wages minus jury fees, as long as the employer has at least 5 employees, and the employee is not a temporary worker who has been employed for less than 6 months.

Additional employee protections: Employer may not demote, suspend, or discriminate against employee. Night shift employees are excused from shift work during and for the night before the first day of jury service.

Notice employee must give: Employee must show summons to supervisor the next workday after receiving it.

Employer penalty for firing or penalizing employee: Employees are entitled to reinstatement and reimbursement for lost wages and work benefits. Violating employee rights or any provisions of this law is a Class A misdemeanor, punishable by up to 11 months, 29 days' imprisonment or a fine up to $2,500, or both. Liable to employee for lost wages and benefits and must reinstate employee.

Texas

Tex. Civ. Prac. & Rem. Code Ann. §§ 122.001, 122.002

Unpaid leave: Yes.

Notice employee must give: Employee must notify employer of intent to return after completion of jury service.

Employer penalty for firing or penalizing employee: Liable to employee for not less than one year's nor more than 5 years' compensation and attorneys' fees. Must reinstate employee.

Note: Only applies to permanent employees.

Utah

Utah Code Ann. § 78B-1-116

Unpaid leave: Yes.

Additional employee protections: Employer may not threaten or coerce employee or take any adverse employment action against employee. Employee may not be requested or required to use annual or sick leave or vacation.

State Laws on Jury Duty (continued)

Employer penalty for firing or penalizing employee: May be found guilty of criminal contempt, punishable by a fine of up to $500 or up to 6 months' imprisonment, or both. Liable to employee for up to 6 weeks' lost wages and attorneys' fees and may be required to reinstate the fired employee.

Vermont

Vt. Stat. Ann. tit. 21, § 499

Unpaid leave: Yes.

Additional employee protections: Employee may not be penalized or lose any benefit available to other employees; may not lose seniority, vacation credit, or any fringe benefits.

Employer penalty for firing or penalizing employee: Fine of up to $200.

Virginia

Va. Code Ann. § 18.2-465.1

Unpaid leave: Yes.

Additional employee protections: Employee may not be subject to any adverse personnel action and may not be forced to use sick leave or vacation. Employee who has appeared for 4 or more hours cannot be required to start a shift after 5 p.m. that day or before 3 a.m. the next morning.

Notice employee must give: Reasonable notice.

Employer penalty for firing or penalizing employee: Class 3 misdemeanor, punishable by a fine of up to $500.

Washington

Wash. Rev. Code Ann. § 2.36.165

Unpaid leave: Yes.

Additional employee protections: Employee may not be threatened, coerced, harassed, or denied promotion.

Employer penalty for firing or penalizing employee: Intentional violation is a misdemeanor, punishable by a fine of up to $1,000 or up to 90 days' imprisonment, or both; also liable to employee for damages and attorneys' fees and may be required to reinstate the fired employee.

West Virginia

W.Va. Code § 52-3-1

Unpaid leave: Yes.

Additional employee protections: Employee may not be threatened or discriminated against; regular pay cannot be cut.

Employer penalty for firing or penalizing employee: May be found guilty of civil contempt, punishable by a fine of $100 to $500. May be required to reinstate the fired employee. May be liable for back pay and for attorneys' fees.

Wisconsin

Wis. Stat. Ann. § 756.255

Unpaid leave: Yes.

Additional employee protections: Employee may not lose seniority or pay raises; may not be disciplined.

Employer penalty for firing or penalizing employee: Fine of up to $200. May be required to reinstate the fired employee with back pay.

Wyoming

Wyo. Stat. § 1-11-401

Unpaid leave: Yes.

Additional employee protections: Employee may not be threatened, intimidated, or coerced.

Employer penalty for firing or penalizing employee: Liable to employee for up to $1,000 damages for each violation, costs, and attorneys' fees. May be required to reinstate the fired employee with no loss of seniority.

State Laws on Taking Time Off to Vote

Note: Certain states are not listed in this chart because they do not have laws or regulations on time off to vote that govern private employers. Check with your state department of labor if you need more information. (See the appendix for contact list.)

Alabama

Ala. Code § 17-1-5

Time off work for voting: Necessary time up to one hour. The employer may decide when hours may be taken.

Time off not required if: Employee has 2 nonwork hours before polls open or one nonwork hour after polls are open.

Time off is paid: No.

Employee must request leave in advance: "Reasonable notice."

Alaska

Alaska Stat. § 15.56.100

Time off work for voting: Not specified.

Time off not required if: Employee has 2 consecutive nonwork hours at beginning or end of shift when polls are open.

Time off is paid: Yes.

Arizona

Ariz. Rev. Stat. § 16-402

Time off work for voting: As much time as will add up to 3 hours when combined with nonwork time. Employer may decide when hours are taken.

Time off not required if: Employee has 3 consecutive nonwork hours at beginning or end of shift when polls are open.

Time off is paid: Yes.

Employee must request leave in advance: Prior to the day of the election.

Arkansas

Ark. Code Ann. § 7-1-102

Time off work for voting: Employer must schedule employees' work schedules on election days to enable employees to vote.

Time off is paid: No.

California

Cal. Elec. Code § 14000

Time off work for voting: Up to 2 hours at beginning or end of shift, whichever gives employee most time to vote and takes least time off work.

Time off not required if: Employee has sufficient time to vote during nonwork time.

Time off is paid: Yes (up to 2 hours).

Employee must request leave in advance: 2 working days before election.

Colorado

Colo. Rev. Stat. § 1-7-102

Time off work for voting: Up to 2 hours. Employer may decide when hours are taken, but employer must permit employee to take time at beginning or end of shift, if employee requests it.

Time off not required if: Employee has 3 nonwork hours when polls are open.

Time off is paid: Yes (up to 2 hours).

Employee must request leave in advance: Prior to election day.

Georgia

Ga. Code Ann. § 21-2-404

Time off work for voting: Up to 2 hours. Employer may decide when hours are taken.

Time off not required if: Employee has 2 nonwork hours at beginning or end of shift when polls are open.

State Laws on Taking Time Off to Vote (continued)

Time off is paid: No.

Employee must request leave in advance: "Reasonable notice."

Hawaii
Haw. Rev. Stat. § 11-95

Time off work for voting: 2 consecutive hours excluding meal or rest breaks. Employer may not change employee's regular work schedule.

Time off not required if: Employee has 2 consecutive nonwork hours when polls are open.

Time off is paid: Yes.

Employee required to show proof of voting: Only if employer is verifying whether employee voted when they took time off to vote. A voter's receipt is proof of voting by the employee. If employer verifies that employee did not vote, hours off may be deducted from pay.

Illinois
10 Ill. Comp. Stat. §§ 5/7-42, 5/17-15

Time off work for voting: 2 hours. Employer may decide when hours are taken except that employer must permit a 2-hour absence during working hours if employee's working hours begin less than 2 hours after opening of polls and end less than 2 hours before closing of polls.

Time off is paid: Yes.

Employee must request leave in advance: Prior to the day of election. One day in advance (for general or state election). Employer must give consent (for primary).

Iowa
Iowa Code § 49.109

Time off work for voting: As much time as will add up to 3 hours when combined with nonwork time. Employer may decide when hours are taken.

Time off not required if: Employee has 3 consecutive nonwork hours when polls are open.

Time off is paid: Yes.

Employee must request leave in advance: In writing "prior to the date of the election."

Kansas
Kan. Stat. Ann. § 25-418

Time off work for voting: Up to 2 hours or as much time as will add up to 2 hours when combined with nonwork time. Employer may decide when hours are taken, but it may not be during a regular meal break.

Time off not required if: Employee has 2 consecutive nonwork hours when polls are open.

Time off is paid: Yes.

Kentucky
Ky. Const. § 148; Ky. Rev. Stat. Ann. § 118.035

Time off work for voting: "Reasonable time," but not less than 4 hours. Employer may decide when hours are taken.

Time off is paid: No.

Employee must request leave in advance: One day before election.

Employee required to show proof of voting: No proof specified, but employee who takes time off and does not vote may be subject to disciplinary action.

Maryland
Md. Code Ann. [Elec. Law] § 10-315

Time off work for voting: 2 hours.

Time off not required if: Employee has 2 consecutive nonwork hours when polls are open.

Time off is paid: Yes.

Employee required to show proof of voting: Yes; also includes attempting to vote. Must use state board of elections form.

State Laws on Taking Time Off to Vote (continued)

Massachusetts

Mass. Gen. Laws ch. 149, § 178

Time off work for voting: First 2 hours that polls are open. (Applies to workers in manufacturing, mechanical, or retail industries.)

Time off is paid: No.

Employee must request leave in advance: Must apply for leave of absence (no time specified).

Minnesota

Minn. Stat. Ann. § 204C.04

Time off work for voting: May be absent during the morning of election day.

Time off is paid: Yes.

Missouri

Mo. Rev. Stat. § 115.639

Time off work for voting: 3 hours. Employer may decide when hours are taken.

Time off not required if: Employee has 3 consecutive nonwork hours when polls are open.

Time off is paid: Yes (if employee votes).

Employee must request leave in advance: "Prior to the day of election."

Employee required to show proof of voting: None specified, but pay contingent on employee actually voting.

Nebraska

Neb. Rev. Stat. § 32-922

Time off work for voting: As much time as will add up to 2 consecutive hours when combined with nonwork time. Employer may decide when hours are taken.

Time off not required if: Employee has 2 consecutive nonwork hours when polls are open.

Time off is paid: Yes.

Employee must request leave in advance: Prior to or on election day.

Nevada

Nev. Rev. Stat. Ann. § 293.463

Time off work for voting: If it is impracticable to vote before or after work: Employee who works 2 miles or less from polling place may take 1 hour; 2 to 10 miles, 2 hours; more than 10 miles, 3 hours. Employer will decide when hours are taken.

Time off not required if: Employee has sufficient nonwork time when polls are open.

Time off is paid: Yes.

Employee must request leave in advance: Prior to election day.

New Mexico

N.M. Stat. Ann. § 1-12-42

Time off work for voting: 2 hours. (Includes Indian nation, tribal, and pueblo elections.) Employer may decide when hours are taken.

Time off not required if: Employee's workday begins more than 2 hours after polls open or ends more than 3 hours before polls close.

Time off is paid: Yes.

New York

N.Y. Elec. Law § 3-110

Time off work for voting: As many hours at beginning or end of shift as will give employee enough time to vote when combined with nonwork time. Employer may decide when hours are taken.

Time off not required if: Employee has 4 consecutive nonwork hours at beginning or end of shift when polls are open.

Time off is paid: Yes (up to 2 hours).

Employee must request leave in advance: Not more than 10 or less than 2 working days before election.

State Laws on Taking Time Off to Vote (continued)

North Dakota
N.D. Cent. Code § 16.1-01-02.1

Time off work for voting: Employers are encouraged to give employees time off to vote when regular work schedule conflicts with times polls are open.

Time off is paid: No.

Ohio
Ohio Rev. Code Ann. § 3599.06

Time off work for voting: "Reasonable time."

Time off is paid: Yes.

Oklahoma
Okla. Stat. Ann. tit. 26, § 7-101

Time off work for voting: 2 hours, unless employee lives so far from polling place that more time is needed. Employer may decide when hours are taken or may change employee's schedule to give employee nonwork time to vote.

Time off not required if: Employee's workday begins at least 3 hours after polls open or ends at least 3 hours before polls close.

Time off is paid: Yes.

Employee must request leave in advance: One day before election.

Employee required to show proof of voting: Yes.

South Dakota
S.D. Codified Laws Ann. § 12-3-5

Time off work for voting: 2 consecutive hours. Employer may decide when hours are taken.

Time off not required if: Employee has 2 consecutive nonwork hours when polls are open.

Time off is paid: Yes.

Tennessee
Tenn. Code Ann. § 2-1-106

Time off work for voting: "Reasonable time" up to 3 hours during the time polls are open. Employer may decide when hours are taken.

Time off not required if: Employee's workday begins at least 3 hours after polls open or ends at least 3 hours before polls close.

Time off is paid: Yes.

Employee must request leave in advance: Before noon on the day before the election.

Texas
Tex. Elec. Code Ann. § 276.004

Time off work for voting: Employer may not refuse to allow employee to take time off to vote, but no time limit specified.

Time off not required if: Employee has 2 consecutive nonwork hours when polls are open.

Time off is paid: Yes.

Utah
Utah Code Ann. § 20A-3-103

Time off work for voting: 2 hours at beginning or end of shift. Employer may decide when hours are taken.

Time off not required if: Employee has at least 3 nonwork hours when polls are open.

Time off is paid: Yes.

Employee must request leave in advance: "Before election day."

West Virginia
W.Va. Code § 3-1-42

Time off work for voting: Up to 3 hours. (Employers in health, transportation, communication, production, and processing facilities may change employee's schedule so that time off doesn't impair essential operations but must allow employee sufficient and convenient time to vote.)

State Laws on Taking Time Off to Vote (continued)

Time off not required if: Employee has at least 3 nonwork hours when polls are open.

Time off is paid: Yes (if employee votes).

Employee must request leave in advance: Written request at least 3 days before election.

Employee required to show proof of voting: None specified, but time off will be deducted from pay if employee does not vote.

Wisconsin

Wis. Stat. Ann. § 6.76

Time off work for voting: Up to 3 consecutive hours. Employer may decide when hours are taken.

Time off is paid: No.

Employee must request leave in advance: "Before election day."

Wyoming

Wyo. Stat. § 22-2-111

Time off work for voting: One hour, other than a meal break. Employer may decide when the hour is taken.

Time off not required if: Employee has at least 3 consecutive nonwork hours when polls are open.

Time off is paid: Yes (if employee votes).

Employee required to show proof of voting: None specified, but pay contingent on employee voting.

State Laws on Military Leave

Alabama

Alabama Stat. §§ 31-12-1 to 31-12-4

Members of the Alabama National Guard, or the national guard of another state, called to active duty or for federally funded duty for service other than training have the same leave and reinstatement rights and benefits guaranteed under USERRA (doesn't apply to normal annual training, weekend drills, and required schools).

Alaska

Alaska Stat. § 26.05.075

Employees called to active service in the state militia are entitled to unlimited unpaid leave and reinstatement to their former or a comparable position, with the pay, seniority, and benefits the employee would have had if not absent for service. Employee must return to work on next workday, after time required for travel. Disabled employee must request reemployment within 30 days of release; if disability leaves the employee unable to do the job, employee must be offered a position with similar pay and benefits.

Arizona

Ariz. Rev. Stat. §§ 26-167, 26-168

Members of the National Guard, Arizona National Guard, and U.S. armed forces reserves called to training or active duty have the same leave and reinstatement rights and benefits guaranteed under USERRA. Members of the National Guard called for active duty or to attend camps, formations, maneuvers, or drills are entitled to unlimited unpaid leave and reinstatement to their former or a higher position with the same seniority and vacation benefits. Employer may not dissuade employees from enlisting in state or national military forces by threatening economic reprisal.

Arkansas

Ark. Code Ann. § 12-62-413

Employees called to active state duty as a member of the armed forces (which includes the National Guard, militia, and reserves) of Arkansas or any other state have the same leave and reinstatement rights and benefits guaranteed under USERRA.

California

Cal. Mil. & Vet. Code §§ 394, 394.5, 395.06

Members of the California National Guard, or the national guard of any state, called to active duty are entitled to unlimited unpaid leave and reinstatement to their former position or to a position of similar seniority, status, and pay. Full-time employees must be reinstated (without loss of retirement or other benefits), unless the employer's circumstances have so changed as to make reinstatement impossible or unreasonable. Part-time employees must be reinstated if an open position exists. Reinstated employees cannot be terminated without cause for one year. Full-time employees must apply for reinstatement within 40 days of discharge, while part-time employees must apply for reinstatement within 5 days of discharge.

Employees in the U.S. armed forces reserves, National Guard, or Naval Militia are entitled to 17 days' unpaid leave per year for military training, drills, encampment, naval cruises, special exercises, or similar activities. Employer may not terminate employee or limit any benefits or seniority because of a temporary disability resulting from duty in the National Guard or Naval Militia (up to 52 weeks). Employer cannot discriminate against employee in the terms, conditions, or privileges of employment due to membership in the military services.

State Laws on Military Leave (continued)

Colorado

Colo. Rev. Stat. §§ 28-3-609, 28-3-610, 28-3-610.5

Members of the Colorado National Guard or U.S. armed force reserves are entitled to 15 days' unpaid leave per year for training. Employees called to active state duty in the Colorado National Guard are entitled to unlimited unpaid leave. Employees on leave for training and active duty must be reinstated to their former positions or a similar position with the same status, pay, and seniority, and they must receive the same vacation, sick leave, bonuses, benefits, and other advantages they would have had if not absent for service.

Connecticut

Conn. Gen. Stat. Ann. §§ 27-33a, 27-34a

Members of the Connecticut National Guard, or the national guard of any state, ordered into active state service by the governor are entitled to the same rights and benefits guaranteed under USERRA, except those pertaining to life insurance. Employees who are members of the state armed forces, any reserve component of the U.S. armed forces, or the national guard of any states, are entitled to take leave to perform ordered military duty, including meetings or drills, that take place during regular work hours, without loss or reduction of vacation or holiday benefits. Employer may not discriminate in terms of promotion or continued employment.

Delaware

Del. Code Ann. tit. 20 § 905

National Guard members who are called to state active duty shall be entitled to the same rights, privileges, and protections as they would have had if called for military training under federal law protecting reservists and National Guard members.

Florida

Fla. Stat. Ann. §§ 250.481, 250.482, 252.55, 627.6692(5)

Employees who are called to active duty in the National Guard, or into active duty by the laws of any other state, may not be penalized for absence from work. Upon return from service, employees are entitled to reinstatement with full benefits unless employer's circumstances have changed to make reinstatement impossible or unreasonable or it would impose an undue hardship. Reinstated employees may not be terminated without cause for one year.

If a member of the National Guard or Reserves is receiving COBRA benefits when called to active duty, the period of time when that service member is covered by TRICARE (military health benefits) won't count against his or her COBRA entitlement. Discrimination against members of the National Guard or reserves is prohibited.

Employers with 15 or more employees must provide up to 15 days of unpaid leave to members of the Civil Air Patrol. Employers must reinstate an employee after the leave, unless the employer's circumstances have changed such that it would be unreasonable or impossible or it would cause an undue hardship. Returning employees may not be fired without cause for one year.

Georgia

Ga. Code Ann. § 38-2-280

Discrimination against members of the U.S. military reserves or state militia is prohibited. Employees called to active duty in the U.S. uniformed services, the Georgia National Guard, or the national guard of any other state, are entitled to unlimited unpaid leave for active service and up to 6 months' leave in any 4-year period for service school or annual training.

State Laws on Military Leave (continued)

Employee is entitled to reinstatement with full benefits unless employer's circumstances have changed to make reinstatement impossible or unreasonable. Employee must apply for reinstatement within 90 days of discharge or within 10 days of completing school or training.

Hawaii

Haw. Rev. Stat. § 121-43

Members of the National Guard are entitled to unlimited unpaid leave while performing ordered National Guard service and while going to and returning from service, and reinstatement to the same or a position comparable in seniority, status, and pay. If an employee is not qualified for his or her former position because of a disability sustained during service but is qualified for another position, the employee is entitled to the position that is most similar to his or her former position, unless employer's circumstances have changed to make reinstatement impossible or unreasonable. Employee cannot be terminated without cause for one year after reinstatement. Employer cannot discriminate against employee because of any obligation as a member of the National Guard.

Idaho

Idaho Code §§ 46-224, 46-225, 46-407, 46-409

Members of the Idaho National Guard, or the national guard of another state, who are called to active duty by the governor or president in time of war, armed conflict, or emergency, are entitled to the same protections as USERRA. Once their leave is over, employees are entitled to reinstatement to their former position or a comparable position with like seniority, status, and pay. If an employee is not qualified for his or her former position because of a disability sustained during service, the employee is entitled to the position that is

most similar to his or her former position in terms of seniority, status, and pay (provided that the employee is qualified). Reinstated employees may not be fired without cause for one year.

Members of the National Guard and U.S. armed forces reserves may take up to 15 days' unpaid leave per year for training without affecting the employee's rights to vacation, sick leave, bonus, advancement, and other advantages of employment. Employees must give 90 days' notice of training dates.

Illinois

20 Ill. Comp. Stat. §§ 1805/30.15, 1805/30.20; 330 Ill. Comp. Stat. § 60/4; 820 Ill. Comp. Stat. Ann. §§ 148/10, 148/15, 148/20

Members of the National Guard called to active state duty by order of the governor are entitled to leave and reinstatement with the same increases in status, seniority, and wages that were earned during the employee's military duty by employees in like positions, or to a position of like seniority, status, and pay, unless employer's circumstances have changed so that reinstatement would be unreasonable or impossible or impose an undue hardship. If employee is no longer qualified for the position because of a disability acquired during service but is qualified for any other position, then the employee is entitled to the position that will provide like seniority, status, and pay. If reasonably possible, employee must give advance notice of military service. Members of the National Guard must submit request for reemployment the day after finishing duty if duty lasted less than 31 days, within 14 days if duty lasted longer than 30 days, or within 90 days if duty lasted longer than 180 days. Members of the U.S. uniformed services must submit request for reemployment within 90 days. Employee can't be discharged without cause for

State Laws on Military Leave (continued)

one year. Employees who quit their jobs to enter military service are entitled to restoration after receiving an honorable discharge.

Employers with at least 15 employees must provide up to 15 days of unpaid Civil Air Patrol leave to employees performing a civil air patrol mission. Employers with at least 50 employees must provide up to 30 days of unpaid leave for the same purposes. Employees must be reinstated to the same position with the same pay, benefits, and seniority.

Indiana

Ind. Code Ann. §§ 10-16-7-4, 10-16-7-6, 10-16-7-23; 10-17-4-1 to 10-17-4-5

Members of the Indiana National Guard, or the national guard of any other state, who are called to state active duty have the same leave and reinstatement rights and benefits guaranteed under USERRA. Employers may not refuse to allow members of the Indiana National Guard to attend assembly for drills, training, or other duties.

Members of the U.S. armed force reserves may take up to 15 days' unpaid leave per year for training. Employees must provide evidence of dates of departure and return 90 days in advance, and proof of completion of the training upon return. Leave does not affect vacation, sick leave, bonus, or promotion rights. At the end of training, employee must be reinstated to former or a similar position with no loss of seniority or benefits.

Iowa

Iowa Code § 29A.43

Members of the Iowa National Guard, the national guard of any other state, the organized reserves of the U.S. armed forces, or the Civil Air Patrol who are called into temporary duty are entitled to reinstatement to former or a similar position. Leave does not affect vacation, sick

leave, bonuses, or other benefits. Employee must provide evidence of satisfactory completion of duty and of qualifications to perform the job's duties. Employers may not discriminate against these employees or discharge them due to their military affiliations.

Kansas

Kan. Stat. Ann. §§ 48-222, 48-517

Employees called into active duty by the state of Kansas, or any other state, are entitled to unlimited leave and reinstatement to the same position or a comparable position with like seniority, status, and pay. Reemployment not required if employer's circumstances have changed so as to make reemployment impossible/unreasonable or if reemployment would impose undue hardship on employer. Reinstated employees may not be discharged without cause for one year. Members of the Kansas National Guard are entitled to 5 to 10 days' leave each year to attend annual muster and camp of instruction. Employer's failure to allow employee to attend or punishing employee who attends is a misdemeanor.

Kentucky

Ky. Rev. Stat. Ann. §§ 38.238, 38.460

Members of National Guard are entitled to unlimited unpaid leave for active duty or training and reinstatement to former position with no loss of seniority or benefits. Employer may not in any way discriminate against employee or use threats to prevent employee from enlisting in the Kentucky National Guard or active militia.

Louisiana

La. Rev. Stat. Ann. §§ 29:38, 29:38.1

Employees called into active duty in National Guard, state militia, or any branch of the state military forces of Louisiana or any other state are

State Laws on Military Leave (continued)

entitled to reinstatement to same or comparable position with same seniority, status, benefits, and pay. If employee is not qualified for former position because of disability sustained during active duty, but is otherwise qualified to perform another position, employer or successor shall employ person in other or comparable position with like seniority, status, benefits, and pay provided the employment does not pose a direct threat or significant risk to the health and safety of the individual or others that cannot be eliminated by reasonable accommodation. Employees on leave are entitled to the benefits offered to employees who take leave for other reasons. Employee must report to work within 72 hours of release or recovery from service-related injury or illness and cannot be fired, except for cause, for one year after reinstatement. Employer cannot discriminate against employee because of any obligation as a member of the state National Guard or U.S. reserves.

Maine

Me. Rev. Stat. Ann. tit. 37-B, § 342; tit. 26, §§ 811–813

Employer may not discriminate against employee for membership or service in National Guard or United States armed forces reserves. Employees in the National Guard or reserves are entitled to military leave in response to state or federal military orders. Upon completion of service, employees must be reinstated, at the same pay, seniority, benefits, and status, and must receive all other employment advantages as if they had been continuously employed.

For the first 30 days of an employee's military leave, the employer must continue the employee's health, dental, and life insurance at no additional cost to the employee. After 30 days, the employee may continue these benefits at his or her own expense (paying the employer's group rates).

Maryland

Md. Code Ann., [Public Safety], § 13-704; Md. Code Ann., Lab. & Empl., § 3-1001 to 3-1007

Members of the state National Guard and Maryland Defense Force ordered to military duty have the same leave and reinstatement rights and benefits guaranteed under USERRA. Maryland employers with 15 or more employees must allow employees who have been employed for at least 90 days to take at least 15 days off each year to respond to an emergency mission of the Maryland Wing of the Civil Air Patrol. Employees must give as much notice as possible of their need for this leave. After arriving at the emergency location, employees must notify their employer and estimate how long the mission will take. Employees are entitled to reinstatement upon their return from this type of leave. Employers may not penalize employees for exercising their rights under this law, nor may they retaliate against employees who complain that an employer has violated the law.

Massachusetts

Mass. Gen. Laws ch. 151B, § 4; ch 33 § 13

Employers may not discriminate against employees and applicants based on their membership in, application to perform, or obligation to perform military service, including service in the National Guard. Employees who are members of the armed forces are entitled to the same rights and protections granted under USERRA.

Michigan

Mich. Comp. Laws §§ 32.271 to 32.274

Employees who are called to active duty in the U.S. uniformed services, the National Guard, or the military or naval forces of Michigan or any other state, are entitled to take unpaid leave, and

State Laws on Military Leave (continued)

to be reinstated when their service has ended. Reinstatement is not required for military service that exceeds five years, except in certain cases. Employers may not discriminate against employees based on their military service, use threats to prevent employees from enlisting, or prevent employees from attending military encampments or other places of drills or instruction.

Minnesota

Minn. Stat. Ann. § 192.34

Employer may not discharge employee, interfere with military service, or dissuade employee from enlisting by threatening employee's job. Applies to employees who are members of the U.S., Minnesota, or any other state military or naval forces.

Mississippi

Miss. Code Ann. §§ 33-1-15, 33-1-19

Employers may not discriminate against employees or applicants based on their current membership in the reserves of the U.S. armed forces or their former membership in the U.S. armed forces. Employers may not threaten employees to dissuade them from enlisting. Members of the U.S. armed forces reserves or U.S. military veterans may take time off for state or federal military training or duty, with reinstatement to their former position (or a similar position) once their leave is over. Employees must provide evidence that they have completed their training.

Missouri

Mo. Rev. Stat. §§ 40.490, 41.730

Members of the Missouri military forces, the national guard of any other state, or a reserve component of the U.S. armed forces, who are called to active duty are entitled to the same leave and reinstatement rights provided

under USERRA. Employers may not discharge employees, interfere with their military service, or use threats to dissuade employee from enlisting in the state organized militia.

Montana

Mont. Code Ann. §§ 10-1-1005, 10-1-1006, 10-1-1007

Employees who are ordered to federally funded military service are entitled to all rights available under USERRA. Members of the Montana National Guard, or the national guard of any other state, who are called to state military duty are entitled to leave for duration of service. Leave may not be deducted from sick leave, vacation, or other leave, although employee may voluntarily use that leave. Returning employee is entitled to reinstatement to same or similar position with the same seniority, status, pay, health insurance, pension, and other benefits, provided that the employee told the employer of membership in the military at the time of hire, or if the employee enlisted during employment, at the time of enlistment. Employer may not in any way discriminate against employee or dissuade employee from enlisting in the state organized militia.

Nebraska

Neb. Rev. Stat. § 55-161

Employees who are called into active duty in the Nebraska National Guard, or the national guard of any other state, have the same leave and reinstatement rights and benefits guaranteed under USERRA.

Nevada

Nev. Rev. Stat. Ann. §§ 412.139, 412.606

Employers may not discriminate against members of the Nevada National Guard or the national guard of another state and may not discharge any employee because he or she assembles for

State Laws on Military Leave (continued)

training, participates in field training, is called to active duty, or otherwise meets as required for ceremonies, maneuvers, and other military duties.

New Hampshire

N.H. Rev. Stat. Ann. §§ 110-B:65, 110-C:1

Members of the state National Guard or militia called to active duty by the governor have the same leave and reinstatement rights and benefits guaranteed under USERRA. Employer may not discriminate against employee because of connection or service with state National Guard or militia; may not dissuade employee from enlisting by threatening job.

New Jersey

N.J. Stat. Ann. § 38:23C-20

An employee is entitled to take unpaid leave for active service in the U.S. or state military services. Upon return, employee must be reinstated to the same or a similar position, unless employer's circumstances have changed to make reinstatement impossible or unreasonable. If same or similar position is not possible, employer shall restore such person to any available position, if requested by such person, for which the person is capable and qualified to perform the duties. Employee must apply for reinstatement within 90 days of release from service. Employee may not be fired without cause for one year after returning from service. Employee is also entitled to take up to 3 months' leave in 4-year period for annual training or assemblies relating to military service, or to attend service schools conducted by the U.S. armed forces. Employee must apply for reinstatement within 10 days.

New Mexico

N.M. Stat. Ann. §§ 28-15-1, 28-15-2, 20-4-6

Members of the U.S. armed forces, organized reserves, or National Guard of any state may take unpaid leave for service (or for up to 1 year of hospitalization after discharge). Employee who is still qualified must be reinstated in former or similar position with like status, seniority, and pay unless employer's circumstances have changed to make reinstatement impossible or unreasonable. Employee may not be fired without cause for one year after returning from service. Employee must request reinstatement within 90 days. Employer may not discriminate against or discharge employee because of membership in the National Guard; may not prevent employee from performing military service.

Members of the U.S. armed forces, organized reserves, or National Guard of any state may take unpaid leave for service for up to five years. Employee who is still qualified must be reinstated in former or similar position with like status, seniority, and pay unless employer's circumstances have changed to make reinstatement impossible or unreasonable. Employee may not be fired without cause for one year after returning from service.

Employee must request reinstatement within 90 days after being released from duty or after being released from continuing hospitalization following duty (hospitalization can last no longer than two years). Employer may not discriminate against or discharge employee because of membership in the National Guard; may not prevent employee from performing military service.

New York

N.Y. Mil. Law §§ 251, 252, 317, 318

Members of the U.S. armed forces or organized militia are entitled to unpaid leave for active service; reserve drills or annual training; service school; initial full-time or active duty training. Returning employee is entitled to reinstatement to previous position, or to one with the same seniority, status, and pay,

State Laws on Military Leave (continued)

unless the employer's circumstances have changed and reemployment is impossible or unreasonable. Employee must apply for reinstatement within 90 days of discharge from active service, 10 days of completing school, reserve drills, or annual training, or 60 days of completing initial full-time or active duty training. Employee may not be discharged without cause for one year after reinstatement. Employers may not discriminate against persons subject to state or federal military duty.

North Carolina

N.C. Gen. Stat. §§ 127A-201, 127A-202, 127A-202.1, 127B-14

Members of the North Carolina National Guard, or the national guard of any other state, who are called to active state duty by a state governor are entitled to take unpaid leave. Within five days of release from state duty, employee must be restored to previous position or one of comparable seniority, status, and salary, unless the employer's circumstances now make it unreasonable. Employees who are no longer qualified for their jobs must be placed in another position with appropriate seniority, status, and salary. For service of 30 days or less, the employee must apply for reinstatement in writing on the next regularly scheduled workday at least eight hours after traveling home. For service of more than 30 days, the employee must apply in writing within 14 days of release from duty. (If the employee is hospitalized due to an injury or illness sustained in active duty, different rules apply.)

Employers may not discriminate against or fire an employee because of membership in the national guard of any state or fire an employee called up for emergency military service.

North Dakota

N.D. Cent. Code §§ 37-29-01, 37-29-03

Employers may not terminate, demote, or otherwise discriminate against volunteer members of the North Dakota army national guard or North Dakota air national guard, or volunteer civilian members of the civil air patrol. The employer must allow such employees to be absent or tardy from work for up to 20 days in a calendar year because they are responding to a disaster or national emergency (20-day limit does not apply to involuntarily activated members of the North Dakota National Guard). An employee who needs this leave must make a reasonable effort to notify the employer. Upon request, the employee must also provide written verification of the dates and times of service.

Ohio

Ohio Rev. Code Ann. §§ 5903.01, 5903.02

Employees who are members of the Ohio organized militia or National Guard or in the organized militia of another state called for active duty or training; members of the commissioned public health service corps; or any other uniformed service called up in time of war or emergency; have the same leave and reinstatement rights and benefits guaranteed under USERRA.

Oklahoma

Okla. Stat. Ann. tit. 44, §§ 71, 208.1

Employees in the Oklahoma National Guard who are ordered to state active duty or full-time National Guard duty have the same reinstatement rights and other benefits guaranteed by USERRA. Members of the state National Guard must be allowed to take time off to attend state National

State Laws on Military Leave (continued)

Guard drills, instruction, encampment, maneuvers, ceremonies, exercises, or other duties.

Oregon

Ore. Rev. Stat. §§ 659A.082, 659A.086

Members of Oregon or other states' organized militias called into active state service or state active duty may take unpaid leave for term of service. Returning employee is entitled to reinstatement with no loss of seniority or benefits including sick leave, vacation, or service credits under a pension plan. Employee must return to work within 7 calendar days of release from service.

Pennsylvania

51 Pa. Cons. Stat. Ann. §§ 7301 to 7309

Employees who enlist or are drafted during a time of war or emergency called by the president or governor, along with reservists or members of Pennsylvania National Guard called into active duty, are entitled to unpaid military leave. Leave expires 90 days after enlistment/draft period, 90 days after military duty for reservists, 30 days after state duty for Pennsylvania National Guard members. Returning employee must be reinstated to same or similar position with same status, seniority, and pay. If no longer qualified due to disability sustained during military duty, employer must restore to position with like seniority, status, and pay unless employer or successor's circumstances have changed so as to make it impossible or unreasonable to do so. Employers may not discharge or discriminate against any employee because of membership or service in the military. Employees called to active duty are entitled to 30 days' health insurance continuation benefits at no cost.

Rhode Island

R.I. Gen. Laws §§ 30-11-2 to 30-11-9, 30-21-1

Members of state military forces and the National Guard of Rhode Island or any other state who are called to active duty have the same leave and reinstatement rights and benefits guaranteed under USERRA. Members of the National Guard or U.S. armed forces reserves are entitled to unpaid leave for training and are entitled to reinstatement with the same status, pay, and seniority. Employees in the U.S. armed forces are entitled to reinstatement to the same position or a position with similar seniority, status, and pay unless the employer's circumstances make reinstatement impossible or unreasonable. Employee must request reinstatement within 40 days. Employer may not discriminate against or discharge employee because of membership in the state military forces or U.S. reserves, interfere with employee's military service, or dissuade employee from enlisting by threatening employee's job.

South Carolina

S.C. Code Ann. §§ 25-1-2310 to 25-1-2340, 25-1-2350

Members of the South Carolina National Guard or State Guard, or the national or state guard of any state, who are called to active duty by a state governor are entitled to unpaid leave for service. Upon honorable discharge from service, the employee must be reinstated to the same position or a position with similar seniority, status, and pay. Employee must apply for reinstatement in writing, within 5 days of release from service or related hospitalization. Employer has no duty to reinstate if the employer's circumstances make reinstatement unreasonable.

State Laws on Military Leave (continued)

South Dakota

S.D. Codified Laws Ann. § 33A-2-9

Members of the South Dakota National Guard, or the national guard of any state, ordered to active duty by the governor or president have the same leave and reinstatement rights and benefits guaranteed under USERRA.

Tennessee

Tenn. Code Ann. § 58-1-604

Employer may not terminate or refuse to hire an employee because of Tennessee National Guard membership or because employee is absent for a required drill, including annual field training.

Texas

Tex. Govt. Code Ann. §§ 437.204, 437.213

Members of the state military forces are entitled to the same leave and reinstatement protections granted under USERRA. Employers may not discriminate against members of the Texas military forces, or the military forces of any other state, and have the right to be reinstated following a call to active duty or training. Employees are entitled to be reinstated to the same position they held before leaving, with no loss of time, efficiency rating, vacation time, or other benefits. An employee must give notice of his or her intent to return to work as soon as practicable after release from duty.

Utah

Utah Code Ann. § 39-1-36

Members of U.S. armed forces reserves who are called to active duty, active duty for training, inactive duty training, or state active duty may take up to 5 years of unpaid leave. Upon return, employee is entitled to reinstatement to previous employment with same seniority, status, pay, and vacation rights. Employer may not discriminate

against an employee based on membership in armed forces reserves.

Vermont

Vt. Stat. Ann. tit. 21, § 491, Vt. Stat. Ann. tit. 20, § 608

Employees who are members of U.S. armed forces reserves, an organized unit of the National Guard of Vermont or any other state, or the ready reserves are entitled to 15 days per year of unpaid leave for military drills, training, or other temporary duty under military authority. Returning employee must be reinstated to former position with the same status, pay, and seniority, including any seniority that accrued during the leave of absence. Employer may not discriminate against an employee who is a member or an applicant for membership in the National Guard of Vermont or any other state. Members of the National Guard of Vermont or any other state ordered to state active duty by the governor have the right to take unpaid leave from civilian employment, and cannot be required to exhaust their vacation or other accrued leave.

Virginia

Va. Code Ann. §§ 44-93.2 to 44-93.4

Members of the Virginia National Guard, Virginia Defense Force, or the national guard of another state, called to active duty by the governor are entitled to take unpaid leave and may not be required to use vacation or any other accrued leave (unless employee wishes). Returning employee whose absence does not exceed five years must be reinstated to previous position or one with same seniority, status, and pay; if position no longer exists, then to a comparable position unless employer's circumstances would make reemployment unreasonable. Employee must apply for reinstatement, in writing, within (a) 14 days of release from service or related hospitalization

State Laws on Military Leave (continued)

if service length did not exceed 180 days, or (b) 90 days of release from service or related hospitalization if service length exceeded 180 days. Employer cannot discriminate against employees because of membership in state military service.

Washington

Wash. Rev. Code Ann. §§ 73.16.032 to 73.16.035

Employees in Washington who are members of the armed forces or the national guard of any state are entitled to take leave when called to active duty for training, inactive duty training, full-time national guard duty, or state active duty. Employees are entitled to be reinstated, following their military duty, to the position they previously held or one with like seniority, status, and pay. The time limit for requesting reinstatement depends on the length of the employee's military leave.

Employers may not discriminate against employees based on their membership in any branch of the uniformed services.

West Virginia

W.Va. Code § 15-1F-8

Employees who are members of the organized militia in active service of the state of West Virginia or any other state have the same leave and reinstatement rights and benefits guaranteed under USERRA.

Wisconsin

Wis. Stat. Ann. §§ 111.321, 321.64, 321.65, 321.66

Employees who enlist, are inducted, or are ordered to serve in the U.S. armed forces for 90 days or more, or civilian employees who are asked to perform national defense work during an officially proclaimed emergency, may take leave for military service and/or training. Employees who are called to state active duty in the Wisconsin National Guard or the national guard of any other state, or called to active service with the state laboratory of

hygiene during a public health emergency, are also entitled to take military leave. Upon completion of military leave, employees are entitled to reinstatement to their prior position or to one with equivalent seniority, status, and pay. A reinstated employee may not be discharged without cause for up to one year. Employers may not discriminate against employees based on their military service.

Employers with 11 or more employees must provide up to 15 days of unpaid leave (but not more than five consecutive days at a time) to members of the Civil Air Patrol for an emergency service operation, if it wouldn't unduly disrupt the employers' operations.

Wyoming

Wyo. Stat. §§ 19-11-103, 19-11-104, 19-11-107, 19-11-111

Employees of the armed forces or national guard of any state who report for active duty, training, or a qualifying physical exam may take up to 5 years' leave of absence. Employee must give advance notice of service. Employee may use vacation or any other accrued leave but is not required to do so. Returning employee is entitled to reemployment with the same seniority, rights, and benefits, plus any additional seniority and benefits that employee would have earned if there had been no absence, unless employer's circumstances have changed so that reemployment is impossible or unreasonable or would impose an undue hardship. Time limits set forth governing written application for reinstatement based on length of uniformed service. Employee is entitled to complete any training program that would have been available to employee's former position during period of absence. Employee may not be terminated without cause for one year after returning to work. Employer cannot discriminate against applicant or member of the uniformed services.

Health Insurance

I n 2010, President Obama signed the Patient Protection and Affordable Care Act into law. Also known as the Affordable Care Act, the ACA, or simply Obamacare, this sweeping health care law is one of the most important workplace reforms in decades. Along with imposing coverage requirements on insurance companies and mandating that everyone carry health insurance or pay a penalty, Obamacare requires larger employers to offer affordable, quality coverage to their full-time employees. Employers that don't provide the benefits required by law must pay a penalty (which is why this employer mandate is sometimes referred to as "pay or play.")

To say Obamacare has been controversial would be putting it very mildly. Congressional Republicans have made multiple attempts to repeal it, employer advocates complain that it increases costs and suppresses hiring, and consumers argue that the insurance plans available in some areas are anything but affordable. However, supporters of the law argue that the benefits outweigh the costs, as health coverage has become more affordable and widely available to millions of Americans.

Political views aside, the Affordable Care Act is still law, and the employer mandate is still in effect. In fact, the IRS recently announced that it will be issuing its first "pay or play" penalties for the year 2015.

This chapter explains what Obamacare requires of employers. It also covers your right to continue health coverage once you leave your job.

CAUTION

More changes might be in store. To keep up to date on legal changes, check the online companion page for this book.

Coverage for Current Employees

Obamacare requires certain employers to either make affordable, quality health care benefits available to employees or pay a fine. But not all employers are subject to this mandate, nor are all employees protected by it.

Which Employers and Employees Are Covered by Obamacare

Obamacare requires employers with at least 50 full-time employees (or their equivalent) to offer health care coverage to their full-time employees or pay a fine.

Employer Coverage

You'd think it would be easy enough to count up to 50, but legal math is different than what they teach in school. The law requires employers to offer coverage once they have at least 50 full-time or full-time equivalent employees. Independent contractors are not included in the count.

Any employee who works at least 30 hours per week is considered full time. To come up with a figure for full-time equivalent (FTE) employees, the employer must add up all of the hours worked in a month by employees who work less than 30 hours per week, then divide the total by 120. For example, if an employer had two employees who each worked 15 hours a week, and the month consisted of four work weeks, those two part-time employees would add up to one FTE employee.

To find out whether an employer is subject to the mandate, you must:

- add up all full-time and FTE employees for each month of the prior year
- divide that total by 12, and
- round the total down to the nearest whole number.

Employers with fewer than 50 employees aren't subject to the employer mandate. Of course, they are free to offer health insurance if they wish, and Obamacare provides some help, in the form of tax credits and a special marketplace for small businesses.

Employee Coverage

Covered employers must offer health insurance to at least 95% of full-time employees and their dependents. Employers are not required to provide health insurance to part-time employees—those working less than 30 hours—even though those employees are counted in the FTE calculation for determining employer coverage.

What Employers Must Offer

Employers that want to avoid paying a fine have to provide insurance that meets certain standards. The health insurance they offer you must be affordable and must provide minimum value. If either of these requirements isn't met, the employer will be

subject to financial penalties if its employees choose to instead buy their own insurance through the state health care exchanges.

Individual Mandate Under Obamacare Repealed

When it was originally passed, the Affordable Care Act also had an individual mandate: All Americans were required to have health insurance or pay an individual fine. Employees who didn't receive health insurance through work had to secure it through another source. If they didn't, they owed a fine of $695 or 2.5% of their household income, whichever was higher.

However, in late 2017, this portion of Obamacare was repealed. Beginning in 2019, people will not be required to pay a fine if they don't have health insurance. The individual mandate is still in effect for the year 2018, however.

Affordable Coverage

Although employers have to make coverage available to employees, Obamacare does not require employers to pay the full cost. Under Obamacare, employers can continue the common practice of passing some of the premium costs on to employees. However, there's a limit to how much employees can be required to pay.

A plan is considered "affordable" under Obamacare as long as an employee doesn't have to pay more than 9.56% of his or her annual household income for self-only coverage (that is, coverage for the employee only, not for the employee's spouse, partner, or children). This percentage is subject to change each year.

Minimum Value

A plan meets the minimum value standards if it pays at least 60% of covered costs. In other words, your plan can require you to pay up to 40% of your health care costs and still meet this requirement. The official Obamacare website—www.healthcare.gov—suggests asking your employer whether its plan meets this standard.

If Your Employer's Plan Falls Short

Ordinarily, people who buy their own insurance can qualify for a tax credit to keep costs down. Those who earn less than about $48,000 qualify for some savings; the less you earn, the higher your credit. If your employer's plan doesn't meet the affordability or minimum value tests, you are eligible for these tax credits for purchasing insurance on your own. If your employer's plan does meet Obamacare standards, you can still shop around for your own insurance, but you won't qualify for any savings if you decide to pass on your employer's coverage.

Employer Penalties

The employer penalties only kick in if at least one employee receives the premium tax credit for purchasing insurance through the exchange. Obamacare has two different penalties, depending on the type of violation:

- **No coverage.** If an employer fails to provide coverage to 95% of its full-time employees, and at least one employee receives the tax credit for buying insurance through the exchange, it must pay an annual penalty of $2,260 for each full-time employee that it has. However, the first 30 full-time employees are "free" and not included in the calculation. For example, an employer with 60 full-time employees would owe a penalty of $67,800 ($2,260 x 30 employees).

- **Employer offers coverage.** An employer that offers coverage to 95% of its full-time employees will still owe a penalty if the coverage isn't affordable or doesn't provide minimum value. The penalty also kicks in if an employee purchases insurance through the exchange because he or she was not one of the 95% of employees who were offered coverage. In any of these situations, the penalty is $3,390, but only for each employee who received the premium tax credit.

The penalty amounts are adjusted for inflation each year; the figures above are for 2017.

Coverage for Former Employees

A federal workplace law, the Consolidated Omnibus Budget Reconciliation Act, or

COBRA (29 U.S.C. § 1162), requires your employer to offer you—and your spouse and dependents—continuing insurance coverage in either of the following situations:

- You lose insurance coverage because your number of work hours is reduced.
- You lose your job for any reason other than gross misconduct. Courts are still grappling with the question of how egregious the workplace behavior must be to qualify as gross misconduct. So far, courts have ruled that inefficiency, poor performance, negligence, or errors in judgment on the job are not enough. There must be some deliberate, wrongful violations of workplace standards to qualify as gross misconduct.

COBRA was intended to extend access to group health insurance coverage to people who would otherwise be totally unprotected and unlikely to be able to secure coverage on their own. When COBRA passed in 1986, no one had a right to—or a legal obligation to purchase—health insurance. But now, Obamacare is the law of the land. If you lose coverage through your job these days, you have a choice: Continue your health insurance through COBRA or buy your own coverage on the private market or through the state insurance exchanges. To decide which option makes more sense, you'll have to compare coverage, benefits, and cost. Often, an employer-provided plan is more comprehensive, and might have seemed generous when your employer was footing part of the bill. However, as explained below, you have to pay the full premium cost for COBRA coverage.

COBRA applies to all employers with 20 or more employees although, as noted below, some states have passed "mini-COBRA" laws that apply to smaller workplaces. Under the law, employers need only make the insurance available; they need not pay for it. Employers may charge up to 102% of the base premium for continued coverage (the extra 2% is thrown in to cover administrative costs).

Those covered under COBRA include:

- all individuals who are or were provided insurance coverage under an employer's group plan, and
- those individuals' beneficiaries, who typically include a spouse and dependent children.

Continuing Coverage

Qualified employees may elect to continue coverage up to 18 months after they quit, are laid off, or are fired (other than for gross misconduct), or after a reduction in hours that makes them ineligible for coverage. Those who become disabled, however, can get COBRA coverage for 29 months.

No one can choose to enroll in an employer-provided insurance plan upon becoming ineligible for workplace coverage. COBRA extends only to those already enrolled when their health insurance coverage ceases.

Coverage for Dependents

Beneficiaries or dependents may also elect to continue coverage under the same circumstances mentioned above. However, they may opt to have coverage continued for up to 36 months if any of the following occurs:

- The covered employee dies.
- The covered employee becomes entitled to Medicare.
- There is a divorce or legal separation.
- A dependent child loses "dependent" child status under the plan.

Enforcing COBRA

COBRA provides for a number of fines for employers and health insurance plan administrators that violate its requirements. However, the Act has so many complexities that no one can agree on exactly what circumstances release an employer from its requirements. And, frustratingly, there is no one place you can call to get help if you think your rights under COBRA have been violated. Parts of the law are administered by the U.S. Labor Department and other parts fall under the Internal Revenue Service.

If you have a COBRA-related question or complaint, you can try calling your local office of either of those agencies, but neither has a track record of actively enforcing COBRA requirements. Your employer is required to provide you with an explanation of your COBRA rights when you are enrolled in a group health care plan covering 20 or more employees. However, these materials are seldom well written or easy to understand.

In general, COBRA can be enforced only through an expensive lawsuit. That means that the statute typically can be used only by large groups of former employees who have been denied their rights to continue group health insurance coverage, and who can share the expense of hiring a lawyer and filing a lawsuit to enforce that right. (In Chapter 17, see "Class Action Lawsuits.")

State Laws on Insurance Continuation

Because COBRA generally cannot be enforced by any means other than a complex and expensive lawsuit, state laws that give former employees the right to continue group health insurance coverage after leaving a job are often a better alternative. State laws often provide interesting twists that make it easier to get continued coverage.

However, for an employee to be eligible for continued coverage, most state laws require that he or she must be covered for a certain time—three months is common—just before being terminated. In nearly all instances, any continuation of coverage will be at your expense, just as it would be under COBRA.

However, the specific requirements of these laws and how they are enforced vary tremendously. For more specific information, contact your state's insurance department. In addition, the plant closing laws of a few states may give you the right to continue group health insurance coverage. (In Chapter 9, see "Plant Closings.")

State Health Insurance Continuation Laws

Alabama

Ala. Code § 27-55-3(a)(4)

Special Situations: 18 months for subjects of domestic abuse who have lost coverage they had under abuser's insurance and who do not qualify for COBRA.

Arizona

Ariz. Rev. Stat. §§ 20-1377, 20-1408

Employers affected: All employers that offer group disability insurance.

Length of coverage for dependents: Insurer must either continue coverage for dependents or convert to individual policy upon death of covered employee or divorce. Coverage must be the same unless the insured chooses a lesser plan.

Qualifying event: Death of an employee; change in marital status; any other reason stated in policy (other than failure to pay premium).

Time employer has to notify employee: No provisions for employer. Insurance policy must include notice of conversion privilege. Clerk of court must provide notice to anyone filing for divorce that dependent spouse entitled to convert health insurance coverage.

Time employee has to apply: 31 days after termination of existing coverage.

Arkansas

Ark. Code Ann. §§ 23-86-114 to 23-86-116

Employers affected: All employers that offer group health insurance.

Eligible employees: Employees continuously insured for previous 3 months.

Length of coverage for employee: 120 days.

Length of coverage for dependents: 120 days.

Qualifying event: Termination of employment; change in insured's marital status. Employer may

—but is not required to—continue benefits on death of employee.

Time employee has to apply: 10 days.

California

*Cal. Health & Safety Code §§ 1373.6, 1373.621;
Cal. Ins. Code §§ 10128.50 to 10128.59*

Employers affected: Employers that offer group health insurance and have 2 to 19 employees.

Eligible employees: All covered employees are eligible.

Length of coverage for employee: 36 months.

Length of coverage for dependents: 36 months.

Qualifying event: Termination of employment; reduction in hours; death of employee; change in marital status; loss of dependent status; covered employee's eligibility for Medicare (for dependents only).

Time employer has to notify employee: 15 days.

Time employee has to apply: 60 days.

Special situations: Employee who is at least 60 years old and has worked for employer for previous 5 years may continue benefits for self and spouse beyond COBRA or Cal-COBRA limits (also applies to COBRA employers). Employee who began receiving COBRA coverage on or after 1/1/03 and whose COBRA coverage is for less than 36 months may use Cal-COBRA to bring total coverage up to 36 months.

Colorado

Colo. Rev. Stat. § 10-16-108

Employers affected: All employers that offer group health insurance.

Eligible employees: Employees continuously insured for previous 6 months.

Length of coverage for employee: 18 months.

Length of coverage for dependents: 18 months.

State Health Insurance Continuation Laws (continued)

Qualifying event: Termination of employment; reduction in hours; death of employee; change in marital status.

Time employer has to notify employee: 60 days.

Time employee has to apply: 30 days after termination; 60 days if employer fails to give notice.

Connecticut

Conn. Gen. Stat. Ann. §§ 38a-512a, 31-51n, 31-51o

Employers affected: All employers that offer group health insurance.

Eligible employees: All covered employees are eligible.

Length of coverage for employee: 30 months, or until eligible for Medicare benefits.

Length of coverage for dependents: 30 months, or until eligible for Medicare benefits; 36 months in case of employee's death, divorce, or loss of dependent status.

Qualifying event: Layoff; reduction in hours; termination of employment; death of employee; change in marital status; loss of dependent status.

Special situations: When facility closes or relocates, employers with 100 or more employees must pay for insurance for employee and dependents for 120 days or until employee is eligible for other group coverage, whichever comes first. (Does not affect employee's right to conventional continuation coverage, which begins when 120-day period ends.)

Delaware

18 Del. Code Ann. § 3571F

Employers affected: Employers that offer group health insurance and have 1 to 19 employees.

Eligible employees: Employees continuously insured for previous three months.

Length of coverage for employee: 9 months.

Length of coverage for dependents: 9 months.

Qualifying event: Employee's death; termination of employment; divorce or legal separation; employee's eligibility for Medicare; loss of dependent status.

Time employer has to notify employee: Within 30 days of the qualifying event.

Time employee has to apply: 30 days.

District of Columbia

D.C. Code Ann. §§ 32-731 to 32-732

Employers affected: Employers with fewer than 20 employees.

Eligible employees: All covered employees are eligible.

Length of coverage for employee: Three months.

Length of coverage for dependents: Three months.

Qualifying event: Any reason employee or dependent becomes ineligible for coverage, except employee's termination for gross misconduct.

Time employer has to notify employee: Within 15 days of termination of coverage.

Time employee has to apply: 45 days after termination of coverage.

Florida

Fla. Stat. Ann. § 627.6692

Employers affected: Employers with fewer than 20 employees.

Eligible employees: Full-time (25 or more hours per week) employees covered by employer's health insurance plan.

Length of coverage for employee: 18 months.

Length of coverage for dependents: 18 months.

Qualifying event: Layoff; reduction in hours; termination of employment; death of employee; change in marital status.

State Health Insurance Continuation Laws (continued)

Time employer has to notify employee: Carrier notifies within 14 days of learning of qualifying event (beneficiary has 63 days to notify carrier of qualifying event).

Time employee has to apply: 30 days from receipt of carrier's notice.

Georgia

Ga. Code Ann. §§ 33-24-21.1 to 33-24-21.2

Employers affected: All employers that offer group health insurance.

Eligible employees: Employees continuously insured for previous 6 months.

Length of coverage for employee: 3 months plus any part of the month remaining at termination.

Length of coverage for dependents: 3 months plus any part of the month remaining at termination.

Qualifying event: Termination of employment (except for cause).

Special situations: Employee, spouse, or former spouse, who is 60 years old and who has been covered for previous 6 months may continue coverage until eligible for Medicare. (Applies to companies with more than 20 employees; does not apply when employee quits for reasons other than health.)

Hawaii

Haw. Rev. Stat. §§ 393-11, 393-15

Employers affected: All employers required to offer health insurance (those paying a regular employee a monthly wage at least 86.67 times state hourly minimum—about $542).

Length of coverage for employee: If employee is hospitalized or prevented from working by sickness, employer must pay insurance premiums for 3 months or for as long as employer continues to pay wages, whichever is longer.

Qualifying event: Employee is hospitalized or prevented by sickness from working.

Idaho

Idaho Code § 41-2213

Employers affected: All employers that offer group disability insurance.

Eligible employees: Employees or dependents who are totally disabled at the time the policy ends. (Applies to policies that provide benefits for loss of time during periods of hospitalization, benefits for hospital or medical expenses, or benefits for dismemberment.)

Length of coverage for employee: Must provide a reasonable extension of coverage (in the case of medical and hospital expenses, a reasonable extension is at least 12 months).

Length of coverage for dependents: Must provide a reasonable extension of coverage (in the case of medical and hospital expenses, a reasonable extension is at least 12 months).

Illinois

215 Ill. Comp. Stat. §§ 5/367e, 5/367.2, 5/367.2-5

Employers affected: All employers that offer group health insurance.

Eligible employees: Employees continuously insured for previous 3 months.

Length of coverage for employee: 12 months.

Length of coverage for dependents: Upon death or divorce, 2 years' coverage for spouse under 55 and eligible dependents who were on employee's plan; until eligible for Medicare or other group coverage for spouse over 55 and eligible dependents who were on employee's plan. A dependent child who has reached plan age limit or who was not already covered by plan, is also entitled to 2 years' continuation coverage.

State Health Insurance Continuation Laws (continued)

Qualifying event: Termination of employment; reduction in hours; death of employee; divorce.

Time employer has to notify employee: 10 days.

Time employee has to apply: 30 days after termination or reduction in hours or receiving notice from employer, whichever is later, but not more than 60 days from termination or reduction in hours.

Iowa

Iowa Code §§ 509B.3, 509B.5

Employers affected: All employers that offer group health insurance.

Eligible employees: Employees continuously insured for previous 3 months.

Length of coverage for employee: 9 months.

Length of coverage for dependents: 9 months.

Qualifying event: Any reason employee or dependent becomes ineligible for coverage.

Time employer has to notify employee: 10 days after termination of coverage.

Time employee has to apply: 10 days after termination of coverage or receiving notice from employer, whichever is later, but not more than 31 days from termination of coverage.

Kansas

Kan. Stat. Ann. § 40-2209(i)

Employers affected: All employers that offer group health insurance.

Eligible employees: Employees continuously insured for previous 3 months.

Length of coverage for employee: 18 months.

Length of coverage for dependents: 18 months.

Qualifying event: Any reason employee or dependent becomes ineligible for coverage.

Time employer has to notify employee: Reasonable notice.

Kentucky

Ky. Rev. Stat. Ann. § 304.18-110

Employers affected: All employers that offer group health insurance.

Eligible employees: Employees continuously insured for previous 3 months.

Length of coverage for employee: 18 months.

Length of coverage for dependents: 18 months.

Qualifying event: Any reason employee or dependent becomes ineligible for coverage.

Time employer has to notify employee: Employer must notify insurer as soon as employee's coverage ends; insurer then notifies employee.

Time employee has to apply: 31 days from receipt of insurer's notice, but not more than 90 days after termination of group coverage.

Louisiana

La. Rev. Stat. Ann. §§ 22:1045, 22:1046

Employers affected: All employers that offer group health insurance and have fewer than 20 employees.

Eligible employees: Employees continuously insured for previous 3 months.

Length of coverage for employee: 12 months.

Length of coverage for dependents: 12 months.

Qualifying event: Termination of employment; death of insured; divorce.

Time employee has to apply: By the end of the month following the month in which the qualifying event occurred.

Special situations: Surviving spouse who is 50 or older may have coverage until remarriage or eligibility for Medicare or other insurance.

State Health Insurance Continuation Laws (continued)

Maine

Me. Rev. Stat. Ann. tit. 24-A, § 2809-A

Employers affected: All employers that offer group health insurance and are not subject to COBRA.

Eligible employees: Employees employed for at least 6 months.

Length of coverage for employee: One year.

Length of coverage for dependents: One year.

Qualifying event: Temporary layoff; permanent layoff if employee is eligible for federal premium assistance for laid-off employees who continue coverage; loss of employment because of a work-related injury or disease.

Time employee has to apply: 31 days from termination of coverage.

Maryland

Md. Code Ann., [Ins.] §§ 15-407 to 15-409

Employers affected: All employers that offer group health insurance.

Eligible employees: Employees continuously insured for previous 3 months.

Length of coverage for employee: 18 months.

Length of coverage for dependents: 18 months upon death of employee; upon change in marital status, 18 months or until spouse remarries or becomes eligible for other coverage.

Qualifying event: Termination of employment; death of employee; change in marital status.

Time employer has to notify employee: Must notify insurer within 14 days of receiving employee's continuation request.

Time employee has to apply: 45 days from termination of coverage. Employee begins application process by requesting an election of continuation notification form from employer.

Massachusetts

Mass. Gen. Laws ch. 175, §§ 110G, 110I; ch. 176J, § 9

Employers affected: All employers that offer group health insurance and have fewer than 20 employees.

Eligible employees: All covered employees are eligible.

Length of coverage for employee: 18 months; 29 months if disabled.

Length of coverage for dependents: 18 months upon termination or reduction in hours; 29 months if disabled; 36 months upon divorce, death of employee, employee's eligibility for Medicare, or employer's bankruptcy.

Qualifying event: Involuntary layoff; death of insured employee; change in marital status.

Time employer has to notify employee: Carrier must notify beneficiary within 14 days of learning of qualifying event.

Time employee has to apply: 60 days.

Special situations: Termination due to plant closing: 90 days' coverage for employee and dependents, at the same payment terms as before closing.

Minnesota

Minn. Stat. Ann. §§ 62A.17; 62A.20; 62A.21

Employers affected: All employers that offer group health insurance and have 2 or more employees.

Eligible employees: All covered employees are eligible.

Length of coverage for employee: 18 months; indefinitely if employee becomes totally disabled while employed.

Length of coverage for dependents: 18 months for current spouse or child after termination of

State Health Insurance Continuation Laws (continued)

employment; divorced or widowed spouse can continue until eligible for Medicare or other group health insurance. Upon divorce or death of employee, dependent children can continue until they no longer qualify as dependents under plan.

Qualifying event: Termination of employment; reduction in hours.

Time employer has to notify employee: Within 14 days of termination of coverage.

Time employee has to apply: 60 days from termination of coverage or receipt of employer's notice, whichever is later.

Mississippi

Miss. Code Ann. § 83-9-51

Employers affected: All employers that offer group health insurance and have fewer than 20 employees.

Eligible employees: Employees continuously insured for previous 3 months.

Length of coverage for employee: 12 months.

Length of coverage for dependents: 12 months.

Qualifying event: Termination of employment; divorce; employee's death; employee's eligibility for Medicare; loss of dependent status.

Time employer has to notify employee: Insurer must notify former or deceased employee's dependent child or divorced spouse of option to continue insurance within 14 days of their becoming ineligible for coverage on employee's policy.

Time employee has to apply: Employee must apply and submit payment before group coverage ends; dependents or former spouse must elect continuation coverage within 30 days of receiving insurer's notice.

Missouri

Mo. Rev. Stat. § 376.428

Employers affected: All employers that offer group health insurance and are not subject to COBRA.

Eligible employees: All employees.

Length of coverage for employee: 18 months.

Length of coverage for dependents: 18 months if eligible due to termination or reduction in hours; 36 months if eligible due to death or divorce.

Qualifying event: Termination of employment; death of employee; divorce; reduction in hours; employee's eligibility for Medicare; loss of dependent status.

Time employer has to notify employee: Same rules as COBRA.

Time employee has to apply: Same rules as COBRA.

Montana

Mont. Code Ann. §§ 33-22-506 to 33-22-507

Employers affected: All employers that offer group disability insurance.

Eligible employees: All employees.

Length of coverage for employee: One year (with employer's consent).

Qualifying event: Reduction in hours.

Special situations: Insurer may not discontinue benefits to child with a disability after child exceeds age limit for dependent status..

Nebraska

Neb. Rev. Stat. §§ 44-1640 and following, 44-7406

Employers affected: Employers not subject to federal COBRA laws.

Eligible employees: All covered employees.

Length of coverage for employee: Six months.

State Health Insurance Continuation Laws (continued)

Length of coverage for dependents: 1 year upon death of insured employee. Subjects of domestic abuse who have lost coverage under abuser's plan and who do not qualify for COBRA may have 18 months' coverage (applies to all employers).

Qualifying event: Involuntary termination of employment (layoff due to labor dispute not considered involuntary).

Time employer has to notify employee: Within 10 days of termination of employment must send notice by certified mail.

Time employee has to apply: 10 days from receipt of employer's notice.

Nevada

Nev. Rev. Stat. Ann. § 689B.0345

Employers affected: All employers that offer group health insurance.

Eligible employees: Employees who are on unpaid leave due to total disability.

Length of coverage for employee: Coverage must continue for 12 months, unless one of the following events occurs sooner: the employee is terminated, the employee obtains another health insurance policy, or the group health insurance policy is terminated.

Length of coverage for dependents: Coverage must continue for 12 months, unless one of the following events occurs sooner: the employee is terminated, the employee obtains another health insurance policy, or the group health insurance policy is terminated.

New Hampshire

N.H. Rev. Stat. Ann. § 415:18

Employers affected: All employers that offer group health insurance.

Eligible employees: All insured employees are eligible.

Length of coverage for employee: 18 months; 29 months if disabled at termination or during first 60 days of continuation coverage.

Length of coverage for dependents: 18 months; 29 months if disabled at termination or during first 60 days of continuation coverage; 36 months upon death of employee, divorce or legal separation, loss of dependent status, or employee's eligibility for Medicare.

Qualifying event: Any reason employee or dependent becomes ineligible for coverage.

Time employer has to notify employee: Carrier must notify beneficiary within 30 days of receiving notice of loss of coverage.

Time employee has to apply: Within 45 days of receipt of notice.

Special situations: Layoff or termination due to strike: 6 months' coverage with option to extend for an additional 12 months. Surviving, divorced, or legally separated spouse who is 55 or older may continue benefits available until eligible for Medicare or another employer-based group insurance.

New Jersey

N.J. Stat. Ann. §§ 17B:27-51.12, 17B:27A-27

Employers affected: Employers with 2 to 50 employees.

Eligible employees: Employed full time (25 or more hours).

Length of coverage for employee: 18 months; 29 months if disabled at termination or during first 60 days of continuation coverage.

Length of coverage for dependents: 18 months; 36 months upon death of employee, divorce or legal separation, loss of dependent status, or employee's eligibility for Medicare.

State Health Insurance Continuation Laws (continued)

Qualifying event: Termination of employment; reduction in hours; change in marital status; death.

Time employer has to notify employee: At time of qualifying event.

Time employee has to apply: Within 30 days of qualifying event.

Special benefits: Coverage must be identical to that offered to current employees.

Special situations: Total disability: employee who has been insured for previous 3 months and employee's dependents, entitled to continuation coverage that includes all benefits offered by group policy (applies to all employers).

New Mexico

N.M. Stat. Ann. § 59A-18-16

Employers affected: All employers that offer group health insurance.

Eligible employees: All insured employees are eligible.

Length of coverage for employee: 6 months.

Length of coverage for dependents: 6 months for termination of employment. May continue group coverage or convert to individual policies upon death of covered employee or divorce or legal separation.

Qualifying event: Termination of employment.

Time employer has to notify employee: Insurer or employer must give written notice at time of termination.

Time employee has to apply: 30 days after receiving notice.

New York

N.Y. Ins. Law § 3221(m)

Employers affected: All employers that offer group health insurance.

Eligible employees: All covered employees are eligible.

Length of coverage for employee: 36 months.

Length of coverage for dependents: 36 months.

Qualifying event: Termination of employment; death of employee; divorce or legal separation; loss of dependent status; employee's eligibility for Medicare.

Time employee has to apply: 60 days after termination or receipt of notice, whichever is later.

North Carolina

N.C. Gen. Stat. §§ 58-53-5 to 58-53-40

Employers affected: All employers that offer group health insurance.

Eligible employees: Employees continuously insured for previous 3 months.

Length of coverage for employee: 18 months.

Length of coverage for dependents: 18 months.

Qualifying event: Termination of employment.

Time employer has to notify employee: Employer has option of notifying employee as part of the exit process.

Time employee has to apply: 60 days.

North Dakota

N.D. Cent. Code §§ 26.1-36-23, 26.1-36-23.1

Employers affected: All employers that offer group health insurance.

Eligible employees: Employees continuously insured for previous 3 months.

Length of coverage for employee: 39 weeks.

Length of coverage for dependents: 39 weeks; 36 months if required by divorce or annulment decree.

State Health Insurance Continuation Laws (continued)

Qualifying event: Termination of employment; change in marital status, if divorce or annulment decree requires employee to continue coverage.

Time employee has to apply: Within 10 days of termination or of receiving notice of continuation rights, whichever is later, but not more than 31 days from termination.

Ohio

Ohio Rev. Code Ann. §§ 1751.53, 3923.38

Employers affected: All employers that offer group health insurance.

Eligible employees: Employees continuously insured for previous 3 months who were involuntarily terminated for reasons other than gross misconduct on the part of the employee.

Length of coverage for employee: 12 months.

Length of coverage for dependents: 12 months.

Qualifying event: Involuntary termination of employment.

Time employer has to notify employee: At termination of employment.

Time employee has to apply: Whichever is earlier: 31 days after coverage terminates; 10 days after coverage terminates if employer notified employee of continuation rights prior to termination; 10 days after employer notified employee of continuation rights, if notice was given after coverage terminated.

Oklahoma

Okla. Stat. Ann. tit. 36, § 4509

Employers affected: All employers that offer group health insurance.

Eligible employees: Employees insured for at least 6 months; (all other employees and their dependents entitled to 30 days' continuation coverage).

Length of coverage for employee: 63 days for basic coverage; 6 months for major medical at the same premium rate prior to termination of coverage (only for losses or conditions that began while group policy in effect).

Length of coverage for dependents: 63 days for basic coverage; 6 months for major medical at the same premium rate prior to termination of coverage (only for losses or conditions that began while group policy in effect).

Qualifying event: Any reason coverage terminates (except employment termination for gross misconduct).

Time employer has to notify employee: Carrier must notify employee in writing within 30 days of receiving notice of termination of employee's coverage.

Time employee has to apply: 31 days after receipt of notice.

Special benefits: Includes maternity care for pregnancy begun while group policy was in effect.

Oregon

Ore. Rev. Stat. §§ 743B.343 to 743B.347

Employers affected: Employers not subject to federal COBRA laws.

Eligible employees: Employees continuously insured for previous 3 months.

Length of coverage for employee: 9 months.

Length of coverage for dependents: 9 months.

Qualifying event: Termination of employment; reduction in hours; employee's eligibility for Medicare; loss of dependent status; termination of membership in group covered by policy; death of employee.

Time employer has to notify employee: 10 days after qualifying event.

State Health Insurance Continuation Laws (continued)

Time employee has to apply: Within the time limit determined by the insurer, which must be at least 10 days after the qualifying event or employee's receipt of notice, whichever is later.

Special situations: Surviving, divorced, or legally separated spouse who is 55 or older and dependent children entitled to continuation coverage until spouse remarries or is eligible for other coverage; must include dental, vision, or prescription drug benefits, if they were offered in original plan (applies to employers with 20 or more employees).

Pennsylvania
Pa. Stat. 40 P.S. § 764j

Employers affected: Employers that offer group health insurance and have 2 to 19 employees.

Eligible employees: Employees continuously insured for at least 3 months.

Length of coverage for employee: 9 months.

Length of coverage for dependents: 9 months.

Qualifying event: Termination of employment; reduction in hours; death of employee; change in marital status; employer's bankruptcy.

Time employer has to notify employee: 30 days after qualifying event.

Time employee has to apply: 30 days after receiving notice.

Rhode Island
R.I. Gen. Laws §§ 27-19.1-1, 27-20.4-1 to 27-20-4-2

Employers affected: All employers that offer group health insurance.

Eligible employees: All insured employees are eligible.

Length of coverage for employee: 18 months (but not longer than continuous employment); cannot be required to pay more than one month premium at a time.

Length of coverage for dependents: 18 months (but not longer than continuous employment); cannot be required to pay more than one month premium at a time.

Qualifying event: Involuntary termination of employment; death of employee; change in marital status; permanent reduction in workforce; employer's going out of business.

Time employer has to notify employee: Employers must post a conspicuous notice of employee continuation rights.

Time employee has to apply: 30 days from termination of coverage.

Special situations: If right to receiving continuing health insurance is stated in the divorce judgment, divorced spouse has right to continue coverage as long as employee remains covered or until divorced spouse remarries or becomes eligible for other group insurance.

South Carolina
S.C. Code Ann. § 38-71-770

Employers affected: All employers that offer group health insurance.

Eligible employees: Employees continuously insured for previous 6 months.

Length of coverage for employee: Six months (in addition to part of month remaining at termination).

Length of coverage for dependents: Six months (in addition to part of month remaining at termination).

Qualifying event: Any reason employee or dependent becomes ineligible for coverage.

Time employer has to notify employee: At time of termination, employer must clearly and meaningfully advise employee of continuation rights.

State Health Insurance Continuation Laws (continued)

South Dakota

S.D. Codified Laws Ann. §§ 58-18-7.5, 58-18-7.12, 58-18C-1

Employers affected: All employers that offer group health insurance.

Eligible employees: All covered employees.

Length of coverage for employee: 18 months; 29 months if disabled at termination or during first 60 days of continuation coverage.

Length of coverage for dependents: 18 months; 29 months if disabled at termination or during first 60 days of continuation coverage; 36 months upon death of employee, divorce or legal separation, loss of dependent status, or employee's eligibility for Medicare.

Qualifying event: Termination of employment; death of employee; divorce or legal separation; loss of dependent status; employee's eligibility for Medicare.

Special situations: When employer goes out of business: 12 months' continuation coverage available to all employees. Employer must notify employees within 10 days of termination of benefits; employees must apply within 60 days of receipt of employer's notice or within 90 days of termination of benefits if no notice given.

Tennessee

Tenn. Code Ann. § 56-7-2312

Employers affected: All employers that offer group health insurance.

Eligible employees: Employees continuously insured for previous 3 months.

Length of coverage for employee: Three months (in addition to part of month remaining at termination).

Length of coverage for dependents: 3 months

(in addition to part of month remaining at termination); 15 months upon death of employee or divorce (in addition to part of month remaining at termination).

Qualifying event: Termination of employment; death of employee; change in marital status.

Special situations: Employee or dependent who is pregnant at time of termination entitled to continuation benefits for 6 months following the end of pregnancy.

Texas

Tex. Ins. Code Ann. §§ 1251.252 to 1251.255; 1251.301 to 1251.310.

Employers affected: All employers that offer group health insurance.

Eligible employees: Employees continuously insured for previous 3 months.

Length of coverage for employee: Nine months; for employees eligible for COBRA, 6 months after COBRA coverage ends.

Length of coverage for dependents: 9 months; for employees eligible for COBRA, 6 months after COBRA coverage ends. Three years for dependents with coverage due to the death or retirement of employee or severance of the family relationship.

Qualifying event: Termination of employment (except for cause); employee leaves for health reasons; severance of family relationship; retirement or death of employee.

Time employee has to apply: 60 days from termination of coverage or receiving notice of continuation rights from employer or insurer, whichever is later. Must give notice within 15 days of severance of family relationship. Within 60 days of death or retirement of family member or severance of family relationship, dependent must give notice of intent to continue coverage.

State Health Insurance Continuation Laws (continued)

Utah

Utah Code Ann. § 31A-22-722

Employers affected: All employers that offer group health insurance.

Eligible employees: Employees continuously insured for previous 3 months.

Length of coverage for employee: 12 months.

Length of coverage for dependents: 12 months.

Qualifying event: Termination of employment; retirement; death; divorce; reduction in hours; sabbatical; disability; loss of dependent status.

Time employer has to notify employee: In writing within 30 days of termination of coverage.

Time employee has to apply: Within 60 days of qualifying event.

Vermont

Vt. Stat. Ann. tit. 8, §§ 4090a to 4090c

Employers affected: All employers that offer group health insurance.

Eligible employees: All covered employees are eligible.

Length of coverage for employee: 18 months.

Length of coverage for dependents: 18 months.

Qualifying event: Termination of employment; reduction in hours; death of employee; change of marital status; loss of dependent status.

Time employer has to notify employee: Within 30 days of qualifying event.

Time employee has to apply: Within 60 days of receiving notice following the occurrence of a qualifying event.

Virginia

Va. Code Ann. §§ 38.2-3541 to 38.2-3542

Employers affected: All employers that offer group health insurance.

Eligible employees: Employees continuously insured for previous 3 months.

Length of coverage for employee: 12 months.

Length of coverage for dependents: 12 months.

Qualifying event: Any reason employee or dependent becomes ineligible for coverage.

Time employer has to notify employee: 14 days from termination of coverage.

Time employee has to apply: Within 31 days of receiving notice of eligibility, but no more than 60 days following termination.

Special situations: Employee may convert to an individual policy instead of applying for continuation coverage (must apply within 31 days of termination of coverage).

Washington

Wash. Rev. Code Ann. § 48.21.075

Employers affected: All employers that offer disability insurance.

Eligible employees: Insured employees on strike.

Length of coverage for employee: Six months if employee goes on strike.

Length of coverage for dependents: Six months if employee goes on strike.

Qualifying event: If employee goes on strike.

Special situations: All employers have option of offering continued group health benefits.

West Virginia

W. Va. Code §§ 33-16-2, 33-16-3(e);
W. Va. Code St. R. 114-93-3

Employers affected: Employers providing insurance for between 2 and 20 employees.

Eligible employees: All employees are eligible.

Length of coverage for employee: 18 months in case of involuntary layoff.

State Health Insurance Continuation Laws (continued)

Qualifying event: Involuntary layoff.

Time employer has to notify employee: Carrier must notify beneficiaries within 15 days of receiving notice from beneficiary of intent to apply.

Time employee has to apply: 20 days to send notice of intention to apply; 30 days to apply after receiving election and premium notice.

Wisconsin

Wis. Stat. Ann. § 632.897

Employers affected: All employers that offer group health insurance.

Eligible employees: Employees continuously insured for previous 3 months.

Length of coverage for employee: 18 months (or longer at insurer's option).

Length of coverage for dependents: 18 months (or longer at insurer's option).

Qualifying event: Any reason employee or dependent becomes ineligible for coverage (except employment termination due to misconduct).

Time employer has to notify employee: 5 days from termination of coverage.

Time employee has to apply: 30 days after receiving employer's notice.

Wyoming

Wyo. Stat. § 26-19-113

Employers affected: Employers not subject to federal COBRA laws.

Eligible employees: Employees continuously insured for previous 3 months.

Length of coverage for employee: 12 months.

Length of coverage for dependents: 12 months.

Time employee has to apply: 31 days from termination of coverage.

Family and Medical Leave

The typical American household has changed dramatically in the decades since the 1950s, when many families were rigidly organized around a wage-earning father and a housekeeping, stay-at-home mother.

The workforce, too, has changed dramatically, as women, single parents, and two-paycheck couples have entered in droves.

And, partially due to the astronomical costs of medical care, more workers are responsible for providing at least some of the care for sick or injured family members and aging parents.

There have been some additions to workplace legal rights that recognize these grand changes. But, by and large, legislation has not quite kept up with societal shifts. Fortunately for employees, some states are stepping in to provide additional protections to working parents and other caregivers—for example, in the form of paid family leave benefits or reasonable accommodations for pregnant workers.

The Family and Medical Leave Act

The most sweeping federal law to help workers balance work and family is the Family and Medical Leave Act, or FMLA. Passed by Congress in 1993, this law provides important rights to employees who need to take time off from a job due to illness or family needs. But these rights under the FMLA are limited, and the time off is unpaid.

The FMLA requires larger employers to give their workers up to 12 weeks off per year to care for a seriously ill family member, recuperate from a serious illness, care for a new child, or handle issues arising from a family member's call to active military duty. It gives employees the right to take up to 26 weeks of leave in a year to care for a family member who is seriously injured or becomes seriously ill while on active military duty.

Employers that are subject to the FMLA have certain responsibilities to employees who take FMLA leave. Employers must reinstate most employees to their former positions (or equivalent ones, in some cases), provide employees with continued health insurance while on leave, and allow employees to use paid time off (such as vacation and sick time) during unpaid FMLA leave under certain circumstances.

Who Is Covered

Employers must comply with the FMLA if they have 50 or more employees. All employees on the payroll—including part-time workers and workers out on leave—count toward the total.

An employee is entitled to FMLA leave if all three of the following conditions are met:

- **Length of time employed.** The employee has worked for the employer for at least 12 months.
- **Hours worked.** The employee has worked at least 1,250 hours (about 25 hours a week) during the 12 months immediately preceding the leave.

- **Worksite.** The employee works at a location where the employer has at least 50 employees within a 75-mile radius.

Reasons for Leave

Even if all three of these requirements are met, you can take FMLA leave only for specified reasons. Not every personal or family emergency qualifies for FMLA leave. You must be seeking leave for:

- **Birth, adoption, or foster care.** If you become a new parent, including an adoptive or foster parent, you may take FMLA leave within one year after the child is born or placed in your home. You can start your leave before the child arrives, if necessary, for prenatal care, to attend court proceedings, or to otherwise finalize the adoption or foster placement.

- **The employee's serious health condition.** You can take leave to recuperate from your own serious health problem. Generally, an employee who requires inpatient treatment, has a chronic serious health problem, or is unable to perform normal activities for three days while under the care of a doctor has a serious health condition.

- **A family member's serious health condition.** You are entitled to take leave to care for a seriously ill family member. However, only parents, spouses, and children are covered. (Adult children do not count unless they have a disability.) Grandparents, domestic partners, in-laws, and siblings are not covered.

(However, they might be covered under a similar state law.)

- **Qualifying exigencies related to a family member's active duty.** You are entitled to take leave to handle certain urgent matters arising from a family member's active duty or call to active duty in the military (for purposes of military family leave only, adult children are covered family members). Only certain activities are covered, including attending military events, arranging child care, seeking counseling, and spending time with the family member who is about to be deployed or is on temporary rest and recuperation leave.

- **Military caregiver leave.** You can take leave to care for a family member who has suffered a serious injury or illness while on active military duty. A family member is a spouse, parent, child (of any age), and someone for whom the employee is "next of kin" (the nearest blood relative). The family member must be a current servicemember, or a veteran who was discharged—under conditions other than dishonorable—in the five years prior to the employee taking FMLA.

FMLA leave is available for up to 12 weeks each year for any of the first four reasons mentioned above: bonding with a child, the employee's serious health condition, a family member's serious health condition, or qualifying exigencies. This entitlement renews each year. Military caregiver leave, on the other hand, is available for up to

What Is a Serious Health Condition?

The FMLA divides serious health conditions for which FMLA leave may be taken into these six categories:

- inpatient care
- incapacity for more than three days with continuing treatment by a health care provider
- incapacity relating to pregnancy or prenatal care
- chronic serious health conditions
- permanent or long-term incapacity, and
- certain conditions requiring multiple treatments.

The FMLA doesn't definitively state that particular illnesses or diseases are always, or never, serious health conditions. Instead, the facts of each situation must be considered on their own. After all, one person's bout with bronchitis might result in a missed day of work and some coughing; another person's might result in an extended hospital stay for pneumonia. In this case, the first person would not have a serious health condition, but the second would.

Nonetheless, there are certain ailments that don't typically qualify as serious health conditions, including:

- colds and flu
- earaches
- upset stomachs and minor ulcers
- headaches (other than migraines)
- routine dental or orthodontic problems or periodontal disease, and
- cosmetic treatments (other than for restorative purposes), unless complications arise or inpatient care is required.

26 weeks in a 12-month period. However, this entitlement does not renew each year; you can take it once for a particular servicemember (or veteran) for a particular injury. The entire 26 weeks may be used for military caregiver leave, or up to 12 of those weeks may be used for any other FMLA-qualifying reason.

Reinstatement to Your Position

When your leave ends, your employer must immediately reinstate you to the same position you held when you went out on leave or an equivalent position that is virtually identical in pay, benefits, and other working conditions. However, the following limitations apply:

- **You have no greater right to reinstatement than you would have had if you had not taken leave.** If your position is legitimately eliminated while you are out on leave, you don't have the right to be reinstated. However, this is true only if the elimination of your job is unrelated to your leave. For example, if you work in the accounting department and your employer decides, while you are on leave, to lay off the entire department and outsource the company's bookkeeping needs, you are not entitled to reinstatement.

- **Employers can refuse to reinstate certain highly paid, "key" employees.** Your employer can refuse to reinstate you if: (1) you are among the 10% most highly paid of the employer's salaried workforce within a 75-mile radius of your workplace, and (2) reinstating you would cause "substantial and grievous economic injury" to the company. However, your employer must warn you ahead of time that you are considered a key employee and give you a reasonable opportunity to return.

Continued Health Insurance

If your employer provides a group health plan, you are entitled to continued health insurance coverage while you are on leave. If you usually have to pay part of the premium, you will have to pay this amount during your FMLA leave. Your employer still has to pay its usual share, as well.

If you decide voluntarily not to return to work when your leave ends, your employer can require you to reimburse it for the health care premiums it paid on your behalf during your leave. However, your employer cannot require this if you are unable to return to work after taking leave because the serious health condition continued or recurred or because of other circumstances beyond your control. For example, if you have a healthy baby and decide to quit your job so you can

stay home with your child, your employer can require you to pay for your benefits. On the other hand, if you have a baby with a serious disability, and you quit your job because your child needs round-the-clock care, your employer may not seek reimbursement.

Spouses Who Work for the Same Employer

The FMLA allows employers to limit how much leave a married couple may take for certain types of time off. When both spouses work for the same employer, they are entitled to a combined 12 weeks of leave for bonding with a child and caring for a parent with a serious health condition.

A similar limit applies to military caregiver leave: Spouses are entitled to a combined 26 weeks of leave to care for a military family member with a serious illness or injury, if each spouse is the parent, spouse, child, or next of kin of the servicemember.

However, each spouse retains his or her own allotment of leave for other FMLA-qualifying reasons. For example, if Bob and Alice have a child, Alice might take eight weeks of parenting leave while Bob takes four. This would use up their combined 12 weeks of FMLA parenting leave. However, if Alice had to stop working a couple of weeks before the baby was born, and was incapacitated for a couple of weeks after giving birth, she would be entitled to those additional four weeks as FMLA leave for her own serious health condition.

Scheduling and Notice Requirements

The FMLA requires you to give 30 days' notice of the need for leave if it is foreseeable. This is most often the case if you plan to take leave for the birth or adoption of a child or to care for a family member recovering from surgery or other planned medical treatment.

If your need for leave is not foreseeable, you are required to give as much notice as is both possible and practical under the circumstances. If you have a medical emergency, for example, it might not be possible for you to give any advance notice at all, but you should notify your employer as soon as you are able to do so.

Some employees may want to take leave intermittently rather than all at once. If you need physical therapy for a serious injury, for example, or you need to care for a spouse receiving periodic medical treatments such as chemotherapy, you might want to take a few hours off per week rather than 12 weeks at a clip. You may take FMLA leave intermittently when medically necessary to care for an injured servicemember, for your own serious health condition, or for the serious health condition of your child, parent, or spouse. You may also take intermittent leave for qualifying exigencies. You may not take intermittent leave to bond with a new child, however, unless your employer agrees.

Using Paid Time Off

Although FMLA leave is unpaid, you are entitled to use your accrued paid vacation or PTO during FMLA leave. You can use other types of paid leave only if the reasons for the leave are covered by your employer's leave policy. For example, you cannot use paid sick leave during FMLA leave to care for an ill family member unless your employer's sick policy allows employees to take sick leave to care for others who are ill. Your employer can require you to use accrued paid leave in the same fashion, even if you don't agree.

You must follow your company's usual rules and procedures for taking paid leave, even if you are using it while on FMLA leave. For example, if your company requires one week's notice before employees can take vacation time, and you have to go out on emergency FMLA leave, your employer can make you wait one week before applying your paid vacation. The first week still counts as FMLA leave, during which you are protected from retaliation and are entitled to continuation of benefits.

Enforcing Your Rights

FMLA violations are all too common, even decades after the law passed. Some employers retaliate against employees who exercise their rights by refusing to reinstate them, reinstating them to a position with fewer responsibilities, or making their work lives miserable before they go out on a scheduled FMLA leave. Some employers are just careless or ignorant of the law, resulting in failing to give employees required information about their rights, cutting off benefits while employees are on leave, or postponing an employee's reinstatement until it's convenient for the company.

Employers that violate the FMLA may be liable for a number of monetary damages, including:

- wages, employment benefits, or other compensation an employee has lost due to the violation
- the cost of securing care for a baby or ill family member (if the employee was prevented from taking leave and had to pay someone else to provide care)
- interest on the above amounts
- liquidated damages: a sum equal to the unpaid wages, benefits, other costs, and interest, and
- reasonable attorneys' fees and costs.

Instead of, or in addition to, some of these monetary damages, an employee can also receive an order from the court to be reinstated to a particular job.

If your employer violates the FMLA, you have two years from the date of the violation to file a lawsuit. This deadline is three years for "willful" violations, for example, when an employer intentionally retaliates against an employee for taking FMLA leave. However, it's up to a court to decide whether the violation was willful, so it's best not to rely on the longer time frame.

Another option is to file an administrative complaint with the Department of Labor, the agency responsible for enforcing the FMLA. A complaint may be filed in the same manner as a wage and hour complaint; to learn more, see "Filing a Wage Complaint or Lawsuit" in Chapter 2.

The Department of Labor recommends that you take the following commonsense steps if you are denied family and medical leave to which you are entitled:

- **Write down what happened.** Write down the date, time, and place. Include what was said and who was there. Keep a copy of these notes at home. They will be useful if you decide to file a complaint or lawsuit against your employer.
- **Get emotional support from friends and family.** It can be very upsetting to feel treated unfairly at work. Take care of yourself. Think about what you want to do. Get help to do it.
- **Talk to your union representative.** If you belong to a union, your union representative can help you file a grievance if you are denied family leave.
- **See what your company can do to help.** Your company may have an internal complaint procedure and a method of resolving disputes, such as mediation. Check your employee handbook for procedures that may be available.
- **Find out if other workers have been denied leave.** Talk with anyone else who had the same problem. Join with them to try to work out fitting solutions.
- **Keep doing a good job and keep a record of your work.** Keep copies at home of your performance evaluations and any letters or memos that show that you do a good job at work. Your boss might criticize

your job performance later on in order to defend what he or she did to you.

- **File a complaint.** Remember, the law has a time limit on how long you can wait to file a complaint against your company.
- **Contact community resources.** If you and several other workers are being denied rights to leave by the same boss, you might be able to file a lawsuit as a group. Call a women's or disability rights group. You might be able to help other people in the future.
- **Talk to a lawyer.** You don't need a lawyer to file an administrative complaint with the Department of Labor. However, you will need one if you plan on filing a lawsuit. If you're not sure what route to take, an employment lawyer can assess your case and advise you on your options.

State Family and Medical Leave Laws

Many states have their own family and medical leave laws in addition to the federal FMLA. Sometimes, the law parallels the protections provided by the FMLA. Other times, however, the law provides greater benefits or protections than the federal FMLA. For example, state law might cover smaller employers that aren't covered by the FMLA or employees who have worked for an employer for less time than the FMLA requires. Some states provide greater total

job-protected time off than the 12 weeks the FMLA provides—especially for women giving birth, who might be entitled to time off for their own pregnancy disabilities, plus time off to care for their newborn after the birth.

Types of State Leave Laws

There is wide variety in state family and medical leave laws, but they can generally be divided into a handful of broad categories. Employees are entitled to the rights set out in the most protective law that applies in any given situation, whether that's the state's law or the federal FMLA.

Here are the most common types of state family and medical leave laws; to learn more about your state's laws, check the chart at the end of this chapter, "State Family and Medical Leave Laws":

- **Comprehensive family and medical leave laws.** About a dozen states have laws that are quite similar to the FMLA, requiring employers to provide medical, caretaking, and/or parental leave. Typically, these laws overlap with the FMLA in many respects but also offer additional benefits. For example, some laws apply to smaller employers, cover more family members, or allow longer periods of leave.
- **Pregnancy disability leave laws.** Some states require employers to provide time off for pregnancy disability: the length of time when a woman is temporarily unable to work due to pregnancy and

childbirth. Typically, these laws don't provide for a set amount of time off per year or per pregnancy. Instead, they require employers to provide either a "reasonable" amount of leave or leave for the period of disability, often with a maximum time limit.

- **Adoption leave laws.** A handful of states require employers to offer the same leave to adoptive parents as to biological parents. Generally, these laws don't require an employer to offer parental leave. However, employers that choose to offer some form of parental leave must make it equally available to adoptive parents.
- **Small necessities laws.** Some states require employers to allow time off for various family needs, such as attending a child's school functions, taking a child to routine dental or medical appointments, or helping with eldercare. These laws have come to be known as "small necessities" laws, to recognize needs that don't take up much time but are important to employees.
- **Domestic violence leave laws.** Some states allow employees to take time off for issues relating to domestic violence, such as seeking a restraining order, getting medical care or counseling, or relocating to a safe environment.
- **Organ and bone marrow donation.** Several states have laws that give employees time off to donate organs or bone marrow.

Paid Leave Under State Laws

In addition to laws that allow employees to take unpaid time off, some states and local governments provide some form of paid leave. Common types of paid leave include:

- **Paid family leave.** In the last few years, paid family leave has become a national topic of discussion, as public support for these types of benefits continues to grow. To date, around five states and the District of Columbia have passed such laws, providing benefits to employees who take time off work to bond with a new child or care for an ill family member. These benefits are typically funded through employee payroll deductions and administered and paid by the state. Benefits are around one-half to two-thirds of an employee's wages for around four to 12 weeks.
- **Paid short-term disability.** A handful of states provide benefits to workers who are temporarily unable to work due to their own medical conditions, including pregnancy and childbirth. These benefits are typically administered by the state and funded through some combination of employee and employer contributions. Benefit amounts vary, but employees can generally expect to receive at least half of their wages for up to six months or a year.
- **Paid sick leave.** A growing number of states have passed paid sick leave

laws since 2011. Around seven states and the District of Columbia require employers to provide a small number of paid sick leave days each year, usually between three and five. Paid sick leave can typically be used for the employee's illness, to care for an ill family member, or for reasons relating to domestic violence. Several cities and counties have passed similar laws.

To find out what your state provides, see the chart at the end of this chapter, "State Family and Medical Leave Laws."

The Pregnancy Discrimination Act

Additional workplace rights for new parents come from the Pregnancy Discrimination Act, or PDA passed in 1978 as an amendment to Title VII of the Civil Rights Act of 1964. The PDA outlaws discrimination based on pregnancy, childbirth, or any related medical condition. Most states have similar laws.

Who Is Covered

Like other provisions of Title VII, the PDA applies to all workplaces that:

- engage in some type of interstate commerce (today, broadly construed to include all employers that use the mails, telephones, or computers), and
- have 15 or more employees for any 20 weeks of a calendar year. (See "Title VII

of the Civil Rights Act," in Chapter 7, for more on these protections.)

Available Protections

The PDA prohibits employers from discriminating against employees because of pregnancy, childbirth, or a related medical condition. For example, employers cannot do any of the following:

- fire an employee because she becomes pregnant
- limit job opportunities for pregnant women or women of childbearing age
- move pregnant employees to light-duty jobs even though they are capable of performing their normal jobs, or
- force pregnant employees to take leave once they reach a certain stage in their pregnancy.

When it comes to leave, benefits, and other terms and conditions of work, the rule is this: Employers must treat pregnant employees the same as employees who are temporarily disabled by other conditions, unless they have a legitimate and nondiscriminatory reason for the different treatment. The employer's reasons must be sufficiently strong to justify the burden put on pregnant employees. The fact that it is more expensive or inconvenient to accommodate pregnant employees is not a good enough reason.

On the flip side, this law may also help sanction the denial of a benefit to a pregnant worker if that benefit has been denied to other temporarily disabled workers. If it is company policy, for example, to suspend seniority rights and benefits for employees who require extended medical leave, those work benefits may also be denied to pregnant workers on leave.

State Law Might Require Reasonable Accommodation for Pregnant Employees

Almost half of the states have passed laws requiring employers to provide reasonable accommodations to pregnant employees, even if such accommodations are not provided to other employees. These laws generally require employers to accommodate pregnancy, childbirth, lactation, or other related medical conditions. For example, an employer might be required to:

- modify an employee's work duties to accommodate a lifting restriction
- provide additional breaks for eating or resting
- allow employees to work more flexible hours due to morning sickness
- allow changes to the company uniform or dress code
- provide a stool, foot rest, or other necessary support
- temporarily assign the employee to light duty, or
- provide unpaid time off.

Most state laws include an exception where the reasonable accommodation would cause an undue hardship for the employer, typically defined as a significant expense or burden on the employer, given its size, resources, and other factors.

The protections in the Act sound sensible and absolute. But, in truth, pregnancy discrimination is still alive and well in the workplace. And it spans across all industries and sectors of employment, including childcare, health care, legal, retail, education, construction, manufacturing, finance, real estate, hospitality, and more. In 2017, the EEOC received 3,174 charges of pregnancy discrimination. That figure does not include similar charges filed with state agencies or employees who went directly to court.

Forced Leaves

The PDA bars mandatory maternity leaves, as well as those that are prescribed for a set time and duration. The focus instead is on individual work capabilities. A pregnant woman cannot be required to take a leave from work during her pregnancy as long as she remains able to do her job.

> EXAMPLE: Jody's pregnancy is proceeding without problems, and she has no difficulty performing her job as an office manager. Even though she is a week past her delivery due date according to her doctor's calculations, her employer cannot force her to take off work in anticipation of labor.

Hiring and Promotion Discrimination

In addition, an employer cannot refuse to hire or promote a woman solely because she is pregnant or because of stereotyped notions of what work is proper for a pregnant woman to do or not to do.

EXAMPLE: Marsha is the most qualified applicant for a job but is six months pregnant at the time of her job interview. The company cannot choose another applicant simply because it does not want to find a replacement for Marsha when she takes a leave to give birth.

Insurance Discrimination

The PDA also states that an employer cannot refuse to provide health care insurance benefits that cover pregnancy if it provides such benefits to cover other medical conditions.

EXAMPLE: The Dumont Company provides complete hospitalization insurance to spouses of female employees but has a $500 cap on childbirth coverage for spouses of male employees. This policy is illegal under the PDA.

Men's Rights to Leaves

Under Title VII, an employer must grant men the same options for taking leaves from their jobs to care for children as it grants to women. To do otherwise would constitute illegal discrimination based on gender.

EXAMPLE: Steven works for a company that provides a 12-week unpaid leave for women who give birth to or adopt a child. If his employer refuses to allow Steven to take such a leave afte the birth or adoption of his child, he can file a complaint against his employer under Title VII, alleging gender discrimination.

For details about who is covered by Title VII and how to file a complaint under it, see "Title VII of the Civil Rights Act" in Chapter 7. Also, see the appendix for organizations that provide information on work and family issues.

Work/Life Balance

Some companies help employees juggle work and family responsibilities and help increase their health and enjoyment of life in various ways, including:

- allowing employees to work part time or to share a job
- allowing employees to work from home
- allowing flexible on-site work hours
- allocating dependent care spending accounts
- providing specific child care benefits, including emergency care programs, on-site care centers, employer-arranged discounts with local care providers, and
- providing additional assistance to employees, such as counseling and seminars on work and family issues.

If you feel that one of these options is feasible in your workplace and would make your life more manageable, talk with your employer. Better still, come to the talk armed with success stories of similar setups in local companies. (See the appendix for agencies you can contact.)

Work-at-Home Agreements

These days, many workers depend on computers as essential tools. And computers can easily be transported or hooked up to communicate with the main worksite from various locales. Many other kinds of work are also portable and may lend themselves well to work-at-home arrangements for employees.

These arrangements often involve an agreement between the worker and the company that spells out who is responsible for any legal liabilities that arise from the work-at-home arrangement and how worktime will be measured.

For example, a work-at-home agreement may specify that you are responsible for any damage that occurs to a company-owned laptop computer while it is being used in your home. Most homeowners' and renters' insurance policies do not automatically cover business equipment, so you may have to purchase additional coverage.

Also, check the agreement against the wage and hour laws (discussed in Chapter 2) to make sure that your work-at-home plan doesn't violate the Fair Labor Standards Act.

In general, if you are not an exempt employee (as most employees are not), the wages and hours provisions of the Act still apply even when you are working at home.

Flexible Work Hours

In many urban workplaces, where rush hour commuting makes for immense amounts of downtime, 9-to-5 workdays are all but extinct. In fact, a growing number of employers everywhere are putting less credence in the rigid Monday to Friday, 9-to-5 workweek and allowing employees to adopt more flexible work schedules.

When this idea was newer, it was referred to by the high-tech appellation of flextime. Flextime is not a reduction in hours, but simply a shift in the times employees are required to clock in and out of work. An increasingly popular flextime option, for example, is the ten-hour/four-day workweek, as it gives employees at least the illusion of a three-day weekend. Since flextime employees usually maintain 40-hour workweeks, they lose no benefits—such as health care coverage or vacation time—in the bargain.

State Family and Medical Leave Laws

Arizona

A.R.S. § 23-371 and following.

Paid Leave: Paid Sick Leave: All employers must provide one hour paid sick time for every 30 hours worked. Employers with 15 or more employees may cap accrual and use at 40 hours per year; employers with fewer than 15 employees may cap accrual and use at 24 hours per year. Sick leave may be used for the employee's illness, to care for an ill family member, to seek assistance relating to domestic violence, or due to the closure of the employee's work or a child's school due to a public health emergency.

Arkansas

Ark. Code Ann. §§ 9-9-105, 11-3-205

Family and Medical Leave: Employers that allow employees to take leave for the birth of a child must give the same leave to employees adopting a child no older than 18 (does not apply to stepparent or foster parent adoptions).

Organ and Bone Marrow Donation: All employers must provide up to 90 days of unpaid leave for organ or bone marrow donation to employees who are not eligible for FMLA leave.

California

Cal. Govt. Code §§ 12945, 12945.2, and 12945.6; Cal. Lab. Code §§ 230 and following; Cal. Unemp. Ins. Code §§ 3300 and following; Cal. Lab. Code §§ 245.5, 246 and 246.5

Family and Medical Leave: Employers with 50 or more employees must provide up to 12 weeks of leave each year to care for seriously ill family member, for employee's own serious illness, or to bond with new child. Employees are eligible if they have worked for the employer for at least 12 months, have worked 1,250 hours in the year prior to the start of leave, and work at a location within 75-mile radius of 50 more employees. Employers with 20 to 49 employees must provide up to 12 weeks of leave each year for employees to bond with a new child only. The same eligibility requirements apply, except the employee must work within a 75-mile radius of 20 employees.

Pregnancy Disability Leave: Employers with 5 or more employees must provide up to 4 months of pregnancy disability leave to employees who are unable to work due to pregnancy or childbirth. This time is in addition to 12 weeks of bonding leave under state family leave law.

School Activities: Employers with 25 or more employees must provide up to 40 hours per year, but not more than 8 hours per calendar month, to enroll a child in a school or a licensed child care provider or to participate in activities related to the school or licensed child care provider.

Domestic Violence: Employers with 25 or more employees must provide employees with a reasonable amount of time off to obtain medical treatment counseling, take safety measures, or deal with other issues related to domestic violence, stalking, or sexual assault.

Paid Leave: Paid Sick Leave: All employers must provide employees with one hour of sick leave for every 30 hours worked. Employers may cap sick leave at 24 hours per year. Employees are eligible if they have worked at least 30 days for the employer. Employees may use sick leave for their own illnesses, to care for an ill family member, or to deal with the effects of domestic violence.

Paid Family Leave: Employees may receive 6 weeks of paid family leave benefits from the state when taking leave to bond with a new child or care for a seriously ill family member.

Temporary Disability Insurance: Employees may receive up to 52 weeks of short-term disability

State Family and Medical Leave Laws (continued)

from the state when unable to work due to disability (including pregnancy).

Colorado

Colo. Rev. Stat. §§ 19-5-211; 24-34-402.7

Family and Medical Leave: Employers that offer leave for the birth of a child must give the same leave for adoption (doesn't apply to stepparent adoption).

School Activities: Colorado's previous law requiring employers to provide time off to employees for a child's school activities expired in 2015.

Domestic Violence: Employers with 50 or more employees must provide up to 3 days in a year to seek a restraining order, obtain medical care or counseling, relocate, or seek legal assistance relating to domestic violence, sexual assault, or stalking. Employees are eligible if they have worked for the employer for one year.

Connecticut

Conn. Gen. Stat. Ann. §§ 31-51kk to 31-51qq; 46a-60

Family and Medical Leave: Employers with 75 or more employees must provide up to 16 weeks during any 24-month period for childbirth, adoption, the employee's serious health condition, a family member's serious health condition, bone marrow or organ donation, or a qualifying exigency arising out of a family member's active duty in the military. Employee may take up to 26 weeks in a 12-month period for a family member who is a current member of the armed forces and is undergoing medical treatment for a serious illness or injury. Employees are eligible if they have worked for the employer for one year and have worked 1,000 hours in the last year.

Pregnancy Disability Leave: Employers with 3 or more employees must provide a reasonable amount of leave to employees who are unable to

work due to pregnancy.

Paid Leave: Paid Sick Leave: Employers in the service industry with 50 or more employees must provide employees with one hour of paid sick leave for every 40 hours worked, but may cap accrual at 40 hours per year. Employees may use leave for their own illness or to care for an ill family member.

District of Columbia

D.C. Code Ann. §§ 32-501 and following; 32-1202, 32-131.01 and following.

Family and Medical Leave: Employers with 20 or more employees must provide up to 16 weeks in a 24-month period for the birth of a child, adoption, foster care, placement of a child with the employee for whom the employee permanently assumes and discharges parental responsibility, or to care for family member with a serious health condition. Employees may take an additional 16 weeks in a 24-month period for their own serious health conditions. Employees must have worked for the employer for at least one year and worked at least 1,000 hours in the year before the start of leave.

School Activities: All employers must provide up to 24 hours of unpaid leave per year for an employee to attend a child's school activities.

Domestic Violence: Paid sick leave may also be used for employee or family member who is a victim of stalking, domestic violence, or abuse to get medical attention, get services, seek counseling, relocate, take legal action, or take steps to enhance health and safety.

Paid Leave: Paid Sick Leave: All employers must provide paid sick leave for employees to use for their own illness or to care for a family member. Amount of paid leave ranges from three days to seven days per year, depending on size of the employer. Sick leave may be used for the employee's illness, to care for an ill family member, or to deal

State Family and Medical Leave Laws (continued)

with the effects of stalking, domestic violence, or abuse against the employee or a family member.

Paid Family Leave: Beginning on July 1, 2020, employees will be eligible to receive paid family leave benefits from the district when taking leave for their own serious health conditions (2 weeks), to care for a family member with a serious health condition (6 weeks), or to bond with a new child (8 weeks).

Florida

Fla. Stat. § 741.313

Domestic Violence: Employers with at least 50 employees must provide up to 3 days of unpaid leave each year to employees who are the victims of domestic violence or sexual abuse or whose family members are victims. Employees are eligible if they have worked for the employer for at least 3 months.

Georgia

Ga. Code § 34-1-10

Family and Medical Leave: No requirement to provide sick leave, but employers with 25 or more employees that choose to do so must allow up to five days each year to be used to care for a sick immediate family member.

Hawaii

Haw. Rev. Stat. §§ 378-1, 378-71 to 378-74; 398-1 to 398-11

Family and Medical Leave: Employers with 100 or more employees must provide up to 4 weeks of unpaid leave each year for the birth of a child or adoption, or to care for family member with a serious health condition. (If employer provides paid sick leave, up to 10 days may be used for these purposes.) Employees are eligible if they have worked for the employer for six months.

Pregnancy Disability Leave: All employers must provide a reasonable period of time off for disability resulting from pregnancy, childbirth, or a related condition.

Domestic Violence: All employers must provide domestic violence leave. Employers with 50 or more employees must allow up to 30 days' unpaid leave per year for employee who is a victim of domestic or sexual violence or if employee's minor child is a victim. Employer with 49 or fewer employees must allow up to 5 days' leave.

Organ and Bone Marrow Donation: Employers with 50 or more employees must provide up to 7 days of unpaid leave for bone marrow donation and 30 days' unpaid leave for organ donation.

Paid Leave: Temporary Disability Insurance: Eligible employees who are temporarily unable to work because of illness or injury (including pregnancy) may collect up to 26 weeks of benefits through the state disability insurance program.

Illinois

820 Ill. Comp. Stat. §§ 147/1 and following; 180/1 and following

School Activities: Employers with 50 or more employees must provide 8 hours per year, but not more than 4 hours in a day, for employees to participate in a child's school activities. Employees are eligible if they have worked for the employer at least half time for 6 months and have no paid leave available.

Domestic Violence: All employers must provide unpaid leave each year to an employee who is a victim of domestic violence or sexual assault or whose family or household member is a victim. Employers with 50 or more employees must provide 12 weeks of leave; employers with 15 to 49 employees must provide 8 weeks of leave; and employers with 14 or fewer employees must provide 4 weeks of leave.

State Family and Medical Leave Laws (continued)

Iowa

Iowa Code § 216.6

Pregnancy Disability Leave: Employers with 4 or more employees must provide 8 weeks of leave for disability due to pregnancy, childbirth, or related conditions.

Kentucky

Ky. Rev. Stat. Ann. § 337.015

Family Medical Leave: All employers must provide 6 weeks of leave to employees adopting a child under 7 years old.

Louisiana

La. Rev. Stat. Ann. §§ 23:341 to 23:342; 23:1015 and following; 40:1299.124

Pregnancy Disability Leave: Employers with 25 or more employees must provide a reasonable period of time off for disability due to pregnancy and childbirth, not to exceed 6 weeks for normal pregnancy or 8 weeks for complicated pregnancy.

School Activities: All employers must provide 16 hours of leave each year to attend a child's school or daycare activities.

Organ and Bone Marrow Donation: Employers with 20 or more employees must provide 40 hours of paid leave each year for employees to donate bone marrow. Employees are eligible if they work at least 20 hours per week.

Maine

Me. Rev. Stat. Ann. tit. 26, §§ 843 and following

Family and Medical Leave: Employers with 15 or more employees at one location must provide 10 weeks of leave in a two-year period for the birth of a child, adoption (for child 16 or younger), the employee's serious health condition, a family member's serious health condition, organ donation, or the death or serious health condition

of a family member incurred while on active military duty. Employees are eligible if they have worked for the employer for at least one year.

Domestic Violence: All employers must provide reasonable and necessary leave to an employee who is the victim of domestic violence, sexual assault, or stalking, or whose parent, spouse, or child is a victim. Leave may be used to prepare for and attend court, for medical treatment, and for other necessary services.

Maryland

Md. Code Ann., [Lab. & Empl.] §§ 3-801, 3-802, 3-803

Family Medical Leave: Employers with 15 or more employees must provide the same leave for adoption as allowed for the birth of a child. Employers with 50 or more employees must give employees a day off when an immediate family member leaves for or returns from active military duty outside the United States. Employees are eligible if they have worked for the employer for at least 12 months and worked at least 1,250 hours in the last year.

Massachusetts

Mass. Gen. Laws ch. 149, §§ 52D, 105D, 148C; ch. 151B, § 1(5)

Family and Medical Leave: Employers with 6 or more employees must provide eight weeks of unpaid leave to employees for the birth of a child or the adoption of a minor. Employees are eligible once they have completed their initial probationary period of employment, as long as it doesn't exceed three months. Employers with 50 or more employees must provide 24 hours of leave each year to take a minor child or relative who is 60 or older to medical or dental appointment (combined with school activities leave). Employees must meet the same eligibility requirements of the FMLA.

State Family and Medical Leave Laws (continued)

School Activities: Employers with 50 or more employees must provide 24 hours of leave each year for an employee to attend a child's school activities (combined with family and medical leave for medical appointments). Employees must meet the same eligibility requirements of the FMLA.

Domestic Violence: Employers with 50 or more employees must provide 15 days of unpaid leave in a 12-month period if the employee, or the employee's family member, is a victim of abusive behavior. Leave may be used to seek medical attention or counseling, obtain a protective order from a court, attend child custody proceedings, and other related purposes. Employees must meet the same eligibility requirements of the FMLA.

Paid Leave: Paid Sick Leave: All employers must provide one hour of sick leave for every thirty hours worked, although employers may cap annual accrual at 40 hours. Employers with 11 or more employees must provide paid time off; employers with 10 or fewer employees may provide unpaid time off. Employees may use leave for their own illnesses, to care for an ill family member, or domestic violence reasons.

Minnesota

Minn. Stat. Ann. §§ 181.940 and following

Family and Medical Leave: Employers with 21 or more employees at one site must provide 12 weeks of leave for the birth of a child or adoption. Employees may also use accrued sick leave to care for an ill family member. Employees are eligible if they have worked at least half time for one year.

School Activities: All employers must provide 16 hours in a 12-month period to attend a child's activities related to child care, preschool, or special education. Employees are eligible if they have worked half time for at least one year.

Domestic Violence: Employers with 21 or more employees must allow accrued sick leave to be used to seek assistance due to sexual assault, domestic violence, or stalking.

Organ and Bone Marrow Donation: Employers with 20 or more employees must provide 40 hours of paid leave each year to donate bone marrow. Employees are eligible if they work at least 20 hours per week.

Montana

Mont. Code Ann. §§ 49-2-310, 49-2-311

Pregnancy Disability Leave: All employers must provide a reasonable leave of absence for pregnancy disability and childbirth.

Nebraska

Neb. Rev. Stat. § 48-234

Family and Medical Leave: Employers that allow employees to take leave for the birth of a child must give the same leave for adoption of a child no older than 8, or a child no older than 18 if the child has special needs (does not apply to stepparent or foster parent adoptions).

Nevada

Nev. Rev. Stat. Ann. §§ 392.920, 392.4577, 613.335; 2017 Nevada Laws Ch. 496 (S.B. 361)

Pregnancy Disability Leave: Employers that provide sick or disability leave to employees with other medical conditions must provide the same leave for pregnancy, miscarriage, childbirth and related medical conditions.

School Activities: Employers with 50 or more employees must provide employees with a child in public school 4 hours of leave per school year to attend parent-teacher conferences, school-related activities during regular school hours, school-sponsored events, or to volunteer or be

State Family and Medical Leave Laws (continued)

involved at the school. All employers may not fire or threaten to fire a parent, guardian, or custodian for attending a school conference or responding to a child's emergency.

Domestic Violence: All employers must provide 160 hours of unpaid leave within one year of an incident of domestic violence for the following purposes: to seek medical treatment, to obtain counseling, to participate in court proceedings, or to create a safety plan. Employees are eligible if they have worked for at least 90 days and if they are victims of domestic violence or have a family member who is a victim.

New Hampshire

N.H. Rev. Stat. Ann. § 354-A:7(VI)

Pregnancy Disability Leave: Employers with 6 or more employees must provide temporary disability leave for pregnancy, childbirth, or a related medical condition.

New Jersey

N.J. Stat. Ann. §§ 34:11B-1 and following; 34-11C and following; 43:21-1 and following

Family and Medical Leave: Employers with 50 or more employees must provide 12 weeks of leave (or 24 weeks reduced leave schedule) in any 24-month period for the birth or adoption of a child or to care for a family member with serious health condition. Employees are eligible if they have worked for at least one year and at least 1,000 hours in previous 12 months.

Domestic Violence: Employers with 25 or more employees must provide 20 unpaid days in one 12-month period for employee who is (or whose family member is) a victim of domestic violence or a sexually violent offense. Employees are eligible if they have worked for at least one year and worked at least 1,000 hours in the last 12 months.

Paid Leave: Paid Family Leave: Employees may receive paid family leave benefits from the state for 6 weeks of leave per year to care for a seriously ill family member (including a registered domestic partner) or to bond with a new child.

Temporary Disability Insurance: Employees may receive temporary disability benefits from the state for up to 26 weeks when they are unable to work due to disability.

New Mexico

N.M. Stat. Ann. §§ 50-4A-1 and following

Domestic Violence: All employers must provide intermittent leave for up to 14 days each calendar year, but no more than eight hours in one day, to obtain an order of protection or other judicial relief from domestic abuse, to meet with law enforcement officials, to consult with attorneys or district attorneys' victim advocates, or to attend court proceedings related to the domestic abuse of an employee or an employee's family member.

New York

N.Y. Lab. Law §§ 201-c, 202-a. N.Y. Workers' Compensation Law § 200 and following

Family and Medical Leave: Employers that allow employees to take leave for the birth of a child must provide the same leave for adoption of a child of preschool age or younger (or no older than 18 if disabled). All employers must provide time off to employees to bond with a new child, take care of a family member with a serious health condition, or for qualifying exigencies arising out of a family member's call to active military duty. The maximum amount of leave in a 52-week period: 8 weeks in 2018, 10 weeks in 2019 and 2020, and 12 weeks in 2021 and beyond. Full-time employees are eligible once they have been employed for 26 weeks; part-time employees are

State Family and Medical Leave Laws (continued)

eligible once they have worked 175 days.

Organ and Bone Marrow Donation: Employers with 20 or more employees at one site must provide 24 hours' leave to donate bone marrow. Employees are eligible if they work at least 20 hours per week.

Paid Leave: Paid Family Leave: Employees may also receive paid family leave benefits from the state when taking leave to care for a family member with a serious health condition, to bond with a new child, or for qualifying exigency arising out of a family member's call to active duty in the military. The maximum benefit in 2018 is 50% of employee's average weekly wage or the state average weekly wage. This increases to 55% in 2019, 60% in 2020, and 67% in 2021.

Temporary Disability Insurance: Employees who have worked for a covered employer for at least 4 consecutive weeks may receive temporary disability insurance benefits from the state for up to 26 weeks while unable to work due to disability (including pregnancy).

North Carolina

N.C. Gen. Stat. §§ 50B-5.5, 95-28.3

School Activities: All employers must give employees 4 hours of leave per year to parents or guardians of school-aged children to participate in school activities.

Domestic Violence: All employers must provide reasonable time off to obtain or attempt to obtain relief from domestic violence and sexual assault.

Oregon

Ore. Rev. Stat. §§ 653.601 and following; 659A.150 and following; 659A.270 and following; 659A.312, 659A.029

Family and Medical Leave: Employers with 25 or more employees must provide 12 weeks off per year for the birth or adoption of a child (parental leave), the employee's serious health condition, to care for a family member with a serious health condition, to care for a child with an illness or injury that requires home care (sick child leave), or to deal with the death of a family member (bereavement leave). Bereavement leave is capped at 2 weeks. Employees can take 12 weeks of parental leave and an additional 12 weeks for sick child leave. Employees are eligible if they have worked 25 or more hours per week for at least 180 days (except parental leave, which only requires that the employee has worked 180 days).

Pregnancy Disability Leave: Employers with 25 or more employees must provide 12 weeks off per year for pregnancy disability. This is in addition to 12 weeks for parental leave and 12 weeks for sick child leave. Employees are eligible if they have worked 25 or more hours per week for at least 180 days.

Domestic Violence: Employers with 6 or more employees must provide reasonable leave to employee who is victim of, or whose minor child is a victim of, domestic violence, harassment, sexual assault, or stalking. Leave may be used to seek legal treatment, medical services, counseling, or to relocate or secure existing home.

Organ and Bone Marrow Donation: All employers must allow the employee to use accrued leave or must provide the employee with 40 hours of unpaid leave, whichever is less, to donate bone marrow. Employees are eligible if they work at least 20 hours per week.

Paid Leave: Paid Sick Leave: All employers must provide one hour of sick leave for every 30 hours worked, although employers may cap accrual and use at 40 hours per year. Up to 40 hours of accrued leave must carry over to the next year. Employers with 10 or more employees must provide paid time off; employers with 9 or fewer employees

State Family and Medical Leave Laws (continued)

may provide unpaid time off. Employees may use leave for their own illnesses, to care for an ill family member, to deal with domestic violence issues, or for any purpose described under the "Family Medical Leave" section.

Rhode Island

R.I. Gen. Laws §§ 28-48-1 and following; 28-41-34 through 28-41-42

Family Medical Leave: Employers with 50 or more employees must provide 13 weeks of leave in a two-year period for the birth of a child, adoption of child up to 16 years old, the employee's serious health condition, or to care for family member with serious health condition. Employees must have worked an average of 30 or more hours a week for at least 12 consecutive months.

School Activities: Employers with 50 or more employees must provide up to 10 hours a year to attend a child's school conferences or other activities.

Paid Leave: Paid Sick Leave: Employers with 18 or more employees must provide one hour of paid sick leave for every 35 hours worked, up to a maximum of 24 hours in 2018, 32 hours in 2019, and 40 hours in 2020 and beyond. Employers with fewer than 18 employees must provide the same amount of unpaid sick leave. Sick leave may be used for the employee's own illness, to care for an ill family member, for reasons relating to domestic violence, or due to the closure of the employee's work or a child's school due to a public health emergency.

Paid Family Leave: Employees who take time off to bond with a new child or care for a family member with a serious health condition may receive four weeks of temporary caregiver benefits from the state.

Temporary Disability Insurance: Employees who are unable to work due to illness, injury, or

pregnancy may collect up to 30 weeks of benefits from the state through its short-term disability insurance program (temporary caregiver benefits are counted against the 30 weeks).

South Carolina

S.C. Code Ann. § 44-43-80

Organ and Bone Marrow Donation: Employers with 20 or more employees in the state at one site may—but are not required to—allow employees to take up to 40 hours' paid leave per year to donate bone marrow. Employees are eligible if they work at least 20 hours per week.

Tennessee

Tenn. Code Ann. § 4-21-408

Family and Medical Leave: Employers with 100 or more employees must provide up to 4 months of unpaid leave for pregnancy, childbirth, nursing, and adoption. Employees must give 3 months' notice unless a medical emergency requires the leave to begin sooner. Employees are eligible if they have worked full-time for the employer for 12 consecutive months.

Texas

Tex. Lab. Code Ann. § 21.0595

Family and Medical Leave: Employers with 15 or more employees that provide leave to care for a sick child must also allow leave to care for a sick foster child.

Vermont

Vt. Stat. Ann. tit. 21, §§ 471 and following

Family and Medical Leave: Employers with 10 or more employees must provide unpaid leave for pregnancy, childbirth, or parental leave for the birth of a child or adoption of a child 16 or younger. Employers with 15 or more employees must also provide unpaid leave for

State Family and Medical Leave Laws (continued)

the employee's serious health conditions or to care for family member with a serious health condition. Employees may take up to 12 weeks each year for any of these purposes. Employers with 15 employees must provide an additional 4 hours of leave in a 30-day period, but not more than 24 hours per year, to take a family member to a medical, dental, or professional well-care appointment or respond to a family member's medical emergency (combined with school activities leave). Employees are eligible if they have worked an average of 30 hours per week for one year.

School Activities: Employers with 15 or more employees must provide employees with 4 hours of leave in a 30-day period, but not more than 24 hours per year, to participate in a child's school activities (combined with leave to take a family member to medical appointments). Employees are eligible if they have worked an average of 30 hours per week for one year.

Paid Leave: All employers must provide one hour of paid sick leave for every 52 hours worked. Employers may cap accrual at 24 hours per year in 2018 and 40 hours per year in 2019. Employees are eligible if they have worked for a covered employer for an average of 18 hours per week for at least 20 weeks.

Washington

Wash. Rev. Code Ann. §§ 49.12.265 and following; 49.12.350 and following; 49.76.010 and following; 49.78.010 and following

Family and Medical Leave: Employers with 50 or more employees must provide 12 weeks of leave during any 12-month period for the birth or placement of a child (through adoption or foster placement), the employee's serious health condition, or to care for a family member with a serious health condition. Employees are eligible if

they have worked for the employer for at least 12 months and have worked at least 1,250 hours in the previous year.

Pregnancy Disability Leave: Employers with 8 or more employees must provide leave for the period of time when an employee is temporarily disabled due to pregnancy or childbirth. This is in addition to any leave available under federal FMLA and state family and medical leave laws.

Domestic Violence: All employers must provide reasonable leave from work to employees who are victims of domestic violence, sexual assault, or stalking—or whose family member is a victim—to prepare for and attend court, for medical treatment, and for other necessary services.

Paid Leave: All employers must provide one hour of paid sick leave for every 40 hours worked. No annual cap on accrual, but employees may only carry over 40 hours of accrued leave from year to year. Employees may use sick leave for their own illness, the illness of a family member, the closure of a child's school or day care due to a public health emergency, and to seek services relating to domestic violence. Washington has a state-run paid family leave program, but benefits wont be available until January 2020.

Wisconsin

Wis. Stat. Ann. § 103.10

Family and Medical Leave: Employers with 50 or more employees must provide 6 weeks of leave per 12-month period for pregnancy, childbirth, and to bond with a baby arriving by birth or adoption. These employers must provide an additional 2 weeks off each year for the employee's own serious health condition and an additional 2 weeks each year to care for a family member with a serious health condition. Employees are eligible if they have worked for at least one year and have worked 1,000 hours in the preceding 12 months.

Privacy Rights

Technology has made it easier to pry into people's lives and psyches, through computerized record keeping, drug and alcohol testing, videotaping, audiotaping, even collecting and analyzing genetic information. And that has caused more workers to jealously guard their rights to privacy.

Theoretically, at least, employers sit on the other side of the fence. They are understandably concerned about stamping out wrongdoing and waste in the workplace, such as drug and alcohol abuse, theft, incompetence, and low productivity. And, usually, their concerns center on finding and keeping the best-qualified employees. To that end, most employers want to know what workers are doing on the job.

While there are some legal controls on what an employer and prospective employer can find out about you and on how they can use that information, there are still many ways an employer can invade your privacy. But there are also some subtle limits to their reach. In general, employers are entitled to intrude on your personal life no more than is necessary for legitimate business interests.

Most abuses of privacy rights occur when people are not aware of these legal constraints and how to enforce them. This chapter covers these rules and outlines some current workplace privacy issues: access to personnel records, medical and psychological testing, use of credit checks, and surveillance during work.

Your Personnel Records

Your employer is required by law to keep some tabs on you, including information on your wages and hours, workplace injuries and illnesses, and tax withholding, as well as records of accrued vacation and other benefits. That information is usually gathered in one place: your personnel file. Your file will usually contain little information you did not know or provide to your employer in the first place.

But personnel files can sometimes become the catchalls for other kinds of information: references from previous employers, comments from customers or clients, employee reprimands, job performance evaluations, or memos of management's observations about an employee's behavior or productivity. When employment disputes develop, or an employee is demoted, transferred, or fired, the personnel file often provides essential information—often unknown to the employee—about the whys and wherefores.

A federal law, the Privacy Act (5 U.S.C. § 552a), limits the type of information that federal agencies, the military, and other government employers may keep on their workers.

However, private employers have a nearly unfettered hand when it comes to the kind of information they can collect. While many states now have some type of law regulating personnel files, most of these laws control not the content of the files, but, rather:

- whether and how employees and former employees can get access to their personnel files
- whether employees are entitled to copies of the information in them, and
- how employees can contest and correct erroneous information in their files.

Getting Access to Your File

The best way to find out what a company knows about you, or what company representatives are saying about you to outside people who inquire, is to obtain a copy of the contents of your personnel file from your current or former employer.

In some states, the only way you can obtain those files is if they are relevant to a lawsuit you have filed against your employer. And even then, you might be in for a legal battle over what portions of the files must be handed over. But, in many states, you have the right to see the contents of your personnel file—or at least some of the documents in it—without filing a lawsuit.

State laws on employee access to personnel records generally cover procedural matters, such as when your request must be made, how long the employer has to respond, and whether you have the right to dispute information you disagree with. Before you request your file, read the law on procedures for your state. (See "State Laws on Access to Personnel Records," at the end of this chapter.) In general, you should make your request to see your personnel file in writing to your employer or former employer as soon as you decide that you want to see it. If you send your request by certified mail, you will be able to prove when your request was submitted, should you need that evidence later.

Forcing an Employer to Keep Your Secrets

Employers are supposed to collect only information about you that is job related. And only those people with a proven need to know are supposed to have access to your personnel file. For example, your employer cannot tell your coworkers the results of a drug screening test you were required to take. But the truth is that employers frequently give out information about their employees to other people: other employers, unions, police investigators, creditors, insurance agents.

Job applicants or employees who want some personal information to remain private—address and phone number, for example, if they fear physical violence at the hands of a former spouse—should request in writing that the information be kept confidential. That request may end up being worth little more than the paper it is written on. But it may also be the strongest evidence of an employer's carelessness should problems develop later.

If you live in a state that does not have a specific law ensuring you access to your personnel records, all is not lost. If you wish to see and copy your personnel files, ask to do so. If you are met with resistance, make a more formal request in writing. If that request is denied, and you genuinely believe your records may contain information that you need, you should consult with an expert such as a private investigator or an experienced attorney.

Criminal Records

According to recent statistics collected by the Bureau of Justice Statistics, approximately one third of the workforce has a criminal record. And many feel they are approached with wariness, or even subjected to abject discrimination, by employers who learn of their histories.

Arrest and conviction records are public records available to anyone, including an employer, who is willing to search for them. Criminal records are also kept by a number of agencies, including police, prosecutors, courts, the FBI, probation departments, prisons, and parole boards. These record keepers are theoretically barred from releasing this information to anyone other than other criminal justice agencies and a few types of specialized employers (those who help manufacture controlled substances or run child care or elder care facilities for example). In reality, however, slips of the tongue are made and persistent employers can generally find a way to get this information.

Most states have passed at least some type of law restricting an employer's ability to access criminal records. Because our justice system is rooted in the belief that someone is innocent until proven guilty, most states prohibit employers from accessing records of arrests that did not lead to convictions. Criminal records that have been sealed, expunged, or vacated are also often off limits. On the other hand, many states allow employers to inquire about past criminal convictions, especially if they are rationally related to the job at hand—a theft conviction, for example, for any person who will have access to company funds. (To learn your state's law, see "State Laws on Employee Arrest and Conviction Records," at the end of this chapter.)

As many job seekers with a criminal record know, it's not uncommon for employers to take a zero-tolerance approach when it comes to criminal history. Many employers automatically reject applicants upon learning that they have a criminal record, without considering the severity of the crime, how long ago it happened, and other relevant factors. To give ex-offenders a fair shot at finding work, many states have passed "ban-the-box" laws, named after the infamous question found on job applications: "Have you ever been convicted of a crime? Check yes or no." While the details vary, these laws generally prohibit employers from asking applicants about their criminal histories until they have conducted an interview or made a job offer. The idea is that employers will be more likely to assess a candidate's qualifications and then decide whether the conviction would impact his or her ability to do the job.

Criminal Record Screening & Race or National Origin Discrimination

An employer that has a blanket policy of rejecting applicants with criminal records might be violating federal antidiscrimination laws. Under Title VII, a neutral policy can be discriminatory if it has a disproportionate impact on members of a protected class. According to guidance issued by the EEOC in 2012, excluding applicants based on criminal history can qualify as illegal race or national origin discrimination because it might screen out disproportionate numbers of African American or Hispanic applicants. Generally speaking, employers can avoid discrimination by considering an applicant's criminal history on a case-by-case basis, given the nature of the job, the nature of the crime, and how long ago the crime happened, for example. And, applicants should be given a chance to show that they have been rehabilitated or made amends for the crime.

Expunging Your Past

Many states have laws that allow individuals to expunge, or seal, their criminal records. When a record is expunged, it is usually not available to anyone other than criminal justice agencies and the courts. If your criminal record has been expunged, you are generally allowed to deny that you have one when a prospective employer asks about it.

Some states extend the expunging privilege only to a first arrest that did not result in a conviction. Other states are more generous, allowing a conviction for a petty offense to be expunged if probation was successfully completed. Some states limit the procedure to juvenile records. Usually, a request to seal your record will be granted only if you have remained clear of any contacts with the criminal justice system for a specified period of time following your arrest or conviction.

The bottom line: Only small-potato crimes can be easily expunged from your record. Records of truly serious offenses cannot be sealed and are with you for life.

Medical Records

Medical information about employees comes into the workplace a number of ways. It is volunteered by an employee who is calling in sick. It becomes general knowledge after filtering through the gossip mill. It is listed on the insurance application for a group policy, which your employer will likely have on file.

As a general legal rule, employers are not supposed to reveal medical information about employees unless there is a legitimate business reason to do so. That nebulous standard provides little guidance because it is so poorly defined.

In an attempt to curb leaks of medical information in the workplace, the Americans with Disabilities Act, or ADA—the broad federal law prohibiting disability discrimination on the job—imposes strict requirements on how and where employers must keep medical information on employees.

Under the ADA, medical information must be kept in a secure location, separate from nonmedical information—and access to it should be limited to those with a true need to know:

- supervisors of employees whose work duties are limited or who require some accommodation because of a medical condition
- first aid and safety workers who may need to administer emergency treatment or respond during an evacuation, and
- government and insurance officials who are investigating compliance with the ADA.

Despite the confidentiality measures imposed by the ADA, information leaks and abuses still occur. If you are concerned about keeping your medical information

confidential and out of the workplace limelight, you must take active steps to do so. If you confide any medical information to coworkers, ask them not to tell others. Remind all doctors who treat you that they should not reveal anything about your health or treatment to another person without getting a release, or written permission, from you first. (See "Medical Examinations," below, for more on employee medical exams and records.)

Background Checks & Credit Reports

In the last decade, background checks have become a standard part of the job application process. According to a survey by the National Association of Professional Background Screeners conducted in 2016 and 2017, a whopping 96% of responding companies stated that they used at least some type of background screening for new hires, with 83% screening for all full-time positions.

A number of companies have popped up to fill this need, providing a range of background check services—from checking criminal records and driving records to pulling credit reports and verifying résumé information. When an employer hires this type of company, or any other third party, to gather information on an applicant, it must follow the federal Fair Credit Reporting Act (FCRA). Some states have also passed laws that specifically limit an employer's ability to obtain credit reports on applicants.

The Fair Credit Reporting Act

Despite its name, the federal Fair Credit Reporting Act (15 U.S.C. § 1681 and following) applies to much more than just an applicant's credit information. The FCRA applies whenever a consumer reporting agency (CRA) gathers information on a consumer's credit, character, reputation, personal characteristics, or mode of living (called a "consumer report") for employment purposes or to assess eligibility for credit or insurance. Under the FCRA, employers must follow certain procedures before ordering a consumer report on an applicant or employee, including:

- **Notice.** An employer must notify you in writing if it plans to obtain a consumer report on you. The written notice must be separate from other documents; it can't be buried in the middle of a job application, for example.
- **Authorization.** The employer must get your written permission before ordering the report. The notice usually provides a signature line for you to consent.
- **Pre-adverse action notice.** Before taking any negative action against you based on the contents of the report—such as rejecting you for a job or promotion—the employer must send you a copy of the report and a written notice of your rights under the FCRA.
- **Adverse action notice.** After taking the adverse action, the employer must send you a written notice that includes the name of the CRA that provided the report and instructions on how to challenge inaccurate information.

While this sounds like strong stuff at first, the truth is that applicants have little choice but to consent to background checks if they want the job. Employers are free to reject applicants who refuse to authorize a background check. If you don't give your permission, you will leave the impression that you have something to hide and the employer might take you out of the running for the job.

If you're worried about something in your past, you might want to run a background check or credit check on yourself before you apply for a job. If anything negative turns up, you can at least bring the issue up with the employer preemptively and have an opportunity to explain. Many background check companies allow individuals to order reports on themselves for a relatively low fee. Credit reporting agencies are required to provide a free credit report to consumers each year upon request; visit www.annualcreditreport.com to learn more.

Inaccurate information on a consumer or credit report is also more common than you might think. The FCRA imposes additional obligations on CRAs in terms of what type of information they can report and what procedures they must follow to ensure the accuracy of consumer reports. To learn more, including how to dispute inaccurate reports, visit www.ftc.gov/credit.

Some employers have a manager or human resources representative do some Internet digging on applicants before hiring them. If an employer does its own research without hiring a third party, it generally does not have to follow FCRA requirements. However, the employer must still follow other rules, such as state laws restricting consideration of an applicant's criminal records (see "Criminal Records," above).

RESOURCE

Need to know more about fixing your credit? For detailed information—and step-by-step instructions—on cleaning up your credit report before it becomes a problem, see *Credit Repair*, by Amy Loftsgordon and Cara O'Neill (Nolo).

State Credit Discrimination Laws

When the economy took a nosedive a decade ago, some states stepped in to pass laws restricting or prohibiting an employer from considering credit history in making job decisions. These states determined that it's neither fair nor sensible to punish people for past credit mistakes, especially if the penalty affects their ability to earn money—and stay out of financial trouble—in the future.

Currently, about a dozen states, including California, Illinois, and Maryland, put some limits on an employer's right to consider credit information in hiring or retaining employees. In general, these laws prohibit employers from checking an applicant

or employee's credit report, unless credit information has a direct relationship to the job at hand. For example, most laws have exceptions for managerial positions and jobs that provide access to company funds or trade secrets.

Social Media Passwords

Over the years, employers have looked for new ways to vet job applicants and make sure they are hiring the right people for the job. One relatively new trend is asking job applicants and employees to hand over the passwords to their personal social media accounts, such as a Facebook or Twitter account. The first high profile case happened in 2011, when a correctional officer for the state of Maryland was asked to provide his password to his personal Facebook account during a recertification interview with his supervisor. The supervisor scrolled through the employee's posts during the interview, looking for anything that might be improper. After the interview, the employee called the American Civil Liberties Union, which brought national attention to the issue and demanded protections for employee privacy.

The Maryland legislature responded by passing a law that prohibits employers from asking applicants or employees for passwords to their personal social media accounts. Many states followed suit; about twenty-five states now have social media password laws on the books. These laws differ in the details, but they generally ban employers from asking or requiring applicants or employees to provide login information to personal social media accounts, to bring up their social media pages during an interview, to change the privacy settings on their accounts, or to add someone from the company as a friend or contact. Some states' laws apply only to social media profiles, while others apply generally to all online accounts—including an email account or retail website account. To learn whether your state has such as law, see "State Laws on Social Media Passwords," at the end of this chapter.

In most of these states, employers are free to look at information that is publicly available. For example, if a job applicant has a personal Facebook account that is accessible to the public, the employer may look at its contents. However, an employer cannot use any information learned from a social media page to discriminate based on a protected characteristic, such as religion or disability.

Workplace Testing

Ostensibly, prospective employers and employees want the same thing: to match the best person with the most fitting job. These days, there are a number of tests that purport to take the guesswork out of the process. Ploughing through the Information Age and into the Biotech Century, many employers are quick to welcome outside evaluations of

an individual's mental and physical fitness and integrity and to believe in their results, often at the risk of sacrificing individual privacy rights.

Medical Examinations

Employers may require specific physical and mental examinations to ensure a qualified workforce. However, there are strict rules on when those exams can be conducted and who can learn the results.

Courts have ruled that the constitutional right to privacy covers medical information and that honesty is the only policy when it comes to medical tests for prospective and existing employees. That is, employers must identify what conditions they are testing for and get individual consent to perform the test.

Examining Job Applicants

Employers may legally require prospective employees to undergo medical exams to make sure they are physically able to perform their jobs, as long as all employees entering that job category are required to do so. In other words, an employer can't selectively require medical examinations for only certain applicants. The timing of the medical exam is also important. Under the federal Americans with Disabilities Act, or ADA (discussed in Chapter 7), covered employers cannot require medical examinations before offering an individual a job. They are, however, free to make an employment offer contingent upon a person's passing a medical exam.

As discussed above, the ADA also requires your employer to keep your medical history and exam results in a file separate from your other personnel records.

Examining Existing Employees

Once an employee is on the job, employers must have a legitimate business reason for requiring a medical exam. In practice, this means testing of current employees is usually limited to "fitness-for-duty" exams, when there is some reason to doubt whether the employee is able to perform the essential functions of the job. However, other situations might justify an examination, such as where an employee's erratic behavior raises concerns of workplace safety. The examining doctor may take a detailed medical history from the employee and administer any tests necessary to determine whether the employee is capable of performing the job. However, the employer is typically entitled only to the doctor's conclusion as to whether the employee is fit to work.

Drug and Alcohol Testing

Many private employers now test for drug and alcohol use. The laws regulating drug abuse in the workplace and the testing of employees for such abuse, however, are still being shaped by the courts. Currently, there is a hodgepodge of legal rules controlling drug testing, some in the Americans with Disabilities Act (see Chapter 7), some set out in specific state laws (see the chart "State Drug and Alcohol Testing Laws," at the end of this chapter), and a number arrived at through court decisions.

Drug tests take a number of forms. Analyzing urine samples is the method most commonly used, but samples of saliva, blood, hair, and breath can also be tested for the presence of alcohol or other drugs in the body. Typically, state laws set out the testing methods that may be used.

Testing Job Applicants

Although state laws vary, employers generally have the right to test job applicants for traces of drugs in their systems as long as all of the following are true:

- The applicant knows that such testing will be part of the screening process for new employees.
- The employer has already offered the applicant the job.
- All applicants for the same job are tested.
- The tests are administered by a state-certified laboratory.

Today, most companies that intend to conduct drug testing on job candidates include in their job applications an agreement to submit to such testing. If, in the process of applying for a job, you are asked to agree to drug testing, you have little choice but to agree to the test or drop out as an applicant.

Testing Existing Employees

There are a number of employees who, because of their specialized positions or type of work, can be tested more freely for drugs and alcohol use. For example, the Department of Transportation requires drug testing for some critical positions, such as airline pilots. And the Federal Aviation Administration mandates testing of all airline maintenance employees. In addition, courts have routinely approved random drug testing for employees with national security clearances, prison officers, employees at chemical weapons and nuclear power plants, and police officers.

However, many states place legal constraints on testing current employees for drugs or alcohol in private workplaces. In some states, employers cannot conduct blanket drug tests of all employees or random drug testing. In other states, employers have more freedom to test employees, but they still must follow specific procedures—such as having a written drug testing policy, using a certified lab, and allowing an employee to challenge a positive result. (See "State Drug and Alcohol Testing Laws," at the end of this chapter, to learn your state's rules.)

Most states allow employers to drug test employees in the following situations:

- when the employer has reasonable suspicion that an employee is abusing drugs or alcohol
- after a job-related accident
- for certain high-risk or safety-sensitive positions
- as part of a fitness-for-duty exam, and
- as a follow-up to the employee completing a rehabilitation program.

When Is a Suspicion Reasonable?

In most situations, an employer may test you for drugs if there is a reasonable suspicion that you are using them. What suspicion is reasonable and what is not is in the eye and mind of the beholder, which makes it a slippery standard indeed.

But some statutes and courts have attempted to set some guidelines that may be helpful if you are targeted for a test and you believe your employer's suspicions are less than reasonable. A reasonable suspicion of drug use must generally be based on actual facts and logical inferences such as:

- direct observation of drug use or its physical symptoms, including slurred speech, agitated or lethargic demeanor, uncoordinated movement, and inappropriate response to questions
- abnormal conduct or erratic behavior while at work, or significant deterioration in work performance
- a report of drug use provided by a reliable and credible source that has been independently corroborated
- evidence that the employee has tampered with current drug test results
- information that the employee has caused or contributed to an accident at work, or
- evidence that the employee has used, possessed, sold, solicited, or transferred drugs while working or at work.

Employers in all states may not drug test in a discriminatory way, for example, by singling out people based on race or national origin. Employers might also need to reasonably accommodate an employee's or applicant's use of legal prescription drugs for a disability (see Chapter 7 to learn more).

Challenging Drug Tests

As an employee, you can always refuse to take a workplace drug test. But, if you are fired because of your refusal, you may have little recourse. (You might also be denied unemployment benefits if you are fired for failing or refusing to take a drug test.) Your employer needs only to show that he or she had good reason to believe that you were a safety hazard on the job or that you seemed unable to perform the work required. You would be placed in the untenable position of proving that your employer knew no such thing.

If you have been given a drug test and unfairly suspended or demoted because of it, your best bet may be to argue that the testers did not meet with the strict requirements for form and procedure set out in your state law. And note that employers are free to add safeguards to protect against specimen tampering, such as requiring those taking the test to remove their own clothing and don hospital gowns, or providing a test monitor who checks the temperature of the urine and adds dye to toilet water. However, a modicum of discretion is required; while most courts have found it reasonable to

have a monitor listen as a urine test is administered, a number have found it an unreasonable invasion of privacy for the monitor to watch.

In addition, some laws require employers to maintain workplace counseling and outreach programs before they can test employees. While most employers these days are too savvy to slip up on procedural details, many of the laws are so picky and detailed that it may be worth your while to wade through and see whether your test made the grade.

Medical Marijuana

About half of the states have legalized marijuana for medicinal use, at least to treat certain medical conditions (such as cancer, glaucoma, HIV/AIDS, epilepsy, and multiple sclerosis). As mentioned above, the Americans With Disabilities Act requires employers to reasonably accommodate an employee's use of legal drugs for a disability. However, because marijuana use is still illegal under federal law, employees are often not entitled to reasonable accommodation for medical marijuana use.

About a dozen states have passed laws protecting job applicants and employees from discrimination based on their status as medical marijuana cardholders. In these states, employers may not fire employees for using medical marijuana with a valid prescription, as long as they don't bring marijuana to work and aren't under the influence or impaired on the job. However, other states do not have antidiscrimination provisions protecting medical marijuana users. In these states, courts often rule in favor of employers, allowing them to fire employees even for legal, off-duty use. The Colorado Supreme Court, for example, upheld an employer's termination of a quadriplegic employee who used medical marijuana during non-working hours to treat his medical condition. (To learn your state's laws, see "State Laws on Marijuana Use and Employment," at the end of this chapter.) Because this is a rapidly evolving area of law, check with a local employment lawyer if you have questions about your medical marijuana use.

Genetic Testing

While wildly hailed as a law prohibiting discrimination on the job, the Genetic Information Nondiscrimination Act, or GINA, protects a commodity that most people hold near and dear and private: their genes.

GINA broadly prohibits employers with 15 or more employees from using applicants' or employees' genetic information in making employment decisions, restricts how it can be acquired, and strictly limits disclosing it to others.

The law takes the long view that genetic information includes information about an individual's genetic tests and the genetic tests of an individual's family members, as well as any information about any disease, disorder, or condition revealed in an individual's family medical history.

While individuals were initially most concerned that potential employers would use genetic tests to pry out information during the interview and hiring process, the law also forbids discrimination on the basis of genetic information when it comes to any aspect of employment, including pay, job assignments, promotions, layoffs, training, fringe benefits, firing, or any other term or condition of employment.

Generally speaking, employers cannot collect an employee's genetic information or family medical history, except in very narrow circumstances. And, even if an employer receives genetic information in a lawful manner, it may not use the information when making employment decisions and must keep it confidential. (For more on GINA, see "The Genetic Information Nondiscrimination Act" in Chapter 7.)

Personality Testing

A number of people who label themselves as workplace consultants claim they have developed several series of written questions —integrity tests—that can predict whether a person would lie, steal, or be unreliable if hired for a particular job. And a number of other alleged experts claim to have perfected personality tests that allow employers to tell in advance whether an individual is suited by temperament and talent to a particular position. Employers are drawn to these tactics because they seem to short-circuit the process of interviewing and promise some insight

Target Learns What Not to Ask

The first major case to challenge psychological testing of job applicants yielded grand results: a $2 million settlement and a five-year ban on testing.

The settlement came in July 1993, after a class action brought by several people who had applied to the Target stores chain for work as security guards. (*Soroka v. Dayton Hudson Corp.*, 7 Cal. App.4th 203 (1991).) As part of the application process, they had been asked to respond to over 700 true/false statements including:

- I am very strongly attracted by members of my own sex.
- I have never indulged in unusual sex practices.
- I believe my sins are unpardonable.
- I believe in the second coming of Christ.
- I have had no difficulty starting or holding my urine.

About 30% of the 2,500 test takers did not get jobs with Target, either because of the answers they gave or because the results were deemed inconclusive.

But the test made even successful applicants queasy. Robert Marzetta worked at Target for a year before becoming one of the main plaintiffs in the case. He said that while he felt the test questions were "out of line" and made him "uncomfortable," he didn't object at exam time because he needed the job.

Sue Urry joined in the case because, she said, as a Mormon, she found the religious questions particularly offensive.

Another plaintiff, Sibi Soroka found the test questions so unsettling that he copied all 700 of them before turning in his answers, then went to the American Civil Liberties Union and a number of attorneys seeking help. He was on the job only about a month because, he said, "it's kind of difficult to work for a person you're suing."

Target argued that the test, the Rodgers Condensed CPI-MMPI, helped weed out the emotionally unstable from the pool of those who would be subjected to the stressful task of apprehending shoplifting suspects.

The applicants challenged the test as violating their privacy rights and the state labor code, which bans questions about sexual orientation.

They shared in the $2 million in wealth Target lost.

This headline-grabbing case inspired hundreds of other workers around the nation to mount challenges to psychological tests they found offensive or intrusive. So far, the majority of courts have sided with the workers.

into an applicant's personality, which can be tough to assess in an interview setting.

Psychological tests are not a new idea. They were first developed during World War I to help the military decide how to assign soldiers to various jobs. Some legal cutbacks to personality and psychological testing in the workplace began in the 1970s, when employers were banned from questioning prospective employees about age, race, or sex. The tests had a heyday again in the early 1990s, shortly after lie detector screening was curtailed by law. (See "Lie Detector Tests," below.) And, today, legions of test publishers have cropped up online, most of which claim they can forecast everything from a potential employee's likelihood of being honest and hardworking to his or her absence and injury rate on the job. And they promise an analysis fast, often within 48 hours of receiving responses to test questions. Critics say that is a suspiciously tall order to fill so quickly. And there may be legal pitfalls to the tests as well. Despite the doubts that surround them, however, the employee-screening tests remain popular with many employers, most of whom claim to temper their acceptance with a dollop of skepticism and to cast about for information in more subtle ways.

Personality tests are generally allowed, as long as they don't violate other employment laws. For example, a personality test might be illegal if it has a discriminatory impact on members of a protected class or if it is trying to detect a mental disability. Personality tests that delve too deeply into an applicant or employee's personal life or moral views might also violate state privacy laws.

Lie Detector Tests

For decades, lie detectors or polygraphs—now more euphemistically referred to as "psychological stress evaluator tests"—were routinely used on employees and job applicants. Such tests purport to measure the truthfulness of a person's statements by tracking bodily functions, such as blood pressure and perspiration.

Employers could—and often did—ask employees and prospective employees questions about extremely private matters, such as sexual preferences, toilet habits, and family finances, while a machine to which they were hooked passed judgment on the truthfulness of the answers. Push the machine's needle too far by reacting to an offensive question and you could be labeled a liar and denied employment.

The federal Employee Polygraph Protection Act (29 U.S.C. § 2001), passed in 1988, virtually outlawed using lie detectors in connection with employment. That law covers all private employers in interstate commerce, which includes just about every private company that uses a computer, the U.S. mail, or a telephone system to send messages to someone in another state.

Under the Act, it is illegal for employers to:

- require, request, suggest, or cause any employee or job applicant to submit to a lie detector test
- use, accept, refer to, or inquire about the results of any lie detector test conducted on an employee or job applicant, or
- dismiss, discipline, discriminate against, or even threaten to take action against any employee or job applicant who refuses to take a lie detector test.

The law also prohibits employers from discriminating against or firing those who use the law's protections.

When Lie Detector Tests Can Be Used

The Employee Polygraph Protection Act allows polygraph tests to be used only in very limited circumstances. One instance is where the employer is conducting an ongoing investigation into company theft and has reason to believe the employee was involved. However, before you can be required to take such a test as part of an investigation, you must be given a written notice, at least 48 hours before the test, stating that you are a suspect. And there must be a provable, reasonable suspicion that you were involved in the theft or other conduct triggering the investigation.

Limitations on the Tests

Even when testing is allowed, there are a number of restrictions on their format.

Before a lie detector test can be administered, your employer must read to you and ask you to sign a statement that includes:

- a list of topics you cannot be asked about, including questions on religious beliefs, sexual preference, racial matters, lawful activities of labor organizations, and political affiliation
- information on your right to refuse to take the test
- the fact that you cannot be required to take the test as a condition of employment
- an explanation of how the test results can be used, and
- an explanation of your legal rights if the test is not given in keeping with the law.

While the test is being administered, you have the right:

- to stop it at any time, and
- to be asked questions in a way that is not "degrading or needlessly intrusive."

When the test is said and done, results can be disclosed only to the employer that ordered the test, the employee who was tested, a court or government agency, or an arbitrator or mediator if there is a related court order. The law specifically prohibits prospective employers from accessing old test results.

How to Take Action

The Employee Polygraph Protection Act is enforced by the U.S. Department of Labor. If you have questions about whether the Act applies to your job or if you suspect that you have been subjected to illegal polygraph testing, call the office of the U.S. Labor Department's Wage and Hour Division nearest you. (See the appendix for contact details.)

HIV Testing

The disease of Acquired Immune Deficiency Syndrome (AIDS) was first identified in 1981. Fairly early on, researchers isolated its viral cause, the Human Immunodeficiency Virus (HIV), which suppresses the immune systems of those who carry it, making them easy targets for various other infections and diseases. Since then, while great strides have been made in treating AIDS symptoms, there still is no cure. Many of those who have the HIV infection live nearly symptom free. But, ultimately, the disease is still considered fatal.

The impact on American workplaces has been and will continue to be enormous. Not only have hundreds of thousands of workers died, most of them have also suffered from the reactions of others—irrational fear and ostracism—that play in tandem with the AIDS epidemic. Historically, many workplaces responded to the hysteria with more hysteria, developing intrusive policies of isolating workers suspected to have the disease. (See the section in Chapter 7, "Discrimination Against Workers With HIV or AIDS.")

Another offshoot of this hysteria is the practice of testing employees for the HIV virus. While a number of courts have struck down state and local efforts to screen employees for HIV, the practice continues in many workplaces.

Types of Tests

Although medical researchers may develop more methods of testing for HIV, the test first approved for commercial use by the Food and Drug Administration in 1985 is still in use today. Basically, the test measures antibodies in the blood that are stimulated by the virus. If a test is positive, indicating exposure to the deadly virus, a confirmation test is usually performed that uses a more complicated system of measuring molecular weights found in the blood.

However, there are a number of things the HIV antibody testing does not indicate. Tests do not identify people who have AIDS. AIDS is defined by the Centers for Disease Control and Prevention (CDC), and the definition is still evolving. Currently, an individual is considered to have AIDS if he or she has any of the AIDS-related diseases specified by the CDC and has a T-count—or number of infection-fighting white corpuscles—of less than 200 in a cubic milliliter of blood.

Also, tests do not identify every person carrying the HIV virus. The tests are aimed at measuring the antibodies stimulated by HIV, so they do not work effectively on individuals who have been exposed to the virus but have not developed antibodies to it, a process that usually takes about eight weeks, but may take up to a year or more.

Legal Controls on Testing

Originally, HIV blood tests were fashioned to screen blood, not people. But when prospective employees and employees are subjected to testing, the reality is that people are being screened and sometimes labeled as unfit workers.

Because HIV substantially limits the proper functioning of the immune system, it qualifies as a disability under the Americans With Disabilities Act. (See Chapter 7.) Employers therefore may not test job applicants in order to screen out those with HIV or AIDS. However, as discussed earlier in this chapter, employers may require job applicants and employees to undergo a general medical examination in certain situations. If an exam reveals that an applicant or employee has HIV or AIDS, the employer cannot reject the applicant or fire the employee unless:

- the applicant or employee is not able to perform the essential functions of the job, with or without a reasonable accommodation, or
- the applicant or employee would pose a direct threat to health or safety in the workplace.

Legal Actions Against Privacy Violations

There are specific laws that forbid employers from being overly invasive. However, your most powerful weapon may be to file a lawsuit against your employer claiming invasion of privacy. And the most likely way to win such a case is to show that, in the process of collecting information on you, the employer was guilty of one of the following acts.

Deception. Your employer asked you to submit to a routine medical examination, for example, but mentioned nothing about a drug test. However, the urine sample that you gave to the examining physician was tested, and because drugs were found in your urine, you were fired.

Violation of confidentiality. Your former employer asked you to fill in a health questionnaire and assured you that the information would be held in confidence for the company's use only. But you later found out that the health information was divulged to a prospective employer that called to check your references.

Secret, intrusive monitoring. Installing visible video cameras above a supermarket's cash registers is usually considered a legitimate method of ensuring that employees are not stealing from the company. But installing hidden video cameras above the stalls in an employee restroom would probably qualify as an invasion of privacy.

Intrusion on your private life. Your employer hired a private detective, for example, to monitor where you go in the evening when you're not at work. When the company discovered that you are active in a gay rights organization, you were told to resign from that group or risk losing your job.

Either of these standards would be difficult for an employer to meet, though. Because HIV is often controllable with antiviral medications, many people show no outward signs of illness. Others might have minor health issues that can be addressed with a reasonable accommodation. And, because there are a limited number of ways in which HIV is transmitted (through sexual activity or exposure to blood), most people with HIV will not be considered a threat to workplace safety based on HIV-positive status alone. For example, an HIV-positive firefighter, schoolteacher, nurse, or restaurant server would likely not pose a direct threat to others. An orthopedic surgeon, on the other hand, might pose a direct threat because of prolonged contact with a patient's blood and use of sharp tools in a confined space.

Some states and cities have additional rules that apply to HIV testing in employment. Contact your local government for more information. A number of organizations also offer resources for employees with HIV or AIDS. (See the appendix for contact information.)

Surveillance and Monitoring

We have arrived at the place we long feared: Technological advances have made it easy for Big Brother—and anyone else who wants to join him—to watch us. In truth, most employers cannot properly be painted as paranoid Peeping Toms. And the law does require that most workplace monitoring— listening in on telephone calls and audio-taping or videotaping conversations—must have some legitimate business purpose. Other than that, however, there are very few federal legal controls protecting workers from being watched and listened to while at work.

Some states set their own bounds on how much prying you must tolerate. For example, several states have laws specifically restricting searches and surveillance of employees, and some of those laws are quite powerful.

In Connecticut, for example, an employer that repeatedly uses electronic devices, such as video cameras or audiotape recorders, to monitor employees in restrooms, locker rooms, or lounges can be fined and sentenced to jail for 30 days. (Conn. Gen. Stat. § 31-48b.)

Telephone Calls

In general, it is legal for employers to monitor business-related telephone calls to and from their own premises for business reasons (for example, to evaluate the quality of customer service). However, a federal law, the Electronic Communications Privacy Act, or ECPA (18 U.S.C. §§ 2510 to 2720), puts some major limitations on that right. The ECPA restricts individuals and organizations, including employers, from intercepting wire, oral, or electronic communications.

Under the Act, even if a call is being monitored for business reasons, which is perfectly legal, if a personal call comes in, an employer must hang up as soon as he or she realizes the call is personal. An employer may monitor a personal call only if an employee knows the particular call is being monitored and consents to it.

While the federal law seems to put some serious limits on employers' rights to monitor phone calls, some state laws have additional safeguards. A number of them require, for example, that employers inform the employee and the person on the other end of the phone that the call is being monitored.

In general, if your employer has a clear policy notifying you that it monitors phone calls and that you shouldn't use work phones to make personal calls, it won't be violating your privacy rights by listening in.

Computers

Nearly every workplace in America today conducts at least some part of its business on computers. While hailed by many as time-savers and aids to efficiency, computers have lent a new murkiness to workplace privacy laws.

Computer Files

There still is no specific law controlling whether and when the files you create on a workplace computer are legally protected from others' snooping eyes. In legal battles over the issue, employers that claim a right to rummage through employees' computer files must show they have a valid business purpose for doing so. Employees often respond by claiming that they had a valid expectation of privacy: a logical, reasonable belief that others would not retrieve and read the files.

Employers can, however, reduce an employee's expectation of privacy by giving advance notice that computers will be monitored by the company and should be used only for business purposes. If your employer has issued such a policy, it will be nearly impossible to refute.

Email

Well over half of all employers now routinely monitor employee emails. This is easy to do. Some email systems copy all messages that pass through them; others create backup copies of new messages as they arrive on the system servers. And a surprising number of employers assign someone to manually read and review email. Workers who logically assume their messages are gone for good when they delete them are painfully surprised to learn they are wrong.

Technology has now turned on itself as more companies buy into the software and electronic surveillance systems that make it easier to monitor email. In some situations, even the most stalwart privacy advocate can see that the forces behind the monitoring are legitimate. For example, employers may have concerns over poor job performance, quality control, theft of trade secrets, and potential liability for sexual harassment and discrimination claims.

Stories abound of those who abused email privileges at work or were reprimanded or fired for offensive or overindulgent instant messaging. Courts have almost unanimously

Employers That Spy

From email monitoring and website blocking to phone tapping and GPS tracking, employers increasingly combine technology with policy to manage productivity and for a host of other reasons, according to a recent poll.

More than half of the employers surveyed said they have fired workers for what they considered to be a misuse of email or the Internet.

Additional survey findings revealed some of the thought behind the sleuthing.

Email and Internet-Related Terminations

Employers that have fired workers for email misuse cited the following reasons:

- violation of a company policy (64%)
- inappropriate or offensive language (62%)
- excessive personal use (26%)
- breach of confidentiality rules (22%), and
- other (12%).

Those that fired workers for Internet misuse cited:

- viewing, downloading, or uploading inappropriate or offensive content (84%)
- violation of a company policy (48%)
- excessive personal use (34%), and
- other (9%).

Internet, Email, Blogs, and Social Networking

Employers are primarily concerned about inappropriate Internet surfing. To that end:

- 66% monitor Internet connections, and
- 65% use software to block connections to inappropriate websites.

Employers that block access to the Web are concerned about employees visiting:

- adult sites with sexual, romantic, or pornographic content (96%)
- game sites (61%)
- social networking sites (50%)
- entertainment sites (40%)
- shopping/auction sites (27%)
- sports sites (21%), and
- external blogs (18%).

Source: "2007 Electronic Monitoring & Surveillance Survey" from the American Management Association (AMA) and The ePolicy Institute.

---

found in favor of the employer when deciding whether it had the right to review employee emails sent on company equipment or over company networks. As long as the employer does nothing to lead employees to believe it won't read their email, and particularly if the employer has a policy telling employees that it reserves the right to read email, judges have sided with employers on this one.

Again, a growing number of companies—nearly 84% of all larger ones—have taken proactive measures by establishing written policies informing employees of acceptable use of email at work. The policies range from absolutist controls banning personal email on the job completely, to limiting it to reasonable use, to the rare but existing nod that email will not be monitored on the job. A few states

The Dangers of Social Media

As social media becomes an increasing part of our lives, the downsides of spending too much time on Facebook, Twitter, Instagram, and similar websites is becoming apparent. Several studies have emerged on the negative effects of social media on mental health, and social media has often been used as a tool to bully or harass others. When it comes to the workplace, many applicants and employees have found that the words that they post can leave them jobless.

Here are some examples of social media landing employees in hot water:

- A waiter was fired after tweeting that a famous actress skipped out on a bill, only to have her agent pay it the next day with no tip.
- An applicant had a job offer rescinded from a large tech company after tweeting that she was weighing the money against the commute and "hating the work."
- A daycare employee was fired shortly after she posted on Facebook that she hated her job and being around kids.
- An employee of a government contractor was fired after she used a viral picture of her flipping off the presidential motorcade as her profile picture on Twitter and Facebook.

But what about the right to free speech? You might be surprised to learn that the First Amendment applies only to actions by the government, not by private employers.

Employers are generally free to rescind job offers or fire employees based on their social media content. However, there are some federal and state laws that place limits on this right. Some of the most common restrictions are outlined below.

Federal labor law. The National Labor Relations Act (NLRA) is often thought of as a law that applies to unionized workplaces. However, the NLRA also safeguards the right of nonunion employees to get together and discuss the terms and conditions of their employment (called "protected concerted activity"). For example, if an employee posts on Facebook about low wages and dangerous working conditions and tags several coworkers, that post might be protected under the NLRA. (To learn more about the NLRA, see Chapter 15.)

Political beliefs. Some states specifically prohibit employers from discriminating against applicants and employees based on their political beliefs, opinions, or affiliations.

Off-duty conduct laws. Some states have laws making it illegal for an employer to fire an employee for lawful conduct that happens outside of work hours and away from company premises. Unless the conduct somehow harms your employer's business interests, your conduct would be protected. For example, if you posted a photo on Facebook of yourself holding a glass of wine or attending a political rally, your employer might not be able to fire you for it.

(including Connecticut and Delaware) have comprehensive laws requiring employers to inform workers of electronic monitoring including email and Internet use.

Internet Use

Another source of complaints about employers' monitoring computer use on the job is likely to settle on employees' Internet habits. Some former employees have already felt the sting when hit with evidence of site surfing that is hard to pass off as work related. For example, one fellow was recently fired on his third day of work at a large CPA firm after being confronted with company records that revealed repeated visits to a pornography website.

A number of employers say they block employees' access to personal email and Internet sites they deem frivolous or without a sufficient work-related purpose, such as video-streaming and retail websites. Such filters are imperfect at best and counterproductive at worst, particularly if they block access to sites an employee needs to complete a job task. But they are currently legal.

Audiotaping and Videotaping

Almost half of the companies responding to an American Management Association survey reported they use video monitoring to counter theft, violence, and sabotage. Only 7% use video surveillance to track employees' on-the-job performance. But nearly all said they notify employees that the cameras may be rolling beforehand.

But now there's another twist in the on-the-job taping. As the number of lawsuits over workplace disputes has grown, so has an alarming trend: Both employers and employees intent on bolstering their claims have begun to record one another in the hope of capturing some wrongdoing on tape. There are a number of legal and practical problems with this approach to gathering evidence, however.

Federal law appears to allow any person involved in a conversation to tape it without the other person's knowledge or permission— as long as the recording is not made for the purpose of committing a crime, such as extortion. But a number of state laws have much stricter controls. Some, for example, require that everyone involved must consent before a conversation or an action can be taped.

Although our guts might tell us the opposite, audiotapes and videotapes also have questionable value as trial evidence. Before any jury would be allowed to hear or see a tape of a workplace scene, the tape would have to satisfy many picky rules designed to qualify and disqualify trial evidence.

Searches and Seizures

Most employers would claim a legitimate desire to keep workplaces free of illegal drugs, alcohol, and weapons. And most employees would claim that they have a right to expect that their personal belongings will remain safe from the groping hands of their employers.

When faced with an invasion of privacy claim by an employee, a court will weigh the employee's reasonable expectation of privacy against the employer's legitimate business reason for performing the search. The lower the expectation of privacy and the more compelling the reason for the search, the more likely the search is legal. For example, an employer would probably be justified in searching an employee's locker if there were reports that he or she had brought a gun to work.

In general, employees will have a higher expectation of privacy in their bodies, purses or backpacks, or personal cars than their work desks or company cars. Company theft and safety concerns are usually considered legitimate business interests.

> EXAMPLE: Thomas sold household appliances for a department store that provides each employee with a storage cabinet for personal belongings in a room adjacent to the employee lounge. The store's employee handbook states that, although the company does not provide locks for the cabinets and does not take responsibility for any thefts from the storage area, employees may bring in locks of their own to secure their individual cabinets.
>
> One day while at work, Thomas was called to the manager's office, where he was confronted with a letter that

had been written to him from his drug rehabilitation counselor. The manager said the letter had been found in his storage cabinet during a routine search by the company's security force. The manager fired Thomas.

Thomas could likely win an invasion of privacy lawsuit against his former employer. By allowing Thomas to use his own lock to secure his cabinet, the department store had given him a reasonable expectation of privacy for anything kept in that cabinet. His claim would be much weaker, however, if his former employer had furnished the locks and doled out the keys or combinations to them, because Thomas would then be on notice that others could get into his locker.

Another factor that weighs heavily in determining whether an employer's search is legal is the reasonableness of its length and scope. For example, an employer that suspected an employee of stealing foot-long copper piping might be justified in searching a work locker, but not her purse or pockets.

Clothing and Grooming Codes

In general, employers have the right to dictate on-the-job standards for clothing and grooming as a condition of employment. Codes governing employees' appearance may be illegal, however, if they result in a pattern of discrimination against a particular group of employees or potential employees. This type of violation has most often been mounted in companies with different dress and grooming codes for male and female employees.

Dress Codes

Many companies have policies about uniforms for the legitimate purpose of keeping their employees looking neat and identifiable. There is nothing inherently illegal, for example, about a company requiring all employees to wear navy blue slacks during working hours.

Many employers provide workers with some or all of the clothing that they are required to wear on the job. A few companies even rent attire for their employees to ensure that they will be similarly dressed.

Employers have a lot of freedom to set dress codes that meet their business needs, but they must follow a few rules:

No Paint, No Powder, No Job

Darlene Jespersen toiled for nearly 20 years as a bartender at the sports bar in Harrah's Casino in Reno. Along the way, she garnered rave performance reviews from her supervisors, along with a stack of customer feedback forms praising her excellent service and good attitude.

Then Harrah's served up something new: a Beverage Department Image Transformation Program with new appearance standards for employees, called "Personal Best." It required all women who worked in the beverage department to wear makeup, including "foundation or powder, blush, lipstick, and mascara applied neatly in complimentary colors"; stockings; colored nail polish; hair "teased, curled, or styled every day" and "worn down at all times, no exceptions."

Men, on the other hand, were simply forbidden by the policy from wearing any makeup of any kind and required to maintain trimmed hair and fingernails.

According to Jespersen, wearing makeup made her extremely uncomfortable and interfered with her ability to do her job. Harrah's was unwilling to change the policy, so Jespersen left her job.

Jespersen filed a federal lawsuit accusing Harrah's of sex discrimination. But an all-male panel held against her, opining that the grooming requirements, on their face, were not more burdensome for women than men. Jespersen argued that the makeup requirement was more burdensome in practice because it required significantly more time and money for women to comply with. However, the court refused to consider this issue because Jespersen had failed to show evidence to that effect at trial.

(*Jespersen v. Harrah's Operating Co., Inc.*, 444 F.3d 1104 (2006).)

- **Discriminatory dress codes.** Dress codes cannot discriminate based on a protected characteristic, such as race, gender, or religion. Gender-based differences are allowed, but the dress code may not impose a heavier burden on one gender. For example, courts have held that an employer cannot require female employees to wear uniforms if it allows male employees to wear street clothes on the job.

- **Reasonable accommodations.** Employers may also need to provide a modification to a dress code as a reasonable accommodation for an employee's religion or disability. For example, an employer with a "no hats" policy would likely need to accommodate an employee who wears a hijab (a head covering worn by some Muslim women).

- **Cost of uniforms.** As discussed in Chapter 2, federal law allows employers to deduct the cost of uniforms from an employee's paycheck, unless it would result in the employee making less than minimum wage. However, some states require employers to bear the cost of company uniforms as a business expense.

Grooming Codes

The same rules that apply to dress codes apply to grooming codes. Most workplace grooming codes simply require that employees be clean and presentable on the job. And such codes are rarely challenged.

However, several lawsuits challenging workplace grooming codes have been waged by black men with pseudofollicullitis barbae, a race-specific skin disorder making it painful to shave. Several individuals have successfully challenged companies that refuse to hire men with beards or that fire men who do not comply with no-beard rules.

EXAMPLE: Nelson, a black man, was advised by his physician not to shave his facial hair too closely because that would cause his whiskers to become ingrown and infected. Although Nelson brought a doctor's note to this effect to a job interview, he was turned down for employment because of the company's no-beard policy.

Nelson filed a complaint against the company under his state's antidiscrimination laws on the basis of racial discrimination. Medical experts testified in his case that the condition which prevented Nelson from shaving usually affected only black men.

The court ruled in Nelson's favor, saying that the company's failure to lift its ban on beards despite Nelson's well-documented medical problem resulted in illegal racial discrimination. (See Chapter 7 for details on discrimination laws.)

State Laws on Access to Personnel Records

This chart deals with only those states that authorize access to personnel files. Generally, an employee is allowed to see evaluations, performance reviews, and other documents that determine a promotion, bonus, or raise; access usually does not include letters of reference, test results, or records of a criminal or workplace-violation investigation. Under other state laws, employees may have access to their medical records, payroll records, and records of exposure to hazardous substances; these laws are not included in this chart.

Alaska

Alaska Stat. § 23.10.430

Employers affected: All.

Employee access to records: Employee or former employee may view and copy personnel files.

Conditions for viewing records: Employee may view records during regular business hours under reasonable rules.

Copying records: Employee pays (if employer so requests).

California

Cal. Lab. Code §§ 1198.5; 432

Employers affected: All employers subject to wage and hour laws.

Employee access to records: Employee or former employee has right to inspect personnel records relating to performance or to a grievance proceeding, within 30 days of making a written request for records. Employer may redact the names of any nonmanagerial employees. Employer need not comply with more than one request per year from a former employee. If employee files a lawsuit against employer that relates to a personnel matter, the right to review personnel records ceases while the suit is pending.

Written request required: Yes. If employee makes an oral request, the employer must supply a form to make a written request.

Conditions for viewing records: Employee may view personnel file at reasonable times, during break or nonwork hours. If records are kept offsite or employer does not make them available at the workplace, then employee must be allowed to view them at the storage location without loss of pay. If former employee was terminated for reasons relating to harassment or workplace violence, employer may provide copy of records or make them available offsite.

Copying records: Employee or former employee also has a right to a copy of personnel records, at the employee's cost, within 30 days of making a written request.

Colorado

Colo. Rev. Stat. Ann. § 8-2-129

Employers affected: All.

Employee access to records: Upon request, current employee may inspect personnel file at least once per year. Former employee may inspect personnel file once after termination of employment.

Conditions for viewing records: Employer must make personnel file available at its place of business at a time convenient to employee and employer. Employer may have a designated representative present at the time of inspection.

Copying records: Employee or former employee may request a copy of the personnel file. Employer can require the employee to pay reasonable copying costs.

State Laws on Access to Personnel Records (continued)

Connecticut

Conn. Gen. Stat. Ann. §§ 31-128a to 31-128h

Employers affected: All.

Employee access to records: Employee has right to inspect personnel files within 7 business days after making a request, but not more than twice a year. Former employee has right to inspect personnel files within 10 business days after making a request.

Written request required: Yes.

Conditions for viewing records: Employee may view records during regular business hours in a location at or near worksite. Employer may require that files be viewed in the presence of designated official.

Copying records: Employer must provide copies within 7 days (current employee) or 10 days (former employee) after receiving employee's written request; request must identify the materials employee wants copied. Employer may charge a fee that is based on the cost of supplying documents. Employee is entitled to a copy of any disciplinary action against the employee within 1 business day after it is imposed; employer must immediately provide terminated employee with a copy of the termination notice.

Employee's right to insert rebuttal: If employee disagrees with information in personnel file and cannot reach an agreement with employer to remove or correct it, employee may submit an explanatory written statement (a "rebuttal"). Rebuttal must be maintained as part of the file. Employer must inform employee of the right to submit a rebuttal in evaluation, discipline, or termination paperwork.

Delaware

Del. Code Ann. tit. 19, §§ 730 to 735

Employers affected: All.

Employee access to records: Current employee, employee who is laid off with reemployment rights, or employee on leave of absence may inspect personnel record; employee's agent is not entitled to have access to records. Unless there is reasonable cause, employer may limit access to once a year.

Written request required: At employer's discretion. Employer may require employee to file a form and indicate either the purpose of the review or what parts of the record employee wants to inspect.

Conditions for viewing records: Records may be viewed during employer's regular business hours. Employer may require that employees view files on their own time and may also require that files be viewed on the premises and in the presence of a designated official.

Copying records: Employer is not required to permit employee to copy records. Employee may take notes.

Employee's right to insert rebuttal: If employee disagrees with information in personnel file and cannot reach an agreement with employer to remove or correct it, employee may submit an explanatory written statement (a "rebuttal"). Rebuttal must be maintained as part of the personnel file.

Illinois

820 Ill. Comp. Stat. §§ 40/1 to 40/12

Employers affected: Employers with 5 or more employees.

State Laws on Access to Personnel Records (continued)

Employee access to records: Current employee, or former employee terminated within the past year, is permitted to inspect records twice a year at reasonable intervals, unless a collective bargaining agreement provides otherwise. An employee involved in a current grievance may designate a representative of the union or collective bargaining unit, or other agent, to inspect personnel records that may be relevant to resolving the grievance. Employer must make records available within 7 working days after employee makes request (if employer cannot meet deadline, may be allowed an additional 7 days).

Written request required: At employer's discretion. Employer may require use of a form.

Conditions for viewing records: Records may be viewed during normal business hours at or near worksite or, at employer's discretion, during nonworking hours at a different location if more convenient for employee.

Copying records: After reviewing records, employee may get a copy. Employer may charge only actual cost of duplication. If employee is unable to view files at worksite, employer, upon receipt of a written request, must mail employee a copy.

Employee's right to insert rebuttal: If employee disagrees with any information in the personnel file and cannot reach an agreement with employer to remove or correct it, employee may submit an explanatory written statement (a "rebuttal"). Rebuttal must remain in file with no additional comment by employer.

Iowa
Iowa Code §§ 91A.2, 91B.1
Employers affected: All employers with salaried employees or commissioned salespeople.

Employee access to records: Employee may have access to personnel file at time agreed upon by employer and employee.

Conditions for viewing records: Employer's representative may be present.

Copying records: Employer may charge copying fee for each page that is equivalent to a commercial copying service fee.

Maine
Me. Rev. Stat. Ann. tit. 26, § 631
Employers affected: All.

Employee access to records: Within 10 days of submitting request, employee, former employee, or authorized representative may view and copy personnel files.

Written request required: Yes.

Conditions for viewing records: Employee may view records during normal business hours at the location where the files are kept, unless employer, at own discretion, arranges a time and place more convenient for employee. If files are in electronic or any other nonprint format, employer must provide equipment for viewing and copying.

Copying records: Employee entitled to one free copy of personnel file during each calendar year, including any material added to file during that year. Employee must pay for any additional copies.

Massachusetts
Mass. Gen. Laws ch. 149, § 52C
Employers affected: All.

Employee access to records: Employee or former employee must have opportunity to review personnel files within 5 business days of submitting request, but not more than twice a calendar year. (Law does not apply to tenured or tenure-track employees in private colleges and universities.)

State Laws on Access to Personnel Records (continued)

Employer must notify an employee within 10 days of placing in the employee's personnel record any information to the extent that the information is, has been, or may be used, to negatively affect the employee's qualification for employment, promotion, transfer, additional compensation, or the possibility that the employee will be subject to disciplinary action. (This notification does not count toward employee's two allotted opportunities to view personnel file.)

Written request required: Yes.

Conditions for viewing records: Employee may view records at workplace during normal business hours.

Copying records: Employee must be given a copy of record within 5 business days of submitting a written request.

Employee's right to insert rebuttal: If employee disagrees with any information in personnel record and cannot reach an agreement with employer to remove or correct it, employee may submit an explanatory written statement (a "rebuttal"). Rebuttal becomes a part of the personnel file.

Michigan

Mich. Comp. Laws §§ 423.501 to 423.505

Employers affected: Employers with 4 or more employees.

Employee access to records: Current or former employee is entitled to review personnel records at reasonable intervals, generally not more than twice a year, unless a collective bargaining agreement provides otherwise.

Written request required: Yes. Request must describe the record employee wants to review.

Conditions for viewing records: Employee may view records during normal office hours either at or reasonably near the worksite. If these hours would require employee to take time off work, employer must provide another reasonable time for review.

Copying records: After reviewing files, employee may get a copy; employer may charge only actual cost of duplication. If employee is unable to view files at the worksite, employer, upon receipt of a written request, must mail employee a copy.

Employee's right to insert rebuttal: If employee disagrees with any information in personnel record and cannot reach an agreement with employer to remove or correct it, employee may submit a written statement explaining his or her position. Statement may be no longer than five 8½" by 11" pages.

Minnesota

Minn. Stat. Ann. §§ 181.960 to 181.966

Employers affected: Employers with 20 or more employees.

Employee access to records: Current employee may review files once per 6-month period; former employee may have access to records once only during the first year after termination. Employer must comply with written request within 7 working days (14 working days if personnel records kept out of state). Employer may not retaliate against an employee who asserts rights under these laws.

Written request required: Yes.

Conditions for viewing records: Current employee may view records during employer's normal business hours at worksite or a nearby location; does not have to take place during employee's working hours. Employer or employer's representative may be present.

Copying records: Employer must provide copy free of charge. Current employee must first review record and then submit written request for copies.

State Laws on Access to Personnel Records (continued)

Former employee must submit written request; providing former employee with a copy fulfills employer's obligation to allow access to records.

Employee's right to insert rebuttal: If employee disputes specific information in the personnel record, and cannot reach an agreement with employer to remove or revise it, employee may submit a written statement identifying the disputed information and explaining his or her position. Statement may be no longer than 5 pages and must be kept with personnel record as long as it is maintained.

Nevada

Nev. Rev. Stat. Ann. § 613.075

Employers affected: All.

Employee access to records: An employee who has worked at least 60 days, and a former employee within 60 days of termination, must be given a reasonable opportunity to inspect personnel records.

Conditions for viewing records: Employee may view records during employer's normal business hours.

Copying records: Employer may charge only actual cost of providing access and copies.

Employee's right to insert rebuttal: Employee may submit a reasonable written explanation in direct response to any entry in personnel record. Statement must be of reasonable length; employer may specify the format; employer must maintain statement in personnel records.

New Hampshire

N.H. Rev. Stat. Ann. § 275:56

Employers affected: All.

Employee access to records: Employer must provide employees with a reasonable opportunity to inspect records.

Copying records: Employer may charge a fee reasonably related to cost of supplying copies.

Employee's right to insert rebuttal: If employee disagrees with any of the information in personnel record and cannot reach an agreement with the employer to remove or correct it, employee may submit an explanatory written statement along with supporting evidence. Statement must be maintained as part of personnel file.

Oregon

Ore. Rev. Stat. § 652.750

Employers affected: All.

Employee access to records: Within 45 days after receipt of request, employer must provide employee a reasonable opportunity to inspect payroll records and personnel records used to determine qualifications for employment, promotion, or additional compensation, termination, or other disciplinary action.

Conditions for viewing records: Employee may view records at worksite or place of work assignment.

Copying records: Within 45 days after receipt of request, employer must provide a certified copy of requested record to current or former employee (if request made within 60 days of termination). If employee makes request after 60 days from termination, employer shall provide a certified copy of requested records if employer has records at time of the request. May charge amount reasonably calculated to recover actual cost of providing copy.

Pennsylvania

43 Pa. Cons. Stat. Ann. §§ 1321 to 1324

Employers affected: All.

Employee access to records: Employer must allow employee to inspect personnel record at

State Laws on Access to Personnel Records (continued)

reasonable times. (Employee's agent, or employee who is laid off with reemployment rights or on leave of absence, must also be given access.) Unless there is reasonable cause, employer may limit review to once a year by employee and once a year by employee's agent.

Written request required: At employer's discretion. Employer may require the use of a form as well as a written indication of the parts of the record employee wants to inspect or the purpose of the inspection. For employee's agent: Employee must provide signed authorization designating agent; must be for a specific date and indicate the reason for the inspection or the parts of the record the agent is authorized to inspect.

Conditions for viewing records: Employee may view records during regular business hours at the office where records are maintained, when there is enough time for employee to complete the review. Employer may require that employee or agent view records on their own time and may also require that inspection take place on the premises and in the presence of employer's designated official.

Copying records: Employer not obligated to permit copying. Employee may take notes.

Employee's right to insert rebuttal: The Bureau of Labor Standards, after a petition and hearing, may allow employee to place a counterstatement in the personnel file, if employee claims that the file contains an error.

Rhode Island

R.I. Gen. Laws § 28-6.4-1

Employers affected: All.

Employee access to records: Employer must permit employee to inspect personnel file when given at least 7 days' advance notice (excluding weekends and holidays). Employer may limit access to no more than 3 times a year.

Written request required: Yes.

Conditions for viewing records: Employee may view records at any reasonable time other than employee's work hours. Inspection must take place in presence of employer or employer's representative.

Copying records: Employee may not make copies or remove files from place of inspection. Employer may charge a fee reasonably related to cost of supplying copies.

Washington

Wash. Rev. Code Ann. §§ 49.12.240 to 49.12.260

Employers affected: All.

Employee access to records: Employee may have access to personnel records at least once a year within a reasonable time after making a request.

Employee's right to insert rebuttal: Employee may petition annually that employer review all information in employee's personnel file. If there is any irrelevant or incorrect information in the file, employer must remove it. If employee does not agree with employer's review, employee may request to have a statement of rebuttal or correction placed in file. Former employee has right of rebuttal for two years after termination.

Wisconsin

Wis. Stat. Ann. § 103.13

Employers affected: All employers who maintain personnel records.

Employee access to records: Employee and former employee must be allowed to inspect personnel records within 7 working days of making request. Access is permitted twice per calendar year unless a collective bargaining

State Laws on Access to Personnel Records (continued)

agreement provides otherwise. Employee involved in a current grievance may designate a representative of the union or collective bargaining unit, or other agent, to inspect records that may be relevant to resolving the grievance.

Written request required: At employer's discretion.

Conditions for viewing records: Employee may view records during normal working hours at a location reasonably near worksite. If this would require employee to take time off work, employer may provide another reasonable time for review.

Copying records: Employee's right of inspection includes the right to make or receive copies. If employer provides copies, may charge only actual cost of reproduction.

Employee's right to insert rebuttal: If employee disagrees with any information in the personnel record and cannot come to an agreement with the employer to remove or correct it, employee may submit an explanatory written statement. Employer must attach the statement to the disputed portion of the personnel record.

State Laws on Employee Arrest and Conviction Records

The following chart summarizes state laws and regulations on whether an employer can access an employee's or prospective employee's past arrests or convictions. It includes citations to statutes and agency websites, as available.

If your state isn't listed in this chart, then it doesn't have a *general statute* on whether private sector employers can find out about arrests or convictions. There might be a law about your particular industry, though.

It's always a good idea to consult your state's nondiscrimination enforcement agency or labor department. The agency guidelines are designed to help employers comply with state and federal law. For further information, contact your state's agency.

Alabama

Ala. Code §§ 15-27-1, 15-27-6

Rights of employees and applicants: Need not disclose expunged records on employment application.

Arizona

Ariz. Rev. Stat. § 13-904(E)

Rights of employees and applicants: Unless the offense has a reasonable relationship to the occupation, an occupational license may not be denied solely on the basis of a felony or misdemeanor conviction.

Agency guidelines for preemployment inquiries: Office of the Attorney General, Guide to Preemployment Inquiries, at www.azag.gov/sites/default/files/documents/files/PRE-EMPLOYMENT _INQUIRIES.pdf.

California

Cal. Lab. Code §§ 432.7, 432.8; Cal. Gov't Code § 12952

Rules for employers: Employers with five or more employees may not ask about or consider an applicant's criminal history until after making a conditional offer of employment. Once making a conditional offer, an employer may consider the applicant's conviction records. But before rejecting the applicant based on such record, the employer must conduct an individualized assessment as to whether the conviction justifies denying the applicant the job.

All employers may not seek or consider the following at any time: arrests that did not lead to conviction (unless the applicant is awaiting trial); participation in or referral to pretrial or post-trial diversion program; convictions that have been judicially sealed, dismissed, or expunged; non-felony convictions for marijuana possession that are more than two years old; or juvenile criminal history, including arrests, detentions, processings, adjudications, and court dispositions that occurred while applicant was subject to the juvenile court system.

Rights of employees and applicants: When an employer with five or more employees decides to reject an applicant based on a conviction record, the applicant is entitled to written notice. The applicant must be given at least five days to challenge the accuracy of the criminal record or provide mitigating evidence. The employer must take this evidence into account before making a final decision. If the final decision is a rejection, the applicant is entitled to written notice.

Agency guidelines for preemployment inquiries: Department of Fair Employment and Housing, "Employment Inquiries," DFEH-161 at www.dfeh. ca.gov/wp-content/uploads/sites/32/2017/06/ DFEH-161.pdf.

State Laws on Employee Arrest and Conviction Records (continued)

Colorado

Colo. Rev. Stat. §§ 8-3-108(m), 24-72-702(1)(f)(I)

Rules for employers: May not ask an applicant to disclose records of civil or military disobedience, unless the incident resulted in a guilty plea or conviction. May not ask about information contained in sealed criminal records. May not ask about expunged records where employee was arrested due to mistaken identity.

Rights of employees and applicants: Need not disclose any information in a sealed criminal record; may answer questions about sealed arrests or convictions as though they never occurred. Need not disclose information in an expunged record relating to arrest due to mistaken identity.

Agency guidelines for preemployment inquiries: Colorado Civil Rights Division, "Pre-Employment Inquiries" at https://drive.google.com/file/d/0B2RqMM3zUzjtNTdZdklGV2tDS3c/view.

Connecticut

Conn. Gen. Stat. Ann. §§ 46a-79, 46a-80, 31-51i

Rules for employers: Employer may not ask about criminal records in an initial employment application, unless required to by law or the position requires a security or fidelity bond. If exception applies and employment application form contains question concerning criminal history, it must include a notice in clear and conspicuous language that (1) the applicant is not required to disclose the existence of any arrest, criminal charge, or conviction, the records of which have been erased; (2) define what criminal records are subject to erasure; and (3) any person whose criminal records have been erased will be treated as if never arrested or convicted and may swear so under oath. Employers may not

discriminate against applicants or employees on the basis of arrests or convictions that have been erased or for which an employee or applicant has received a provisional pardon or certificate of rehabilitation. Employer may not disclose information about a job applicant's criminal history except to members of the personnel department or, if there is no personnel department, person(s) in charge of hiring or conducting the interview.

Rights of employees and applicants: Employee may file a complaint with the Labor Commissioner if employer asks about criminal records on employment application. May not be asked to disclose information about a criminal record that has been erased; may answer any question as though arrest or conviction never took place.

Special situations: Applicants may not be denied a license, permit, registration, or other authorization to engage in a particular trade solely on the basis of a criminal conviction, unless the agency determines that the applicant isn't suitable based on: the nature of the crime and its relationship to the job; any rehabilitation the person has completed; and how long it has been since the conviction. A consumer reporting agency that issues a consumer report that is used or is expected to be used for employment purposes and that includes in such report criminal matters of public record concerning the consumer shall provide the consumer who is the subject of the consumer report (1) notice that the consumer reporting agency is reporting criminal matters of public record, and (2) the name and address of the person to whom such consumer report is being issued.

State Laws on Employee Arrest and Conviction Records (continued)

Delaware

Del. Code Ann. tit. 11, § 4376

Rights of employees and applicants: Do not have to disclose an arrest or conviction record that has been expunged.

District of Columbia

D.C. Code 32-1342

Rules for employers: Employers with 11 or more employees: May not ask about or require an applicant to disclose any arrest or criminal accusation that is not pending or that did not lead to a conviction. May not ask about or require an applicant to disclose a conviction until after a conditional offer of employment is made. Employer may only withdraw conditional offer based on a legitimate business reason. Employers need not comply for certain positions, including those working with minors and vulnerable adults.

Rights of employees and applicants: If employer withdraws conditional offer based on criminal history, applicant has the right to request within 30 days: all records collected by the employer, including criminal records, and a notice of the applicant's right to file an administrative complaint with the Office of Human Rights.

Florida

Fla. Stat. Ann. §§ 112.011, 768.096, 943.0585, 943.059

Rules for employers: Employers need not conduct criminal background checks. However, employers are legally presumed not to have been negligent in hiring if they conduct a background investigation before hiring employees, including a criminal records check. If the employer conducted such a check and did not discover any information reasonably demonstrating that the employee was unfit for the job (or for employment in general), the employer is entitled to a presumption that it did not act negligently.

Rights of employees and applicants: May not be disqualified to practice or pursue any occupation or profession that requires a license, permit, or certificate because of a prior conviction, unless it was for a felony or first-degree misdemeanor and is directly related to the regulatory standards for that line of work. Employee whose criminal record is expunged or sealed may deny the existence of the arrest, except when seeking employment in certain occupations or obtaining certain licenses.

Georgia

Ga. Code Ann. §§ 35-3-34, 35-3-34.1, 35-3-37, 42-8-62, 42-8-63, 42-8-63.1

Rules for employers: In order to obtain a criminal record from the state Crime Information Center, employer must supply the individual's fingerprints or signed consent. Employer will not be provided with records of arrests, charges, and sentences for first-time offenders where the individual was exonerated. Where, pursuant to Georgia's First Offender Statute, the charges were dismissed without an adjudication of guilt, the discharge may not be used to disqualify candidates except for specific occupations. If an adverse employment decision is made on the basis of the records provided, employer must disclose all information in the record to the employee or applicant and tell how it affected the decision.

Rights of employees and applicants: Probation for a first offense is not a conviction and may not be disqualified for employment once probation is completed, except for certain occupations.

State Laws on Employee Arrest and Conviction Records (continued)

Hawaii

Haw. Rev. Stat. §§ 378-2, 378-2.5, 831-3.2

Rules for employers:

- **Arrest records:** It is a violation of law for any employer to refuse to hire, to discharge, or to discriminate in terms of compensation, conditions, or privileges of employment because of a person's arrest or court record.
- **Convictions:** May inquire into a conviction only after making a conditional offer of employment, may withdraw offer if conviction has a rational relation to job. May not examine any convictions over 10 years old.

Rights of employees and applicants: If an arrest or conviction has been expunged, may state that no record exists and may respond to questions as a person with no record would respond.

Agency guidelines for preemployment inquiries: Hawaii Civil Rights Commission, "Pre-Employment Inquiries (Application Forms and Job Interviews)" at http://labor.hawaii.gov/hcrc/publications.

Idaho

Agency guidelines for preemployment inquiries: Idaho Department of Labor, "A Guide to Lawful Applications and Interviews" at https://labor.idaho.gov/publications/GuidetoLawful.pdf and Idaho Commission on Human Rights, "Pre-Employment Inquiries - Discrimination Pitfalls" at http://humanrights.idaho.gov/discrimination/pre_employment.html.

Illinois

775 Ill. Comp. Stat. § 5/2-103, 20 Ill. Comp. Stat. Ann. 2630/12, 820 Ill. Comp. Stat. Ann. 75/15

Rules for employers: All employers: It is a civil rights violation to ask an applicant about arrests or criminal records that have been expunged or sealed, or to use the fact of an arrest or an expunged or sealed record as a basis for refusing to hire or renew employment. Law does not prohibit employer from using other means to find out if person actually engaged in conduct leading to arrest. Job applications must clearly state that the applicant is not required to provide information about sealed or expunged records of convictions or arrest.

Employers with 15 or more employees: Except in limited situations, employer may not ask about criminal history or criminal records until the applicant is selected for an interview, or if there is none, until a conditional offer of employment has been made.

Indiana

Ind. Code § 35-38-9-10

Rules for employers: Employer may ask about criminal record only in terms that exclude expunged convictions or arrests. It is unlawful discrimination to refuse to employ someone based on a sealed or expunged arrest or conviction record. Information about expunged convictions is not admissible evidence in negligent hiring lawsuit against employer who relied on expungement order in deciding to hire the employee.

Rights of employees and applicants: May answer any question as though expunged arrest or conviction never occurred. May not be discriminated against on the basis of a conviction or arrest that has been expunged or sealed.

Special situations: Sealed or expunged arrest or conviction record may not be used to refuse to grant or renew a license, permit, or certificate necessary to engage in any activity, occupation, or profession.

State Laws on Employee Arrest and Conviction Records (continued)

Iowa

Agency guidelines for preemployment inquiries: Iowa Workforce Development, "Successful Interview Guide, Summary Guide to Application and Pre-Employment Questions," at www.iowaworkforcedevelopment.gov/sites/search.iowaworkforcedevelopment.gov/files/Successful%20Interviewing%20Guide_70-0006.pdf.

Kansas

Kan. Stat. Ann. §§ 12-4516; 22-4710

Rules for employers: Cannot require an employee to inspect or challenge a criminal record in order to obtain a copy of the record to qualify for employment, but may require an applicant to sign a release to allow employer to obtain record to determine fitness for employment. Employers can require access to criminal records for specific businesses. Employer is not liable for making hiring or contracting decision based on applicant's criminal record, as long as it reasonably bears on applicant's trustworthiness or the safety or well-being of customers or other employees.

Rights of employees and applicants: Need not disclose expunged records on employment application except for sensitive positions enumerated in Kan. Stat. Ann. § 12-4516(2) (A)-(K).

Agency guidelines for preemployment inquiries: Kansas Human Rights Commission, "Guidelines on Equal Employment Practices: Preventing Discrimination in Hiring," at www.khrc.net/hiring.html.

Kentucky

Ky. Rev. Stat. Ann. §§ 431.073, 431.076

Rights of employees and applicants: Need not disclose expunged records on employment application.

Louisiana

La. Rev. Stat. Ann. § 37:2950

Rights of employees and applicants: Prior conviction cannot be used as a sole basis to deny an occupational or professional license, unless conviction directly relates to the license being sought and the reasons for denial are stated explicitly, in writing.

Special situations: Protection does not apply to medical, engineering and architecture, or funeral and embalming licenses, among others listed in the statute.

Maine

Me. Rev. Stat. Ann. tit. 5, § 5301

Rights of employees and applicants: A conviction is not an automatic bar to obtaining an occupational or professional license. Only convictions that directly relate to the profession or occupation, that include dishonesty or false statements, that are subject to imprisonment for more than 1 year, or that involve sexual misconduct on the part of a licensee may be considered.

Agency guidelines for preemployment inquiries: The Maine Human Rights Commission, "Pre-Employment Inquiry Guide," at www.maine.gov/mhrc/guidance/pre-employment_inquiry_guide.htm, suggests that asking about arrests is an improper race-based question, but that it is okay to ask about a conviction if related to the job.

Maryland

Md. Code Ann. [Crim. Proc.], §§ 10-109, 10-301, 10-306; Md. Regs. Code § 09.01.10.02

Rules for employers: May not inquire about criminal charges that have been expunged or criminal records that have been shielded under the Maryland Second Chance Act. May not use a

State Laws on Employee Arrest and Conviction Records (continued)

refusal to disclose information as sole basis for not hiring an applicant.

Rights of employees and applicants: Need not refer to or give any information about an expunged charge or shielded record. A professional or occupational license may not be refused or revoked simply because of a conviction; agency must consider the nature of the crime and its relation to the occupation or profession; the conviction's relevance to the applicant's fitness and qualifications; when conviction occurred and other convictions, if any; and the applicant's behavior before and after conviction.

Agency guidelines for preemployment inquiries: DLLR's Office of Fair Practices, "Guidelines for Pre-Employment Inquiries Technical Assistance Guide," at www.dllr.maryland.gov/oeope/preemp.shtml.

Massachusetts

Mass. Gen. Laws ch. 6, § 171A; ch. 151B, § 4; ch. 276, § 100A; Mass. Regs. Code tit. 804, § 3.02

Rules for employers: Unless federal or state law disqualifies applicants with certain convictions from holding position, may not ask about criminal record information of any kind on initial written application. If job application has a question about prior arrests or convictions, it must include a formulated statement (that appears in the statute) that states that an applicant with a sealed record is entitled to answer, "No record." May not ask about arrests that did not result in conviction. May not ask about first-time convictions for drunkenness, simple assault, speeding, minor traffic violations, affray, or disturbing the peace; may not ask about misdemeanor convictions 5 or more years old unless applicant has another conviction within the last 5 years.

Rights of employees and applicants: If criminal record is sealed, may answer, "No record" to any inquiry about past arrests or convictions.

Special situations: Employer must give applicant a copy of criminal record before asking about it. Employer must give applicant a copy of record after making adverse job decision (if it didn't already provide the record). Additional rules apply to employers that conduct 5 or more criminal background checks per year.

Agency guidelines for preemployment inquiries: Massachusetts Commission Against Discrimination, "Employment Discrimination on the Basis of Criminal Record," at www.mass.gov/mcad/resources/employers-businesses/emp-fact-sheet-discrim-criminal-record-gen.html.

Michigan

Mich. Comp. Laws § 37.2205a

Rules for employers: May not request information on any misdemeanor arrests or charges that did not result in conviction. May ask about felony arrests and misdemeanor or felony convictions.

Rights of employees and applicants: Employees or applicants are not making a false statement if they fail to disclose information they have a civil right to withhold.

Agency guidelines for preemployment inquiries: Michigan Department of Civil Rights, "Pre-Employment Inquiry Guide," at www.michigan.gov/documents/mdcr/Preemploymentguide62012_388403_7.pdf.

Minnesota

Minn. Stat. Ann. §§ 181.981, 364.01 to 364.03

Rules for employers: Employers may not ask, consider, or require applicants to disclose criminal record or history until selected for

State Laws on Employee Arrest and Conviction Records (continued)

an interview or, if there is no interview, until a conditional offer of employment is made. However, employer may notify applicants that particular criminal records will disqualify applicants from holding particular jobs.

Rights of employees and applicants: No one can be disqualified from pursuing or practicing an occupation that requires a license, unless the crime directly relates to the occupation. Agency may consider the nature and seriousness of the crime and its relation to the applicant's fitness for the occupation. Even if the crime does relate to the occupation, a person who provides evidence of rehabilitation and present fitness cannot be disqualified.

Special situations: Employee's criminal record is not admissible in any civil lawsuit against the employer based on the employee's actions if: the lawsuit is based on the employer's compliance with the state's "ban the box" law; the employee's record was sealed or pardoned prior to the actions; the employee's record consists only of arrests or charges that did not lead to conviction; or the employee's job duties did not create any greater risk of harm than being employed in general or interacting with the public outside of work.

Agency guidelines for preemployment inquiries: Minnesota Department of Human Rights, "Criminal Background" at http://mn.gov/mdhr/employers/criminal-background.

Mississippi

Miss. Code Ann. § 99-19-71

Rules for employers: Employer may ask applicant if expunction order has been issued regarding the applicant.

Rights of employees and applicants: Applicant need not disclose expunged arrest or conviction when responding to inquiries.

Missouri

Mo. Rev. Stat. § 314.200

Rights of employees and applicants: No one may be denied a license for a profession or occupation primarily on the basis that a prior conviction negates the person's good moral character, if the applicant has been released from incarceration by pardon, parole, or otherwise, or the applicant is on probation with no evidence of violations. The conviction may be considered, but the licensing board must also consider the crime's relation to the license, the date of conviction, the applicant's conduct since the conviction, and other evidence of the applicant's character.

Montana

Mont. Admin. Rule 24.9.1406

Rules for employers: Employer should not ask questions about arrests at any point in the hiring process. Employers may ask about convictions, however.

Nebraska

Neb. Rev. Stat. § 29-3523

Rules for employers: May not obtain access to information regarding arrests after one year if no charges are filed by prosecutor decision; after two years if no charges are filed as a result of completed diversion; or after three years if charges were filed but were dismissed by the court. May not ask about sealed records in an employment application.

Rights of employees and applicants: As to sealed records, employee may respond as if the offense never occurred.

Nevada

Nev. Rev. Stat. Ann. §§ 176A.850, 179A.100(3), 179.285, 179.301

State Laws on Employee Arrest and Conviction Records (continued)

Rules for employers: Unless applicant consents, employer may obtain only records of convictions or incidents for which the applicant or employee is currently within the criminal justice system, including parole or probation.

Special situations: Employees not be required to disclose sealed convictions, or convictions for which they were honorably discharged from probation (except to a gaming establishment or state employer).

Agency guidelines for preemployment inquiries: Nevada Equal Rights Commission, "Guide to Pre-Employment," at http://detr.state.nv.us/Nerc_pages/premployment_guide.htm.

New Hampshire

N.H. Rev. Stat. Ann. § 651:5 (X)

Rules for employers: May ask about a previous criminal record only if question substantially follows this wording, "Have you ever been arrested for or convicted of a crime that has not been annulled by a court?"

New Jersey

N.J. Stat. Ann. §§ 5:5-34.1, 5:12-89, 5:12-91, 32:23-86, 34:6B-11 to 34:6B-19

Rules for employers: Employers with 15 or more employees may not publish a job advertisement that states that applicants who have been arrested or convicted will not be considered for the position. These employers also may not ask applicants about criminal history until after an interview has been conducted. These employers also may not refuse to hire an applicant based on a criminal record that has been expunged or erased through executive pardon.

Special situations: There are specific rules for casino employees, longshoremen and related occupations, horse racing, and other gaming industry jobs.

New Mexico

Criminal Offender Employment Act, N.M. Stat. Ann. §§ 28-2-3, 28-2-4

Special situations: For a license, permit, or other authority to engage in any regulated trade, business, or profession, a regulating agency may consider felony and convictions for misdemeanors involving moral turpitude. Such convictions cannot be an automatic bar to authority to practice in the regulated field, but may be disqualifying if they relate directly to the profession, the agency determines after investigation that the applicant isn't sufficiently rehabilitated to warrant the public's trust, or the field is teaching or child care (for certain offenses).

New York

N.Y. Correct. Law §§ 750 to 754; N.Y. Exec. Law § 296 (15), (16)

Rules for employers: It is unlawful discrimination to ask about any arrests or charges that did not result in conviction, unless they are currently pending. Employers also may not ask about sealed convictions or youthful offender adjudications. Employers with 10 or more employees may not deny employment based on a conviction unless it relates directly to the job or would be an "unreasonable" risk to property or to public or individual safety. Employer must consider 8 factors listed in statute. If employer considers these factors and makes a reasonable, good-faith decision to hire or retain employee, there's a rebuttable presumption that evidence of the employee's criminal history should be excluded in any subsequent lawsuit for negligent hiring or retention.

State Laws on Employee Arrest and Conviction Records (continued)

Rights of employees and applicants: Upon request, applicant must be given, within 30 days, a written statement of the reasons why employment was denied.

Agency guidelines for preemployment inquiries: New York State Division of Human Rights, www.dhr.ny.gov/sites/default/files/pdf/arrest_conviction.pdf.

North Carolina

N.C. Gen. Stat. § 15A-146

Rules for employers: May not ask applicants about expunged arrests, charges, or convictions.

Rights of employees and applicants: Person whose arrest or charge was expunged may omit expunged entries in response to questions.

Special situations: Licensing board may not automatically deny professional or occupational license to applicant based on criminal history. If board is authorized to deny license based on crime of fraud or moral turpitude, must consider: level and seriousness of crime; when crime occurred; age of applicant when crime occurred; circumstances of crime; relationship between crime and profession or occupation; prison, parole, rehabilitation, and employment records since crime was committed; any subsequent criminal activity; and affidavits and other documents, including character references.

North Dakota

N.D. Cent. Code § 12-60-16.6

Rules for employers: May obtain records of arrests (adults only) occurring in the past three years or of convictions, provided the information has not been purged or sealed.

Agency guidelines for preemployment inquiries: North Dakota Department of Labor, "Employment Applications and Interviews," www.nd.gov/labor/publications/docs/employment.pdf.

Ohio

Ohio Rev. Code Ann. §§ 2151.357, 2953.33, 2953.55

Rules for employers: May inquire only into convictions or bail forfeitures that have not been sealed, unless question has a direct and substantial relationship to job.

Rights of employees and applicants: May not be asked about arrest records that are sealed; may respond to inquiry as though arrest did not occur.

Oklahoma

Okla. Stat. Ann. tit. 22, § 19(F)

Rules for employers: May not inquire into any criminal record that has been expunged.

Rights of employees and applicants: If record is expunged, may state that no criminal action ever occurred. May not be denied employment solely for refusing to disclose sealed criminal record information.

Oregon

Ore. Rev. Stat. §§ 181A.230, 181A.240, and 181A.245, 659A.030

Rules for employers: Employer may not ask about criminal convictions on an employment application. Employer may ask about criminal convictions only after an initial interview or after a conditional offer of employment has been made.

Employer may request information from state police department about convictions and arrests in the past year that have not resulted in dismissal or acquittal. Before making request, employer must notify employee or applicant; when submitting request, must tell department when and how person was notified. May not discriminate against an applicant or current employee on the basis of an expunged juvenile record unless there is a "bona fide occupational qualification."

State Laws on Employee Arrest and Conviction Records (continued)

Rights of employees and applicants: Before state police department releases any criminal record information, it must notify employee or applicant and provide a copy of all information that will be sent to employer. Notice must include protections under federal civil rights law and the procedure for challenging information in the record. Record may not be released until 14 days after notice is sent.

Pennsylvania

18 Pa. Cons. Stat. Ann. § 9125

Rules for employers: May consider felony and misdemeanor convictions only if they relate to person's suitability for the job.

Rights of employees and applicants: Must be informed in writing if refusal to hire is based on criminal record information.

Rhode Island

R.I. Gen. Laws §§ 12-1.3-4, 13-8.2-1 through 8, 28-5-7(7)

Rules for employers: It is unlawful to include on an application form or to ask as part of an interview if the applicant has ever been arrested or charged with any crime. Application form may not include questions about arrests, charges, or convictions, except questions about convictions for specific offenses that would legally disqualify the applicant for the position under federal or state law, or would preclude bonding (if bonding is required for the position). May ask about convictions during the first interview or later.

Rights of employees and applicants: Do not have to disclose any conviction that has been expunged. As to sealed records for arrests due to mistaken identity, employee may respond as if the offense never occurred.

Special situations: Those convicted of crimes may apply to the parole board for a Certificate of Recovery and Re-Entry, stating that the holder has achieved certain rehabilitation goals. Parole board will consider applications for a certificate one year or more after conviction of a misdemeanor, or three years or more after conviction of a nonviolent felony. Although the purpose of this certificate is to assist the holder in reentering society, employers are not liable for denying employment based on prior conviction(s), even if the applicant holds a certificate.

Agency guidelines for preemployment inquiries: Rhode Island Commission for Human Rights, "Pre-Employment Inquiries Guidelines," at www.richr.state.ri.us/pei.pdf.

South Carolina

S.C. Code Ann. § 40-1-140

Rights of employees and applicants: Person may not be denied authorization to practice, pursue, or engage in regulated profession or occupation based on prior conviction, unless it relates directly to the profession or occupation or the applicant is found unfit or unsuitable based on all available information, including the prior conviction.

South Dakota

Agency guidelines for preemployment inquiries: South Dakota Division of Human Rights, "Pre-Employment Inquiry Guide," at www.sdra.org/dwnld/preemplo.htm suggests that an employer shouldn't ask or check into arrests or convictions if they are not substantially related to the job.

Texas

Tex. Crim. Proc. Code Ann. § 55.03;
Tex. Fam. Code Ann. § 58.261

State Laws on Employee Arrest and Conviction Records (continued)

Rights of employees and applicants: Employee may deny the occurrence of any arrest that has been expunged. An employee whose juvenile records have been sealed is not required to disclose in a job application that the employee was the subject of a juvenile court proceeding.

Vermont

13 Vt. Stat. Ann. §§ 7606 to 7607; 21 Vt. Stat. Ann. § 495j

Rules for employers: May not ask about criminal history on an employment application, except for specific offenses that would disqualify the applicant for the position under state or federal law. Employer may ask about criminal history during an interview or once the applicant has been deemed qualified for the position.

Rights of employees and applicants: Need not disclose arrests or convictions that have been expunged or sealed.

Virginia

Va. Code Ann. § 19.2-392.4

Rules for employers: May not require an applicant to disclose information about any arrest or criminal charge that has been expunged.

Rights of employees and applicants: Need not refer to any expunged charges if asked about criminal record.

Washington

Wash. Rev. Code Ann. §§ 9.94A.640(3), 9.96.060(3), 9.96A.020, 43.43.815; Wash. Admin. Code § 162-12-140; 2017 Washington H.B. 1298, 65th Legislature (2018)

Rules for employers:
- **Arrest records:** An employer may not ask about, seek, or consider an applicant's criminal history until after it has determined

that the applicant is "otherwise qualified" for the job. At a minimum, the employer must first determine that the applicant meets the basic criteria of the job. After that, employers may seek out criminal history, subject to the limitations below.

- **Convictions:** An employer that obtains a conviction record must notify the applicant within 30 days of receiving it and must allow the employee to examine it. And, according to the Human Rights Commission, employers with eight or more employees must consider certain information before rejecting an applicant based on criminal history. With respect to arrest records, these employers must ask whether the charges are still pending, have been dismissed, or led to conviction that would adversely affect job performance and whether the arrest occurred in the last 10 years. These employers may make an employment decision based on a conviction record, but only if the conviction or the applicant's release from prison occurred within the last ten years and the crime reasonably relates to the job duties.

Rights of employees and applicants: If a conviction record is cleared or vacated, may answer questions as though the conviction never occurred. A person convicted of a felony cannot be refused an occupational license unless the conviction is less than 10 years old and the felony relates specifically to the occupation or business.

Special situations: Employers are entitled to obtain complete criminal record information for positions that require bonding, or that have access to information affecting national security, trade secrets, confidential or proprietary business information, money, or items of value. Employers may also obtain record to assist an investigation

State Laws on Employee Arrest and Conviction Records (continued)

of suspected employee misconduct that may also be a penal offense under federal or state law.

Agency guidelines for preemployment inquiries: Washington Human Rights Commission, "Pre-employment inquiry guide," at http://apps.leg.wa.gov/WAC/default.aspx?cite=162-12.

West Virginia

W.Va. Code § 49-4-723

Rules for employers: Employers may not discriminate on the basis of juvenile criminal records that have been expunged.

Agency guidelines for preemployment inquirles: West Virginia Bureau of Employment Programs, "Pre-employment Inquiries Technical Assistance Guide," at www.wvcommerce.org/App_Media/assets/pdf/workforce/WFWV_Afirmative_Action_Pre-employment_Inquiries.pdf. The state's website says that employers can only make inquiries about convictions directly related to the job.

Wisconsin

Wis. Stat. Ann. §§ 111.31 and 111.335

Rules for employers: It is a violation of state civil rights law to discriminate against an employee

on the basis of a prior arrest or conviction record. Arrest records: May not ask about arrests unless there are pending charges. May not reject applicant unless pending charges are substantially related to the job or would preclude required bonding. Convictions: May not ask about convictions unless charges substantially relate to job or would preclude required bonding.

Special situations: Employers are entitled to obtain complete criminal record information for positions that require bonding and for burglar alarm installers.

Agency guidelines for preemployment inquiries: Wisconsin Department of Workforce Development, Equal Rights Division, Civil Rights Bureau, "Fair Hiring & Avoiding Loaded Interview Questions," at dwd.wisconsin.gov/er/civil_rights/discrimination/avoiding_discriminatory_interview_questions.htm.

Wyoming

Wyo. Stat. § 7-13-1401

Rights of employees and applicants: If an arrest or charge has been expunged, may respond to questions as if arrest or charge never occurred.

State Drug and Alcohol Testing Laws

Note: This chart lists statutes that regulate workplace drug and alcohol testing. However, because workplace testing implicates an applicant's or employee's right to privacy, court cases also create law that addresses this issue. Court cases that place general limits on workplace testing are included in this chart; however, additional laws might apply. Check with your state department of labor for more information.

Alabama

Ala. Code §§ 25-5-330 to 25-5-340

Employers affected: Employers that establish a drug-free workplace program to qualify for a workers' compensation rate discount.

Testing applicants: Employer must test applicants upon conditional offer of employment. May test only those applying for certain positions, if based on reasonable job classifications. Job ads must include notice that drug and alcohol testing required.

Testing employees: Random testing permitted. Must test after an accident that results in lost work time; upon reasonable suspicion (reasons for suspicion must be documented and made available to employee upon request; as required by employer's routinely scheduled fitness for duty exams; and as follow-up to a required rehabilitation program.

Employee rights: Employees have 5 days to contest or explain a positive test result. Employer must have an employee assistance program or maintain a resource file of outside programs.

Notice and policy requirements: All employees must have written notice of drug policy. Must give 60 days' advance notice before implementing testing program. Policy must include consequences of refusing to take test or testing positive.

Alaska

Alaska Stat. §§ 23.10.600 to 23.10.699

Employers affected: Employers with one or more full-time employees.

Testing applicants: Employer may test applicants for any job-related purpose consistent with business necessity and the terms of the employer's policy.

Testing employees: Employers are not required to test. Random testing permitted. Employer may test: for any job-related purpose consistent with business necessity; to maintain productivity or safety; as part of an accident investigation or investigation of possible employee impairment; or upon reasonable suspicion.

Employee rights: Employer must provide written test results within 5 working days. Employee has 10 working days to request opportunity to explain positive test results; employer must grant request within 72 hours or before taking any adverse employment action.

Notice and policy requirements: Before implementing a testing program employer must distribute a written drug policy to all employees and must give 30 days' advance notice. Policy must include consequences of a positive test or refusal to submit to testing.

Arizona

Ariz. Rev. Stat. §§ 23-493 to 23-493.11

Employers affected: Employers with one or more full-time employees.

Testing applicants: Employer must inform prospective hires that they will undergo drug testing as a condition of employment.

Testing employees: Statute does not encourage, discourage, restrict, prohibit or require testing. Random testing permitted. Employees may be

State Drug and Alcohol Testing Laws (continued)

tested: for any job-related purpose; to maintain productivity or safety; as part of an accident investigation or investigation of individual employee impairment; or upon reasonable suspicion. If employer tests, all compensated employees must be included in the program, including officers, directors, and supervisors.

Employee rights: Policy must inform employees of their right to explain positive results.

Notice and policy requirements: Before conducting tests employer must give employees a copy of the written policy. Policy must state the consequences of a positive test or refusal to submit to testing.

Arkansas

Ark. Code Ann. §§ 11-3-203, 11-14-101 to 11-14-112

Employers affected: All employers.

Testing applicants: Employers who establish a drug-free workplace program to qualify for a workers' compensation rate discount: must test for drug use upon conditional offer of employment. May test only those applying for certain positions, if based on reasonable job classifications. Employer may test for alcohol. Job ads must include notice that testing is required.

All employers: may not test applicant unless employer pays for the cost of the test, and upon written request, provides a free copy of the report to the employee or applicant.

Testing employees: Employers who establish a drug-free workplace program to qualify for a workers' compensation rate discount: employer must test any employee: upon reasonable suspicion; as part of a routine fitness-for-duty medical exam; after an accident that results in injury; and as follow-up to a required rehabilitation program. Employer may test for any other lawful reason.

All employers: may not test employee unless employer pays for the cost of the test, and upon written request, provides a free copy of the report to the employee or applicant.

Employee rights: Employer may not refuse to hire applicant or take adverse personnel action against an employee on the basis of a single positive test that has not been verified by a confirmation test and a medical review officer. An applicant or employee has 5 days after receiving test results to contest or explain them.

Notice and policy requirements: Employer must give all employees a written statement of drug policy, including the consequences of a positive test or refusal to submit to testing. Employer must give 60 days' advance notice before implementing program.

California

No statute on drug and alcohol testing, but court cases have defined some limitations (Smith v. Fresno Irrigation Dist., 72 Cal.App.4th 147 (1999); Loder v. City of Glendale, 14 Cal.4th 846 (1997)).

Employers affected: All employers.

Testing applicants: Employers may test applicants as part of a post-offer preemployment medical examination, as long as all applicants are tested.

Testing employees: Random drug testing or testing of all current employees is generally illegal in California. Employers must have individualized suspicion of drug or alcohol use in order to test, except for safety- or security-sensitive positions.

Connecticut

Conn. Gen. Stat. Ann. §§ 31-51t to 31-51bb

Employers affected: All employers.

Testing applicants: Employer must inform job applicants in writing if drug testing is required

State Drug and Alcohol Testing Laws (continued)

as a condition of employment. Employer must provide copy of positive test result.

Testing employees: Employer may test: when there is reasonable suspicion that employee is under the influence of drugs or alcohol and job performance is or could be impaired. Random testing is allowed only: when authorized by federal law; when employee's position is dangerous or safety sensitive; when employee drives a school bus or student transportation vehicle; or as part of a voluntary employee-assistance program.

Employee rights: Employer may not take any adverse personnel action on the basis of a single positive test that has not been verified by a confirmation test.

District of Columbia

D.C. Code Ann. § 32-931

Employers affected: All employers.

Testing applicants: Employers may test applicants for marijuana only after a conditional offer of employment has been made.

Florida

Fla. Stat. Ann. §§ 440.101 to 440.102

Employers affected: Employers who establish a drug-free workplace program to qualify for a workers' compensation rate discount.

Testing applicants: Employers must test job applicants upon conditional employment offer. May test only those applying for certain positions, if based on reasonable job classifications. Job ads must include notice that testing is required.

Testing employees: Must test employee: upon reasonable suspicion; as part of a routine fitness-for-duty medical exam; or as part of a required rehabilitation program. Random testing and testing for any other reason is neither required nor precluded by the law.

Employee rights: Employees who voluntarily seek treatment for substance abuse cannot be fired, disciplined, or discriminated against, unless they have tested positive or have been in treatment in the past. All employees have the right to explain positive results within 5 days. Employer may not take any adverse personnel action on the basis of an initial positive result that has not been verified by a confirmation test and a medical review officer.

Notice and policy requirements: Prior to implementing testing, employer must give 60 days' advance notice and must give employees written copy of drug policy. Policy must include consequences of a positive test result or refusal to submit to testing.

Georgia

Ga. Code Ann. §§ 34-9-410 to 34-9-421

Employers affected: Employers that establish a drug-free workplace program to qualify for a workers' compensation rate discount.

Testing applicants: Employer must test on conditional offer of employment. May test only those applying for certain positions, if based on reasonable job classifications. Job ads must include notice that testing is required.

Testing employees: Must test any employee: upon reasonable suspicion; as part of a routine fitness-for-duty medical exam; after an accident that results in an injury; or as part of a required rehabilitation program. Random testing and testing for any other lawful reason is neither required nor prohibited.

Employee rights: Employees have 5 days to explain or contest a positive result. Employer must have an employee assistance program or maintain a resource file of outside programs. Initial positive result must be confirmed.

State Drug and Alcohol Testing Laws (continued)

Notice and policy requirements: Employer must give applicants and employees notice of testing and must give 60 days' notice before implementing program. All employees must receive a written policy statement; policy must state the consequences of refusing to submit to a drug test or of testing positive.

Hawaii

Haw. Rev. Stat. §§ 329B-1 to 329B-5.5

Employers affected: All employers.

Testing applicants: Same conditions as current employees.

Testing employees: Employer may test employees only if these conditions are met: employer pays all costs including confirming test; tests are performed by a licensed laboratory; employee receives a list of the substances being tested for (and medications that could cause a positive result); there is a form for disclosing medicines and legal drugs; and the results are kept confidential.

Notice and policy requirements: If employer uses an on-site screening test, it must follow the instructions on the package. If an employee or applicant tests positive in an on-site test, the employer must direct the employee or applicant to go to a licensed laboratory, within four hours, for a follow-up test. If the employee or applicant doesn't go to the lab, the employer can fire, refuse to hire, or take other adverse action against the employee or applicant only if the employer provided written notice that: the employer followed the required procedures for the on-site test; and the employee or applicant could refuse to take the test. If the employee or applicant refused or failed to take the test, the employer can take adverse action.

Idaho

Idaho Code §§ 72-1701 to 72-1716

Employers affected: Employers that establish a drug-free workplace program to qualify for a workers' compensation rate discount and/or prohibit employees fired for drug or alcohol use from qualifying for unemployment compensation.

Testing applicants: Employer may test as a condition of hiring.

Testing employees: May test for variety of reasons, including: following a workplace accident; based on reasonable suspicion; as part of a return-to-duty exam; at random; and as a condition of continued employment. An employer who follows drug-free workplace guidelines may fire employees who refuse to submit to testing or who test positive for drugs or alcohol. Employees will be fired for misconduct and denied unemployment benefits.

Employee rights: An employee or applicant who receives notice of a positive test may request a retest within 7 working days. Employee must have opportunity to explain positive result. If the retest results are negative, the employer must pay for the cost; if they are positive, the employee must pay. Employer may not take any adverse employment action on the basis of an initial positive result that has not been verified by a confirmation test.

Notice and policy requirements: Employer must have a written policy that includes a statement that violation of the policy may result in termination due to misconduct, as well as what types of testing employees may be subject to.

State Drug and Alcohol Testing Laws (continued)

Illinois

775 Ill. Comp. Stat. § 5/2-104(C)(2)

Employers affected: Employers with 15 or more employees.

Testing employees: Statute does not "encourage, prohibit, or authorize" drug testing, but employers may test employees who have been in rehabilitation.

Indiana

Ind. Code Ann. §§ 22-9-5-6(b), 22-9-5-24

Employers affected: Employers with 15 or more employees.

Testing employees: Statute does not "encourage, prohibit, or authorize" drug testing, but employers may test employees who have been in rehabilitation.

Iowa

Iowa Code § 730.5

Employers affected: Employers with one or more full-time employees.

Testing applicants: Employer may test as a condition of hiring.

Testing employees: Statute does not encourage, discourage, restrict, limit, prohibit, or require testing. Employer may conduct unannounced, random testing of employees selected from the entire workforce at one site, all full-time employees at one site, or all employees in safety-sensitive positions. Employers may also test: upon reasonable suspicion; during and after rehabilitation; or following an accident that caused a reportable injury or more than $1,000 property damage.

Employee rights: Employee has 7 days to request a retest. Employers with 50 or more employees must provide rehabilitation for any employee testing positive for alcohol use who has worked for at least 12 of the last 18 months and has not previously violated the substance abuse policy. Employer must have an employee assistance program or maintain a resource file of outside programs.

Notice and policy requirements: Must have written drug test policy that includes consequences of positive result and refusal to take test. Employer may take action only on confirmed positive result.

Kentucky

Ky. Rev. Stat. 304.13-167; 803 Ky. Admin. Code 25:280

Employers affected: Employers that establish a drug-free workplace to qualify for a workers' compensation premium discount.

Testing applicants: Must test for drugs and alcohol after conditional offer of employment.

Testing employees: Must test for drugs: upon reasonable suspicion; following a workplace accident that requires medical care; as a follow-up to an Employee Assistance Program (EAP) or rehabilitation program for drug use; and upon being selected using a statistically valid, random, unannounced selection procedure. Must test for alcohol: upon reasonable suspicion, following a workplace accident that required medical care; and as a follow-up to an EAP or rehabilitation program for alcohol use.

Employee rights: Employee must have an opportunity to report use of prescription or over-the-counter medicines after receiving a positive test result.

Notice and policy requirements: Employer must have a written drug-free workplace policy. Employer must distribute and post notice of how it will determine whether employees have violated the policy and the consequences of violating the policy.

State Drug and Alcohol Testing Laws (continued)

Louisiana

La. Rev. Stat. Ann. §§ 49:1001 to 49:1012

Employers affected: Employers with one or more full-time employees. (Does not apply to oil drilling, exploration, or production.)

Testing applicants: Employer may require all applicants to submit to drug and alcohol test. An employer must use certified laboratories and specified procedures for testing if it will base its hiring decisions on the results of the test.

Testing employees: Employer may require employees to submit to drug and alcohol test. An employer that will take negative action against an employee based on a positive test result must use certified laboratories and specified procedures for testing.

Employee rights: Employees with confirmed positive results have 7 working days to request access to all records relating to the drug test. Employer may allow employee to undergo rehabilitation without termination of employment.

Maine

Me. Rev. Stat. Ann. tit. 26, §§ 681 to 690

Employers affected: Employers with one or more full-time employees.

Testing applicants: Employer may require applicant to take a drug test only if offered employment or placed on an eligibility list.

Testing employees: Statute does not require or encourage testing. Employer may test based upon probable cause but may not base belief on a single accident, an anonymous informant, or off-duty possession or use (unless it occurs on the employer's premises or nearby, during or right before work hours); must document the facts and give employee a copy. May test randomly

when there could be an unreasonable threat to the health and safety of coworkers or the public. Testing is also allowed when an employee returns to work following a positive test.

Employee rights: Employee who tests positive has 3 days to explain or contest results. Employee must be given an opportunity to participate in a rehabilitation program for up to 6 months; an employer with more than 20 full-time employees must pay for half of any out-of-pocket costs. After successfully completing the program, employee is entitled to return to previous job with full pay and benefits.

Notice and policy requirements: All employers must have a written policy, which includes the consequences of a positive result or refusing to submit to testing. Policy must be approved by the state department of labor. Policy must be distributed to each employee at least 30 days before it takes effect. Any changes to policy require 60 days' advance notice. An employer with more than 20 full-time employees must have an employee assistance program certified by the state office of substance abuse before implementing a testing program.

Maryland

Md. Code Ann., [Health-Gen.] § 17-214

Employers affected: All employers.

Testing applicants: May use preliminary screening to test applicant. If initial result is positive, may make job offer conditional on confirmation of test results.

Testing employees: Employer may require substance abuse testing for legitimate business purposes only.

Employee rights: The sample must be tested by a certified laboratory; at the time of testing employee

State Drug and Alcohol Testing Laws (continued)

may request laboratory's name and address. An employee who tests positive must be given:

- a copy of the test results
- a copy of the employer's written drug and alcohol policy
- a written notice of any adverse action employer intends to take, and
- a statement of employee's right to an independent confirmation test at own expense.

Massachusetts

No statute on drug or alcohol testing, but court cases have defined some limitations (Webster v. Motorola, Inc., 418 Mass. 425 (1994))

Employers affected: All employers.

Testing employees: Random drug testing that doesn't distinguish between safety-sensitive positions and other positions is not allowed.

Minnesota

Minn. Stat. Ann. §§ 181.950 to 181.957

Employers affected: Employers with one or more employees.

Testing applicants: Employers may require applicants to submit to a drug or alcohol test only after they have been given a job offer and have seen a written notice of testing policy. May only test if required of all applicants for same position.

Testing employees: Employers are not required to test. Employers may require drug or alcohol testing only according to a written testing policy. Testing may be done if there is a reasonable suspicion that employee: is under the influence of drugs or alcohol; has violated drug and alcohol policy; has been involved in a work-related accident; or has sustained or caused another employee to sustain a personal injury. Random tests permitted only for employees in safety-sensitive positions. With 2 weeks' notice, employers may also test as part of

an annual routine physical exam. Employer may test, without notice, an employee referred by the employer for chemical dependency treatment or evaluation or participating in a chemical dependency treatment program under an employee benefit plan. Testing is allowed during and for two years following treatment.

Employee rights: If test is positive, employee has 3 days to explain the results; employee must notify employer within 5 days of intention to obtain a retest. Employer may not discharge employee for a first-time positive test without offering counseling or rehabilitation; employee who refuses or does not complete program successfully may be discharged.

Notice and policy requirements: Employees must be given a written notice of testing policy that includes consequences of refusing to take test or having a positive test result. Two weeks' notice required before testing as part of an annual routine physical exam.

Mississippi

Miss. Code Ann. §§ 71-3-121, 71-3-205 to 71-3-225, 71-7-1 to 71-7-33

Employers affected: Employers with one or more full-time employees. Employers that establish a drug-free workplace program to qualify for a workers' compensation rate discount must implement testing procedures.

Testing applicants: May test all applicants as part of employment application process. Employer may request a signed statement that applicant has read and understands the drug and alcohol testing policy or notice.

Testing employees: May require drug and alcohol testing of all employees: upon reasonable suspicion; as part of a routinely scheduled fitness-

State Drug and Alcohol Testing Laws (continued)

for-duty medical examination; as a follow-up to a rehabilitation program; or if they have tested positive within the previous 12 months. May also require drug and alcohol testing following an employee's work-related injury, for purposes of determining workers' compensation coverage. Testing is also allowed on a neutral selection basis.

Employee rights: Employer must inform an employee in writing within 5 working days of receipt of a positive confirmed test result; employee may request and receive a copy of the test result report. Employee has 10 working days after receiving notice to explain the positive test results. Employer may not discharge or take any adverse personnel action on the basis of an initial positive test result that has not been verified by a confirmation test. Private employer who elects to establish a drug-free workplace program must have an employee assistance program or maintain a resource file of outside programs.

Notice and policy requirements: 30 days before implementing testing program employer must give employees written notice of drug and alcohol policy that includes consequences:
- of a positive confirmed result
- of refusing to take test, and
- of other violations of the policy.

Montana

Mont. Code Ann. §§ 39-2-205 to 39-2-211

Employers affected: Employers with one or more employees.

Testing applicants: May test as a condition of hire, but only for applicants who will work in a hazardous work environment; a security position; a position that affects public safety or health; a position with a fiduciary relationship to the employer, or a position that requires driving.

Testing employees: Same job restrictions apply to employees as to applicants. Employees in these positions may be tested: upon reasonable suspicion; after involvement in an accident that causes personal injury or more than $1,500 property damage; as a follow-up to a previous positive test; or as a follow-up to treatment or a rehabilitation program. Employer may conduct random tests as long as there is an established date, all personnel are subject to testing, the employer has signed statements from each employee confirming receipt of a written description of the random selection process, and the random selection process is conducted by a scientifically valid method. Employer may require an employee who tests positive to undergo treatment as a condition of continued employment.

Employee rights: After a positive result, employee may request additional confirmation by an independent laboratory; if the results are negative, employer must pay the test costs. Employer may not take action or conduct follow-up testing if the employee presents a reasonable explanation or medical opinion that the original results were not caused by illegal drug use; employer must also remove results from employee's record.

Notice and policy requirements: Written policy must be available for review 60 days before testing. Policy must include consequences of a positive test result.

Nebraska

Neb. Rev. Stat. §§ 48-1901 to 48-1910

Employers affected: Employers with 6 or more full-time and part-time employees.

Testing employees: Employers are not required to test. Employer may require employees to submit to drug or alcohol testing and may

State Drug and Alcohol Testing Laws (continued)

discipline or discharge any employee who refuses, tests positive, or tampers with the test sample.

Employee rights: Employer may not take adverse action on the basis of an initial positive result unless it is confirmed according to state and federal guidelines.

New Hampshire

N.H. Rev. Stat. Ann. § 275:3

Employers affected: All employers.

Testing employees: May not require applicants to pay the costs of testing.

Employee rights: May not require employees to pay the costs of testing.

New Jersey

No statute on drug or alcohol testing, but court cases place some limitations (Hennessey v. Coastal Eagle Point Oil Co., 129 N.J. 81 (1992); Vargo v. Nat'l Exch. Carriers Ass'n, Inc., 376 N.J. Super. 364 (App. Div. 2005))

Employers affected: All employers.

Testing employees: Employer may require applicants to undergo preemployment testing.

Employee rights: Random drug testing allowed for safety-sensitive positions.

North Carolina

N.C. Gen. Stat. §§ 95-230 to 95-235

Employers affected: All employers.

Testing applicants: May test as a condition of hire. Applicant has right to retest a confirmed positive sample at own expense. If first screening test produces a positive result, applicant may waive a second examination that is intended to confirm the results.

Testing employees: Employers may, but are not required to, test. Testing must be performed under reasonable, sanitary conditions, and must

respect individual dignity to the extent possible. Employer must preserve samples for at least 90 days after confirmed test results are released.

Employee rights: Employee has right to retest a confirmed positive sample at own expense.

North Dakota

N.D. Cent. Code §§ 34-01-15, 65-01-11

Employers affected: All employers.

Testing applicants: May test as a condition of hire.

Testing employees: Employer may test following an accident or injury that will result in a workers' compensation claim, if employer has a mandatory policy of testing under these circumstances, or if employer or physician has reasonable grounds to suspect injury was caused by impairment due to alcohol or drug use.

Employee rights: Employer that requires drug testing of any applicant or employee must pay for the test.

Ohio

Ohio Admin. Code § 4123-17-58

Employers affected: Employers that establish a drug-free safety program may qualify for a workers' compensation rate bonus.

Testing applicants: Must test all applicants and new hires.

Testing employees: Must test employees: upon reasonable suspicion; following a return to work after a positive test; after an accident that results in an injury requiring off-site medical attention or property damage. Employers must test at random to meet requirements for greater discounts.

Employee rights: Employer must have an employee assistance plan. Employers who test at random to qualify for greater discount must

State Drug and Alcohol Testing Laws (continued)

not terminate employee who tests positive for the first time, comes forward voluntarily, or is referred by a supervisor. For these employees, employer must pay costs of substance abuse assessment.

Notice and policy requirements: Policy must state consequences for refusing to submit to testing or for violating guidelines. Policy must include a commitment to rehabilitation.

Oklahoma

Okla. Stat. Ann. tit. 40, §§ 551 to 565

Employers affected: Employers with one or more employees.

Testing applicants: May test applicants.

Testing employees: Statute does not require or encourage testing. Before requiring testing, employer must provide an employee assistance program. Random testing is allowed. May test employees: upon reasonable suspicion; after an accident resulting in injury or property damage; on a random selection basis; as part of a routine fitness-for-duty examination; or as follow-up to a rehabilitation program.

Employee rights: Employee has right to retest a positive result at own expense; if the confirmation test is negative, employer must reimburse costs.

Notice and policy requirements: Before requiring testing employer must: adopt a written policy; give a copy to each employee and to any applicant offered a job; and allow 10 days' notice. Policy must state consequences of a positive test result or refusing to submit to testing.

Oregon

Ore. Rev. Stat. §§ 438.435, 659.840, 659A.300

Employers affected: Law applies to all employers.

Testing applicants: Unless there is reasonable suspicion that an applicant is under the influence of alcohol, no employer may require a breathalyzer test as a condition of employment. Employer is not prohibited from conducting a test if applicant consents.

Testing employees: Unless there is reasonable suspicion that an employee is under the influence of alcohol, no employer may require a breathalyzer or blood alcohol test as a condition of continuing employment. Employer is not prohibited from conducting a test if employee consents.

Employee rights: No action may be taken based on the results of an on-site drug test without a confirming test performed according to state health division regulations. Upon written request, test results will be reported to the employee.

Rhode Island

R.I. Gen. Laws §§ 28-6.5-1 to 28-6.5-2

Employers affected: Law applies to all employers.

Testing applicants: May test as a condition of hire.

Testing employees: May require employee to submit to a drug test only if there are reasonable grounds, based on specific, documented observations, to believe employee may be under the influence of a controlled substance that is impairing job performance.

Employee rights: Employee must be allowed to provide sample in private, outside the presence of any person. Employee who tests positive may have the sample retested at employer's expense and must be given opportunity to explain or refute results. Employee may not be terminated on the basis of a positive result but must be referred to a licensed substance abuse professional. After referral, employer may require additional testing and may terminate employee if test results are positive.

State Drug and Alcohol Testing Laws (continued)

South Carolina

S.C. Code Ann. §§ 38-73-500, 41-1-15

Employers affected: Employers that establish a drug-free workplace program to qualify for a workers' compensation rate discount.

Testing applicants: Employer is not required to test applicants to qualify for discount.

Testing employees: Must conduct random testing among all employees.

Employee rights: Employee must receive positive test results in writing within 24 hours.

Notice and policy requirements: Employer must notify all employees of the drug-free workplace program at the time it is established or at the time of hiring, whichever is earlier. Program must include a policy statement that balances respect for individuals with the need to maintain a safe, drug-free environment.

Tennessee

Tenn. Code Ann. §§ 50-9-101 to 50-9-114

Employers affected: Employers that establish a drug-free workplace program to qualify for a workers' compensation rate discount.

Testing applicants: Must test applicants for drugs upon conditional offer of employment. May test only those applying for certain positions, if based on reasonable job classifications. May test for alcohol after conditional offer of employment. Job ads must include notice that drug and alcohol testing is required.

Testing employees: Employer must test upon reasonable suspicion; must document behavior on which the suspicion is based within 24 hours or before test results are released, whichever is earlier; and must give a copy to the employee upon request. Employer must test employees: if required by employer policy as part of a routine fitness-for-duty medical exam; after an accident that results in injury; or as a follow-up to a required rehabilitation program. May test employees who are not in safety-sensitive positions for alcohol only if based on reasonable suspicion.

Employee rights: Employee has the right to explain or contest a positive result within 5 days. Employee may not be fired, disciplined, or discriminated against for voluntarily seeking treatment unless employee has previously tested positive or been in a rehabilitation program.

Notice and policy requirements: Before implementing testing program, employer must provide 60 days' notice and must give all employees a written drug and alcohol policy statement. Policy must include consequences of a positive test or refusing to submit to testing.

Utah

Utah Code Ann. §§ 34-38-1 to 34-38-15

Employers affected: Employers with one or more employees.

Testing applicants: Employer may test any applicant for drugs or alcohol as long as management also submits to periodic testing.

Testing employees: Employer may test employee for drugs or alcohol as long as management also submits to periodic testing. Employer may require testing to:

- investigate possible individual employee impairment
- investigate an accident or theft
- maintain employee or public safety; or
- ensure productivity, quality, or security.

Employer may suspend, discipline, discharge, or require treatment on the basis of a failed test (confirmed positive result, adulterated sample, or substituted sample) or a refusal to take test.

State Drug and Alcohol Testing Laws (continued)

Notice and policy requirements: Testing must be conducted according to a written policy that has been distributed to employees and is available for review by prospective employees.

Vermont

Vt. Stat. Ann. tit. 21, §§ 511 to 520

Employers affected: Employers with one or more employees.

Testing applicants: Employer may not test applicants for drugs or alcohol unless there is a job offer conditional on a negative test result and applicant is given written notice of the testing procedure and a list of the drugs to be tested for.

Testing employees: Random testing not permitted unless required by federal law. Employer may not require testing unless:

- there is probable cause to believe an employee is using or is under the influence
- employer has an employee assistance program which provides rehabilitation, and
- employee who tests positive and agrees to enter employee assistance program is not terminated.

Employee rights: Employer must contract with a medical review officer who will review all test results and keep them confidential. Medical review officer is to contact employee or applicant to explain a positive test result. Employee or applicant has right to an independent retest at own expense. Employee who successfully completes employee assistance program may not be terminated, although employee may be suspended for up to 3 months to complete program. Employee who tests positive after completing treatment may be fired.

Notice and policy requirements: Must provide written policy that states consequences of a positive test.

Virginia

Va. Code Ann. § 65.2-813.2

Employers affected: Employers that establish drug-free workplace programs to qualify for workers' compensation insurance discount.

Testing applicants: State law gives insurers the authority to establish guidelines and criteria for testing.

Testing employees: State law gives insurers the authority to establish guidelines and criteria for testing.

West Virginia

W.Va. Code §§ 21-3E-1 to 21-3E-16

Employers affected: Employers with one or more full-time employees.

Testing applicants: Same conditions as current employees.

Testing employees: Employers may test for a wide variety of reasons, including: following a workplace accident; to deter or detect substance abuse; to investigate employee theft or misconduct; to protect the safety of employees, customers, or the general public; to maintain productivity or quality of services; or to protect company property or information. Testing must be paid for by the employer and conducted by an approved laboratory.

Employee rights: Employees and applicants must be given the opportunity to provide information relevant to the test, such as current prescription drug use or medical information. They also have the right to challenge the result and order retesting of the sample at their own cost.

Notice and policy requirements: Employers must have a written testing policy in place and distribute it to employees and applicants.

State Drug and Alcohol Testing Laws (continued)

Wyoming

Wy. Stat. Ann. 27-14-201; Wy. Rules & Regulations, WSD WCD Ch. 2, § 8

Employers affected: Employers that establish a drug and alcohol testing program approved by the state Department of Workforce Services may receive a workers' compensation discount of up to 5% of the base rate for the employer's classification.

Testing applicants: Must test applicants for drugs; may test applicants for alcohol. Job announcements must state that testing is required.

Testing employees: Must test employees: upon reasonable suspicion; following a workplace accident; at random. Must follow testing protocols prescribed in regulations (including "strong recommendation" that postaccident testing be done by blood sample).

Employee rights: Employee has 5 days to contest or explain a positive result.

Notice and policy requirements: Employer must have written policy including consequence of positive result or refusing to submit to test. Must give notice 60 days prior to testing.

State Laws on Socia Media Passwords

Arkansas

Ark. Code Ann. § 11-2-124; Code Ark. R. 010.14.1-500

Accounts Covered: A personal online account where users create, share, or view user-generated content, including videos, photographs, blogs, podcasts, messages, emails, and website profiles or locations. Does not include an account provided to an employee by the employer or created by the employee at the request of the employer or on behalf of the employer.

Employers Covered: All

Employees Covered: All current and prospective employees

Restrictions: Employers may not ask or require employees or applicants to: disclose their user names or passwords; change the privacy settings on their accounts; or add another employee, supervisor, or administrator to their contacts.

If an employer inadvertently receives an employee's login information for a social media account, the employer is not liable but may not use the information to access the accounts.

Violations: If an employer violates the law, the state Department of Labor may assess civil monetary penalties or seek injunctive relief.

California

Cal. Lab. Code § 980

Accounts Covered: A personal online service, account, or content, including videos, photographs, blogs, video blogs, podcasts, instant and text messages, email, or website profiles or locations.

Employers Covered: All

Employees Covered: All current and prospective employees

Restrictions: Employers may not request or require employees or applicants to: disclose user names or passwords to social media accounts;

access their social media accounts in the presence of the employer; or disclose any personal social media content.

Permitted Actions: Employers may ask employees to disclose personal social media that is reasonably believed to be relevant to an investigation into employee misconduct or violation of the law, as long as the information is used solely for the purpose of the investigation or a related proceeding.

Employers may ask employees to disclose user names, passwords, or other login information in order to access an employer-issued electronic device.

Colorado

Colo. Rev. Stat. Ann. § 8-2-127

Accounts Covered: Personal accounts or services on a personal electronic communication device.

Employers Covered: All

Employees Covered: All current and prospective employees

Restrictions: Employers may not suggest, request, or require employees or applicants to disclose user names, passwords, or other means of accessing a personal account through a personal electronic communication device. Employers may not ask or require employees or applicants to change their privacy settings or force them to add anyone, including the employer or its agent, to their contact list.

Permitted Actions: Employers may require employees to disclose login information to any nonpersonal accounts that provide access to the employer's internal computer or information systems.

Employers may investigate employees to ensure compliance with applicable securities or financial

State Laws on Social Media Passwords (continued)

laws based on information about an employee's use of a personal website or account for business purposes.

Employers may investigate employees with regard to unauthorized downloading of employer's proprietary information or financial data to a personal website or account.

Violations: Employees and applicants may file a complaint with the state Department of Labor and Employment. Employers can be fined up to $1,000 for the first violation and up to $5,000 for each subsequent violation.

Connecticut
Conn. Gen. Stat. Ann. § 31-40x

Accounts Covered: Any online account that is used exclusively for personal purposes, including email, social media, and retail websites. Does not include any account created or used by an employee for business purposes of the employer.

Employers Covered: All

Employees Covered: All current and prospective employees

Restrictions: Employers may not ask or require employees or applicants to: disclose user names, passwords, or other login information; or authenticate or access a personal online account in the presence of the employer. Employers may not require employees or applicants to invite, or accept an invitation from, an employer to join a group affiliated with a personal online account.

Permitted Actions: Employers may request or require an employee to provide user names and passwords in order to access an employer-issued electronic device or an account created by the employer or used by the employee for the employer's business purposes.

Employers may require employees or applicants to provide access to personal online accounts as part of an investigation into employee misconduct, violation of the law, or unauthorized transfer of the employer's confidential or financial data. However, the employer must have specific information relating to the employee's activity on a personal account, and the employee cannot be required to disclose the user name or password for the account.

Violations: Employees and applicants may file a complaint with the state labor commissioner. Employers can be fined up to $500 for the first violation and between $500 and $1,000 for each subsequent violation. Employees can be awarded relief, including job reinstatement, payment of back wages, reestablishment of employee benefits, and reasonable attorneys' fees and costs.

Delaware
Del. Code Ann. tit. 19, § 709A

Accounts Covered: Any account on a social networking website that is used exclusively for personal use. Does not include accounts created by or operated by the employer and used by employees as part of their employment.

Employers Covered: All

Employees Covered: All current and prospective employees

Restrictions: Employers may not ask or require employees or applicants to: disclose user names or passwords; access social media in the presence of the employer; change the privacy settings to their social media accounts; use personal social media as a condition of employment; or add anyone, including the employer, to their contacts.

Permitted Actions: Employers may require employees to provide user names and passwords

State Laws on Social Media Passwords (continued)

in order to access an employer-issued electronic device or an account created by the employer or used by the employee for the employer's business purposes.

Violations: Employers may require employees to disclose user names, passwords, or social media reasonably believed to be relevant to an investigation into employee misconduct or violation of the law, as long as the social media is used solely for such purposes.

Illinois

820 Ill. Comp. Stat. Ann. 55/10; Ill. Admin. Code tit. 56, §§ 360.110, 360.120

Accounts Covered: An online account that is used primarily for personal reasons. Does not include an account created or used by a person for the business purposes of the employer.

Employers Covered: All

Employees Covered: All current and prospective employees

Restrictions: Employers may not request, require, or coerce employees or applicants to: disclose user names or passwords or otherwise provide access to personal online accounts; or authenticate or access personal online accounts in the presence of the employer. Employers may not require employees or applicants to: invite the employer to join any group affiliated with the personal online account; join an online account established by an employer; or add an employer or employment agency to their contact lists.

If an employer inadvertently receives login information to access an employee's or applicant's personal social media, the employer may not use the information to access the accounts and must delete the information as soon as reasonably possible.

Permitted Actions: Employers may require that an employee share specific content (but not user names and passwords) that has been reported to the employer from a personal online account for a variety of reasons, including: to comply with laws and regulations; to investigate specific allegations of the unauthorized transfer of the employer's proprietary information; to investigate specific allegations of employee workplace misconduct or violation of the law; and to prohibit employees from using a personal account for business purposes, or during business hours while on company property and using the company's network or equipment.

Violations: If an employer violates the law, employees and applicants can file a complaint with the state Department of Labor.

Louisiana

La. Stat. Ann. §§ 51:1951 to 51:1953, and 51:1955

Accounts Covered: Any online account used exclusively for personal, non-business communications.

Employers Covered: All

Employees Covered: All current and prospective employees

Restrictions: Employers may not request or require employees or applicants to disclose user names and passwords or other login information for their personal accounts.

If an employer inadvertently receives user names, passwords, or other login credentials, the employer may not use the information to access the accounts.

Permitted Actions: Employers may request or require employees or applicants to disclose user names, passwords, or other login information to

State Laws on Social Media Passwords (continued)

access an employer-issued electronic device or account used for business purposes.

Employers may require employees to share the contents of their personal online accounts as part of an investigation, based on specific information relating to activity on the employee's personal account, into workplace misconduct, violation of law, or unauthorized transfer of the employer's confidential or financial data. However, employers may not require the employee to provide the user name and password to the account.

Maine

Me. Rev. Stat. tit. 26, §§ 615 to 619

Accounts Covered: A personal online account through which users create, share and view user-generated content including but not limited to videos, photographs, blogs, video blogs, podcasts, instant and text messages, email, online service accounts, and website profiles and locations. Does not include accounts opened by an employee at the employer's instruction or accounts intended for use primarily on behalf of the employer.

Employers Covered: All

Employees Covered: All current and prospective employees

Restrictions: Employers may not request, require, coerce employees or applicants to: disclose passwords or other means of access to personal social media accounts; access social media accounts in the presence of the employer; or change the privacy settings to their social media accounts. Employers may not require employees to disclose any personal social media information or add anyone to their contact list.

Permitted Actions: Employers may require employees to disclose personal social media account information that is reasonably believed

to be relevant to an investigation into workplace misconduct or a work-related violation of the law, as long as the information is used solely for such purposes.

Violations: An employer that violates the law is subject to a fine from the Department of Labor of at least $100 for the first violation, $250 for the second violation, and $500 for subsequent violations.

Maryland

Md. Code Ann., Lab. & Empl. § 3-712

Accounts Covered: Any personal account accessed through a computer, phone, or other electronic device.

Employers Covered: All

Employees Covered: All current and prospective employees

Restrictions: Employers may not ask or require employees or applicants to disclose user names, passwords, or other information to access personal accounts through an electronic device.

Permitted Actions: Employers may conduct an investigation when: receiving information about an employee's use of a personal account for business reasons, in order to ensure compliance with applicable securities or financial laws; or when receiving information about an employee's unauthorized transfer of the employer's proprietary information to a personal account.

Employers may request user names and passwords for purposes of accessing nonpersonal accounts that provide access to the employer's internal computer or information systems.

Violations: Whenever the state Labor Commissioner determines that this section has been violated, the Commissioner will try to resolve the

State Laws on Social Media Passwords (continued)

issue informally through mediation or ask the state Attorney General to bring an action on behalf of the applicant or employee for damages or other relief.

Michigan
Mich. Comp. Laws Ann. §§ 37.271 to 37.278

Accounts Covered: A personal account created through an Internet-based service that requires a user to input or store login information on an electronic device to view, create, utilize, or edit the user's account information, profile, display, communications, or stored data.

Employers Covered: All

Employees Covered: All current and prospective employees

Restrictions: Employers may not ask employees or applicants to grant access to, allow observation of, or disclose information that allows access to personal Internet accounts.

Permitted Actions: Employers may require employees to disclose information to gain access to an electronic device supplied by the employer or to an online account provided by the employer or used for business purposes.

Employers may conduct an investigation when: receiving specific information about activity on the employee's personal Internet account, in order to ensure compliance with the law, regulations, or workplace misconduct rules; or when receiving specific information about an employee's unauthorized transfer of the employer's proprietary information or financial data to a personal account.

Violations: Employers that violate the law can be convicted of a misdemeanor and fined up to $1,000.

Employees and applicants may also file a civil claim and recover up to $1,000 in damages plus attorneys' fees and court costs.

Montana
Mont. Code Ann. § 39-2-307

Accounts Covered: A personal password-protected electronic service or account containing electronic content, including but not limited to email, videos, photographs, blogs, video blogs, podcasts, instant and text messages, website profiles or locations, and online services or accounts. Does not include an account opened for, or provided by, an employer and intended solely for business use.

Employers Covered: All

Employees Covered: All current and prospective employees

Restrictions: Employers may not ask or require employees or applicants to: disclose user names or passwords to personal social media accounts; access personal social media in the presence of the employer; or reveal personal social media or any information contained in a personal social media account.

Permitted Actions: Employers may request an employee's user name or password to access personal social media when such access is necessary to make a factual determination in an investigation of workplace misconduct, criminal defamation, the unauthorized transfer of the employer's proprietary information or financial data to a personal account, or compliance with applicable laws or regulations.

Violations: An employee or applicant may bring an action against an employer in small claims court. If successful, an employee or applicant can receive $500 or actual damages up to $7,000, as well as legal costs.

State Laws on Social Media Passwords (continued)

Nebraska

Neb. Rev. Stat. Ann. §§ 48-3501 to 48-3511

Accounts Covered: Any personal online account that requires login information in order to access or control the account. Does not include an account supplied by the employer or exclusively used for the employer's business purposes.

Employers Covered: All

Employees Covered: All current and prospective employees

Restrictions: Employers may not ask or require employees or applicants to: disclose user names, passwords, or other access information to a personal Internet account; or access a personal Internet account in the presence of the employer. Employers may not require employees or applicants to change the privacy settings to their personal Internet accounts or add anyone to their contact lists.

If an employer inadvertently receives login credentials to access an employee's or applicant's personal Internet account, the employer may not use the information to access the account or share the information with anyone. The employer must delete the information as soon as practical.

Permitted Actions: Employers may ask or require employees to disclose login information to an employer-issued electronic device or to online accounts that are provided by the employer or used for the employer's business purposes.

Employers may require employees to cooperate when investigating specific information about workplace misconduct, violation of applicable laws or regulations, or the unauthorized transfer of the employer's proprietary information or financial data to a personal online account.

Violations: An employee or applicant may file a lawsuit in court and receive appropriate relief, including temporary or permanent injunctive relief, general and special damages, reasonable attorneys' fees, and costs.

Nevada

Nev. Rev. Stat. Ann. § 613.135

Accounts Covered: Any personal electronic service or account or electronic content, including videos, photographs, blogs, video blogs, podcasts, instant and text messages, email, or website profiles.

Employers Covered: All

Employees Covered: All current and prospective employees

Restrictions: Employers may not request, require, or suggest employees or applicants to disclose user names, passwords, or other information providing access to personal social media accounts.

Permitted Actions: Employers may require employees to disclose login information to an electronic account or service, other than a personal social media account, for the purpose of accessing the employer's own internal computer or information system.

New Hampshire

N.H. Rev. Stat. Ann. §§ 275:73 to 275:75

Accounts Covered: An account, service, or profile on a social networking website that is used primarily for personal communications unrelated to any business purposes of the employer.

Employers Covered: All

Employees Covered: All current and prospective employees

State Laws on Social Media Passwords (continued)

Restrictions: Employers may not ask or require employees or applicants to disclose user names, passwords, or other login information to any personal account or service through an electronic device. Employers may not require employees or applicants to change the privacy settings on their email or social media accounts or add anyone to their email or social media contact lists.

If an employer inadvertently receives login credentials to access an employee's or applicant's personal social media, the employer may not use the information to access the accounts.

Permitted Actions: Employers may ask or require employees to disclose login information to an employer-issued electronic device or online accounts that were provided by virtue of the employment relationship.

Employers may conduct investigations when: receiving information about an employee's activity on a personal account, in order to ensure compliance with laws, regulations, or workplace misconduct rules; or when receiving specific information about the unauthorized transfer of proprietary, confidential, or financial data to an employee's personal account. However, employers may only require that the employee provide the content received by the employer, in order to make a factual determination.

Violations: Employers that violate the law are subject to a fine of up to $2,500 from the state Labor Commissioner.

New Jersey

N.J. Stat. Ann. §§ 34:6B-5 to 34:6B-10

Accounts Covered: An account, service or profile on a social networking website used exclusively for personal communications unrelated to any business purpose of the employer.

Employers Covered: All

Employees Covered: All current and prospective employees

Restrictions: Employers may not ask or require employees or applicants to disclose user names or passwords, or provide the employer with access in any other manner, to personal online accounts.

Permitted Actions: Employers may conduct an investigation: when receiving specific information about an employee's activity on a personal account, in order to ensure compliance with laws, regulations, and workplace misconduct rules; or when receiving specific information about the unauthorized transfer of proprietary, confidential, or financial data to an employee's personal account.

Violations: Employers that violate the law are subject to a fine of up to $1,000 for the first violation and up to $2,500 for each subsequent violation from the state Labor Commissioner.

New Mexico

N.M. Stat. Ann. § 50-4-34

Accounts Covered: An Internet-based service that allows individuals to: construct a public or semi-public profile within a bounded system created by the service; create a list of other users with whom they share a connection within the system; and view and navigate their list of connections and those made by others within the system.

Employers Covered: All

Employees Covered: Prospective employees only

Restrictions: Employers may not ask or require applicants to disclose passwords to, or otherwise demand access to, personal accounts on social media networking websites.

State Laws on Social Media Passwords (continued)

Oklahoma

Okla. Stat. Ann. tit. 40, § 173.2

Accounts Covered: An online account used exclusively for personal communications and used to generate or store content, including videos, photographs, blogs, video blogs, instant messages, audio recordings, or email.

Employers Covered: All

Employees Covered: All current and prospective employees

Restrictions: Employers may not require employees or applicants to disclose passwords or other information that will provide access to personal online social media accounts or require employees to access personal social media in the presence of the employer.

If an employer inadvertently receives login credentials to access an employee's or applicant's social media account, the employer may not use the information to access the accounts.

Permitted Actions: Employers may require employees to disclose access information to an employer-issued electronic device or online accounts that are provided by the employer or used for the employer's business purposes.

Employers may review or access personal social media accounts that an employee uses on the employer's computer system, network, or an employer-issued electronic device.

Employers may conduct an investigation: when receiving specific information about an employee's activity on a personal social media account, in order to ensure compliance with laws, regulations, or workplace misconduct rules; or when receiving specific information about the unauthorized transfer of proprietary or financial data to an employee's personal social media account. Such investigation may include requiring the employee to share the content that has been provided to the employer, in order to make a factual determination.

Violations: An employee or applicant can file a lawsuit and receive injunctive relief and $500 in damages per violation.

Oregon

Ore. Rev. Stat. Ann. § 659A.330

Accounts Covered: A social media account that is used exclusively for personal purposes unrelated to any business purpose of the employer and that is not provided by, or paid for by, the employer. Social media means an online medium for users to create and share user-generated content, such as videos, photographs, blogs, podcasts, instant messages, email or website profiles or locations.

Employers Covered: All

Employees Covered: All current and prospective employees

Restrictions: Employers may not ask or require employees or applicants to establish or maintain a personal social media account or to disclose user names and passwords to personal social media accounts. Employers may not require employees or applicants to allow the employer to authorize on their personal social media accounts; to access social media in the presence of the employer; or to add the employer or an employment agency to their contacts.

If an employer inadvertently receives login credentials to access an employee's or applicant's social media, the employer may not use the information to access the accounts.

Permitted Actions: Employers may require an employee to disclose any user name and password or other access information in order to

State Laws on Social Media Passwords (continued)

access an account provided by, or used on behalf of, the employer.

Employers may conduct an investigation when receiving specific information about an employee's activity on a personal social media account, in order to ensure compliance with laws, regulations, or workplace misconduct rules. As part of such investigation, the employer may require the employee to share content that has been reported to the employer in order to make a factual determination. However, the employer may not require the employee or applicant to disclose user names or passwords.

Rhode Island

R.I. Gen. Laws §§ 28-56-1 to 28-56-6

Accounts Covered: A online service or account, or electronic content, including, but not limited to, videos, photographs, blogs, video blogs, podcasts, instant and text messages, email, online service or accounts, or website profiles or locations. Does not include accounts provided by the employer, opened at the instruction of the employer, or intended to be used primarily on behalf of the employer.

Employers Covered: All

Employees Covered: All current and prospective employees

Restrictions: Employers may not ask, require, or coerce employees or applicants to: disclose passwords or other means for gaining access to personal social media accounts; or access social media accounts in the presence of the employer. Employers may not require employees or applicants to disclose any personal social media account information; change the privacy settings to their social media accounts; or add anyone to their contacts.

Permitted Actions: Employers may require an employee or applicant to disclose personal social media account information only when reasonably believed relevant to an investigation of employee misconduct or a work-related violation of laws or regulations. Such information may be used only to the extent necessary for purposes of the investigation or a related proceeding.

Violations: Employees and applicants may file a civil lawsuit. The court can award declaratory relief, damages, reasonable attorneys' fees and costs, and injunctive relief against the employer.

Tennessee

Tenn. Code Ann. §§ 50-1-1001 to 50-1-1004

Accounts Covered: An online account used exclusively for personal communications unrelated to any business purpose of the employer, including any online service where users may create, share or view content, including, emails, instant messages, text messages, blogs, podcasts, photographs, videos, or user-created profiles.

Employers Covered: All

Employees Covered: All current and prospective employees

Restrictions: Employers may not ask or require employees or applicants to disclose passwords to personal online accounts. Employers may not force employees or applicants to personal online accounts in the presence of the employer or add the employer or an employment agency to their contact list.

Permitted Actions: Employers may ask or require employees to disclose user names or passwords to access employer-issued electronic devices or accounts provided by the employer or used for the employer's business purposes.

State Laws on Social Media Passwords (continued)

Employers may conduct investigations: when receiving specific information about activity on an employee's personal online account, in order to ensure compliance with laws, regulations, and workplace misconduct rules; or when receiving specific information about the unauthorized transfer of the employer's proprietary of financial data to a personal online account. During such investigations, employers may require employees to share content from a personal online account in order to make a factual determination.

Utah

Utah Code Ann. §§ 34-48-101 to 34-48-301

Accounts Covered: Any online account that is used exclusively for personal communications unrelated to any business purpose of the employer.

Employers Covered: All

Employees Covered: All current and prospective employees

Restrictions: Employers may not ask employees or applicants to disclose user names or passwords to personal online accounts.

Permitted Actions: Employers may ask or require employees to disclose user names or passwords to access employer-owned electronic devices or accounts provided by the employer or used for the employer's business purposes.

Employers may conduct investigations: when receiving specific information about activity on an employee's personal online account, in order to ensure compliance with laws, regulations, and workplace misconduct rules; or when receiving specific information about the unauthorized transfer of the employer's proprietary of financial data to a personal online account. During such investigations, employers may require employees to share content from a personal online account in order to make a factual determination.

Violations: Employees and applicants may file a civil lawsuit against the employer, with a maximum award of $500.

Virginia

Va. Code Ann. § 40.1-28.7:5

Accounts Covered: A personal online account or service where users may create, share, or view user-generated content, including, videos, photographs, blogs, podcasts, messages, emails, or website profiles or locations. Does not include accounts provided by the employer; created by an employee at the request of the employer; or created by an employee on behalf of the employer or to impersonate the employer through use of the employer's logo and trademarks.

Employers Covered: All

Employees Covered: All current and prospective employees

Restrictions: Employers may not require employees or applicants to disclose user names or passwords to personal social media accounts or add the employer, a supervisor, or administrator to their contact list.

If an employer inadvertently receives login information to access an employee's or applicant's social media account, the employer may not use the information to access the account.

Permitted Actions: Employers may ask for an employee's user name or password to access a personal social media account that is reasonably believed to be relevant to an investigation into the employee's violation of any laws, regulations, or the employer's written policies. The employee's user name and password may only be used for the purpose of the investigation or a related proceeding.

State Laws on Social Media Passwords (continued)

Washington

Wash. Rev. Code Ann. §§ 49.44.200 and 49.44.205

Accounts Covered: Personal social networking accounts.

Employers Covered: All

Employees Covered: All current and prospective employees

Restrictions: Employers may not request, require, or coerce employees or applicants to: disclose passwords or other login information for a personal social media account; access social media in the presence of the employer; or change the privacy settings on their social media accounts. Employers also may not force an employee or applicant to add anyone to their contact lists.

If an employer inadvertently receives login information for an employee's social media account, the employer may not use the information to access the account.

Permitted Actions: Employers may ask or require employees to disclose user names or passwords to access employer-owned electronic devices or accounts provided by the employer or used for the employer's business purposes.

Employers may conduct investigations: when receiving information about activity on an employee's personal social media account, in order to ensure compliance with laws, regulations, and workplace misconduct rules; or when receiving information about the unauthorized transfer of the employer's proprietary of financial data to a personal social media account. During such investigations, employers may require employees to share content from a personal social media account in order to make a factual determination relevant to the investigation. However, they may not require the employee or applicant to disclose user names or passwords to the account.

Violations: Employees and applicants may file a civil lawsuit against the employer and obtain injunctive relief, actual damages, a penalty of $500, and reasonable attorneys' fees and costs.

West Virginia

W. Va. Code Ann. § 21-5H-1

Accounts Covered: A personal account, service or profile on a social networking website that is used exclusively for personal communications unrelated to the employer's business purposes.

Employers Covered: All

Employees Covered: All current and prospective employees

Restrictions: Employers may not request, require, or coerce employees or applicants to disclose passwords or other login information to personal social media accounts or access social media in the presence of the employer. Employers may not force employees or applicants to add the employer or an employment agency to their contact lists.

If an employer inadvertently receives login information for an employee's or applicant's social media, the employer may not use the information to gain access to the account and must delete the information as soon as reasonably possible.

Permitted Actions: Employers may ask or require employees to disclose user names or passwords to access employer-issued electronic devices or accounts provided by the employer or used for the employer's business purposes.

State Laws on Social Media Passwords (continued)

Employers may ask an employee to share specific content from a personal online account in order to comply with laws, regulations, or workplace misconduct rules.

Employers may investigate when receiving specific information about the unauthorized transfer of the employer's proprietary or financial data to a personal online account. As part of such investigation, employers may ask employees to share content from a personal social media account in order to make a factual determination.

Wisconsin

Wis. Stat. Ann. § 995.55

Accounts Covered: A personal online account that is created and used by an individual exclusively for purposes of personal communications.

Employers Covered: All

Employees Covered: All current or prospective employees

Restrictions: Employers may not ask or require employees or applicants, as a condition of employment, to disclose login information to personal social media accounts or allow observation of personal social media accounts.

If an employer inadvertently receives login credentials to access an employee's or applicant's social media, the employer may not use the information to access the account.

Permitted Actions: Employers may require employees to disclose user names or passwords to access employer-issued electronic devices or accounts provided by the employer or used for the employer's business purposes.

Employers may investigate, based on reasonable cause, the unauthorized transfer of the employer's proprietary or financial data to a personal online account or the employee's violation of laws, regulations, or workplace rules in an employee handbook. As part of such investigation, employers may ask an employee to share content or information from a personal online account but may not ask for login information.

Violations: Employees and applicants may file a complaint with the state Department of Workforce Development and receive appropriate relief.

State Laws on Marijuana Use and Employment

Note: States that are not listed below do not have medical or recreational marijuana laws that address employment. Some of the statutes listed below specifically protect off-duty medical marijuana use, as long as the employee doesn't use marijuana on company property or show up to work under the influence of marijuana. Other statutes specifically allow employers to fire or discipline employees for off-duty use. And several statutes use more ambiguous language that does not spell out whether off-duty use must be permitted.

Alaska

Alaska Stat. Ann. §§ 17.37.010 to 17.37.080; 17.38.010 to 17.38.050

Covered Employers: All employers.

Legal Marijuana Use: Medical and recreational marijuana

Rules for Employers: Employer not required to accommodate use of medical or recreational marijuana in the workplace.

Arizona

Ariz. Rev. Stat. Ann. §§ 36-2801 to 36-2819

Covered Employers: All employers.

Legal Marijuana Use: Medical marijuana only

Rules for Employers: Employer may not discriminate against medical marijuana users based on status as a cardholder or a positive drug test, unless it would cause the employer to lose money or licensing benefits under federal law. Employer may fire or take other negative action against employee who uses, possesses, or is impaired by medical marijuana on company property or during work hours.

Arkansas

Ark. Const. amend. XCVIII, §§ 3, 6

Covered Employers: Employers with 9 or more employees.

Legal Marijuana Use: Medical marijuana only

Rules for Employers: Employer may not discriminate against applicant or employee based on past or present status as a medical marijuana cardholder or designated caregiver for a physically disabled medical marijuana patient. Employer may take negative action against employee based on a good faith belief that the employee used, possessed, or was impaired by medical marijuana on company property or during work hours. A positive drug test alone is not sufficient grounds for a good faith belief. Employer may exclude employees from safety-sensitive positions based on a positive drug test.

California

Cal. Health & Safety Code §§ 11362.5; 11362.7 to 11362.9; Cal. Health & Safety Code §§ 11362.1 to 11362.45; Ross v. RagingWire Telecommunications, Inc., 42 Cal.4th 920 (2008)

Covered Employers: All employers.

Legal Marijuana Use: Medical and recreational marijuana

Rules for Employers: Employer not required to accommodate use of medical or recreational marijuana in the workplace. Employer may fire employees who test positive for marijuana, even for off-duty use.

Colorado

Colo. Const. art. XVIII, §§ 14, 16; Coats v. Dish Network, LLC, 350 P.3d 849 (2015)

Covered Employers: All employers.

Legal Marijuana Use: Medical and recreational marijuana

State Laws on Marijuana Use and Employment (continued)

Rules for Employers: Employer not required to accommodate use of medical or recreational marijuana in the workplace. Employer may fire employees who test positive for marijuana, even for off-duty use.

Connecticut

Conn. Gen. Stat. Ann. §§ 21a-408 to 21a-408v

Covered Employers: All employers.

Legal Marijuana Use: Medical marijuana only

Rules for Employers: Employer may not discriminate against applicants or employees based on status as a qualifying patient or primary caregiver of a qualifying patient under medical marijuana laws. Employer may prohibit employees from using marijuana during work hours and discipline employees for being under the influence of marijuana during work hours.

Delaware

Del. Code Ann. tit. 16, §§ 4901A to 4928a

Covered Employers: All employers.

Legal Marijuana Use: Medical marijuana only

Rules for Employers: Employer may not discriminate against medical marijuana user based on status as a cardholder or a positive drug test, unless it would cause the employer to lose money or other licensing-related benefits under federal law. Employer may take negative action against employee who uses, possesses, or is impaired by marijuana on company property or during work hours.

District of Columbia

D.C. Code Ann. §§ 7-1671.01 to 7-1671.13; 48-904.01

Covered Employers: All employers.

Legal Marijuana Use: Medical and recreational marijuana

Rules for Employers: Medical marijuana statute does not address employment. Recreational marijuana law does not require employers to allow or accommodate the use or possession of marijuana in the workplace. Employer may enforce policies restricting use of recreational marijuana by employees.

Florida

Fla. Stat. Ann. § 381.986

Covered Employers: All employers.

Legal Marijuana Use: Medical marijuana only

Rules for Employers: Employer not required to accommodate the use of medical marijuana in the workplace or an employee working under the influence of marijuana.

Georgia

Ga. Code Ann. §§ 16-12-190, 16-12-191, 31-2A-18

Covered Employers: All employers.

Legal Marijuana Use: Medical marijuana only

Rules for Employers: Employer not required to allow or accommodate the use or possession of marijuana in the workplace. Employer may enforce a zero-tolerance drug policy and terminate employees for testing positive for marijuana, even for off-duty use.

Hawaii

Haw. Rev. Stat. Ann. §§ 329-121 to 329-131

Covered Employers: All employers.

Legal Marijuana Use: Medical marijuana only

Rules for Employers: Medical marijuana law does not authorize use in the workplace.

Illinois

410 Ill. Comp. Stat. Ann. 130/30, 130/40, 130/50

Covered Employers: All employers.

Legal Marijuana Use: Medical marijuana only

State Laws on Marijuana Use and Employment (continued)

Rules for Employers: Employer may not discriminate on the basis of status as a registered medical marijuana patient or designated caregiver of a medical marijuana patient, unless it would cause the employer to violate federal law or lose money or licensing-related benefits under federal law. Employer may take negative action based on a good faith belief that employee used or possessed marijuana on company property or during work hours. Employer may also take negative action based on a good faith belief that employee was impaired while working on company property during work hours, but the employee must be given a chance to challenge the basis for the determination.

Maine

Me. Rev. Stat. tit. 22, §§ 2421 to 2430-B; Me. Rev. Stat. tit. 7, §§ 2441 to 2455

Covered Employers: All employers.

Legal Marijuana Use: Medical and recreational marijuana

Rules for Employers: Medical marijuana: Employer may not discriminate on the basis of status as a medical marijuana patient or primary caregiver of a medical marijuana patient, unless it would cause the employer to violate federal law or lose a federal contract or funding. Employer not required to allow employee to smoke marijuana on company premises or allow employee to work under the influence of marijuana. Recreational marijuana: Employer not required to accommodate use or possession of marijuana at the workplace and may discipline employees who are under the influence of marijuana at work. Employer may not discriminate against applicants or employees based on off-duty marijuana use.

Massachusetts

Mass. Gen. Laws Ann. ch. 94I §§ 1 to 8; 105 Mass. Code Regs. 725.650; Barbuto v. Advantage Sales and Marketing, LLC, 477 Mass. 456 (2017); Mass. Gen. Laws Ann. ch. 94G, § 2

Covered Employers: All employers, except as otherwise noted.

Legal Marijuana Use: Medical and recreational marijuana

Rules for Employers: Medical marijuana: Employer not required to accommodate on-site use of medical marijuana at the workplace. However, an employee who uses medical marijuana to treat a disability is entitled to reasonable accommodation under state disability discrimination law. Under that law, employers with 6 or more employees must accommodate off-site, off-duty use, unless there is an equally effective treatment available or it would cause the employer undue hardship. Recreational marijuana: Employer not required to accommodate recreational marijuana use in the workplace. Employer may enforce workplace policies restricting marijuana consumption by employees.

Michigan

Mich. Comp. Law §§ 333.26421 to 333.26430; 333.26424, 333.26427; Casias v. Wal-Mart Stores, Inc., 695 F.3d 428 (2012)

Covered Employers: All employers.

Legal Marijuana Use: Medical marijuana only

Rules for Employers: Employer not required to accommodate marijuana use at the workplace or an employee working under the influence of marijuana. Employer may fire employee for testing positive for marijuana on a drug test, even when the use was off-duty.

State Laws on Marijuana Use and Employment (continued)

Minnesota

Minn. Stat. Ann. §§ 152.21 to 152.37

Covered Employers: All employers.

Legal Marijuana Use: Medical marijuana only

Rules for Employers: Employer may not discriminate against applicants or employees based on status as a registered medical marijuana patient or a positive drug test, unless it would cause the employer to violate federal law or lose money or licensing-related benefits under federal law. Employer may take negative action against an employee who uses, possesses, or was impaired by marijuana on company property or during work hours.

Montana

Mont. Code Ann. §§ 50-46-301 to 50-46-345

Covered Employers: All employers.

Legal Marijuana Use: Medical marijuana only

Rules for Employers: Employer not required to accommodate the use of marijuana by a registered cardholder. As part of an employment contract, employer may include a provision prohibiting an employee's use of medical marijuana.

Nevada

Nev. Rev. Stat. Ann. §§ 453A.800, 453D.100

Covered Employers: All employers.

Legal Marijuana Use: Medical and recreational marijuana

Rules for Employers: Medical marijuana: Employer not required to allow use of medical marijuana in the workplace. Employer must try to make reasonable accommodations for registered medical marijuana patient, as long as it would not pose a safety threat to people or property, cause an undue hardship, or prevent the employee from fulfilling his or her job responsibilities. Recreational marijuana: Employer may enforce workplace policy prohibiting or restricting use of recreational marijuana by employees.

New Hampshire

N.H. Rev. Stat. Ann. §§ 126-X:1 to 126-X:11

Covered Employers: All employers.

Legal Marijuana Use: Medical marijuana only

Rules for Employers: Employer not required to accommodate use of medical marijuana on company property. Employers may discipline employees for using marijuana in the workplace or for working while under the influence of marijuana.

New Jersey

N.J. Stat. Ann. §§ 24:6I-1 to 24:6I-16

Covered Employers: All employers.

Legal Marijuana Use: Medical marijuana only

Rules for Employers: Employer not required to accommodate use of medical marijuana in the workplace.

New Mexico

N.M. Stat. Ann. §§ 26-2B-1 to 26-2B-7; Garcia v. Tractor Supply Company, 154 F.Supp.3d 1225 (2016)

Covered Employers: All employers.

Legal Marijuana Use: Medical marijuana only

Rules for Employers: Employer may fire or discipline medical marijuana users based on positive drug test.

New York

N.Y. Pub. Health Law §§ 3360 to 3369-E; N.Y. Comp. Codes R. & Regs. tit. 10, § 1004.18

Covered Employers: All employers, except as otherwise noted.

State Laws on Marijuana Use and Employment (continued)

Legal Marijuana Use: Medical marijuana only

Rules for Employers: Employer may not discriminate based on status as medical marijuana patient, but may enforce a policy that prohibits employees from working while impaired by marijuana. Employers with four or more employees must also provide reasonable accommodations to medical marijuana users. Employer not required to take any action that would cause it to violate federal law or lose a federal contract or funding.

North Dakota

N.D. Cent. Code Ann. §§ 19-24.1-01 to 19-24.1-40

Covered Employers: All employers.

Legal Marijuana Use: Medical marijuana only

Rules for Employers: Employer may discipline employee for possessing or using marijuana in the workplace or for working while under the influence of marijuana.

Ohio

Ohio Rev. Code Ann. §§ 3796.01 to 3796.30

Covered Employers: All employers.

Legal Marijuana Use: Medical marijuana only

Rules for Employers: Employer not required to accommodate an employees use or possession of medical marijuana. Employer may enforce zero-tolerance drug policy and discipline, fire, or refuse to hire medical marijuana users.

Oregon

Ore. Rev. Stat. Ann. § 475B.413; Emerald Steel Fabricators, Inc. v. Bureau of Labor and Industries, 230 P.3d 518 (2010); Ore. Rev. Stat. Ann. § 475B.020

Covered Employers: All employers.

Legal Marijuana Use: Medical and recreational marijuana

Rules for Employers: Medical marijuana:

Employer not required to accommodate the use of medical marijuana in the workplace. Employer may fire or discipline employees for testing positive for marijuana, even if use was off-duty and with a valid medical marijuana card. Recreational marijuana law does not impose any restrictions on employers.

Pennsylvania

35 Pa. Stat. Ann. §§ 10231.510, 10231.1309, 10231.2103

Covered Employers: All employers.

Legal Marijuana Use: Medical marijuana only

Rules for Employers: Employer may not discriminate based on status as a medical marijuana patient. Employer may discipline employees for being under the influence of marijuana at the workplace, or for working while under the influence of medical marijuana, when the employees' conduct falls below the normally accepted standard of care for that job. Employer not required to accommodate medical marijuana use on company property and may prohibit employee from performing any duty that would pose a health or safety risk. Employer not required to take any action that would violate federal law.

Rhode Island

R.I. Gen. Laws §§ 21-28.6-4, 21-28.6-7; Callaghan v. Darlington Fabrics Corp., No. PC-2014-5680 (R.I. Super. 2017)

Covered Employers: All employers.

Legal Marijuana Use: Medical marijuana only

Rules for Employers: Employer not required to accommodate the medical use of marijuana in the workplace. However, employer may not refuse to hire or otherwise penalize a person based solely upon the person's status as a

State Laws on Marijuana Use and Employment (continued)

medical marijuana patient or for testing positive for marijuana on a drug test.

Vermont

Vt. Stat. Ann. tit. 18, §§ 4230a, 4471 to 4474m

Covered Employers: All employers.

Legal Marijuana Use: Medical and recreational marijuana

Rules for Employers: Medical marijuana: Law does not address employment. Recreational marijuana: Employer not required to accommodate, and may regulate or prohibit, use or possession of marijuana in the workplace.

Washington

Wash. Rev. Code Ann. § 69.51A.060; Roe v. TeleTech Customer Care Mgt. (Colorado) LLC, 257 P.3d 586 (Wash. 2011); Wash. Rev. Code Ann. § 69.50.4013

Covered Employers: All employers.

Legal Marijuana Use: Medical and recreational marijuana

Rules for Employers: Medical marijuana: Employer may establish a drug-free workplace policy, in which case no accommodation for medical marijuana use is required. Employer may refuse to hire or fire medical marijuana users for a positive drug test, even if use was off-duty. Recreational marijuana: Law does not address employment.

West Virginia

W. Va. Code Ann. §§ 16A-5-10, 16A-15-4

Covered Employers: All employers.

Legal Marijuana Use: Medical marijuana only

Rules for Employers: Employer may not discriminate against an employee solely on the basis of status as certified to use medical marijuana. Employer may discipline an employee for falling below normally accepted standard of care while under the influence of medical marijuana. Employer may also prohibit employee from performing any duty that would be life-threatening, or would pose a public health or safety risk, while under the influence of marijuana. Employer not required to take any action that would violate federal law.

Health and Safety

Workers in the past 30 years have pushed strongly for laws to protect their health and safety on the job. And they have been successful. Several laws, notably the Occupational Safety and Health Act (OSH Act), now establish basic safety standards aimed at reducing the number of illnesses, injuries, and deaths in workplaces. Because most workplace safety laws are enforced by employees who are willing to report on-the-job hazards, most laws also prevent employers from firing or discriminating against employees who report unsafe conditions to proper authorities.

An invention of the federal government, OSH Act standards are particularly sensitive to political shifts. In March 2001, for example, one of the first major pieces of legislation signed by President George W. Bush was to repeal the previously hard-fought workplace ergonomics standard. The Bush administration largely replaced the process of issuing mandatory regulations with voluntary guidelines and put additional resources into other, previously existing voluntary programs. During the Obama administration, enforcement of the OSH Act became a higher priority. With more funding for inspectors and other resources, OSHA significantly increased workplace inspections and employer penalties from 2008 to 2016. The administration also passed more regulations to improve workplace safety, including making workplace injury and illness statistics public to encourage employers to increase safety. Since taking over in 2016, the Trump administration appears to be reverting back to an approach of deregulation.

The Occupational Safety and Health Act

The main federal law covering threats to workplace safety, the OSH Act (29 U.S.C. §§ 651 to 678), created the Occupational Safety and Health Administration (OSHA) to enforce workplace safety. And it created the National Institute for Occupational Safety and Health (NIOSH) to research ways to increase workplace safety. (See the appendix for contact details.)

The OSH Act broadly requires employers to provide a safe workplace for employees, one that is free of dangers that could physically harm those who work there. The law implements this directive by requiring employers to inform employees about potential hazards, to train them in how to deal with hazards, and to keep records of workplace injuries and deaths.

Sometimes, workplace dangers are caught and corrected during unannounced inspections by OSHA. But the vast majority of OSHA's actions against workplace hazards are initiated by complaints from employees or labor unions.

CAUTION

States have workplace safety laws, too. About half the states now have their own laws similar to the OSH Act. The legal requirements for workplace health and safety in the state laws are generally similar to the federal law. In some cases, the state laws are more strict. (See "State and Local Health and Safety Laws," below.)

Who Is Covered

Unlike many other laws, which cover only companies with a minimum number of employees, the OSH Act covers nearly all private employers engaged in interstate commerce. That includes employers that use the U.S. Postal Service to send mail to other states or make telephone calls to other states, or use the Internet to conduct business.

The OSH Act does not apply to state and local government employers, however, government employees have some protection if their state or local government has a safety plan. About half of the states have an OSHA-approved state plan. Farms owned and operated by a family are the only significant private employers exempted from OSH Act coverage.

RESOURCE

For more information, see "All About OSHA" and "Worker's Rights." You can download these publications for free from the agency's website at www.osha.gov/pls/publications.

OSH Act Requirements

The Occupational Safety and Health Act requires all private employers to maintain a workplace that is free from serious hazards. Under the OSH Act, all employers are charged with this general safety duty. In addition, the law sets specific workplace safety standards for four major categories of work: general industry, maritime, construction, and agriculture.

Safety regulations are usually concerned with preventing a one-time injury, such as falling from an unsafe ladder or tripping on an irregular walkway.

The Act's health concerns are in preventing employee illnesses related to potential health dangers in the workplace—exposure to toxic fumes or asbestos, for example—and cumulative trauma such as carpal tunnel syndrome. (In Chapter 12, see "Conditions Covered" for more about carpal tunnel syndrome.)

The law quite simply, but frustratingly, requires employers to protect workers from "recognized hazards." It does not specify or limit the types of dangers covered, so hazards ranging from things that cause simple cuts and bruises, to the unhealthy effects of long-term exposure to some types of radiation, are all arguably covered.

But proving the law was violated is not easy. To prove an OSH Act violation, you must produce evidence of both of the following:

- Your employer failed to keep the workplace free of a hazard.
- The particular hazard was likely to cause death or serious physical injury.

Under the OSH Act, the definition of a workplace is not limited to the inside of an office or factory. The Act requires that work conditions be safe no matter where the work is performed, even if the workplace is an open field or a moving vehicle.

In addition to the general duty to maintain a safe workplace, employers are required to meet OSHA's safety standards for their specific industries. Depending on the types of hazards and workplaces involved, the employer's responsibility for creating and maintaining a healthy and safe workplace can include informing workers about—and labeling—potentially hazardous substances, upgrading or removing machinery that poses a danger, providing employees with a special breathing apparatus to keep dust created by a manufacturing process from entering workers' lungs, improving lighting above work areas, providing emergency exits and fire protection systems, vaccinating against diseases that can be contracted at work, or even tracking the effects of workplace conditions on employees' health through periodic medical examinations.

Finally, the OSH Act requires employers to display a poster explaining workers' rights to a safe workplace in a conspicuous spot. If the workplace is outdoors, the poster must be displayed where employees are most likely to see it, such as in a trailer at a construction site where workers use a time clock to punch in and out. An employer's failure to display such posters is itself a violation of the law.

Injury and Illness Reports

All employers must report to OSHA:

- within eight hours of a death resulting from a workplace accident, or
- within 24 hours of any inpatient hospitalization, amputation, or eye loss due to a workplace accident.

The report must include certain details, including the names of the affected employees, the time and place of the accident, the nature of the injuries, and a description of the accident.

Companies employing ten or more people must also keep records of work-related injuries and illnesses that have caused death or days off work and post a report on those injuries and illnesses.

Enforcing OSH Act Rights

If you believe that your workplace is unsafe, your first action should be to make your supervisor at work aware as soon as possible. If your employer has designated a particular person or department as responsible for workplace safety, inform the appropriate person of the danger.

In general, your complaint will get more attention if you present it on behalf of a group of employees who all see the situation as a safety threat. And, as for filing a complaint, there is safety in numbers. An employer that becomes angry over a safety complaint is much less likely to retaliate against a group of employees than against an individual. (See "Penalties for Retaliation," below.)

When You Suspect a Lurking Health Hazard

A Health Hazard Evaluation, or HHE, is a study of a workplace conducted by representatives at the National Institute for Occupational Safety and Health. It is conducted, free of charge, to learn whether workers are exposed to hazardous materials or harmful conditions. The aim with such inspections is to diagnose a problem whose cause is not obvious rather than to punish an employer for causing it; NIOSH officials do not have any punishment or enforcement authority. Three or more employees, a union rep, or an employer may seek these workplace evaluations.

HHEs are intended to root out systemic health and safety problems in a workplace, rather than an immediate danger or hazard; the latter should be reported to OSHA by following the steps described above, in "Enforcing OSH Act Rights." But it is appropriate to seek an HHE instead if:

- Employees in your workplace have an illness from an unknown cause.
- Employees are exposed to an agent or working condition that is not regulated by OSHA.
- Employees experience adverse health effects from exposure to a regulated or unregulated agent or working condition, even though the permissible exposure limit is not being exceeded.
- Medical or epidemiological investigations are needed to evaluate the hazard.
- The incidence of a particular disease or injury is higher than expected in a group of employees.
- The exposure is to a new or previously unrecognized hazard.
- The hazard seems to result from the combined effects of several agents.

Recent HHE investigations were requested, for example, because of an alarming number of cases of cancer, hearing loss, and sickness alleged from workplace exposure to diesel fuel, smoke, and chemicals.

NIOSH may respond to an HHE request by writing to you with a referral to another agency that may be able to help, calling to discuss possible solutions to the problem, or visiting the workplace one or more times to talk with affected employees and conduct studies. This process can take from a few months to a few years, depending on the type of evaluation.

For more information on HHEs, visit the NIOSH website at www.cdc.gov/niosh.

This Law Swings Both Ways

Although neither federal nor state workplace safety laws cite employees for violations of their responsibilities, the laws generally require that workers comply with all standards, rules, regulations, and orders issued under the Act. The unspoken inference here is that workers who do not hold up their end of the safety law bargain might jeopardize their own protections under health and safety laws.

Specifically, according to OSHA, an employee should:

- read the OSHA poster at the job site
- comply with all applicable OSH Act standards
- follow all employer safety and health regulations and wear or use prescribed protective equipment while working
- report hazardous conditions to a supervisor
- report any job-related injury or illness to the employer and seek treatment promptly
- cooperate with the OSHA compliance officer conducting an inspection if he or she inquires about safety and health conditions in the workplace, and
- exercise rights under the Act in a responsible manner.

While some of these responsibilities sound a bit nebulous, you should be prepared to show that you did your best to carry them out before claiming protection under any workplace safety law.

Filing a Complaint

If you have not been successful in getting your employer to correct a workplace safety hazard, you can file a complaint with OSHA.

To learn how to file a complaint, go to www.osha.gov/workers/file_complaint.html. While you may file a complaint online, these types of complaints are less likely to result in an on-site inspection than a written and signed complaint sent by fax or mail. In general, file online for less serious complaints, or when you are not interested in an on-site inspection of your workplace.

However you opt to file, it is wise to make a copy of the paperwork or send it to yourself as an email. If you mail in the form, send it by certified mail.

If you ask, OSHA must keep confidential your identity and that of any other employees involved in the complaint. If you want your identity to be kept secret, be sure to check the section on the complaint form that states: "Do not reveal my name to the employer." And if you file online, you may want to take the precaution of using your home computer or one in a library or other public facility rather than using workplace equipment.

Upon receiving your complaint, OSHA will assign a compliance officer to investigate. The compliance officer will likely talk with you and your employer and inspect the work conditions that you have reported.

How Complaints Are Resolved

OSHA can respond to a complaint in two ways. Agency workers can either perform an on-site inspection or an off-site investigation, also quaintly known as a "phone/fax investigation."

OSHA responds more quickly to lower priority hazards using a phone/fax approach. The agency claims that this allows it to concentrate resources on the most serious workplace hazards.

If an off-site investigation is appropriate, the agency telephones the employer, describes the alleged hazards and then follows up with a fax or letter. The employer must respond in writing within five days, identifying any problems found and noting corrective actions it has taken or is planning to take. If the response is adequate, OSHA generally will not conduct an inspection. The person who filed the original complaint will receive a copy of the employer's response and, if still not satisfied, may then request an on-site inspection.

If the employee or employee representative files a written complaint, then OSHA may conduct an on-site inspection. Inspections are generally conducted where: There are claims of serious physical harm that have resulted in disabling injuries or illnesses or claims of imminent danger; written, signed complaints request inspections; and an employer has provided an inadequate response to a phone/fax investigation.

During an inspection, if a compliance officer finds that the condition about which you complained poses an immediate danger to you and your coworkers, the officer can order your employer to immediately remove the danger from the workplace or order the workers to leave the dangerous environment.

Where the danger is particularly urgent or the employer has a record of violations, OSHA may get tough by asking the courts to issue an injunction: a court order requiring the employer to eliminate workplace hazards.

> EXAMPLE: A group of pipeline workers complained to OSHA that the earth walls of the excavation in which they were working were not well supported and could collapse on them. The OSHA compliance officer tried unsuccessfully to talk the employer into improving the situation. OSHA obtained a court injunction forbidding work to continue within the excavation until the walls were shored up with steel supports.

If the danger is less immediate, the compliance officer will file a formal report on your complaint with the director of OSHA for your region. If the facts gathered by the compliance officer support your complaint, the regional director may issue a citation to your employer.

The citation will specify what work conditions must be changed to ensure the safety of the employees, the timetable that OSHA is allowing for those changes to be made—usually known as an abatement plan—and any fines that have been levied against your employer.

EXAMPLE: Leslie is a machine operator in an old woodworking shop that uses lathes that throw a large quantity of wood dust into the air inside the shop. The wood dust appeared to be a hazard to the employees who breathed it, and Leslie was unsuccessful in resolving the problem with the shop's owner. She filed a complaint with OSHA.

OSHA studied the air pollution in the shop and agreed that it was a threat to workers' health. It ordered the shop's owner to install enclosures on the lathes to cut down on the amount of dust put into the air and filter-equipped fans throughout the shop to capture any wood dust that escaped from the enclosures. Because the lathe enclosures and fans needed to be custom-designed and installed, OSHA allowed the shop's owner six months to correct the situation.

In the meantime, OSHA ordered the shop's owner to immediately provide Leslie and all the other people employed there with dust-filtering masks to wear over their mouths and noses. Because OSHA regulations generally require employers to make the workplace safe and not just protect workers from an unsafe work situation, the masks were considered merely a temporary part of the long-term abatement plan.

An OSHA inspector who finds a workplace safety hazard or other violation will tell all affected employees about it and post a danger notice before leaving the workplace. This public notice of an unsafe condition is often the impetus an employer needs to take the hazard seriously and correct it.

CAUTION

The importance of being specific. Like many other government agencies, OSHA is a huge bureaucracy that is organized and operated according to computerized file numbers. The best way to get prompt service and accurate information from OSHA is to be as specific as possible. In your dealings with OSHA, be sure to mention the name of your employer, the relevant department, the number assigned to the complaint that you are tracking, and the date on which it was filed. Jot down the names and numbers of those you speak with. And keep detailed notes of your conversations, complete with dates and times.

Contesting an Abatement Plan

You have the right to contest an abatement plan OSHA designs to correct a workplace hazard (for example, if you feel the suggested plan is insufficient). To do so, send a letter expressing your intent to contest the plan to your local OSHA director within 15 days after the OSHA citation and announcement of the plan is posted in your workplace. You need not list specific reasons for contesting the plan in this letter; all you need to make clear is that you think the plan is unreasonable.

Preventing Additional Injuries

Workplace hazards often become obvious only after they cause an injury. For example, an unguarded machine part that spins at high speed might not seem dangerous until someone's clothing or hair becomes caught in it. But, even after a worker has been injured, employers sometimes fail—or even refuse—to make changes necessary to prevent further harm.

If you have been injured at work by a hazard that should be eliminated before it injures someone else, take the following steps as quickly as possible after obtaining the proper medical treatment:

- If you believe the hazard presents an immediate life-threatening danger to you and your coworkers, call OSHA's emergency reporting line at 800-321-6742.
- File a claim for workers' compensation benefits so that your medical bills will be paid and you will be compensated for your lost wages and injury. (See Chapter 12.) Workers' compensation claims can cost a company a lot of money; filing such a claim tends to quickly focus an employer's attention on safety problems. In some states, the amount you receive from a workers' comp claim will be larger if your injury was due to a violation of a state workplace safety law.
- Point out to your employer the continuing hazard created by the cause of your injury. As with most workplace safety complaints, the odds of getting action will be greater if you can organize a group of employees to do this.
- If your employer does not eliminate the hazard promptly, file a complaint with OSHA and any state or local agency that you think may be able to help.

After it receives your letter, OSHA will refer the matter to the Occupational Safety and Health Review Commission in Washington, DC, an agency independent of OSHA. That commission will send your employer a notice that the abatement plan is being contested.

This letter will order the employer to post a notice at the workplace stating that the plan is being contested. It will also require the employer to send the commission a form that certifies the date on which that announcement was made along with a copy to OSHA, you, and any other employees who have contested the plan.

Then, everyone involved in the case has ten days from the date the contest notice was posted to file an explanation of their viewpoints on the abatement plan with the commission. Copies must also be sent to all others involved in the case.

TIP

There really is strength in numbers.
If other employees feel the abatement plan is
unfair or insufficient, encourage them to register
their protests with OSHA as well.

Sample Letter

April 10, 20xx

Ms. Mary Official
Regional Director
Occupational Safety and Health
Administration
321 Main Street
Anycity, USA 12345

Dear Ms. Official:

As allowed by 29 U.S.C. Section 659(c), I wish
to contest the abatement plan agreed to by
your agency and my employer, the Oldtime
Mousetrap Company. This abatement
program resulted from a complaint that I
filed with your office on April 3, 20xx. That
complaint was assigned number A-123456 by
your office.

I contest this agreement because I believe
that it is unreasonable.

Sincerely,

Elmer Springmaker
Elmer Springmaker
456 Central Road
Anycity, USA 12340
123-555-5555

Administrative Review

When attempts to reach a resolution are
unsuccessful, the commission submits the
case to an administrative law judge for a
hearing. These proceedings usually take
several months—and sometimes years—
depending upon the complexity of the
workplace hazards involved.

Hearings before administrative law
judges are very much like a trial. Much time
and money can be consumed in gathering
evidence, and the hearings are usually
scheduled during daytime hours, when most
employees are at work. You will probably
have to hire a lawyer to help if you decide to
pursue your safety complaint at this level.
(See Chapter 17.)

You also have the right to appeal a decision
by an administrative law judge to the full
commission (a panel of three commissioners)
or in federal court, but you will probably have
to hire a lawyer to help you at these levels
as well.

Refusal to Work

The OSH Act gives you the right to refuse
to continue doing your job in extreme
circumstances that pose an immediate and
substantial danger to your safety.

This right is limited. You cannot refuse
to work due to just any workplace safety
dispute. This tactic also cannot be used to
protest general working conditions. But the
OSH Act gives you the right to walk off the

Tips on Presenting Your Views

The explanation you file on the abatement plan need not be elaborate. It should be as clear, brief, and precise as possible. For example, if you have made a list of employee injuries that have already resulted from the hazard in your workplace, include the date, time, location, and identity of the worker injured for each incident in your explanation.

Your explanation need not be typewritten, but your odds of communicating your viewpoint effectively will be increased if it is easy to read.

Send your explanation by certified mail to:

Executive Secretary
Occupational Safety and Health Review
   Commission
1120 20th Street, NW, 9th Floor
Washington, DC 20036

Be sure to include a cover letter—and to specify in it the name of the company involved, the number assigned to the case by the review commission and OSHA, and your mailing address and telephone number. Send a copy to the OSHA office where you filed your original complaint, to your employer, and to any people identified as parties in the case in the paperwork the commission sent to you. Also, be sure to save a copy of your cover letter, your explanation, and any supporting documentation for your personal files.

After it has gathered all the statements on the case, the commission will typically turn them over to U.S. Labor Department lawyers, who will attempt to meet with everyone who submitted statements and negotiate a resolution that is agreeable to all. The commission tries to negotiate settlements whenever possible, and by this point, everyone involved will have had an opportunity to read and think about each other's viewpoints. So the odds are that your complaint will be resolved at this stage.

job without being fired by your employer if the situation is a true workplace safety emergency.

A refusal to work will be legally protected only if your situation meets all of the following conditions:

- You asked your employer to eliminate the hazard and your request was ignored or denied. To protect your rights, it's best to tell more than one supervisor about the hazard or to tell the same supervisor at least twice, preferably in front of witnesses.
- You did not have time to pursue normal enforcement channels, such a filing a complaint with OSHA, because the threat was so urgent.
- You have a reasonable and honest belief that there is a real danger of death or serious injury.

• You had no other reasonable alternative to refusing to work, such as asking for a reassignment to another area.

EXAMPLE: Mike is a welder in a truck building plant. Shortly after starting work one day, he noticed that a large electrical cable running along the plant's ceiling had broken overnight, was coming loose from the hardware attaching it to the ceiling, and was dangling closer and closer to the plant floor. He and several of his coworkers immediately told their supervisor about the broken cable, but the supervisor did nothing about it. The group also told the supervisor's boss about the danger, but still nothing was done to correct it.

By about 11 a.m., the broken cable had dropped to the point where it was brushing against the truck body that Mike was welding. Sparks flew each time the cable and the truck body touched. Because he had a reasonable fear that an electrical shock transmitted from the broken cable could seriously injure or kill him, Mike refused to work until the hazard was fixed. His supervisor fired him for refusing to work. But, because the hazard fit OSHA's definitions of an imminent danger, OSHA ordered the company to reinstate Mike to his job with back wages once the cable was repaired.

If you are faced with an immediate danger at work, don't walk off the job. Instead, ask your employer to correct the hazard and assign you to other work in the meantime. If your employer refuses, stay at the worksite until your employer orders you to leave. Be sure to report the hazard to OSHA as soon as possible; reports of imminent danger are given top priority. Jot down the name of the OSHA officer you speak with and the time that you report the hazard. That will preserve your right to be paid back wages and other losses from the time that the hazard forced you to walk away from work.

Tracking OSHA Actions

Any citation issued by OSHA must be posted for at least three days in a conspicuous place within the workplace it affects. If the hazard specified in the citation is not corrected within three days after the citation is issued, then the citation must remain posted until it is corrected.

Compliance officers are required to inform those who originally filed a complaint of the action taken on it. If you need more information about the outcome of an OSHA investigation that affects your workplace, call, write, or visit your local OSHA office.

If OSHA has given your employer an extended time to remedy a workplace hazard, then you also have a right to request a copy of that abatement plan from your employer. Your other recourse is to obtain a copy from the OSHA compliance officer who handled your complaint.

Penalties for Retaliation

Under the OSH Act, it is illegal for an employer to fire or otherwise retaliate against you for filing an OSHA complaint or participating in an OSHA investigation. OSHA can order an employer that violates this rule to return you to your job and to reimburse you for damages, including lost wages, the value of lost benefit coverages, and the cost of searching for a new job. A number of state laws also protect against retaliation for reporting workplace health and safety violations. (See "State and Local Health and Safety Laws," below.)

However, you cannot enforce this restriction against retaliation by going directly to court; you must ask OSHA to intercede.

If you suspect illegal retaliation, you have 30 days from the time the illegal action took place to file a complaint with your local OSHA office. The outcome of your retaliation complaint may turn on whether you can prove that you were fired or demoted because you contacted authorities, not because your performance slipped or because economic cutbacks made the firing necessary. Be sure to back up your complaint with as much documentation as possible. (For details on how to document a dismissal, see "Getting Documentation" in Chapter 9.)

Once you have filed a complaint about retaliation, OSHA has 90 days to respond. If you have shown that you were fired or otherwise punished because of complaining to OSHA, the compliance officer handling your complaint will attempt to convince your employer to take the proper action to remedy the situation. For example, if you were demoted, the OSHA compliance officer would probably ask your employer to reinstate you to your original position and give you the back pay to which you are entitled.

If OSHA is unsuccessful in getting your employer to reverse the effects of the retaliation, it can sue your employer in federal court on your behalf.

Criminal Actions for OSH Act Violations

As noted, the enforcement arm of OSHA has the power in some situations to pursue criminal prosecutions against employers that fail to maintain a safe workplace, but it rarely does.

However, state prosecutors are increasingly bringing criminal charges, such as reckless endangerment and even manslaughter, against employers whose behavior seriously endangers workers.

You may want to contact your state's attorney general about the possibility of criminal action if your work conditions pose a serious threat of injury or death to you or your coworkers and you are not able to resolve your concerns through OSHA or other civil actions.

While employers can be prosecuted for criminal negligence when an employee dies as a result of violations of OSHA regulations, such convictions are rare. In fact, in the first 20 years the law was in effect, only one employer was convicted and sent to jail for such a death. The main reason for this low conviction rate is that, under the OSH Act, prosecutors must show that an employer's violation of workplace safety rules was willful —that is, done on purpose—a subjective standard that can be tough to meet.

State and Local Health and Safety Laws

Many states and municipalities have laws that mandate a certain level of safety in the workplace. These laws vary greatly in what they require, how they are enforced, and even which employers they cover.

Early on, California began enforcing the most powerful of these laws: It requires every employer in the state to have a written plan to prevent workplace injuries. A number of states have followed the lead, putting teeth and nails into the laws that protect workplace safety. For example, Texas maintains a 24-hour hotline for telephone reports of workplace safety violations and prohibits employers from discriminating against workers who use it.

A number of state laws specifically forbid employers from firing employees who assert their rights under workplace health and safety rules. (In Chapter 9, see "Violations of Public Policy.") Some state laws, like the OSH Act, give workers the right to refuse to work under certain conditions, although the workers may need to report the condition

first. And some states protect workers from retaliation for using state "right to know" laws: statutes that require employers to give workers information about hazardous substances on the job.

Still another group of state laws extends beyond the workplace to protect employees who report violations of laws and rules that create specific dangers to public health and safety. These laws, commonly referred to as whistleblower statutes, generally protect employees who are attempting to uphold a public policy of the state. For example, typical whistleblower statutes prohibit employees from being fired for reporting toxic dumping or fraudulent use of government funds. (In Chapter 9, see "Whistleblowing Violations," for more information.)

Sanitation Laws

Many state and local health and building codes offer guidance in how to keep your workplace safe. While not intended specifically to ensure workplace safety, these laws often include programs designed to ensure good sanitation and public safety in general.

For example, the health department of the city in which you work probably has the power to order an employer to improve restroom facilities that are leaking and causing unsanitary workplace conditions. And your local building inspector typically can order an employer to straighten out faulty electrical wiring that presents a shock or fire hazard to people working near that wiring.

When the Boss Doubles as a Bathroom Monitor

It wasn't big news to many when government health authorities slapped a $332,500 fine on Hudson Foods, a poultry processing plant in the town of Noel, Missouri. The plant had been inspected by the Occupational Safety and Health Administration (OSHA) 23 times in 24 years—a healthy number for an agency notoriously backlogged and selective in carrying out its charge of ferreting out workplace health and safety violations.

A number of news sources dutifully recounted the parade of transgressions OSHA inspectors had noted: blocked and restricted fire exits, failure to provide training in and enforce use of eye protective equipment, failure to provide training and issue procedures for handling hazardous chemicals, and failure to securely anchor machines.

Less widely reported was one innocuous sounding violation: insufficient toilet facilities. But few could fathom the human humiliation behind it all. Hudson workers claim they were required to ask permission before being allowed bathroom breaks; permission was denied as often as granted. Some say they were forced to urinate in their clothes or wear diapers to absorb the inevitable. Thom Hanson, chief regulatory compliance officer at Hudson, defended the company's position: The workers simply "need to ask supervisors to release them," he explained. "Normally, a relief person comes by and takes their place."

But relief was not always in sight, according to one woman who worked five years as a packer at Hudson. "It matters how good you get along with your supervisor. Sometimes they'll say no," she said. "And it's pretty hard to leave the line when you've got thousands of chickens coming at you."

OSHA regulations have long required that employers provide toilets in the workplace: at least six for the first 150 workers, and one more for each additional 40 workers. But in a twist of semantics that defies logic, the regulations mandate only the presence of toilets on the scene, not employees' rights to use them. In considering the Hudson complaints, OSHA officials found for the first time that the company in effect denied workers toilet facilities when it denied them the right to use them.

In the wake of the *Hudson* case and the ensuing public outcry, OSHA officials dictated at last that employers must give workers prompt and reasonable access to toilet facilities, even though the regulations do not specifically require it.

An official Standards and Compliance Letter issued by OSHA noted: "Toilets that employees are not allowed to use for extended periods cannot be said to be 'available' to those employees."

In other words, employers can no longer hide behind the lacking letter of the law. Employers that do not allow employees reasonable access to workplace toilets may now be cited and sanctioned by OSHA inspectors.

You can find state and local health and building codes at your city hall or county courthouse.

Tobacco Smoke in the Workplace

OSHA rules apply to tobacco smoke only in the most rare and extreme circumstances, such as when contaminants created by a manufacturing process combine with tobacco smoke to create a dangerous workplace air supply that fails OSHA standards. Workplace air quality standards and measurement techniques are so technical that typically only OSHA agents or consultants who specialize in environmental testing are able to determine when the air quality falls below allowable limits. But, when asked to intercede on early workplace complaints about tobacco smoke, Environmental Protection Agency (EPA) officials typically hedge that "exposures to the carbon monoxide or other toxic substances in the tobacco smoke rarely exceed current OSHA permissible exposure limits or PELs." (OSHA Standards Interpretation and Compliance Letter, 10/26/98.)

But the torturous effects of tobacco smoke on human health have now been clearly established and even certified by the government. A recent report by the Surgeon General, for example, estimated that secondhand tobacco smoke has caused the deaths of 2.5 million nonsmokers since 1964.

Although there is no federal law that directly controls smoking at work, a majority of states protect workers from unwanted smoke in the workplace. In addition, hundreds of city and county ordinances restrict smoking in the workplace. (See the appendix for contact details for organizations with current information on laws that restrict smoking in your workplace.)

At the same time, over half the states make it illegal to discriminate against employees or potential employees because they smoke off duty during nonworking hours.

Protections for Nonsmokers

The sentiment against smoking in the workplace and any other shared space has grown so strong that some companies increase their attractiveness to job seekers by mentioning in their Help Wanted advertising that they maintain a smokefree workplace.

Many states now ban smoking in all places of employment; others allow employers to set aside designated smoking areas if they wish. However, smoking areas typically must be outdoors or must be ventilated and segregated in a way that prevents smoke from entering the rest of the workplace. And in many states, smoking is not allowed within a certain distance of the entrance to a workplace.

Clearing the Air in the Workplace

If you work in a state and facility where others may smoke, and your health problems are severely aggravated by coworkers' smoking, there are a number of steps you can take:

- **Ask your employer for an accommodation.** Successful accommodations for smoke-sensitive workers have included installing additional ventilation systems, restricting smoking areas to outdoor areas or special rooms, and segregating smokers and nonsmokers.

    EXAMPLE: Carmelita's sinus problems were made almost unbearable by the smoke created by her coworkers in an insurance claims processing office. Because her job involves primarily individual work on a computer terminal and no contact with people outside the company, Carmelita convinced her employer to allow her to start her workday at 4 p.m., just an hour before her coworkers leave for home. When Carmelita needs to discuss something with coworkers or her supervisor, she does so via email or at occasional one-hour staff meetings that begin at 4 p.m., at which smoking is not allowed.

- **Check local and state laws.** As indicated, a growing number of local and state laws prohibit smoking in the workplace. Most of them also set out specific procedures for pursuing complaints. If you are unable to locate local laws on smoking, check with a nonsmokers' rights group. (See the appendix for contact details.)

- **File a federal complaint.** If you have a disability that is exacerbated by secondhand smoke, and your employer refuses to provide a reasonable accommodation, you might want to file a complaint under the Americans With Disabilities Act. (See Chapter 7.)

- **Workers' compensation.** If you develop an injury or illness due to secondhand smoke in the workplace, you can typically file a workers' compensation claim. In addition to receiving covered medical treatment, you can receive partial wage loss benefits. (See Chapter 12.)

- **Unemployment insurance.** If you are forced to leave a job because of the dangers of secondhand smoke, you might be eligible for unemployment benefits depending on your state's rules. (See Chapter 11.)

There are also common exceptions written into antismoking laws. Often, their protections do not apply to:

- places where private social functions are typically held, such as rented banquet rooms in hotels
- private offices occupied exclusively by smokers
- bars and casinos, and
- inmates at correctional facilities and hospital patients, who usually must comply with the rules of the institution while they are confined.

Protections for Smokers

Because of the potentially higher costs of health care insurance, absenteeism, unemployment insurance, and workers' compensation insurance associated with employees who smoke, some companies now refuse to hire anyone who admits to being a smoker on a job application or in prehiring interviews.

Some states protect both smokers and nonsmokers by insisting that employers provide a smokefree environment for nonsmokers and by prohibiting discrimination against an employee who smokes off the job or otherwise in compliance with a workplace smoking policy.

Protection for smokers may be couched in off-duty conduct laws that prohibit discrimination against employees who use "lawful products" or engage in lawful activities outside the workplace before or after workhours. Wisconsin law goes

an extra step and forbids employers from discriminating against both workers who use and workers who do not use lawful products.

Several of the state laws that prohibit discrimination against smokers do not apply if not smoking is truly a job requirement. In these states it is likely, for example, that a worker in the front office of the American Cancer Society—a group outspoken in its disdain of tobacco—could be fired for taking up smoking.

And even in those states that offer some protection to smokers, employers are often free to charge smokers higher health insurance premiums than nonsmoking employees.

Pesticide Laws

Misused and overused pesticides are one of the greatest safety threats to people who work on farms, in other parts of the food industry, and in gardening and lawn care companies, to name just a few. Heavy exposure to some of these chemicals can cause serious health problems and even death. For people with certain types of allergies, even small doses of some pesticides can cause severe illness.

However, as early as 1975, a federal court ruled that the U.S. Environmental Protection Agency (EPA)—not the OSH Act—is responsible for making sure that workers are not injured by exposure to pesticides at work. (*Organized Migrants in Community Action, Inc. v. Brennan,* 520 F.2d 1161.)

There have been some disputes between the EPA and OSHA over this ruling in recent years; and the question of enforcement responsibility remains unsettled decades later. If you believe that you or your coworkers are being exposed to dangerous doses of pesticides at work, the best thing to do is to file complaints with both OSHA and the EPA and let them decide who gets to handle the matter. To find the nearest EPA office, visit www.epa.gov/aboutepa and select "Regional Offices."

Hazardous Substances Laws

Most states now have laws that restrict or regulate the use, storage, and handling of hazardous substances in the workplace. These laws vary greatly from state to state. The identification of toxic and otherwise hazardous substances is a very technical matter that most often is the responsibility of the state's labor department.

In some cases, workers detect that they are being exposed to a hazardous substance when one or more of them notices that a health problem—a skin rash or eye irritation for example—coincides with work hours.

If you think that you are being subjected to hazardous substances in your workplace, follow up your complaint to OSHA with a call to your state's labor department. (See the appendix for contact details.)

EXAMPLE: Hanchung took a job as a forklift driver in a metal plating plant. After his first few hours at work, his eyes began to water and became badly irritated. On the way home from work, Hanchung visited a walk-in medical clinic, where the doctor used a cotton swab to take samples of skin residues from his face. A few days later, the doctor told Hanchung that the problem with his eyes was a reaction to sulfuric acid that apparently was in the air where he worked and had settled on his skin and eyes.

Hanchung filed a complaint with OSHA and his state's labor department. As a result of the joint investigation, OSHA ordered his employer to construct an enclosure around processing areas that used sulfuric acid and to provide Hanchung and his coworkers with protective clothing to wear at work while the enclosures were being built. ●

Illegal Discrimination

It is almost always illegal for employers to discriminate against workers because of their race, skin color, gender, religious beliefs, national origin, genetic information, disability, or age (if the employee is at least 40 years old). In many states, it is also illegal for employers to discriminate against workers based on sexual orientation, marital status, or other traits.

The most powerful antidiscrimination law governing the workplace is Title VII of the federal Civil Rights Act of 1964. It originally outlawed discrimination based on race, skin color, gender, religious beliefs, or national origin, and it created the Equal Employment Opportunity Commission (EEOC) to administer and enforce the legal standards it set.

Today, a number of additional federal laws—several of them amendments to Title VII—are used to fight unfair workplace discrimination:

- The Equal Pay Act of 1963 specifically outlaws discrimination in wages on the basis of gender. (See "Title VII of the Civil Rights Act," below.)
- The Age Discrimination in Employment Act (ADEA) outlaws workplace discrimination on the basis of age (40 and older). (See "The Age Discrimination in Employment Act," below.)
- The Older Workers Benefit Protection Act is an amendment to the ADEA, passed in 1990, that specifically outlaws discrimination in employment benefit programs on the basis of an employee's age. It too applies only to employees age 40 and older. It also puts restrictions on employers' use of waivers in which employees sign away their rights to take legal action against age-based discrimination. (See "The Older Workers Benefit Protection Act," below.)
- The Pregnancy Discrimination Act (PDA), which makes it illegal for an employer to refuse to hire a pregnant woman, to terminate her employment, or to compel her to take maternity leave, was passed in 1978 as an additional amendment to Title VII. (In Chapter 4, see "The Pregnancy Discrimination Act," for more on pregnancy-related leave.)
- The Americans with Disabilities Act (ADA), enacted in 1990, makes it illegal to discriminate against people because of their physical or mental disabilities. (See "The Americans with Disabilities Act," below.)
- The Labor Management Relations Act and amendments, passed as a patchwork of protections, generally makes it illegal to discriminate against workers for belonging to or refusing to join a labor union. (See Chapter 15.)
- The Genetic Information Nondiscrimination Act (GINA), which took effect in 2009, prohibits discrimination against employees or applicants because of genetic information. GINA also requires employers to keep

this information confidential. (In Chapter 5, see "Workplace Testing," and "The Genetic Information Nondiscrimination Act," below.)

Title VII of the Civil Rights Act

Most of the laws that broadly protect employees from discrimination in the workplace have been enacted through the years as amendments to the Civil Rights Act, also known as Title VII. (42 U.S.C. §§ 2000 and following.)

Who Is Covered

Title VII applies to all companies and labor unions with 15 or more employees. It also governs employment agencies, state and local governments, and apprenticeship programs.

Title VII does not cover:

- federal government employees (special procedures have been established to enforce antidiscrimination laws for them) and
- independent contractors.

Illegal Discrimination

Under Title VII, employers may not use race, skin color, gender, pregnancy, religious beliefs, or national origin as the basis for decisions on hirings, promotions, dismissals, pay raises, benefits, work assignments, leaves of absence, or just about any other aspect of employment. Title VII covers everything about the

employment relationship, from prehiring ads to working conditions, performance reviews, and postemployment references.

Counting Employees: Not as Easy as It Sounds

The Civil Rights Act is clearly written to apply to employers with 15 or more employees. But courts across the nation have been of differing minds when it comes to deciding which employees should stand up and be counted.

Most courts used a counting system in which both hourly and part-time employees were considered in the total, but only on the days they were at work or on paid leave.

However, the U.S. Supreme Court ruled that this is a disingenuous shell game. The Court held that employees should be defined and tallied for purposes of Title VII according to the payroll method. Under the payroll method, employers are covered if they have 15 or more employees on the payroll for each working day in 20 or more weeks, regardless of the actual work the employees perform or whether they are compensated for each of those days. (*Walters v. Metropolitan Educational Enterprises, Inc.*, 519 U.S. 202 (1997).)

This judicial clarification can be important if your discrimination claim is dismissed because your employer is too small. You may be able to successfully argue that part-time workers and those on leave should be included in the final tally of employees.

Remedies Available

There are a number of remedies that an employee who suffers the effects of discrimination on the job can obtain.

Reinstatement and promotion. A court can order that the employee be rehired, promoted, or reassigned to whatever job was lost because of the discrimination.

Wages and job-connected losses. A court can award any salary and benefits the employee lost as a result of being fired, demoted, or forced to quit because of discrimination. This can include loss of wages, pension contributions, medical benefits, overtime pay, bonuses, back pay, shift differential pay, vacation pay, and participation in a company profit-sharing plan.

Compensatory and punitive damages. A court can award compensatory damages to the employee for the emotional harm caused by the discrimination, as well as any out-of-pocket expenses the employee incurred (such as medical bills or job search costs). A court can also award punitive damages, which are aimed at punishing the employer and deterring future discrimination. However, Title VII places a combined cap on compensatory and punitive damages. The cap is between $50,000 and $300,000, depending on the size of the employer.

Injunctive relief. A court can direct the company to change its policies to stop discrimination and to prevent similar incidents in the future.

Attorneys' fees. If the employee wins a case, a court can order the company to pay attorneys' fees and legal costs.

Filing a Complaint With the EEOC

Compared to most other government agencies, the EEOC has very well-defined procedures for filing complaints. But the EEOC also operates through a complex hierarchy of offices and has strict time limits for filing complaints, which usually range from a few months to nearly a year. Pay particular attention to timing if you decide to take action against what you believe is illegal workplace discrimination. (See "When to File," below.)

Employees must file a complaint with the EEOC before they can pursue a discrimination lawsuit against an employer in court.

Where to File

Title VII complaints can be filed at:
- state and regional offices of the EEOC, and
- local fair employment practice (FEP) agency offices. These are not federal offices, but state and local agencies that have been designated as representatives of the EEOC. (See "State Agencies That Enforce Laws Prohibiting Discrimination in Employment," in the appendix, for contact information.)

There are EEOC offices throughout the United States. Normally, it is best to file a complaint at the office nearest to you or your place of employment. But, if there is no office nearby or in your state, you can legally file a complaint in any office. To find the nearest office, go to the EEOC's website, www.eeoc.gov; you can find a list of local offices under the "Contact Us" tab.

Tips for Dealing With the EEOC

There are a number of things to keep in mind when helping to shuttle your claim through the EEOC bureaucracy most efficiently:

- **Stay vigilant.** Do not assume that the EEOC will do everything and that you don't have to monitor what is going on. Check periodically with the EEOC to find out what is happening with your case.
- **Be assertive.** If some EEOC action—or, more likely, inaction—is causing you serious problems, call that to the attention of the people handling your case.
- **Read—and reread—the fine print.** When you file a charge with the EEOC, a worker there will ask you to read and sign a written statement summarizing your claim. Be sure to scrutinize the form carefully before signing. Some later argue that their words were twisted or misstated on the EEOC charge form, which can be hard to prove once the signed form wends its way into the system.
- **Keep your options open.** Filing a claim with the EEOC does not prevent you from taking other action to deal with your case. You still have a right to try to solve the problem on your own or use a company complaint procedure. You also have the right to hire an attorney to file a lawsuit, if that is appropriate for your situation.

When to File

If your state has its own equal employment opportunity laws that protect against the type of discrimination you are facing, you will typically be allowed 300 days after the act of discrimination occurred to file a complaint. But, if your state has no law covering your situation, you have only 180 days to file. (See "State Laws Prohibiting Discrimination in Employment," at the end of this chapter.) The safest way to proceed is to assume that 180 days is the limit in your case and file your complaint as soon as possible.

In some cases, you will not be able to recognize illegal discrimination from a single action by an employer. If you discern a pattern of illegal discrimination that extends back more than 180 days, the safest way to proceed is to assume that the clock began to run with the event that caused you to recognize the pattern and file a complaint as soon as possible. These cases are often complicated, so you should consider consulting a lawyer for help. (In Chapter 17, see "Hiring a Lawyer.")

EXAMPLE: A woman who worked with Jan in a pharmaceutical lab was fired in January. Two months later, the lab fired another woman. In June, a third woman was fired.

When the third woman was fired, Jan began to notice that the firings seemed to have nothing to do with job performance. Although the lab employed several men with less experience and whose job performance was not as good as the three women who had been fired, no men had been fired.

After consistently receiving positive performance reviews, Jan's supervisor informed her the lab staff was being reduced and she should start looking for another job. Jan took a few weeks to gather evidence to support her belief that the company was illegally discriminating against women on the basis of gender and then filed a complaint with the EEOC in September.

Organizing Your Evidence

Because illegal discrimination rarely takes the form of one simple event, it is important to organize your evidence of illegal discrimination before contacting the EEOC to file a complaint.

Whenever possible, keep a log of the date, time, location, people involved, and nature of actions that demonstrate any pattern of illegal discrimination. Keep a file of any documents that your employer gives you, such as written performance reviews or disciplinary notices. (See "Documenting the Problem" in Chapter 1.)

If you present your evidence to the EEOC in an organized way—without yielding to the temptation to vent your displeasure with your employer's policies and practices—you will raise the chances of your complaint getting full attention and consideration from the EEOC investigators.

How the EEOC Handles Complaints

When you file a complaint, an EEOC staff lawyer or investigator will typically interview you and evaluate whether your employer's actions appear to violate Title VII. If the interviewer does not feel that the incident warrants a complaint, he or she will tell you so. You may have to think about other options, such as pursuing a complaint through your company's established complaint procedure.

If the interviewer feels your complaint states a violation of Title VII, he or she will fill out an EEOC Charge of Discrimination form and send it to you to review and sign. After receiving your complaint, the EEOC should interview your employer and then try to mediate a settlement.

That is what the EEOC's operating regulations provide. And, for the most part, the EEOC does what it is supposed to do. But do not expect every claim to proceed as described. EEOC offices differ in caseloads, local procedures, and the quality of their personnel. Investigations are usually slow, sometimes taking years. The EEOC takes only a tiny fraction of its cases to court. These and other factors can have an impact on how a case is actually handled.

Penalties for Retaliation

It is illegal for your employer to retaliate against you either for filing a Title VII complaint or for cooperating in the investigation of one. But, to take advantage of this protection, you must be able to prove that

BFOQs: Jobs That Require Discrimination

Under Title VII and many state and local antidiscrimination laws, an employer may intentionally use gender, religious beliefs, or national origin as the basis for employment decisions but only if the employer can show that the job has special requirements that make such discrimination necessary.

When an employer establishes that such a special circumstance exists, it is called a bona fide occupational qualification (BFOQ).

EXAMPLE: A religious denomination employs counselors who answer telephone inquiries from those interested in becoming members of that religion. The employer could likely refuse to hire people who did not believe in that religion.

In general, the courts, the EEOC, and state equal employment opportunity agencies prohibit the use of BFOQs except where clearly necessary. They typically require any employer using a BFOQ in employment decisions to prove conclusively that the BFOQ is essential to the successful operation of the company or organization. Typically, this type of permissible discrimination turns on gender. The classic example is the job of a wet nurse, who must be female. But theaters, cosmetic companies, and modeling agencies have also succeeded in arguing that workers hired needed to be of a particular gender to get the job done.

You are most likely to encounter a BFOQ on a job application, in which case the employer must state on the application that the employment qualification covered by the questions would otherwise be illegal but has been approved by the EEOC.

the retaliation occurred because you filed a complaint. (In Chapter 9, see "Retaliation.")

And historically, you were required to prove that the retaliation was work-related. However, in 2006, the U.S. Supreme Court dramatically changed and expanded the scope of such claims by redefining retaliation, holding for the first time that an employer's harmful actions need not be related to employment or the workplace to qualify as Title VII retaliation.

The same case also resolved the question of how serious the harm must be before it qualifies as retaliation. In the case, the employer, Burlington Northern, reassigned Sheila White, the only female forklift operator, to a less desirable position and suspended her without pay for more than a month after she complained of workplace discrimination. Burlington then claimed White was not sufficiently harmed, since the new position was within the same work classification and her back pay was eventually reinstated. The justices, however, were persuaded by the reality that the new position was less prestigious and "by all accounts more arduous and dirtier." They also underscored that while she was eventually repaid, White and her family had to live for 37 days without income, noting her testimony at trial: "That was the worst Christmas I had out of my life. No money, no income—and that made all of us feel bad." The Court held that as long as "a reasonable employee" finds an action to be "materially adverse," it can qualify as retaliation in a Title VII claim. (*Burlington Northern & Santa Fe Ry. Co. v. White*, 548 U.S. 53 (2006).)

Filing a Title VII Lawsuit

In the very likely event that the EEOC does not complete its investigation of your complaint within 180 days, you can request a right-to-sue letter that authorizes you to file a lawsuit in court against the offending employer. Because filing a lawsuit requires detailed knowledge of the law and court procedures, you will probably need to hire a lawyer. (In Chapter 17, see "Hiring a Lawyer.") A number of specialized organizations offer legal referrals and advice on workplace discrimination. (See the appendix for contact details.) Once you receive a right-to-sue letter, you have only 90 days to file a lawsuit, so deadlines are very important at this point of the Title VII process.

The Equal Pay Act

A federal law, the Equal Pay Act (29 U.S.C. § 206), requires employers to pay all employees equally for equal work, regardless of their gender. It was passed in 1963 as an amendment to the Fair Labor Standards Act. (In Chapter 2, see "Rights Under the FLSA.")

While the Act technically protects both women and men from gender discrimination in pay rates, it was passed to help rectify the pay disparity that female workers faced due to sex discrimination. And, in practice, this law almost always has been applied to situations where women are being paid less than men for doing similar jobs.

The wage gap has narrowed slowly since 1980, when women's weekly earnings were only 64% of men's. Today, women make closer to 80% of what men make on a nationwide basis. And the figure is significantly lower for African American women (63%) and Hispanic women (54%).

In reality, the Equal Pay Act probably hasn't had an overwhelming impact on the gender pay gap. The law's biggest weakness is that it is strictly applied only when men and women are doing the same work. Because women have historically been banned from many types of work and have had only limited entree to managerial positions, the Equal Pay Act in reality helps a small number of women.

To successfully raise a claim under the Equal Pay Act, you must show that you and an employee of the opposite sex:

Keeping the Faith at Work

Claims of religious discrimination have been on the rise: In the last four years, the EEOC has received more than 3,400 religion claims annually. Theologians hail this burst in litigation as a sign that Americans are returning to the fold. Pessimists say that workers are just looking for another excuse to work less. And politicians point to politics.

Title VII of the Civil Rights Act and most state laws prohibit employers from discriminating on the basis of religious beliefs. Where workers articulate a need to express their religious beliefs and practice in the workplace, employers are generally required to accommodate them, unless doing so would cause the employer undue hardship.

As in all other claims where the term comes up, the meaning of undue hardship in this context gives employers and courts cause for pause. The U.S. Supreme Court has pronounced twice on the issue.

In *Trans World Airlines Inc. v. Hardison*, 432 U.S. 63 (1977), an airline employee claimed that his religion, the Worldwide Church of God, forbade him from working on Saturdays. TWA union officials argued that allowing the employee to change shifts would violate a collective bargaining agreement that banned the arrangement for workers without sufficient seniority. The Court agreed, holding that the union agreement was more sacrosanct than the religious practices.

Nearly a decade later, the Court again heard the pleas of a member of the Worldwide Church of God. This time, a high school teacher argued that he needed six days off per school year for religious observance. The sticking point again was a collective bargaining agreement providing only three days of paid leave for religious observation. The Court waffled some in its opinion, holding that the court below could decide whether providing unpaid leave to make up the balance was a reasonable accommodation. (*Ansonia Board of Education v. Philbrook*, 479 U.S. 60 (1986).)

Since then, the lower courts that have faced the issue have reached grandly differing conclusions about what is an undue burden for employers. A Florida police officer's request for Saturdays off was denied "for public safety reasons." A Tennessee jury upheld the denial of a request by Muslim factory workers to take a break for sunset prayers; this would have required temporarily shutting down a production line. But a New Mexico court ruled that a truck driver was illegally denied a job because of his practice of smoking peyote during a Native American ritual. And a California court shot down an employer's order that banned religious artifacts in all workers' cubicles and prevented them from any type of "religious advocacy" on the job.

For now, employers and employees grappling with the issue would be best served to work together to reach a mutually agreeable accommodation and keep the issue out of the uncharted territory of court decisions.

- are working in the same place
- are doing equal work under similar working conditions, and
- are receiving unequal pay.

The difference in pay must be based on gender rather than seniority, merit or some other legitimate performance-based reason.

Who Is Covered

The Equal Pay Act applies to all employees covered by the Fair Labor Standards Act, which means virtually all employees are covered. (In Chapter 2, see "The Fair Labor Standards Act.")

Determining Equal Work

Jobs do not have to be identical for the courts to consider them equal. In general, two jobs are equal for the purposes of the Equal Pay Act when both require equal levels of skill, effort, and responsibility and are performed under similar conditions.

There is a lot of room for interpretation here, of course. But the general rule is that, if there are only small differences in the skill, effort, or responsibility required, two jobs should still be regarded as equal. The focus is on the duties actually performed. Job titles, classifications, and descriptions may weigh in to the determination but are not all that is considered.

The biggest problems arise where two jobs are basically the same, but one includes a few extra duties. It is perfectly legal to award higher pay for the extra duties, but some courts have looked askance at workplaces in which the higher-paying jobs with extra duties are consistently reserved for workers of one gender.

Doing the Math on the Gender Gap

According to the WAGE Project, the difference between women's and men's earnings can really add up over a lifetime of work. Female high school graduates earn $700,000 less than their male counterparts over their work life; college graduates earn $1.2 million less; and women with a professional postgraduate degree earn a whopping $2 million less than men with the same credentials. Check out all of the figures—and what you can do to change them—at www.wageproject.org.

Determining Equal Pay

In general, pay systems that result in employees of one gender being paid less than the other gender for doing equal work are allowed under the Equal Pay Act if the pay system is actually based on a factor other than gender, such as a merit or seniority system.

EXAMPLE: In 1990, the Ace Widget Company was founded and initially hired 50 male widget makers. Many of those men are still working there. Since its founding, the company has expanded and hired 50 more widget makers, half of them female. All of the widget makers at Ace are doing equal work, but because the company awards raises systematically based on seniority or length of employment, many of the older male workers earn substantially more per hour than their female coworkers. Nevertheless, the pay system at Ace Widget does not violate the Equal Pay Act because its pay differences are based on a factor other than gender.

How to Take Action

The Equal Pay Act (EPA) was passed one year before Title VII of the Civil Rights Act. Both laws prohibit wage discrimination based on gender, but Title VII goes beyond ensuring equal pay for equal work, as it also

---

State Equal Pay Laws

Equal pay has received a fair amount of attention, at least at the state level, in recent years. The gender pay gap remains steady, despite federal law outlawing wage discrimination decades ago. As a result, many states have stepped up to adopt new laws aimed at narrowing the pay gap. Most states have some form of equal pay law on the books. These laws, which apply to almost all employers in the state, take one or more of the following approaches:

- Some state laws loosen the standard for equal pay violations—for example, it might be illegal to pay different wages for "substantially similar" or "comparable" work, instead of the stricter "equal work" standard required by the federal Equal Pay Act.
- Some state laws shift the burden of proof to the employer, making it easier for employees to bring claims. For example, an employee might need to show only that another employee of the opposite sex who holds a similar position is being paid more. The employer is then required to show a legitimate reason for the difference.
- Because wage secrecy can lead to continuing disparities, some state laws prohibit employers from barring employees from discussing their wages.
- A few states have banned employers from asking job applicants about their prior salaries. These laws are meant to prevent employers from perpetuating wage discrimination by previous employers.

To learn more, contact your state department of labor. Contact information is in the appendix.

bars discrimination in hiring, firing, and promotions. In addition, Title VII broadly prohibits other forms of discrimination, including that based on race, color, religion, and national origin. (See "Title VII of the Civil Rights Act," above, for a detailed discussion of how to take action.)

EXAMPLE: Suzanne works as a reservations agent for an airline, answering calls on the company's toll-free telephone number. About half of the other reservations agents in her office are men, who are typically paid $1 per hour more than Suzanne and the other female agents. What's more, the company has established a dress code for female reservations agents, but not for the male agents.

If Suzanne decides to file a discrimination complaint against her employer, the EPA would apply to the pay difference between females and males. Title VII would apply to both the pay difference and the fact that only the female employees in her office are held to a dress code.

In cases where both Title VII and the Equal Pay Act apply, the EPA offers one big advantage: You can file a lawsuit under the EPA without first filing a complaint with the EEOC.

However, you also stand to gain less compensation in an EPA claim. Damages are limited to back pay, an additional sum equal to your back pay award (called "liquidated damages"), and attorneys' fees and court costs. You are entitled to no additional damages for emotional distress to punish the wrongdoing employer.

EPA claims are also subject to different time limits than Title VII claims. A lawsuit under the Equal Pay Act must typically be filed within two years from the date of the violation (or three years, if the violation is deemed willful by the court). Title VII claims, on the other hand, must be filed with the EEOC within 180 days from the violation. In 2007, one employee learned the hard way how short the 180-day deadline can be. Lilly Ledbetter, a production supervisor at a Goodyear tire plant in Alabama, sued her employer for gender discrimination. She claimed that over the years, she had received lower performance reviews and smaller pay increases than her male colleagues because of her gender. The cumulative effect of Goodyear's gender bias behavior, Ledbetter alleged, was that her salary near to her retirement was 20% lower than that of her male counterparts.

But the Court never even got to the merits of her case, dismissing it as filed too late. The Court held that the 180-day time limit for presenting a wage discrimination claim begins at the date the pay was agreed upon, not the date of the most recent paycheck. (*Ledbetter v. Goodyear Tire & Rubber Co., Inc.*, 550 U.S. 618 (2007).)

In an effort to correct this harsh result, the Lilly Ledbetter Fair Pay Act was signed into law in 2009. The law declares that each discriminatory paycheck is a violation of wage discrimination laws, which restarts the 180-day clock for filing claims. In other words, an employee like Lilly Ledbetter can now file a claim within 180 days of her most recent discriminatory paycheck, even though her employer set the discriminatory pay long ago.

The Genetic Information Nondiscrimination Act

The Genetic Information Nondiscrimination Act (GINA), makes it illegal to discriminate against employees or applicants based on their genetic information. The law also forbids using genetic information in making employment decisions, restricts how and when employers can acquire genetic information, and strictly limits disclosing it to others.

Who Is Covered

GINA's protections apply to workplaces with 15 or more employees.

Defining Genetic Information

Under the law, "genetic information" broadly includes information from an individual's genetic tests and the genetic tests of an individual's family members, as well as information about any disease, disorder, or condition of an individual's family members.

Family medical history is protected because it is often used to determine whether someone has an increased risk of getting a disease, disorder, or condition in the future, yet it realistically tells nothing about an individual's current ability to work.

Prohibited Behavior

GINA forbids discrimination based on genetic information in all aspects of employment, including hiring, firing, pay, job assignments, promotions, layoffs, training, fringe benefits, or any other term or condition of employment.

The law also makes it illegal to harass a person because of his or her genetic information. Harassment can include making offensive or derogatory remarks about an applicant or employee's genetic information, or about the genetic information of a relative of the applicant or employee. The EEOC makes clear that, as with other types of harassment on the job, the law doesn't prohibit occasional teasing, offhand comments, or isolated incidents that are not very serious.

It is also illegal to fire, demote, harass, or otherwise retaliate against an applicant or employee for filing a charge of discrimination, participating in a discrimination proceeding (such as a discrimination investigation or lawsuit) or otherwise opposing discrimination.

GINA prohibits employers from requiring or requesting that employees provide genetic information. For example, an employer may not ask applicants to take genetic tests or inquire about family health history during an interview. If an employer acquires genetic information about an employee (through one of the exceptions discussed below), the employer must keep that information confidential and must not consider it in making job decisions.

Exceptions to the Law

While GINA generally makes it illegal for employers to plumb for genetic information about applicants and employees, there are several narrow exceptions to this prohibition:

- Inadvertent acquisitions of genetic information do not violate GINA (for example, if a manager or supervisor overhears someone talking about a family member's illness).
- Genetic information may be obtained as part of voluntary health or genetic services offered by the employer, but only if the employee consents in writing and the employer receives the results in aggregate terms that don't identify specific employees.
- Family medical history may be acquired as part of the certification process for FMLA leave or leave under similar state or local laws, if an employee is asking for leave for a serious health condition.

- Learning about the genetic information through commercially and publicly available documents, such as newspapers, is permitted, as long as the employer is not searching those sources with the intent of finding it.
- Acquiring the information through a genetic monitoring program that monitors the biological effects of toxic substances in the workplace is permitted if the monitoring is required by law or the employee consents in writing.
- And finally, employers that engage in DNA testing for law enforcement purposes as a forensic lab or for purposes of human remains identification may acquire genetic information, but may use the DNA markers only for quality control to detect sample contamination.

The Age Discrimination in Employment Act

The federal Age Discrimination in Employment Act (ADEA) is the single most important law protecting the rights of older workers. It provides that workers who are 40 or older cannot be harassed because of their age or discriminated against because of age in any employment decision. Perhaps the single most important rule under the ADEA is that no worker can be forced to retire.

The Act prohibits age discrimination in hiring, discharges, layoffs, promotion, wages, health care coverage, pension accrual, other terms and conditions of employment, referrals by employment agencies, and membership in and the activities of unions.

Of all the possible claims of workplace discrimination, age discrimination has the broadest potential reach; most workers will live to be 40. And the protection is likely to become even more important. We live in a time where life expectancy is increasing, the older population is expanding rapidly, and many older workers stay in the workforce for a long time, many past age 70.

An amendment to the ADEA, the Older Workers Benefit Protection Act (discussed below), sets out specifics of how and when ADEA protections can be waived.

The ADEA is enforced, along with other discrimination complaints, by the EEOC. (See "Title VII of the Civil Rights Act," above, for more on procedure.) A number of national organizations can also provide legal referrals and help in evaluating age discrimination complaints. (See the appendix for contact information.)

Who Is Covered

The ADEA applies only to employees age 40 and older, and only to workplaces with 20 or more employees. The ADEA covers employees of labor organizations and local and federal governments. State workers are protected by the law but are limited to having the EEOC act to enforce it on their behalf.

There are a number of exceptions to the broad protection of the ADEA:

- Executives or people "in high policy-making positions" can be forced to retire at age 65 if they would receive annual retirement pension benefits worth $44,000 or more.
- There are special exceptions for police and fire personnel, tenured university faculty, and certain federal employees in the fields of law enforcement and air traffic control. If you are in one of these categories, check with your personnel office or benefits plan office for details.
- Another exception to the federal age discrimination law occurs when age is an essential part of a particular job. This exception is called a bona fide occupational qualification (BFOQ). An employer that sets age limits on a particular job must be able to prove: the limit is reasonably necessary to the essence of the employer's business; all or substantially all people over the age limit would be unable to do the job safely or efficiently; and it would be highly impractical for the employer to assess each person's ability to do the job on an individual basis.

State Laws

Most states have laws banning age discrimination in employment. (See the chart, "State Laws Prohibiting Discrimination in

Employment," at the end of the chapter.) An individual working in a state with such a law can choose to file a complaint under state law, federal law (ADEA), or both.

In many cases, the state law can provide greater protection than the federal law. For example, several states provide age discrimination protection to workers who are younger than 40, and some state laws apply to employers with fewer than 20 employees. Even if the protection offered by your state law is the same as that provided by the federal law, you may get better results pursuing your rights under state law. A state agency entrusted with investigating and enforcing its own age discrimination law may provide easier, quicker, and more aggressive prosecution of your complaint than the overburdened EEOC.

The Older Workers Benefit Protection Act

The main purpose of the Older Workers Benefit Protection Act, an amendment to the ADEA that passed in 1990, is to make it clearly illegal:

- to use an employee's age as the basis for discrimination in benefits, and
- to target older workers for their staff-cutting programs.

Some parts of this law are very difficult for anyone but a benefits administrator to understand. However, one provision of the law that you are most likely to run into is the restriction on legal waivers of ADEA claims.

By signing a waiver—often called a release or covenant not to sue—an employee agrees not to take any legal action, such as filing an age discrimination lawsuit, against the employer. In return for signing the waiver, the employer gives the employee an incentive to leave voluntarily, such as a severance pay package that exceeds the company's standard policy.

This type of transaction was very popular in the early 1990s among large corporations that wanted to reduce their payroll costs. Because older workers who have been with a company a long time typically cost more in salary and benefits than younger workers, most staff-cutting programs were directed at older workers. But cutting only older workers constitutes illegal age discrimination, so companies commonly induced the older workers to sign away their rights to sue their former employers. In colloquial parlance, these deals are often referred to as Golden Handshakes. This cruel squeeze play is now somewhat limited.

Under the Older Workers Benefit Protection Act, you must be given at least 21 days to decide whether or not to sign such a waiver that has been presented to you individually. If the waiver is presented to a group of employees, each of you must be given at least 45 days to decide whether or not to sign. In either case, you have seven days after agreeing to such a waiver to revoke your decision.

Who Is Covered

The Older Workers Benefit Protection Act applies to nonunion employees in private workplaces who are at least 40 years old.

Restrictions on Agreements Not to Sue

There are a number of other key restrictions the Older Workers Benefit Protection Act places on agreements not to sue.

- Your employer must make the waiver understandable to the average individual eligible for the program in which the waiver is being used.
- The waiver may not cover any rights or claims that you discover after you sign it, and it must specify that it covers your rights under the ADEA.
- Your employer must offer you something of value—over and above what is already owed to you—in exchange for your signature on the waiver.
- Your employer must advise you, in writing, that you have the right to consult an attorney before you sign the waiver.
- If the offer is being made to a class of employees (as part of an early retirement incentive program, for example), your employer must inform you in writing how the class of employees is defined, the job titles and ages of all the individuals to whom the offer is being made, and the ages of all the employees in the same job classification or unit of the company to whom the offer is not being made.

Employers are allowed no room to hedge on any one of these requirements. A waiver that does not comply with all the absolute requirements is invalid. The U.S. Supreme Court reaffirmed this in a case decision, holding that an employee who signed a deficient waiver could not only sue for age discrimination, but also did not have to return the severance pay she received from her former employer for signing the invalid waiver. *(Oubre v. Entergy Operations, Inc., 522 U.S. 422 (1998).)*

Negotiating a Better Deal

The Older Workers Benefits Protection Act gives additional legal protections if your employer offers you the opportunity to participate in a staff reduction program. The Act indirectly puts you in a position to negotiate the terms of your departure.

The fact that your employer has offered an incentive tells you that the company wants you gone and is worried that you might file a lawsuit for wrongful discharge. (In Chapter 9, see "When a Firing May Be Illegal.") Although company heads may say that you have only two choices—accept or reject the offer—there is nothing preventing you from making a counteroffer. For example, after taking a week or two to think, you might go back to your employer and agree to leave voluntarily if your severance pay is doubled.

As in all employment transactions, it is wise to advise your employer of your decision in writing and to keep a copy of that letter, along with copies of all documents given to you by your employer as part of the staff reduction program. If you refuse to accept such an offer and are later dismissed, you may be able to allege illegal age discrimination as a basis for challenging your dismissal.

How to Take Action

If you believe that an employer has violated your rights under the Older Workers Benefit Protection Act, you can file a complaint with the EEOC just as you would for any other workplace discrimination prohibited by Title VII, discussed above. Note, however, that money damages are limited to back pay, an additional sum equal to your back pay (called "liquidated damages"), and attorneys' fees and court costs.

If the EEOC does not resolve your complaint to your satisfaction, you may decide to pursue your complaint through a lawsuit. (See "Filing a Title VII Lawsuit," above.)

The Americans with Disabilities Act

The Americans with Disabilities Act (ADA) prohibits employment discrimination on the basis of workers' disabilities. While debated, haggled over, and honed by both employees and employers before it was passed, the law is not a panacea for either group. The ADA

Amendments Act, however, which took effect in 2009, clarifies that the spirit of the law requires courts and employers to define the term "disability" broadly, to protect as many employees as possible.

Generally, the ADA prohibits employers from:

- discriminating on the basis of any physical or mental disability
- asking job applicants questions about their past or current medical conditions
- requiring job applicants to take preemployment medical exams except under certain circumstances, and
- creating or maintaining worksites that include substantial physical barriers to the movement of people with physical handicaps.

The Act requires that an employer must make reasonable accommodations for qualified individuals with disabilities, unless that would cause the employer undue hardship.

Who Is Covered

The ADA covers employers with 15 or more employees. Its coverage broadly extends to private companies, employment agencies, labor organizations, and state and local governments. State workers, while covered by the Act, cannot sue on their own behalf; they must rely on the EEOC to enforce their rights.

The Act protects workers with disabilities who are still qualified for a particular job. They must be able to perform the essential functions of a job, either with or without some form of accommodation. Whether a worker is deemed qualified for a job depends on whether he or she has appropriate skill, experience, training, or education for the position.

To determine whether a particular function is considered essential for a job, look first at a written job description. If a function is described there, it is more likely to be considered an essential part of the job. But an employer's discretion and the reality of an individual workplace are important, too. For example, if other employees would likely be available to take over some tangential part of a job, only a small portion of the workday is spent on the function, or the work product will not suffer if the function is not performed, that function may not be deemed essential to the job.

Definition of Disability

The ADA's protections extend to those with disabilities, defined as someone who:

- has a physical or mental impairment that substantially limits a major life activity
- has a record of such an impairment, or
- is regarded as having such an impairment.

For an impairment to be a disability under the ADA, it must be long term. Temporary impairments, such as pregnancy or broken bones, are not covered by the ADA (though they may be covered by other laws, such as the FMLA or state pregnancy disability laws).

Impairments Limiting a Major Life Activity

Physical or mental impairments that limit an employee's or applicant's ability to engage in major life activities qualify as disabilities under the ADA.

What's an Impairment?

An impairment can be physical or mental. A physical impairment is a condition, disorder, cosmetic disfigurement, or an anatomical loss that negatively affects the body's functioning. A mental impairment is any psychological or mental disorder, such as a developmental disability, organic brain syndrome, emotional or mental illness, or learning disability.

An impairment is not the same as a condition or trait. Traits and conditions are not disabilities. For example, height and weight (when they are within the normal range) are traits, not impairments. Personality traits, such as a quick temper, are also not impairments (unless they are symptoms of an underlying mental or psychological disorder).

The EEOC's regulations interpreting the ADA provide a list of impairments that will virtually always count as disabilities, because of the way they affect major life activities. The list includes deafness, blindness, intellectual disabilities, autism, cerebral palsy, diabetes, missing limbs or mobility impairments that require the use of a wheelchair, cancer, epilepsy, HIV infection, muscular dystrophy, bipolar disorder, major depressive disorder, schizophrenia, obsessive-compulsive disorder, and posttraumatic stress disorder.

What's a Substantial Limitation?

An impairment must substantially limit a major life activity to count as a disability; not all impairments are protected. Prior to the passage of the ADA Amendments Act (ADAAA), courts sometimes used to find that a person had to be completely unable to perform a major life activity in order to qualify as having a disability. In enacting the ADAAA, however, Congress stated that this definition was too narrow and excluded too many people from the ADA's reach. Congress instructed the EEOC to revise its regulations to redefine "substantially limits" more generously.

In keeping with this directive, the EEOC's regulations interpreting the ADAAA state that the term is "not meant to be a demanding standard." They also clarify that a person can be substantially limited in performing a major life activity even if that person is not prevented, or significantly restricted, from performing that activity. The condition, manner, and duration of the person's performance of the activity should be examined. For example, can the person perform the activity only for a brief period? Must the person expend significant effort to perform the activity? Is it painful or otherwise difficult for the person to perform the activity? Do the side effects of medication or other treatment make it harder for the person to perform the activity?

Conditions that are episodic or in remission are also now covered by the ADA, as long as they would substantially limit a major life activity when active. For example, an employee whose cancer is in remission or who suffers from chronic asthma would likely be covered.

Also, the corrective measures an employee uses to treat or control a disability may not be considered in determining whether the employee is protected. If the employee has an impairment that would substantially limit a major life activity if left untreated or if the employee didn't use mitigating measures (such as a cane or artificial limb), then the employee has a disability. As an exception to this rule, a vision impairment that is corrected by ordinary glasses or contact lenses is not considered a disability.

What Is a Major Life Activity?

Major life activities are activities of essential importance to daily life. They include:

- breathing
- seeing
- walking
- hearing
- speaking
- caring for oneself
- performing manual tasks
- learning, and
- working.

The ADAAA added major bodily functions to the list of major life activities. An impairment that disrupts the proper working of bodily processes, functions, or systems—such as the immune system, normal cell growth, and the digestive, bowel, bladder, neurological, brain, respiratory, circulatory, endocrine, and reproductive functions of the body—will count as a disability. This means that serious conditions that have not yet appeared as outwardly debilitating will be covered. For example, many types of cancer wreak havoc on the body's internal functioning before they substantially limit a person's ability to breathe, walk, or work. These conditions will now be covered by the ADA without question.

Records of Impairment

Because discrimination often continues even after the effects of a disability have abated, the ADA prohibits discrimination against those who have had impairments in the past. This includes workers such as former cancer patients, rehabilitated drug addicts, and recovering alcoholics.

This type of ADA claim is perhaps most difficult to plead and prove, because the discrimination often takes the form of subtler ostracism. One case that succeeded in this way involved an anesthesiologist who was hospitalized for panic disorder and depression, then took a medical leave of absence to deal with side effects of his medication. Although he was later released to work without restrictions, the hospital administration subjected him to more rigorous observation and discipline than appeared to be warranted. After he was fired, an appellate court held that he made out a valid claim for discrimination

based on "a record of impairment in the major life activities of sleeping, eating, thinking, and caring for himself" during his earlier bout with depression. (*Mattice v. Memorial Hospital of South Bend*, 249 F.3d 682 (7th Cir. 2001).)

Regarded as Impaired

In recognition of the fact that discrimination often stems from prejudice or irrational fear, the ADA protects workers who have no actual physical or mental impairment but may be viewed by others as disabled—for example, someone who is badly scarred, walks with a limp, or is erroneously believed to be HIV positive. An employer cannot refuse to hire a person based on misperceptions of the person's ability to do the job.

Under the new ADA definitions, an employee needs to show only that an employer regarded him or her as having a physical or mental disability; the employer need not actually believe that it limited a major life activity. Unlike other claims filed under the ADA, however, those who claim discrimination because they were "regarded as" disabled are not entitled to any accommodation from their employers.

Illegal Discrimination

The ADA prohibits employers from discriminating against job applicants and employees who have disabilities in a number of specific situations.

Screening Tests

Employers may not use preemployment tests or ask interview questions that focus on an applicant's disabilities rather than skills related to the job. Although these questions used to be routine, employers can no longer ask, for example: Have you ever been hospitalized? Have you ever been treated for any of the following listed conditions or diseases? Have you ever been treated for a mental disorder? (In Chapter 5, see "Workplace Testing" for a discussion of when medical exams are allowed.)

However, in screening applicants to find the best match to fill a job opening, employers are free to ask questions about an individual's ability to perform job-related tasks, such as: Can you lift a 40-pound box? Do you have a driver's license? Can you stand for long periods of time?

Insurance Benefits

Employers cannot deny health coverage or other fringe benefits to workers with disabilities. Before the ADA was passed, many employers railed that their insurance costs would skyrocket if they were forced to provide coverage for the special medical needs of those with disabilities. The ADA does not require that all medical conditions be covered; workplace policies can still limit coverage for various treatments. However, employers must provide the same coverage for workers with disabilities as they do for workers without disabilities. (See Chapter 3 for a discussion of health insurance.)

Relatives and Friends

The ADA also attempts to clamp down on the invidious effects of taint by association. Employers are banned from discriminating against people who do not have disabilities but are related to or associated with someone who does. For example, an otherwise qualified worker cannot be denied employment because a sibling, roommate, or close friend has AIDS.

Segregation

On the job, employers cannot segregate or classify workers with disabilities in a way that limits their opportunities or status (for example, by placing them in jobs with different pay, benefits, or promotion opportunities from workers who are not disabled).

Accommodations by Employers

The ADA requires employers to make reasonable accommodations—changes to the work setting or the way jobs are done—so that workers with disabilities can do the job. The law also specifies what employers must do in the sticky situation where two equally qualified candidates, one of whom is disabled, apply for a job. An employer cannot reject a worker solely because he or she would require a reasonable accommodation—a reserved handicapped parking space, a modified work schedule, a telephone voice amplifier—to get the job done.

In reality, a worker with a disability who wants a particular job must become

All in the Mind? The ADA and Mental Disability Claims

In the newest wave of ADA complaints, workers claim that post-traumatic stress makes them hyperactive or short tempered. Others claim that attention deficit disorder, or ADD, makes it difficult for them to concentrate and be productive on the job.

The EEOC last issued formal guidelines on mental illness in 1997, mostly reiterating that the ADA protects workers who have mental impairments that limit "a major life activity" such as learning, thinking, concentrating, interacting with others, caring for himself or herself, or performing manual tasks. The EEOC opined that protected conditions may include major depression, bipolar disorder, panic disorder, obsessive compulsive disorder, schizophrenia, and post-traumatic stress disorder.

In its latest publication on the matter in 2016, the EEOC emphasized that the mental condition does not have to be permanent or severe to qualify for protection. A mental impairment that makes it more difficult, painful, or time-consuming to perform life activities will qualify as a disability. If symptoms come and go, the relevant inquiry is how limiting they are when present. The EEOC also emphasized that employers may not act on stereotypes or assumptions about mental illness; they must rely on objective evidence.

Despite the letter of the law, employees and applicants with mental conditions often face an uphill battle when seeking accommodations. This is, in large part, due to the stigma surrounding mental illness and the belief that people are "faking" it in order to receive special treatment. However, research continues to show that a large number of Americans are affected by mental impairments. According to the National Institute of Mental Health, one in five people will be affected by a mental disability in their lifetime.

The following are some examples of reasonable accommodations for a mental disability:

- allowing an employee to work from home or work flexible hours
- minimizing distractions at the workplace by reducing noise or providing the employee with a more private workspace
- providing time off for therapy or other medical appointments
- providing more frequent breaks, or
- changes in supervisory methods (for example, providing written feedback instead of oral).

The employee's treating doctor can also be a helpful resource in determining what type of accommodation would be reasonable and effective.

something of an activist. Because the law does not require an employer to propose reasonable accommodations—only to provide them—the onus of requesting a reasonable accommodation falls on the worker with a disability. Once you inform your employer that you need a reasonable accommodation for a disability, it must engage in what the law calls an "interactive process": a discussion to determine what accommodation would work in your situation. The employer doesn't have to provide the exact accommodation you request; any reasonable accommodation will do.

What Is a Reasonable Accommodation?

The ADA points to several specific accommodations that are likely to be deemed reasonable. Some of them are changes to the physical setup of the workplace; some of them are changes to how, when, or where work is done. They include:

- making existing facilities accessible to workers with disabilities (for example, by modifying the height of desks and equipment, installing computer screen magnifiers, or installing telecommunications for the hearing impaired)
- restructuring jobs (for example, allowing a ten-hour/four-day workweek so that a worker can receive weekly medical treatments)
- modifying exams and training material (for example, allowing more time for taking an exam, or allowing it to be taken orally instead of in writing)

- providing a reasonable amount of unpaid leave for medical treatment (see also Chapter 4, Family and Medical Leave)
- hiring readers or interpreters to assist an employee
- providing temporary workplace specialists to assist in training, and
- transferring an employee to the same job in another location to obtain better medical care.

These are just a few possible accommodations. The possibilities are limited only by an employee's and employer's imaginations and the financial and practical realities.

What Is an Undue Hardship?

The ADA does not require employers to make accommodations that would cause them an undue hardship: significant difficulty or expense, considering the size and resources of the employer. To show that a particular accommodation would present an undue hardship, an employer would have to demonstrate that it was too costly, extensive, or disruptive to be adopted in that workplace.

The EEOC, in its role as the federal agency responsible for enforcing the ADA, has set out some of the factors that will determine whether a particular accommodation presents an undue hardship on a particular employer:

- the nature and cost of the accommodation
- the financial resources of the employer (a large employer, obviously, can reasonably be asked to foot a larger bill for accommodations than a mom and pop business)

- the nature of the business, including size, composition, and structure, and
- accommodation costs already incurred in a workplace.

It is not easy for employers to prove that an accommodation is an undue hardship, as financial difficulty alone is not usually sufficient. Courts will look at other sources of money, including tax credits and deductions available for making some accommodations and the disabled employee's willingness to pay for all or part of the costs.

How to Take Action

Title I of the ADA is enforced by the Equal Employment Opportunity Commission. (See "Filing a Complaint With the EEOC," above, for specifics on how to file a complaint.) Many state laws protect against discrimination based on physical or mental disability. An individual working in a state with such a law can choose to file a complaint under either state law or the federal law (ADA), or both.

It Helps to Beat Them to the Punch

As one might imagine, the ADA has spawned yet another crop of workplace experts, all eager to give tips to employers on what they must do to comply with the law. Most offer some type of checklist or list of steps to take to help meet the ADA's provisions.

In truth, the checklists are most valuable for employees who want to get or keep a job. If you have a disability, you will be in the best possible bargaining position if you approach a potential employer with information about accommodations.

Here are some things to ponder:

- Analyze the job you want and isolate its essential functions.
- Write down precisely what job-related limitations your condition imposes and note how they can be overcome by accommodations.

- Identify potential accommodations and assess how effective each would be in allowing you to perform the job.
- Estimate how long each accommodation could be used before a change would be required.
- Document all aspects of the accommodation, including cost and availability.

Many accommodations can be provided for free or for a relatively low cost. According to the Job Accommodation Network, employers reported that 59% of accommodations they provided cost them nothing. Many of these accommodations are simple changes to workplace policies. For accommodations that weren't free, the average cost was around $500 (for example, to purchase software or equipment.) For ideas for reasonable accommodations, and help on how to request one, visit www.askjan.org.

Discrimination Against Workers With HIV or AIDS

According to government estimates, more than 1.1 million Americans are currently living with HIV, the virus that leads to Acquired Immune Deficiency Syndrome (AIDS). That population is growing as people become newly infected and as more survive, thanks to evolving drug treatments. The epidemic has hit workplaces hard. In some communities with high-risk populations, such as New York City, Los Angeles, and San Francisco, the infection rate is reported to be as high as one in every 25 workers.

Under the ADA, it is clearly illegal for any company employing 15 or more people to discriminate against workers because they are HIV positive or have AIDS. Employers covered by the ADA must also make reasonable accommodations to allow employees with AIDS or HIV to continue working. Such accommodations include unpaid time off and reassignment to vacant positions that are less physically strenuous or that have flexible work schedules.

RESOURCE

A number of organizations offer publications and specific information on the HIV virus, AIDS, and resources on AIDS in the workplace. The organizations often provide sources of counseling and legal referrals. (See the appendix for contact details.)

In addition, many state and local laws make it illegal to discriminate in employment-related matters on the basis of HIV infection or AIDS. (See "HIV Testing," in Chapter 5, to learn about preemployment testing.)

Discrimination Against LGBT Workers

Gay men and lesbians have been subjected to a long and painful history of discrimination: initiatives barring them from teaching in public schools, local ordinances allowing private clubs to bar them from their doors, loud and heavy lobbying against same-sex marriage laws. On the job, the discrimination often continues with homophobic comments and jokes, lectures about upholding the company image, promotions denied, and jobs lost. And people who are bisexual and transgender have been subjected to similar shuns on the job and off.

Although women, minorities, people older than 40, and people with disabilities now enjoy an umbrella of state and federal protections from discrimination in the workplace, LGBT workers have not been as fortunate, at least at the national level. There is no federal law that specifically outlaws workplace discrimination on the basis of sexual orientation in the private sector.

However, in the last several years, there has been some action at the federal level to protect lesbian, gay, bisexual, and transgender employees. In 2012, the EEOC announced that it would accept and pursue charges of discrimination based on gender identity and sexual orientation. The EEOC based its decision on a string of court cases that interpreted sex discrimination to include holding employees to gender-based stereotypes of how men and women should look or act. This issue has been the subject of much debate in the courts. With respect to sexual orientation, one federal appeals court has ruled that Title VII does not prohibit sexual orientation discrimination, while two other appeals courts have held the opposite. One federal appeals court has held that transgender discrimination is prohibited by Title VII. Only the United States Supreme Court—or a new law passed by Congress—can resolve these issues for good.

At the state level, the rules are much clearer. Almost half of the states now explicitly ban discrimination based on sexual orientation and gender identity. (See "State Laws Prohibiting Discrimination in Employment," at the end of this chapter, to learn whether your state has such a law.) Many cities and counties, especially in large metropolitan areas, have similar laws as well.

According to the National Gay and Lesbian Taskforce, the hodgepodge of laws and ordinances means that the glass is half full. Almost half of the U.S. population now lives in jurisdictions that ban discrimination on the basis of sexual orientation and gender identity.

Finally, a growing number of more enlightened employers have included a clause that they will not discriminate against workers based on sexual orientation or gender identity.

Federal law also now prohibits employers from discriminating against same-sex spouses when it comes to employee benefits. In a landmark case in 2015, the United States Supreme Court held that same-sex marriages must be allowed in all 50 states. (*Obergefell v. Hodges*, 135 S.Ct. 2584 (2015).) As a result, employers that provide benefits to opposite-sex spouses but not same-sex spouses might be breaking the law. For example, it would generally be illegal for an employer to offer group health coverage to opposite-sex spouses only. This is a complicated and evolving area of the law; if you believe you were discriminated against due to your sexual orientation or gender identity, consult with a lawyer.

RESOURCE

For more information on the legal rights of gay and lesbian couples, see *A Legal Guide for Lesbian & Gay Couples*, by Emily Doskow and Frederick Hertz (Nolo). A number of organizations offer publications, counseling, advice, and research on issues gay and lesbian workers face on the job. (See the appendix for contact details.)

State Laws Prohibiting Discrimination

Nearly every state has its own law prohibiting various types of discrimination in employment. Like federal law, state laws usually prohibit discrimination based on race, color, national origin, religion, age, and disability. Some are more protective than federal law. For example, some state laws apply to smaller employers or cover additional types of discrimination, including discrimination based on marital status, sexual orientation, or even physical appearance or homelessness. Many cities and counties have thier own antidiscrimination laws as well.

The charts at the end of this chapter cover each state's discrimination law; in the appendix, you'll find information on each state's fair employment practices (FEP) agency. These state agencies are like the EEOC on the federal level: Typically, they accept complaints of employment discrimination and investigate and try to settle them. The state FEP agency may also decide to sue on behalf of a particular employee, but this is very rare.

In most states, if you file a complaint or charge of discrimination with either the state FEP agency or the local EEOC, it will automatically be filed with the other agency. In other words, if you go to the EEOC and file a charge, your charge will be considered filed with the state agency at the same time. When you file a complaint or charge, ask whether it will be automatically filed at the other agency. This might prove important later, because you may not file a lawsuit alleging discrimination unless you have first filed a claim with the proper agency. For example, if you file a charge at the EEOC, then later decide you would rather proceed under your state's antidiscrimination law, you will have to make sure that your charge has been filed with the state agency as well.

Ordinarily, you must file a charge of discrimination with the EEOC within 180 days of the discriminatory act. If your state has a law covering the same type of discrimination, this time limit is usually extended to 300 days. Check with your local EEOC office or state FEP agency office to make sure you know the rules. (You can find contact information in the appendix.) Because your case could be thrown out if you miss a deadline, it's very important to file as soon as you can.

State Laws Prohibiting Discrimination in Employment

Note: This chart includes characteristics that are expressly listed in the state law. However, related characteristics might be protected even if not listed. For example, pregnancy and breast-feeding are often protected under "gender" and HIV is often protected under "disability." To learn more, contact your state's fair employment practices agency (see the appendix for contact information).

Alabama

Ala. Code §§ 25-1-20, 25-1-21

Law applies to employers with: 20 or more employees

Private employers may not make employment decisions based on:
- Age (40 and older)

Alaska

Alaska Stat. §§ 18.80.220, 18.80.300, 47.30.865

Law applies to employers with: One or more employees

Private employers may not make employment decisions based on:
- Age
- Ancestry or national origin
- Physical or mental disability
- Gender
- Marital status, including changes in status
- Pregnancy, childbirth, and related medical conditions, including parenthood
- Race or color
- Religion or creed
- Mental illness

Arizona

Ariz. Rev. Stat. §§ 41-1461, 41-1463, 41-1465

Law applies to employers with: 15 or more employees

Private employers may not make employment decisions based on:
- Age (40 and older)
- Ancestry or national origin
- Physical or mental disability
- AIDS/HIV
- Gender
- Race or color
- Religion or creed
- Genetic testing information

Arkansas

Ark. Code Ann. §§ 11-4-601, 11-5-403, 16-123-102, 16-123-107

Law applies to employers with: Nine or more employees

Private employers may not make employment decisions based on:
- Ancestry or national origin
- Physical, mental, or sensory disability
- Gender
- Pregnancy, childbirth, and related medical conditions
- Race or color
- Religion or creed
- Genetic testing information

California

Cal. Gov't. Code §§ 12920, 12926.1, 12940, 12941, 12945; Cal. Lab. Code § 1101

Law applies to employers with: Five or more employees

Private employers may not make employment decisions based on:
- Age (40 and older)
- Ancestry or national origin
- Physical or mental disability
- AIDS/HIV
- Gender

State Laws Prohibiting Discrimination in Employment (continued)

- Marital status
- Pregnancy, childbirth, and related medical conditions, including breast-feeding
- Race or color
- Religion or creed
- Sexual orientation
- Genetic testing information
- Gender identity, gender expression
- Medical condition
- Political activities or affiliations
- Status as victim of domestic violence, sexual assault, or stalking
- Military and veteran status

Colorado

Colo. Rev. Stat. §§ 24-34-301, 24-34-401, 24-34-402, 24-34-402.5, 27-65-115; Colo. Code Regs. 708-1:60.1, 708-1:80.8

Law applies to employers with: One or more employees; 25 or more employees (marital status only)

Private employers may not make employment decisions based on:
- Age (40 and older)
- Ancestry or national origin
- Physical, mental, or learning disability
- AIDS/HIV
- Gender
- Marital Status (only applies to marriage to a coworker or plans to marry a coworker)
- Pregnancy, childbirth, and related medical conditions
- Race or color
- Religion or creed
- Sexual orientation, including perceived sexual orientation
- Lawful conduct outside of work
- Mental illness
- Transgender status

Connecticut

Conn. Gen. Stat. Ann. §§ 25-4-1401, 46a-51, 46a-60, 46a-81a, 46a-81c

Law applies to employers with: Three or more employees

Private employers may not make employment decisions based on:
- Age
- Ancestry or national origin
- Present or past physical, mental, learning , or intellectual disability
- AIDS/HIV
- Gender
- Marital status, including civil unions
- Pregnancy, childbirth, and related medical conditions
- Race or color
- Religion or creed
- Sexual orientation, including having a history of such a preference or of being identified with a preference
- Genetic testing information
- Gender identity or expression
- Arrests or convictions that have been erased, pardoned, or rehabilitated
- Status as a veteran

Delaware

Del. Code Ann. tit. 19, §§ 710, 711, 724

Law applies to employers with: Four or more employees

Private employers may not make employment decisions based on:
- Age (40 and older)
- Ancestry or national origin
- Physical or mental disability
- AIDS/HIV
- Gender
- Marital status

State Laws Prohibiting Discrimination in Employment (continued)

- Pregnancy, childbirth, and related medical conditions
- Race or color
- Religion or creed
- Sexual orientation
- Genetic testing information
- Gender identity
- Status as victim of domestic violence, sexual offense, or stalking
- Family responsibilities
- Reproductive health decisions

District of Columbia

D.C. Code Ann. §§ 2-1401.01, 2-1401.02, 2-1401.05, 2-1402.82, 7-1703.03, 32-531.08

Law applies to employers with: One or more employees

Private employers may not make employment decisions based on:

- Age (18 and older)
- Ancestry or national origin
- Physical or mental disability
- Gender (includes reproductive health decisions)
- Marital status, including domestic partnership
- Pregnancy, childbirth, and related medical conditions (includes parenthood and breast-feeding)
- Race or color
- Religion or creed
- Sexual orientation
- Genetic testing information
- Enrollment in vocational, professional, or college education
- Family duties
- Source of income
- Place of residence or business
- Personal appearance
- Political affiliation

- Victim of intrafamily offense
- Gender identity or expression
- Status as unemployed
- Tobacco use
- Credit information
- Any reason other than individual merit

Florida

Fla. Stat. Ann. §§ 448.075, 760.01, 760.02, 760.10, 760.50

Law applies to employers with: 15 or more employees

Private employers may not make employment decisions based on:

- Age
- Ancestry or national origin
- "Handicap"
- AIDS/HIV
- Gender
- Marital status
- Pregnancy, childbirth, and related medical conditions
- Race or color
- Religion or creed
- Sickle cell trait

Georgia

Ga. Code Ann. §§ 34-1-2, 34-5-1, 34-5-2, 34-6A-1 and following

Law applies to employers with: 15 or more employees (disability); 10 or more employees (gender) (domestic and agricultural employees not protected); one or more employees (age)

Private employers may not make employment decisions based on:

- Age (40 to 70)
- Physical, mental, or learning disability
- Gender (wage discrimination only)

State Laws Prohibiting Discrimination in Employment (continued)

Hawaii

Haw. Rev. Stat. §§ 378-1, 378-2, 378-2.5; Hawaii Admin. Rules § 12-46-182

Law applies to employers with: One or more employees

Private employers may not make employment decisions based on:

- Age
- Ancestry or national origin
- Physical or mental disability
- AIDS/HIV
- Gender
- Marital status
- Pregnancy, childbirth, and related medical conditions (includes breast-feeding)
- Race or color
- Religion or creed
- Sexual orientation
- Genetic testing information
- Arrest and court record (unless there is a conviction directly related to job)
- Credit history or credit report, unless the information in the individual's credit history or credit report directly relates to a bona fide occupational qualification
- Gender identity and gender expression
- Status as a victim of domestic or sexual violence (if employer has knowledge or is notified of this status)

Idaho

Idaho Code §§ 39-8303, 67-5902, 67-5909, 67-5910

Law applies to employers with: Five or more employees

Private employers may not make employment decisions based on:

- Age (40 and older)
- Ancestry or national origin
- Physical or mental disability

- Gender
- Pregnancy, childbirth, and related medical conditions
- Race or color
- Religion or creed
- Genetic testing information

Illinois

410 Ill. Comp. Stat. § 513/25; 775 Ill. Comp. Stat. §§ 5/1-102, 5/1-103, 5/1-105, 5/2-101, 5/2-102, 5/2-103; 820 Ill. Comp. Stat. §§ 105/4, 180/30; Ill. Admin. Code tit. 56, § 5210.110

Law applies to employers with: 15 or more employees; one or more employees (disability only)

Private employers may not make employment decisions based on:

- Age (40 and older)
- Ancestry or national origin
- Physical or mental disability
- Gender
- Marital status
- Pregnancy, childbirth, and related medical conditions
- Race or color
- Religion or creed
- Sexual orientation
- Genetic testing information
- Citizenship status
- Military status
- Unfavorable military discharge
- Gender identity
- Arrest record
- Victims of domestic violence
- Order of protection status
- Lack of permanent mailing address or having a mailing address of a shelter or social service provider

State Laws Prohibiting Discrimination in Employment (continued)

Indiana

Ind. Code Ann. §§ 22-9-1-2, 22-9-2-1, 22-9-2-2, 22-9-5-1 and following

Law applies to employers with: 6 or more employees; 1 or more employees (age only); 15 or more employees (disability only)

Private employers may not make employment decisions based on:

- Age (40 to 75)
- Ancestry or national origin
- Physical or mental disability (15 or more employees)
- Gender
- Race or color
- Religion or creed
- Off-duty tobacco use
- Status as a veteran
- Sealed or expunged arrest or conviction record

Iowa

Iowa Code §§ 216.2, 216.6, 216.6A, 729.6

Law applies to employers with: Four or more employees

Private employers may not make employment decisions based on:

- Age (18 or older)
- Ancestry or national origin
- Physical or mental disability
- AIDS/HIV
- Gender
- Pregnancy, childbirth, and related medical conditions
- Race or color
- Religion or creed
- Sexual orientation
- Genetic testing information
- Gender identity
- Wage discrimination

Kansas

Kan. Stat. Ann. §§ 44-1002, 44-1009, 44-1112, 44-1113, 44-1125, 44-1126, 65-6002(e)

Law applies to employers with: Four or more employees

Private employers may not make employment decisions based on:

- Age (40 or older)
- Ancestry or national origin
- Physical or mental disability
- AIDS/HIV
- Gender
- Race or color
- Religion or creed
- Genetic testing information
- Military service or status

Kentucky

Ky. Rev. Stat. Ann. §§ 207.130, 207.135, 207.150, 342.197, 344.010, 344.030, 344.040

Law applies to employers with: Eight or more employees

Private employers may not make employment decisions based on:

- Age (40 or older)
- Ancestry or national origin
- Physical or mental disability
- AIDS/HIV
- Gender
- Pregnancy, childbirth, and related medical conditions
- Race or color
- Religion or creed
- Occupational pneumoconiosis with no respiratory impairment resulting from exposure to coal dust
- Off-duty tobacco use

State Laws Prohibiting Discrimination in Employment (continued)

Louisiana

La. Rev. Stat. Ann. §§ 23:301 to 23:368

Law applies to employers with: 20 or more employees

Private employers may not make employment decisions based on:

- Age (40 or older)
- Ancestry or national origin
- Physical or mental disability
- Gender
- Pregnancy, childbirth, and related medical conditions (applies to employers with 25 or more employees)
- Race or color
- Religion or creed
- Genetic testing information
- Sickle cell trait
- Being a smoker or nonsmoker

Maine

Me. Rev. Stat. Ann. tit. 5, §§ 19302, 4552, 4553, 4571 to 4576; tit. 26, § 833; tit. 39-A, § 353

Law applies to employers with: One or more employees

Private employers may not make employment decisions based on:

- Age
- Ancestry or national origin
- Physical or mental disability
- AIDS/HIV
- Gender
- Pregnancy, childbirth, and related medical conditions
- Race or color
- Religion or creed
- Sexual orientation, including perceived sexual orientation
- Genetic testing information
- Gender identity or expression

- Past workers' compensation claim
- Past whistleblowing
- Medical support notice for child

Maryland

Md. Code, [State Government], §§ 20-101, 20-601 to 20-608; Md. Code Regs. 14.03.02.02

Law applies to employers with: 15 or more employees

Private employers may not make employment decisions based on:

- Age
- Ancestry or national origin
- Physical or mental disability
- AIDS/HIV
- Gender
- Marital status
- Pregnancy, childbirth, and related medical conditions
- Race or color
- Religion or creed
- Sexual orientation
- Genetic testing information
- Civil Air Patrol membership
- Gender identity

Massachusetts

Mass. Gen. Laws ch. 149, § 24A; ch. 151B, §§ 1, 4; Code of Massachusetts Regulations 804 CMR 3.01

Law applies to employers with: Six or more employees

Private employers may not make employment decisions based on:

- Age (40 or older)
- Ancestry or national origin
- Physical or mental disability
- Gender
- Marital status
- Race or color

State Laws Prohibiting Discrimination in Employment (continued)

- Religion or creed
- Sexual orientation
- Genetic testing information
- Military service
- Arrest record
- Gender identity
- Status as a veteran

Michigan

Mich. Comp. Laws §§ 37.1103, 37.1201, 37.1202, 37.2201, 37.2202, 37.2205a, 750.556

Law applies to employers with: One or more employees

Private employers may not make employment decisions based on:
- Age
- Ancestry or national origin
- Physical or mental disability
- AIDS/HIV
- Gender
- Marital status
- Pregnancy, childbirth, and related medical conditions
- Race or color
- Religion or creed
- Genetic testing information
- Height or weight
- Misdemeanor arrest record
- Civil Air Patrol membership

Minnesota

Minn. Stat. Ann. §§ 144.417, 181.81, 181.974, 363A.03, 363A.08

Law applies to employers with: One or more employees

Private employers may not make employment decisions based on:
- Age (18 to 70)
- Ancestry or national origin

- Physical, sensory, or mental disability
- Gender
- Marital status
- Pregnancy, childbirth, and related medical conditions
- Race or color
- Religion or creed
- Sexual orientation, including perceived sexual orientation
- Genetic testing information
- Gender identity
- Member of local commission
- Receiving public assistance
- Familial status (protects parents or guardians living with a minor child)

Mississippi

Miss. Code Ann. § 33-1-15

Law applies to employers with: One or more employees

Private employers may not make employment decisions based on:
- Military status
- No other protected categories unless employer receives public funding

Missouri

Mo. Rev. Stat. §§ 191.665, 213.010, 213.055, 375.1306

Law applies to employers with: Six or more employees

Private employers may not make employment decisions based on:
- Age (40 to 70)
- Ancestry or national origin
- Physical or mental disability
- AIDS/HIV
- Gender
- Race or color
- Religion or creed

State Laws Prohibiting Discrimination in Employment (continued)

- Genetic testing information
- Off-duty use of alcohol or tobacco

Montana

Mont. Code Ann. §§ 49-2-101, 49-2-303, 49-2-310

Law applies to employers with: One or more employees

Private employers may not make employment decisions based on:

- Age
- Ancestry or national origin
- Physical or mental disability
- Gender
- Marital status
- Pregnancy, childbirth, and related medical conditions
- Race or color
- Religion or creed

Nebraska

Neb. Rev. Stat. §§ 20-168, 48-236, 48-1001 to 48-1010, 48-1102, 48-1104

Law applies to employers with: 15 or more employees

Private employers may not make employment decisions based on:

- Age (40 or older—applies to employers with 20 or more employees)
- Ancestry or national origin
- Physical or mental disability
- AIDS/HIV
- Gender
- Marital status
- Pregnancy, childbirth, and related medical conditions
- Race or color
- Religion or creed
- Genetic testing information (applies to all employers)

Nevada

Nev. Rev. Stat. Ann. §§ 613.310 and following; 2017 Nevada Laws Ch. 271 (A.B. 113), 2017 Nevada Laws Ch. 496 (S.B. 361)

Law applies to employers with: 15 or more employees

Private employers may not make employment decisions based on:

- Age (40 or older)
- Ancestry or national origin
- Physical or mental disability
- AIDS/HIV
- Gender
- Pregnancy, childbirth, and related medical conditions (including breast-feeding)
- Race or color
- Religion or creed
- Sexual orientation, including perceived sexual orientation
- Genetic testing information
- Use of service animal
- Gender identity or expression
- Opposing unlawful employment practices
- Credit report or credit information (with some exceptions)
- Requesting leave or reasonable accommodation due to status as victim of domestic violence (applies to all employers)

New Hampshire

N.H. Rev. Stat. Ann. §§ 141-H:3, 354-A:2, 354-A:6, 354-A:7

Law applies to employers with: Six or more employees

Private employers may not make employment decisions based on:

- Age
- Ancestry or national origin
- Physical or mental disability

State Laws Prohibiting Discrimination in Employment (continued)

- Gender
- Marital status
- Pregnancy, childbirth, and related medical conditions
- Race or color
- Religion or creed
- Sexual orientation
- Genetic testing information
- Victims of domestic violence, harassment, sexual assault, or stalking
- Off-duty use of tobacco products

New Jersey

N.J. Stat. Ann. §§ 10:5-1, 10:5-4.1, 10:5-5, 10:5-12, 10:5-29.1, 34:6B-1, 43:21-49

Law applies to employers with: One or more employees

Private employers may not make employment decisions based on:

- Age (18 to 70)
- Ancestry or national origin
- Past or present physical or mental disability
- AIDS/HIV
- Gender
- Marital status, including civil union or domestic partnership status
- Pregnancy, childbirth, and related medical conditions (includes breast-feeding)
- Race or color
- Religion or creed
- Sexual orientation, including affectional orientation and perceived sexual orientation
- Genetic testing information
- Atypical heredity cellular or blood trait
- Accompanied by service or guide dog
- Military service
- Gender identity
- Unemployed status
- Liability for service in the U.S. Armed Forces

- Familial status

New Mexico

N.M. Stat. Ann. §§ 24-21-4, 28-1-2, 28-1-7, 50-4A-4; N.M. Admin Code 9.1.1

Law applies to employers with: Four or more employees

Private employers may not make employment decisions based on:

- Age (40 or older)
- Ancestry or national origin
- Physical or mental disability
- Gender
- Marital status (applies to employers with 50 or more employees)
- Pregnancy, childbirth, and related medical conditions
- Race or color
- Religion or creed
- Sexual orientation, including perceived sexual orientation (applies to employers with 15 or more employees)
- Genetic testing information
- Gender identity (employers with 15 or more employees)
- Serious medical condition
- Domestic abuse leave

New York

N.Y. Exec. Law §§ 292, 296; N.Y. Lab. Law § 201-d

Law applies to employers with: Four or more employees; all employers (sexual harassment only)

Private employers may not make employment decisions based on:

- Age (18 and over)
- Ancestry or national origin
- Physical or mental disability
- Gender
- Marital status

State Laws Prohibiting Discrimination in Employment (continued)

- Pregnancy, childbirth, and related medical conditions
- Race or color
- Religion or creed
- Sexual orientation, including perceived sexual orientation
- Genetic testing information
- Lawful recreational activities when not at work
- Military status or service
- Observance of Sabbath
- Political activities
- Use of service dog
- Arrest or criminal accusation
- Domestic violence victim status
- Familial status
- Gender identity and transgender status

North Carolina

N.C. Gen. Stat. §§ 95-28.1, 95-28.1A, 127B-11, 130A-148, 143-422.2, 168A-5

Law applies to employers with: 15 or more employees

Private employers may not make employment decisions based on:

- Age
- Ancestry or national origin
- Physical or mental disability
- AIDS/HIV
- Gender
- Race or color
- Religion or creed
- Genetic testing information
- Military status or service
- Sickle cell or hemoglobin C trait
- Lawful use of lawful products off site and off duty

North Dakota

N.D. Cent. Code §§ 14-02.4-02, 14-02.4-03, 34-01-17

Law applies to employers with: One or more employees

Private employers may not make employment decisions based on:

- Age (40 or older)
- Ancestry or national origin
- Physical or mental disability
- Gender
- Marital status
- Pregnancy, childbirth, and related medical conditions
- Race or color
- Religion or creed
- Lawful conduct outside of work
- Receiving public assistance
- Keeping and bearing arms (as long as firearm is never exhibited on company property except for lawful defensive purposes)
- Status as a volunteer emergency responder

Ohio

Ohio Rev. Code Ann. §§ 4111.17, 4112.01, 4112.02

Law applies to employers with: Four or more employees

Private employers may not make employment decisions based on:

- Age (40 or older)
- Ancestry or national origin
- Physical, mental, or learning disability
- AIDS/HIV
- Gender
- Pregnancy, childbirth, and related medical conditions
- Race or color
- Religion or creed
- Caring for a sibling, child, parent, or spouse injured while in the armed services
- Military status

State Laws Prohibiting Discrimination in Employment (continued)

Oklahoma

Okla. Stat. Ann. tit. 25, §§ 1301, 1302; tit. 36, § 3614.2; tit. 40, § 500; tit. 44, § 208

Law applies to employers with: One or more employees

Private employers may not make employment decisions based on:
- Age (40 or older)
- Ancestry or national origin
- Physical, mental, or learning disability
- Gender
- Pregnancy, childbirth, and related medical conditions (except abortions where the woman is not in "imminent danger of death")
- Race or color
- Religion or creed
- Genetic testing information
- Military service
- Being a smoker or nonsmoker or using tobacco off duty

Oregon

Ore. Rev. Stat. §§ 25-337, 659A.030, 659A.122 and following, 659A.303

Law applies to employers with: One or more employees

Private employers may not make employment decisions based on:
- Age (18 or older)
- Ancestry or national origin
- Physical or mental disability (applies to employers with 6 or more employees)
- Gender
- Marital status
- Pregnancy, childbirth, and related medical conditions
- Race or color
- Religion or creed

- Sexual orientation
- Genetic testing information
- Parent who has medical support order imposed by court
- Domestic violence victim status
- Refusal to attend an employer-sponsored meeting with the primary purpose of communicating the employer's opinion on religious or political matters
- Credit history
- Whistle-blowers
- Off-duty use of tobacco products

Pennsylvania

Pa. Stat. Ann. tit. 43, §§ 954 to 955

Law applies to employers with: Four or more employees

Private employers may not make employment decisions based on:
- Age (40 to 70)
- Ancestry or national origin
- Physical or mental disability
- Gender
- Pregnancy, childbirth, and related medical conditions
- Race or color
- Religion or creed
- GED rather than high school diploma
- Use of service animal
- Relationship or association with a person with a disability

Rhode Island

R.I. Gen. Laws §§ 12-28-10, 23-6.3-11, 28-5-6, 28-5-7, 28-6-18, 28-6.7-1

Law applies to employers with: Four or more employees; one or more employees (gender-based wage discrimination)

State Laws Prohibiting Discrimination in Employment (continued)

Private employers may not make employment decisions based on:
- Age (40 or older)
- Ancestry or national origin
- Physical or mental disability
- AIDS/HIV
- Gender
- Pregnancy, childbirth, and related medical conditions
- Race or color
- Religion or creed
- Sexual orientation, including perceived sexual orientation
- Genetic testing information
- Domestic abuse victim
- Gender identity or expression
- Homelessness

South Carolina

S.C. Code §§ 1-13-30, 1-13-80

Law applies to employers with: 15 or more employees

Private employers may not make employment decisions based on:
- Age (40 or older)
- Ancestry or national origin
- Physical or mental disability
- AIDS/HIV
- Gender
- Pregnancy, childbirth, and related medical conditions
- Race or color
- Religion or creed

South Dakota

S.D. Codified Laws Ann. §§ 20-13-1, 20-13-10, 60-2-20, 60-12-15, 62-1-17

Law applies to employers with: One or more employees

Private employers may not make employment decisions based on:
- Ancestry or national origin
- Physical or mental disability
- Gender
- Race or color
- Religion or creed
- Genetic testing information
- Preexisting injury
- Off-duty use of tobacco products

Tennessee

Tenn. Code Ann. §§ 4-21-102, 4-21-401 and following, 8-50-103, 50-2-201, 50-2-202

Law applies to employers with: Eight or more employees; one or more employees (gender-based wage discrimination)

Private employers may not make employment decisions based on:
- Age (40 or older)
- Ancestry or national origin
- Physical, mental, or visual disability
- Gender
- Race or color
- Religion or creed
- Use of guide dog
- Volunteer rescue squad worker responding to an emergency

Texas

Tex. Lab. Code Ann. §§ 21.002, 21.051, 21.082, 21.101, 21.106, 21.402

Law applies to employers with: 15 or more employees

Private employers may not make employment decisions based on:
- Age (40 or older)
- Ancestry or national origin
- Physical or mental disability

State Laws Prohibiting Discrimination in Employment (continued)

- Gender
- Pregnancy, childbirth, and related medical conditions
- Race or color
- Religion or creed
- Genetic testing information

Utah

Utah Code Ann. §§ 26-45-103, 34A-5-102, 34A-5-106

Law applies to employers with: 15 or more employees

Private employers may not make employment decisions based on:
- Age (40 or older)
- Ancestry or national origin
- Physical or mental disability
- AIDS/HIV
- Gender
- Pregnancy, childbirth, and related medical conditions (includes breast-feeding)
- Race or color
- Religion or creed
- Sexual orientation
- Genetic testing information
- Gender identity

Vermont

Vt. Stat. Ann. tit. 21, §§ 495, 495d; tit. 18, § 9333

Law applies to employers with: One or more employees

Private employers may not make employment decisions based on:
- Age (18 or older)
- Ancestry or national origin
- Physical, mental, or emotional disability
- AIDS/HIV
- Gender
- Race or color

- Religion or creed
- Sexual orientation
- Genetic testing information
- Gender identity
- Place of birth
- Credit report or credit history

Virginia

Va. Code Ann. §§ 2.2-3900, 2.2-3901, 40.1-28.6, 40.1-28.7:1, 51.5-41

Law applies to employers with: One or more employees

Private employers may not make employment decisions based on:
- Age
- Ancestry or national origin
- Physical or mental disability
- AIDS/HIV
- Gender
- Marital status
- Pregnancy, childbirth, and related medical conditions
- Race or color
- Religion or creed
- Genetic testing information

Washington

Wash. Rev. Code Ann. §§ 38.40.110, 49.12.175, 49.44.090, 49.44.180, 49.60.030, 49.60.040, 49.60.172, 49.60.180, 49.76.120; Wash. Admin. Code § 162-30-020

Law applies to employers with: Eight or more employees; one or more employees (gender-based wage discrimination only)

Private employers may not make employment decisions based on:
- Age (40 or older)
- Ancestry or national origin
- Physical, mental, or sensory disability

State Laws Prohibiting Discrimination in Employment (continued)

- AIDS/HIV
- Gender
- Marital status
- Pregnancy, childbirth, and related medical conditions, including breast-feeding
- Race or color
- Religion or creed
- Sexual orientation
- Genetic testing information
- Hepatitis C infection
- Member of state militia
- Use of service animal
- Gender identity
- Domestic violence victim

West Virginia

W.Va. Code §§ 5-11-3, 5-11-9, 15–1K–4, 16-3C-3, 21-5B-1, 21-5B-3

Law applies to employers with: 12 or more employees; one or more employees (gender-based wage discrimination only)

Private employers may not make employment decisions based on:
- Age (40 or older)
- Ancestry or national origin
- Physical or mental disability, or blindness
- AIDS/HIV
- Gender
- Race or color
- Religion or creed
- Off-duty use of tobacco products
- Membership in the Civil Air Patrol (for employers with 16 or more employees)

Wisconsin

Wis. Stat. Ann. §§ 111.32 and following

Law applies to employers with: One or more employees

Private employers may not make employment decisions based on:
- Age (40 or older)
- Ancestry or national origin
- Physical or mental disability
- Gender
- Marital status
- Pregnancy, childbirth, and related medical conditions
- Race or color
- Religion or creed
- Sexual orientation, including having a history of or being identified with a preference
- Genetic testing information
- Arrest or conviction record
- Military service
- Declining to attend a meeting or to participate in any communication about religious matters or political matters
- Use or nonuse of lawful products off duty and off site

Wyoming

Wyo. Stat. §§ 27-9-102, 27-9-105, 19-11-104

Law applies to employers with: Two or more employees

Private employers may not make employment decisions based on:
- Age (40 or older)
- Ancestry or national origin
- Disability
- Gender
- Pregnancy, childbirth, and related medical conditions
- Race or color
- Religion or creed
- Military service or status

Sexual Harassment

In legal terms, sexual harassment is any unwelcome sex-based conduct on the job that creates an intimidating, hostile, or offensive working environment or that results in an adverse employment action. Simply put, sexual harassment is any offensive conduct related to an employee's gender that a reasonable woman or man should not have to endure while at work.

The laws prohibiting sexual harassment are gender blind; they prevent women from harassing men, men from harassing other men, and women from harassing other women. However, the vast majority of cases involve female workers who have been harassed by male coworkers or supervisors.

The forms that sexual harassment can take range from offensive sexual innuendoes to physical encounters, from dirty jokes to rape. An employee may be confronted with sexual demands to keep a job or obtain a promotion, known in the earliest cases as a quid pro quo harassment. In other forms of sexual harassment, the threat—or the trade-off—is not as blunt. When sexually offensive conduct permeates the workplace, an employee may find it difficult or unpleasant to work there. The term hostile work environment is frequently used to describe this form of sexual harassment.

The definition of sexual harassment is evolving as it passes through courts and legislatures. The most authoritative refinements come from the U.S. Supreme Court, which has issued a number of pronouncements on the subject.

For example, the Court held that a worker need not show psychological injury to prove a case of sexual harassment; it also intimated that one or two offensive remarks are not enough to make a case. (*Harris v. Forklift Sys., Inc.*, 510 U.S. 17 (1993).)

In additional cases, the Court has offered some uncharacteristically homespun advice for both employers and employees entangled in harassment issues: Act reasonably. Use your common sense.

- The Court recognized that illegal harassment can occur between people of the same gender, even if the harassment is not motivated by sexual desire. In that case, a male employee had a valid sexual harassment claim against two male employees who sexually assaulted him in an attempt to intimidate and humiliate him. (*Oncale v. Sundowner Offshore Services, Inc.*, 523 U.S. 75 (1998).)

- The Court also explained an employer's liability for a supervisor's harassment when it had no knowledge of it. If an employee experiences a tangible employment action as a result of the harassment—such as a termination or demotion for refusing to provide sexual favors—the employer will be automatically liable for the supervisor's conduct. If an employee did not suffer a tangible job consequence from the harassment, the employer can defend itself against liability by showing that it exercised reasonable care to prevent

and correct sexual harassment—
for example, by adopting a strong
written antiharassment policy and
investigation procedure—and that
the employee unreasonably failed
to take advantage of the employer's
procedures. (*Burlington Industries,
Inc. v. Ellerth,* 524 U.S. 742 (1998).)

- The Court held that an employee who
speaks out against sexual harassment
while answering questions during a
company's internal investigation of
charges brought by other employees
is also protected from the employer's
retaliation. (*Crawford v. Metropolitan
Gov't of Nashville and Davidson Cty.,
Tennessee,* 555 U.S. 271 (2009).)

The fervor over sexual harassment has
cooled somewhat in the last decade, and the
number of claims alleging it has decreased.
No doubt, this is partially due to laws that
mandate regular training on the topic.
But the workplace problem is far from
solved. In 2017, the EEOC received a little
under 7,000 charges of sexual harassment
and recovered $46.3 million in monetary
damages for those affected; many millions
more were collected in private lawsuits.

The Effects of Sexual Harassment

Sexual harassment on the job can have
a number of serious consequences, both
for the harassed individual and for other
workers who experience it secondhand
and become demoralized or intimidated
at work. (See "Sexual Harassment Under
Federal Law," below, for a discussion of
legal remedies.)

Loss of Job

Sometimes the connection between sexual
harassment and the injuries it causes
is simple and direct: A worker is fired
for refusing to go along with the sexual
demands of a coworker or supervisor.
Often, management uses some other
pretext for the firing, but the reasons are
often quite transparent.

Sometimes the firing technically occurs
because of some other event, but it is still
clearly related to sexual harassment. For
example, if a company downgrades an
employee's job and assignments because
of a harassment complaint and then fires
him or her for complaining about the
demotion, that injury is legally caused by
sexual harassment.

If an employee is temporarily unable
to work as a result of the harassment and
management uses that as an excuse to fire
him or her, that is also considered legally
related to the harassment.

Loss of Wages and Other Benefits

An employee who resists sexual advances
or objects to obscene humor in the office
may suffer work-related consequences
including:

Straight From Hollywood: "The Creative Necessity Defense"

While working as a writers' assistant for the popular television sitcom *Friends*, Amaani Lyle says she got a close-up of the show's writers in action: making sex-related jokes, discussing blow job story lines, discussing the actresses' sexuality, writing sex-related words on scripts, and pantomiming masturbation. After four months, Lyle was fired for her poor typing skills and for her failure to accurately record important jokes and dialogue in her notes.

She sued Warner Bros. Television Production and three individual comedy writers under California's Fair Employment and Housing Act for harassment based on race and gender.

The case itself had impeccable timing, first wending its way through the courts during the season finale of the popular *Friends*, a show about ageless 20/30-somethings coming of age. And it coincided with initial tabloid reports of actor Brad Pitt canoodling with Angelina Jolie, a woman not his wife. His wife was Jennifer Aniston, one of the stars on *Friends*.

And on the legal front, it attracted briefs from writers, employer groups, and unions, pitting the television industry and free speech advocates against some women's rights advocates.

The Los Angeles County Superior Court initially dismissed Lyle's complaint as frivolous. But the appellate court held that the case presented triable issues of fact regarding sexual harassment. It also noted that the court could consider the nature of the defendants' work in determining if their conduct amounted to true harassment, thus fostering The Creative Necessity Defense.

The California Supreme Court agreed, reasoning that while sexual language may constitute harassment, the *Friends* writers' language did not reach that level, as it was not aimed directly at Lyle or at other women because of their gender. In reaching its unanimous decision, the court famously noted: "The FEHA is 'not a civility code' and is not designed to rid the workplace of vulgarity," nor does it "outlaw sexually coarse and vulgar language that merely offends." (*Lyle v. Warner Brothers Television Production,* 38 Cal.4th 264 (2006).) And the court reiterated that a harassing remark must be "objectively and subjectively offensive, one that a reasonable person would find hostile or abusive."

- being denied a promotion
- being demoted, or
- suffering various economic losses.

That employee may also suffer harm to his or her standing within the company, which could jeopardize future pay increases and opportunities for promotion.

A loss of wages usually entails a loss of other job benefits as well, such as pension contributions, medical benefits, overtime pay, bonuses, sick pay, shift differential pay, vacation pay, and participation in any company profit-sharing plan.

Forced Reassignment

Sometimes a company responds to an employee's complaint of sexual harassment by transferring that individual somewhere else in the company and leaving the harasser unpunished. This forced reassignment is another form of job-connected injury, and it may be compounded if it results in a loss of pay or benefits or reduced opportunities for advancement.

Constructive Discharge

Sometimes the sexual harassment causes an employee to quit. If the harassment was so intolerable that it would have led a reasonable person in the same situation to quit, it will be considered a "constructive discharge": the equivalent of an illegal termination. However, this can be a difficult standard to meet. Merely being unhappy or uncomfortable at the job is not enough.

EXAMPLE: A female employee who worked for a film editing company was sexually harassed by the owner of the company for more than a year. The owner made frequent sexually explicit comments, groped her breasts and buttocks, and cornered her alone on multiple occasions. The last straw was when the owner gave the employee an ultimatum to have sex with him or be fired. The owner was leaving for a business trip, but told the employee, "I'll see you when I get back," which she took as a direct threat. Having made complaints of the harassment that went nowhere, the woman decided to quit. A federal court found that the woman was constructively discharged because the working conditions would have made any reasonable person in her situation quit. (*Stockett v. Tolin*, 791 F.Supp. 1536 (S.D. Fla. 1992).)

Penalties for Retaliation

Employees are frequently fired or penalized for reporting sexual harassment or otherwise trying to stop it. Such workplace reprimands are called retaliation. In such cases, the injury is legally considered to be a direct result of the sexual harassment.

Yes, Virgil. Men Get Harassed, Too.

A few years after sexual harassment against women came out of workplace closets across America, a new whisper emerged: "I've been harassed, too. And I'm a man." At first, many people—particularly women—took a dim view of this development. Sexual harassment on the job, after all, had been diagnosed as a social ill stemming from an abuse of power, and men had long dominated the powerful positions in most workplaces.

The popular press and the silver screen seemed titillated by the thought of the role reversal. Michael Crichton was inspired to pen a novel on the theme, *Disclosure*. Still, when the book surfaced inevitably in a film version, even the threat of a besuited Demi Moore pinning a hapless male underling against her mahogany desk seemed less scary than, say, being passed over for a promotion.

The reality is, of course, that abusive behavior in the workplace is not limited by stereotypes of bad boys and good girls. Sexual harassment on the job is not about sex; it's about unwanted, abusive behavior, usually repeated and often

in the face of requests to cut it out. Women as well as men dish out the discriminatory behavior that is sexual harassment, and they'll do it to harass men they want to intimidate, humiliate, or drive out of their workplaces.

Some believe it's worse than we fear: that nearly as many men as women are harassed on the job, but few of them are willing or able to speak up about it.

The exciting development is that gender may not matter in the eyes of the law. Many judges who have considered sexual harassment issues—including the U.S. Supreme Court justices—have edged toward making them gender neutral. For example, most have stopped taking up space in their decisions over whether incidents of alleged harassment should best be viewed from the eyes of a reasonable woman or a reasonable man.

For a growing number of courts these days, the vantage point is common sense, the guiding premise that most workers, men and women, simply want to come to work and do their jobs.

Personal Injuries

In addition to job-connected losses, a sexually harassed worker often suffers serious and costly personal injuries, ranging from stress-related illnesses to serious physical and emotional problems.

Sexual Harassment Under Federal Law

Sexual harassment is illegal under Title VII of the Civil Rights Act, the same federal law that prohibits discrimination based on gender, race, religion, and other protected characteristics. Title VII applies to private employers with 15 or more employees. The procedures and remedies for a sexual harassment claim are generally the same as for other Title VII Claims. (See Chapter 7.)

Sexual harassment occurs when an employee is subjected to unwelcome conduct based on sex. Conduct can still be considered "unwelcome" even if the employee tolerates, or even participates, in the behavior in order to avoid negative consequences. However, that decision is ultimately up to a jury. In most cases, employees fare better when they have clearly told the harasser to stop the conduct and reported the harassment to company officials. The harassing conduct is often sexual in nature, but it doesn't have to be. Courts have found that sexist comments or sabotaging the only woman in a male-dominated job, for example, can qualify as sexual harassment.

Harassment becomes illegal under Title VII when it results in either of the following:

- **A tangible employment action.** A tangible employment action is a significant change in the employee's employment status—for example, when a supervisor fires, demotes, or refuses to promote an employee; takes away opportunities for the employee to earn income; transfers the employee to a less desirable job; or forces the employee to quit

(constructive discharge). As mentioned above, an employer is always liable for sexual harassment that results in a tangible employment action.

- **A hostile work environment.** A hostile work environment occurs where the unwelcome conduct is so severe or pervasive that it alters the conditions of the employee's employment. While a single, extreme incident can be sufficient, a hostile work environment usually involves multiple incidents over a period of time. Occasional teasing or offhand comments do not qualify as sexual harassment. On the other hand, repeated sexual advances, requests for dates, sexual jokes or stories, kissing, or intimate touching (such as massages or long hugs) might qualify as sexual harassment. The harassment does not necessarily need to be directed at the employee either. For example, a woman might be subjected to a hostile work environment when male coworkers frequently discuss their sex lives, refer to other women by demeaning names, and look at pornography at the workplace. While the harasser is often a supervisor or coworker, it can also be a customer, client, vendor, or other nonemployee.

In general, an employer will be responsible for hostile work environment sexual harassment if it knew or should have known that the harassment was occurring and failed to take prompt action to correct it. For example, if you were being harassed by a coworker and reported it to your supervisor or human resources department, your employer will likely be held responsible. As mentioned earlier in the chapter, special rules apply when a supervisor is the one creating the hostile work environment.

Behind Open Doors: How the Battle Was Accidentally Waged

As introduced in Congress, the Civil Rights Act of 1964 only prohibited employment discrimination based on race, color, religion, or national origin. Discrimination on the basis of sex was not included. It was attached to the bill at the last moment by conservative Southern opponents of the bill. They hoped that adding sexual equality was so obviously preposterous that it would scuttle the entire bill when it came to a final vote.

The very idea of prohibiting sex-based discrimination engendered mirth on the floor of Congress and on the editorial pages of major newspapers: Men, it was laughingly argued, could now sue to become Playboy bunnies. The Lyndon Johnson administration, however, wanted the Civil Rights Act passed badly enough that it decided not to oppose the amendment. The Civil Rights Act, including the ban on sex discrimination, became law. Only one of the congressmen who had proposed the sex discrimination amendment actually voted for the bill.

State Laws

Some states have passed their own laws and regulations making sexual harassment illegal, usually called fair employment practices (FEP) laws. But whether a harassed worker has good protection under state law depends on where he or she lives.

On the key issue of compensation for personal injuries, some states have enacted laws that allow employees to recover the full range of remedies for sexual harassment. In some of these states, there is no cap on compensatory and punitive damages like there is under Title VII. However, other states do not allow employees to recover these types of damages at all.

To find out about your state's law, contact your state's fair employment practices agency. (See "State Agencies That Enforce Laws Prohibiting Discrimination in Employment" in the appendix for contact details.)

Other Forms of Illegal Harassment

While sexual harassment is probably the most high-profile type of workplace harassment, other forms of harassment are also illegal. The same laws that prohibit discrimination based on race, color, religion, gender, sex, pregnancy, national origin, age (40 and older), disability, or genetic information also prohibit harassment based on these characteristics. (See Chapter 7 to learn more.) These claims are generally handled in the same manner as sexual harassment claims.

Taking Steps to End Sexual Harassment

The alternatives described here can be viewed as a series of escalating steps you can take to stop sexual harassment. If a particular tactic does not end the objectionable behavior, you can switch to increasingly formal strategies until you find one that is effective.

Confront the Harasser

Often the best strategy for the employee sounds the simplest: Confront the harasser and tell him or her to stop. This is not appropriate or sensible in every case, particularly when you have suffered injuries or are in physical danger. But surprisingly often—workplace experts say up to 90% of the time—it works.

Confronted directly, harassment is especially likely to end if it is at a fairly low level: off-color jokes, inappropriate comments about appearance, repeated requests for dates, sexist cartoons tacked onto the office refrigerator. Saying no makes it clear that you find the behavior unwelcome, which is a critical part of the definition of sexual harassment. It is also a crucial first step if you later decide to take more formal action against the harassment.

Tell the harasser to stop. It is best to deal directly with the harassment when it occurs.

But, if your harasser surprised you with an obnoxious gesture or comment that caught you completely off guard—a common tactic—you may have been too flabbergasted to respond. Or, if you did respond, you may not have expressed yourself clearly. Either way, talk to the harasser the next day.

Here are some tips for telling the harasser to back off:

- **Keep the conversation brief.** Try to speak privately, out of the hearing range of supervisors and coworkers.
- **Do not use humor to make your point.** Joking may be too easily misunderstood or interpreted as a sign that you don't take the situation seriously yourself.
- **Be direct.** It is usually better to make a direct request that a specific kind of behavior stop than to tell your harasser how you feel. For example, saying "I am uncomfortable with this" may be enough to get the point across to some people, but the subtlety may be lost on others. And, of course, making you uncomfortable may be just the effect the harasser was after.
- **Offer no excuses.** Keep in mind that you're not the one whose behavior is inexcusable. Simply make the point and end the conversation. There is no need to offer excuses, such as: "My boyfriend wouldn't like it if we met at your apartment to discuss that new project."

Put it in writing. If your harasser persists, write a letter spelling out the behavior you object to and why. Also specify what you want to happen next. If you feel the situation is serious or bound to escalate, make clear that you will take action against the harassment if it does not stop at once. If your company has a written policy against harassment, attach a copy of it to your letter.

! CAUTION

Beware of retaliation. Do not overlook the possibility that some company witnesses may be blackmailed with the threat—often unspoken —that they will lose their jobs or be demoted if they cooperate with you in documenting or investigating a sexual harassment complaint. While retaliation is illegal, it is difficult to prove. If possible, try to document the harassment by talking with witnesses both inside and outside the company.

Use a Company Complaint Procedure

A court sometimes requires a company to write a comprehensive policy if it finds there has been a problem with sexual harassment. Many businesses also adopt sexual harassment policies on their own, to foster a better atmosphere for employees and to protect themselves from liability.

If you are harassed at work, a sexual harassment policy can help you determine what behavior is inappropriate and how to ensure the harassment is stopped. And, in fact, it is essential for you to heed these policies. The U.S. Supreme Court has ruled in a number of cases that employees can no

longer be coy: If a workplace has a policy or a complaint procedure in place, workers must follow it to complain about or take other action against the bad behavior. Workers who don't take advantage of company procedures for complaining about harassment may lose the legal right to sue the employer.

Find out whether your employer has a sexual harassment policy by contacting the human resources department or the person who handles employee benefits. If there is no policy, lobby to get one.

File a Complaint With a Government Agency

If the sexual harassment does not end after face-to-face meetings or after using the company complaint procedure, consider filing a complaint with the U.S. Equal Employment Opportunities Commission (EEOC) (see Chapter 7) or filing a complaint under a similar state law with a state fair employment practices (FEP) agency. (See "State Laws," above.)

Filing a complaint with these agencies does two important things:

- It sets in motion an investigation by the EEOC or the state FEP agency that may resolve the sexual harassment complaint.
- It is a necessary prerequisite under Title VII and under some state FEP laws if you want to file a lawsuit.

Sometimes the EEOC or a state FEP agency can resolve a sexual harassment dispute at no cost to the employee and with relatively little legal involvement. Almost all of these agencies provide some sort of mediation service: a negotiation between the employer and employee to end the harassment and restore peace in the workplace. Most agencies have the power to expand their investigation to cover more widespread sexual harassment within the company. A few state FEP agencies also provide an administrative hearing, after which a judge or panel can award money to compensate a harassed employee. However, the EEOC and most state agencies do not have this important power.

The EEOC and state FEP agencies can resolve a lot of cases, but not all of them. Investigations sometimes drag on longer than the harassed employee is prepared to wait. Not all cases will be informally resolved; this is particularly true in severe cases of sexual harassment with significant damages.

File a Private Lawsuit

If investigation and mediation by the EEOC or a state FEP agency do not produce satisfactory results, your next step may be to file a lawsuit in federal or state court.

Even if you intend from the beginning to file such a lawsuit, you must first file a claim with a government agency, as described above. An employee must file a claim with the EEOC before bringing a lawsuit under Title VII. Some states also require that the employee first file a claim with the state FEP agency before suing under state law. At some point after such claims are filed and investigated,

the agency will issue you a document—usually referred to as a right-to-sue letter—that allows you to take your case to court. Going to court usually means hiring an attorney who is experienced in these types of cases. (In Chapter 17, see "Hiring a Lawyer.")

Where to Get More Information

Contact your local office of the EEOC and your state FEP agency. Many will send you written materials on sexual harassment and can provide information on local training programs, support groups, and attorneys. A growing number also operate websites listing this information.

Some states and larger cities also have a Commission on the Status of Women or a state or local agency dealing specifically with women's issues; these agencies often offer help to sexually harassed workers. The services these groups provide range from referrals to local groups, to advice and counseling, to legal referrals. Check to see if there is such a group in your area.

Many unions and groups for union members are especially active in the fight against sexual harassment. Contact your union representative to find out about special services or guidance.

Finally, a number of organizations offer specialized information and guidance on evaluating sexual harassment in the workplace, and many also offer legal referrals. (See the appendix for contact details.) ●

Losing or Leaving a Job

The truth will surprise you: No law gives you an automatic right to keep your job. In fact, most of the legal principles and practices of the workplace are indisputably on the side of the employer that fires you.

You can be fired for a host of traditional and obvious reasons: incompetence, excessive absences, violating certain laws or company rules, or sleeping or taking drugs on the job. And other reasons for firings are gaining in popularity, such as economic need occasioned by a downturn in company profits or demands. In most cases, an employer does not need to provide any notice before giving an employee walking papers.

Still, there are limits. The laws do guarantee you some rights on the way out the door. And, because of the grand importance of job security to the majority of Americans, employees are increasingly fighting for and slowly garnering more rights in the workplace.

Even at the tail end of your work relationship, employers do not have the right to discriminate against you illegally (see Chapter 7) or to violate state or federal laws, such as those controlling wages and hours (see Chapter 2). And there are a number of other, more complex reasons that may make it illegal for an employer to fire you.

If you lost your job—or have good reason to think you are about to lose it—it may behoove you to become familiar with the various illegal reasons for firing an employee, discussed in this chapter, and with the services and benefits that may be of assistance

if you do lose your job. (In Chapter 10, see "Collecting Fringe Benefits" and "Replacing Your Income.")

At the very least, understanding how and when laws provide job security and other workplace rights will help you determine whether you should take legal action, in which case you may want to consult a lawyer. (In Chapter 17 see "Hiring a Lawyer," for advice on this.)

The Doctrine of Employment At Will

Once again, for shock value: People employed in private industry have no legal right to their jobs, even if they are reliable, productive employees.

That is because of the long-established legal doctrine of "employment at will," a term you are most likely to hear cited by your boss or your company's lawyers if you speak up and protest your dismissal. An employer's right to unilaterally determine whether or not you should stay on the payroll stems from an 1884 case (*Payne v. Western & Atlantic RR,* 81 Tenn. 507), in which the court ruled that employers do not need a reason to fire employees; they may fire any or all of their workers at will. This means an employee may be fired at any time and for any reason that is not illegal. Even if the reason for dismissal is morally wrong, the court held, no legal wrong has occurred and the government has no basis to intervene.

The management of America's factories was still in the experimental stage in the 1880s when that case was decided. The business community successfully argued then, and in cases that followed, that factories could not be operated profitably unless employers were free to hire and fire as they chose. The employment at will doctrine has been reinforced over and over again by subsequent court rulings. Over time, it has expanded to include not only factories but also virtually all other types of private industry jobs.

But this doesn't mean that employees have no grounds to fight back against getting fired. If that were true, there would be no wrongful termination lawsuits, which is hardly the case. There would be no need for employment lawyers, of which there are many breathing examples. And there would be no need for books about employees' rights! Perish the thought.

Employment at will has been weakened substantially since the 1970s by rulings in wrongful discharge suits and by new laws protecting employees based on certain characteristics (see Chapter 7), for taking protected leave (see Chapter 4), or for reporting workplace safety violations (see Chapter 6), for example.

Nearly all states have adopted the employment at will doctrine. Montana is the only exception. In Montana, employees may be fired only for good cause once they have completed a probationary period.

When a Firing May Be Illegal

A few important exceptions to the employment at will doctrine—and some additional legal theories about unfair treatment on the job—may make it possible for employees to hang onto their jobs or to sue their former employers for wrongful termination.

Written Promises

If you have a written employment contract setting out the terms of your work, pay, and benefits, you may be able to get it enforced against an employer that ignores any one of its provisions.

A written employment contract typically offers job protection by specifying a certain length of employment (for example, a year or two) or by stating that the employee can only be fired for "good cause" or specific offenses.

Employment contracts have become rarer these days, as savvy employers reserve them for the most valuable employees or sensitive situations. For example, employment contracts are often used with executives and high-level managers, employees who will have access to sensitive business information, or employees whose work is essential to the company and who would be hard to replace.

Not all written employment agreements provide job protection, though. Some employers routinely have employees sign "at-will employment agreements." These agreements usually specify some basic terms of the employment agreement—such as job title and starting salary—but they reaffirm the company's right to terminate the employee at any time, for any reason that is not illegal. If you have signed one of these documents, you are not entitled to any greater job protection than the average employee.

An oral contract, while more difficult to prove, is just as legally valid as a written employment contract. For example, if you have evidence that your employer promised during an interview that you would be fired only for good cause, you will be protected against arbitrary and unfair firings.

Implied Promises

Claiming that you and your employer have an implied contract is another way employees can chip away at the doctrine of at-will employment. But it won't be easy. An implied contract is formed based on the words and actions of the employer and employee.

In the past, many employers used terms such as "permanent employment" in their employee manuals, on job application forms, or orally when offering a position to a prospective employee. Today, employees who challenge their firings sometimes argue that, when an employer referred to permanent employment in the hiring process, that created an implied contract between them. They claim that this implied contract means that the company can only fire them for good cause, such as poor performance or misconduct. An employer that fires for less than that, the theory goes, has breached the implied contract. And sometimes, when bolstered by strong evidence, that theory holds up in court.

In addition to making the foolhardy promise of permanent employment, employee handbooks may also offer other fertile grounds for exceptions to employment at will. A few courts have held, for example, that where company manuals state that employees must be given specific forms of progressive discipline before being fired, employers must deliver on those promises. However, most savvy businesses these days are well acquainted with this legal loophole, so few of them now include such promises in their employee manuals. And courts have become more reluctant to find an implied employment contract based on language in an employee manual.

Outside of employee manuals, courts have also found implied contract exceptions to employment at will where employers overtly agree to continue employment for a specific time period, for example: "until the company relocates its main office." And, less commonly, such implied contracts have also been found where employers offer persuasive job negotiations along with letters of reassurance or job offers promising stability.

In determining whether you have a binding implied employment contract with an employer, courts will look at a number of factors, including:

- the duration of your employment
- whether you received regular promotions
- whether you consistently received positive performance reviews
- whether you were assured that you would have continuing employment
- whether your employer violated a usual employment practice in firing you, such as neglecting to give a required warning, or
- whether promises of permanence were made when you were hired.

Breaches of Good Faith and Fair Dealing

While it is an uphill battle to prove that a written or implied promise tantamount to a contract ever existed, it's even tougher to prove that one has been violated. And, barring discrimination or some other egregious wrongdoing in the process, your best hope of fighting a firing may be to claim that your former employer breached what is referred to as a duty of good faith and fair dealing.

Courts have held that employers have committed breaches of good faith and fair dealing by:

- firing or transferring employees to prevent them from collecting sales commissions
- misleading employees about their chances for future promotions and wage increases
- fabricating reasons for firing an employee on the basis of on-the-job performance when the real motivation

is to replace that employee with someone who will work for lower pay
- soft-pedaling the bad aspects of a particular job, such as the need to travel through dangerous neighborhoods late at night, and
- repeatedly transferring an employee to remote, dangerous, or otherwise undesirable assignments to coerce him or her into quitting without collecting the severance pay and other benefits that would otherwise be due.

While their rulings may be subject to change, some courts do not appear to recognize this exception to at-will employment at all. And some states allow employees to sue for breach of good faith and fair dealing only if they have a valid employment contract.

Violations of Public Policy

The employment at will doctrine won't protect an employer from a wrongful discharge claim if a worker is fired for complaining about illegal conduct or a wrong an employer committed, such as failing to pay workers minimum wage or overtime pay when it is required. Indeed, it is illegal to violate public policy when firing a worker: that is, to fire for a reason that harms not only the fired worker, but also the interests of the public in general.

Figuring out whether a court would decide that a particular firing fits into this category can, of course, be an exasperating exercise.

Before allowing an action for a violation of public policy, most courts strictly require that there be some specific law setting out the policy. Many state and federal laws take some of the guesswork out of this issue by specifying employment-related actions that clearly violate public policy, such as firing an employee for:

- disclosing a company practice of refusing to pay employees their earned commissions and accrued vacation pay (in Chapter 2, see "Rights Under the FLSA")
- taking time off work to serve on a jury (in Chapter 2, see "Time Off for Jury Duty")
- taking time off work to vote (in Chapter 2, see "Time Off for Voting")
- serving in the military or National Guard (in Chapter 2, see "Time Off for Military Duty"), or
- notifying authorities about some wrong-doing harmful to the public, generally known as whistleblowing (discussed below).

In addition, a number of state laws protect employees from being fired for asserting a number of more arcane rights, including serving as an election officer, serving as a volunteer firefighter, having certain political opinions, appearing as a witness in a criminal case, or even being elected to the general assembly. Many of these laws, passed in reaction to particular workplace disputes, have become all but dead letters. Few people

know they exist. And very few workers attempt to claim their protections. Still, if you feel that your firing may have violated one of these prohibitions, double-check the laws in your state. (In Chapter 17, see "Legal Research" for detailed guidance.)

Courts have also held that it violates public policy for an employer to fire you because you took advantage of some legal remedies or exercised a legal right. Some states, however, will not recognize this exception unless there is a specific statute conferring a particular right. No matter where you live, it is illegal for your employer to fire you because you:

- file a workers' compensation claim (see Chapter 12)
- file a complaint under the Fair Labor Standards Act (see Chapter 2)
- report a violation of the Occupational Safety and Health Act or state safety law (see Chapter 6)
- claim your rights under Title VII of the Civil Rights Act (see Chapters 7 and 8)
- exercise your right to belong or not to belong to a union (see Chapter 15)
- exercise your right to take a leave from work that was available under state or federal law (see Chapter 4)
- refuse to take a lie detector test or refuse to take a drug test given without good reason (in Chapter 5, see "Workplace Testing"), or
- have your pay subject to an order for child support or a wage garnishment order (see Chapter 2).

Retaliation

Various types of laws—notably, those protecting whistleblowing (see "Whistle-blowing Violations," below) and prohibiting discrimination—specifically forbid employers from retaliating against employees who avail themselves of legal protections.

The broad claim of retaliation is a little more complicated, but somewhat easier to prove, than a charge of workplace discrimination. The reason is that evidence supporting retaliation claims is usually less subjective and more obvious than for cases of discrimination. To make out a case of retaliation, you must prove all of the following:

- You were engaged in a legally protected activity, such as filing a complaint with the Equal Employment Opportunity Commission or formally complaining to your own company officials about harassment or discrimination.

- Your employer took adverse action against you by firing you, denying you a promotion, giving you an unwarranted bad performance review, changing your job duties or responsibilities, overscrutinizing your work, or giving you an inaccurate poor reference.

- There was a direct connection between your activity and your employer's actions. For example, you were demoted just after your employer found out that you filed a charge of sexual harassment.

The employer or former employer is then free to show that there was some legitimate reason—other than retaliation—for its actions. If such evidence is presented, you get one more shot at winning by showing that the employer would not have acted—that is, fired or demoted you—if you had not taken your protected action. This last part is a tad tricky. In seeing whether this link exists, courts are most likely to look at:

- who made the job decision against you (he or she must have known about the action you took)

- your prior work record, especially if you were fired, demoted, or given poor job performance evaluations following your action, and

- the timing of your actions and the employment decision. The shorter the time between them, the more likely a court is to find that they are related.

Fraud

In extreme cases, an employer's actions are so devious and wrong-hearted that they constitute fraud. Fraud can be found at various stages of an employment relationship. It's most common in the recruiting process, where promises are made and broken, or in the final stages, such as when an employee is induced to resign.

Fraud is tough to track and expose, and harder still to prove in court. To win, you must show all of the following:

- The employer made a false representation.

Dream Job Delivers Rude Awakening

Native New Yorker Andrew Lazar uprooted his family to take a California dream job only after a long and agonizing courtship instituted by Rykoff, a restaurant supply and equipment firm.

When Rykoff first set its eyes on Lazar in 1990, he was working in the same family-owned restaurant in which he had worked for more than 18 years, bringing home about $120,000 each year to help cover living expenses for himself, his wife, and their two teens. Rykoff promised him more: a $130,000 salary to start, ample chances for bonuses and increases, a sure shot at becoming department head in a few years, a job with a lifetime guarantee.

Lazar agreed, after being assured that Rykoff was fiscally strong and growing. The company resisted entering a written contract, however, assuring Lazar that "in the Rykoff family, our word is our bond."

But Rykoff's financial picture was not as rosy as painted. While wooing Lazar, it had just experienced its worst year in a long time and was planning to merge with another company, a move that would mean cutting many employees from its staff.

Lazar worked hard and well, exceeding sales goals, increasing sales, and lowering operating costs. But after two years on the job, he was shown the door. Out of work, out of money for home payments, and out of touch with New York job contacts, Lazar sued. He claimed that Rykoff never intended to make him a permanent part of the staff, never intended to pay the wages and bonuses it promised, and so was guilty of fraud. The court agreed. (*Lazar v. Superior Court of Los Angeles County*, 12 Cal. 4th 631 (1996).)

- Someone in charge knew of the false representation.
- Your employer intended to deceive you or induce you to rely on the representation.
- You relied on the representation as the truth.
- You were harmed in some way by your reliance.

The hardest part of proving fraud is connecting the dots to show that the employer acted badly on purpose, in an intentional effort to trick you. That requires good documentation of how, when, to whom, and by what means the false representations were made. If your employer is a large corporation, the task of collecting and proving this information is all the more difficult, because you must usually work through layers of bureaucracy and many individuals. You must be able to name the people who made the fraudulent representations, their authority to speak, whom they spoke to, what they said or wrote, and why you relied on it.

If you are sufficiently lucky and resourceful to present this cogent puzzle after your employer defrauds you, you may be entitled to reimbursement for an array of costs, including the costs of uprooting your family to take the job and the loss of income and security that resulted from leaving your former employer.

Defamation

Defamation is a legal action intended to protect a person's reputation and good standing in the community. There are a lot of opportunities in the typical firing process for an employer to sully an employee's reputation, so it is increasingly common for former employees to bring a defamation charge when they are fired.

A defamation claim is not a challenge to the legitimacy of an employee's dismissal. Rather, it is a way of getting monetary compensation for the reputational harm an employer has caused you.

Defamation is usually difficult to prove. Typically, you must show that, in the process of dismissing you from your job or subsequently providing references to potential new employers, your former employer made

---

Company Makes a Very Expensive Call

Don Hagler had just finished a shift at a Dallas office of Procter & Gamble Co. when a burly security guard stopped him at the front gate, searched a bag he was toting, and confiscated a telephone inside it.

Hagler, who had worked at the detergent plant for 41 years, claimed he had paid for the phone out of his own pocket. But P&G management members saw the phone as their own. They began an intensive investigation, which included posting notices on 11 bulletin boards throughout the plant and over the company email system that read: "It has been determined that the telephone in question is Procter & Gamble's property and that Don had therefore violated Work Rule #12 concerning theft of company property."

Then Hagler was fired.

He sued for defamation, claiming that P&G used him as an example to stem a tide of property pilfering. At trial, a coworker testified that he was with Hagler at a mall when he bought the phone. Hagler testified that he had applied for more than 100 jobs, but no employer would take him on after learning he was fired for theft.

After deliberating for five hours, the jury returned a verdict for Hagler, awarding him $15.6 million in damages.

Hagler became richer, but wistful. "I'm not proud of the fact that I had to sue the company I was dedicated to for 41 years," he told *The Wall Street Journal* just after the verdict. "I sued because they called me a thief and put it on 11 bulletin boards in the plant. I think P&G's a good company. But I think they've changed. They're not as nice to people as they used to be."

a false statement that significantly damaged your good name and jeopardized your chances for gaining new employment.

This commonly entails much legal hair-splitting over the facts surrounding a firing. Most disputes involve whether the employer may communicate the facts surrounding a dismissal to other people. And a number of defamation claims center on whether or not the distribution of the damaging information was intentional and malicious—that is, meant to harm you.

To sue for defamation, you must typically show that your former employer:

- made a false statement of fact about you
- told or wrote that statement to at least one other person
- knew that the statement was false or acted recklessly or negligently with regard to the truth of the statement, and
- harmed you in some way by communicating the statement, such as by causing others to shun you or causing you to lose a job or promotion.

To win a case of defamation, you must prove that the hurtful words were more than petty watercooler gossip. The words must also be more than a personal opinion. Statements that amount to defamation include false claims that an employee:

- committed a crime
- performed job duties incompetently
- improperly used drugs or alcohol, or
- acted in some other way that clearly implied unfitness for a particular job.

Because a few unflattering comments or even a small dose of mean-spiritedness does not usually qualify as defamation, it is extremely important to scrupulously document your employer's false statements. You can do this by writing down not only the exact offensive words that were said and who said them, but also when and where they were said and whether there were any witnesses. Securing this type of documentation may be difficult if you have lost your job and are no longer in the workplace.

Keep in mind that courts will generally be most persuaded by words that clearly damage your work reputation. For example, a former employer's false statement that you stole money would probably qualify as defamation, because most people would probably not hire you because of it. But a false statement that you had stayed at your last job only two months would probably be defamatory only if you could prove that it damaged you severely, by preventing you from getting a new job, causing a landlord to refuse to rent an apartment to you, or otherwise causing you social embarrassment and emotional distress.

Whistleblowing Violations

Whistleblowing is a sort of subset of the public policy violations discussed above. While states differ in the details, whistleblowing laws generally protect individuals who report to proper authorities activities that are unlawful or harm the public interest.

One unique feature about whistleblowing is its foul-crying aspect. The whistleblower is protected for doing the civic duty of pointing out the misdeeds of powers that be. Generally, whistleblowers are protected from retaliation only if they act in good faith and have some good reason to believe that the information they report to authorities is accurate.

Some states protect whistleblowers who complain of any legal violation (that is, who complain that the employer has violated any law, regulation, or ordinance). Others limit whistleblower status to those who report violations of particular laws, such as labor laws or environmental protections. A play-fair provision in a number of state laws requires employees to tell their employers about the wrongdoing first, to allow them an opportunity to fix the problem.

RESOURCE

For more information on whistle-blowing cases and legislation, contact:

National Whistleblower Center
P.O. Box 25074
Washington, DC 20027
202-342-1903

The organization also maintains a robust website at www.whistleblowers.org.

The U.S. Department of Labor also has a Whistleblower Protection Program. For more information, go to www.whistleblowers.gov.

The High Cost of Blowing the Whistle

The story of one of the most famous whistleblowers, Karen Silkwood, was the inspiration for hundreds of articles, several books, and a heavily bankrolled motion picture.

In the early 1970s, Silkwood worked as a lab analyst in an Oklahoma Kerr-McGee plant that manufactured plutonium pins used as fuel for nuclear reactors. Plutonium, a radioactive chemical element, is known to be highly toxic and carcinogenic. Silkwood, an elected union official and outspoken critic of Kerr-McGee's health and safety practices, began collecting and recording information to substantiate her charges that employees at the plant were dangerously exposed.

In early November 1974, Silkwood was found to be contaminated with the chemical. Nine days later, while enroute to meet with a *New York Times* reporter and union leader to turn over her documentation of Kerr-McGee's unsafe work conditions, Silkwood was killed in a car accident with suspicious overtones. The damning documentation she was alleged to have had with her was not recovered from the accident scene.

Silkwood's estate sued Kerr-McGee for the injuries caused by the escaping plutonium. A jury awarded her estate $500,000 for personal injuries, $5,000 for the cost of sanitizing her contaminated apartment, and $10 million in punitive damages. After a series of complicated appeals that went all the way up to the U.S. Supreme Court, the parties settled, with Kerr-McGee agreeing to pay the Silkwood estate $1.38 million.

Tips for Figuring Out Whether You Are Protected

Whistleblower statutes attempt to protect against the too-common occurrence of employees getting fired just after speaking to authorities about some wrongdoing.

Coincidence? Maybe.

What makes the firing questionable—and possibly covered by a whistleblower statute—is often the timing. Pay strict attention to when you were fired. Note whether it was soon after your employer found out that you reported the wrongful behavior. The shorter the time, the more likely that you are protected by a whistleblower statute.

There are also a number of other questions you should ask to help determine whether you may be covered by a whistleblower statute:

- Did you complain to anyone at your own workplace about the wrongful behavior before going outside? If so, what was the response? Were you threatened? Were you offered special benefits for not filing a complaint?

- If your company has a policy of progressively disciplining employees—reprimand, probation, suspension, dismissal—was it speeded up or ignored in your case?
- Were your whistleblowing activities specifically mentioned to you by your supervisor? By company management? By other employees?
- Have other employees been fired for whistleblowing?
- Did you notice management or coworkers treating you differently after you complained about the illegal behavior? Were you suddenly ostracized or ignored, passed over for promotions, or given a less-attractive job assignment?

The more documentation you can produce —memos from management, dated notes summarizing conversations with coworkers, signed statements from other former employees —the stronger your case will be. (For other advice on documenting your dismissal, see "Getting Documentation," below.)

Employees' Rights

The other side of the at-will employment logic is that employees are also free to leave a job at any time; an employer cannot force you to stay in a job you no longer wish to keep. And, while it is customary to give an employer notice before leaving a job, it is not usually required by law (unless you have an employment contract that requires notice). The right to leave a job at any time feels like small recompense for most workers. Obviously, most legal battles are fought by former employees who want their jobs back, not employers demanding that employees stay on.

Finding Out Why You Were Fired

Few job losses—or even disciplinary actions—come as complete surprises. The first step to avoiding termination and deciding whether to take action against a firing is the same: You must delve into the inner workings of your employer's mind to find out the reason. Often this is simple: You are put on probation for missing four deadlines last month. You are being fired for grossly mishandling the company's biggest account. And you are told just so.

But sometimes, discerning the reason or ostensible reason for a disciplining or firing takes more sleuth work.

If You Have Been Disciplined

Although an employer has the right to fire you on the spot for substandard performance or stealing from the company coffer, most employers proceed more gingerly these days, beginning with a verbal warning and progressing to a written warning to probation to suspension, then to dismissal.

There are a number of steps you can take when you suspect the end of your job is near. You are not legally entitled to any progressive warning system unless your employee handbook or other document guarantees it without exception.

But, if you find yourself on the receiving end of a disciplinary notice, there are several steps you can take that might actually save your job:

- Be sure you understand exactly what work behavior is being challenged. If you are unclear, ask for a meeting with your supervisor or human resources staff to discuss the issue more thoroughly.

- If you disagree with allegations that your work performance or behavior is poor, ask for the assessment in writing. You may want to add a written clarification to your own personnel file, but you should do so only if you feel your employer's assessment is inaccurate. First, take some time to reflect and perhaps discuss your situation with friends and family. If your clarification is inaccurate or sounds vengeful, your words could be twisted against you as evidence of your inability to work as a team player or take constructive criticism.

- Look for a written company policy on discipline procedures in the employee handbook or a separate document. If the policy says certain measures "must," "will," or "shall" be followed before an employee will be dismissed, then you have more clout in demanding that they be followed to the letter. Point out the rules and ask why they are being bent in your situation. That may help buy you more time so that you can change your work habits or allow you to wait until a workplace controversy dies down.

• Read between the lines to see whether your disciplining or firing may be discriminatory or otherwise illegal. Pay particular attention to the timing: Were you put on probation shortly before your rights in the company pension plan vested? Look also at uneven applications of discipline: Are women given substandard performance reviews more often than men?

If You Have Been Fired

Unless you are the unfortunate victim of a sudden unforeseen cutback in the workforce, you are likely to have seen the end of your employment coming well before it arrived. This is particularly true if you are fired because your employer claims your work was subpar or that you violated a particular workplace rule. Still, it almost always behooves you to get it in writing.

Before any holes had been punched in the employment at will doctrine, companies often refused to give employees any reasons for being fired. Since a company had the legal right to hire and fire without any justification, most opted not to invite trouble by stating a reason for firing.

Whatever They Call It, It Still Feels Bad

People tend to think that getting fired means that you did something wrong on the job, and that when other terms are used—such as dismissal, discharge, layoff, staff cut, reduction in force, furlough, downsizing, and the all-too-sane-sounding rightsizing—it somehow means something less onerous. In hopes of preventing bad community relations and wrongful discharge lawsuits, many companies use these gentler words to describe firings.

Some companies have gone so far as to announce the firing of large groups of employees by using sterile, institutional terms, such as reorganizational incentives or activity analysis and review. Still other companies have described the process of firing groups of employees as early retirement, even when the people being dismissed are not being given anywhere near enough money to continue to live the rest of their lives without working.

Whenever you are permanently dismissed from a job without being given sufficient income to continue living without working, all these terms mean the same thing: You've been fired. (For more information on layoffs, see "Plant Closings," below.)

Today, many companies have reversed their policies on giving reasons for dismissals. Because courts throughout the country are gradually establishing more rights for fired employees, many companies, particularly large corporations that are attractive targets for wrongful discharge lawsuits, now are careful to provide at least the appearance of fair and evenhanded treatment of employees who are fired. Company owners and managers typically do this by carefully documenting the employee's allegedly unacceptable work performance. Then, the employer can provide the employee—and a court, should it come to that—with specific and tangible documentation of the cause of firing.

If you are fired, make your best effort to obtain a clear statement of the employer's reasons for doing so. Office or factory rumors, your suspicions, or your spouse's hunches just will not suffice. If you eventually decide to challenge your dismissal, the reasons that your former employer stated for firing you will almost certainly become a major point in any legal battle that may develop.

Getting Documentation

Securing the supporting paperwork behind the decision is most important if you have been fired and are considering taking legal action. But, even if you decide not to challenge the legality of your firing, you will be in a much better position to enforce all of your workplace rights if you carefully document the circumstances. For example, if you apply for unemployment insurance benefits and your former employer challenges that application, you will typically need to prove that you were dismissed for reasons beyond your control. (In Chapter 11, see "Filing a Claim.")

There are a number of time-tested ways to document the circumstances leading to your firing.

Keeping a Paper Trail

Long before being fired, you may sense that something has gone wrong in the relationship between you and your employer, even if there has been no formal disciplinary action against you. Perhaps your first clue is that your pay has been stuck at one level with no raises for an unusually long time. Or you may notice that none of your work assignments extend more than a few weeks. Whatever the sign that your job may be in jeopardy, use it as a reason to begin keeping a log of your interactions with your employer.

Record and date each work-related event, such as performance reviews, commendations or reprimands, salary increases or decreases, and even informal comments from your supervisor about your work. Note the date, time, and location for each event, which members of management were involved, and whether or not there were witnesses. Whenever possible, back up your log with written materials your employer has issued, such as copies of the employee handbook, memos, brochures, and employee orientation videos.

In addition, ask to see your personnel file. (In Chapter 5, see "Your Personnel Records," for information on your right to see your file.) Make a copy of all reports and reviews in it. Because personnel administrators are notoriously covetous of employee files, you may have to make repeated requests to see your file or pay reasonable copying costs. It will be money well spent.

Many former employees are startled to learn that their personnel files have been tampered with by unscrupulous former employers. If you fear this might happen, make an additional copy of your file or of relevant reports or performance reviews, and mail them to yourself by certified mail. Then, should matters heat up later—or should a court battle become necessary—you will have dated proof of how the documents looked before any tampering took place.

Getting Written Explanations

There are a number of reasons you might want to get a written explanation of why you were fired from a former employer: to see whether the reason your former employer gives meshes with your own hunches and, in the hardest situations, to use as documentation if you feel your dismissal was discriminatory or otherwise illegal. Written explanations may also help you in a later job search, as you will be better able to assess whether a soon-to-be-former employer is likely to give a good recommendation. (In Chapter 10, see "Getting References" for more on employer references.)

In a rare but possible scenario, you may receive an explanation of your firing that is so shocking, so wrongheaded, and so mean-spirited that it seems that its purpose is to keep you from being hired again. It may indicate that your employer is blacklisting you—a practice that is illegal in many states. (In Chapter 10, see "Blacklisting.")

Information From Former Employers

Many states regulate what an employer may say about a former employee, usually when giving a reference to a prospective employer. In some states, employers may provide information about a former employee only with the employee's consent. And, to protect employers from defamation lawsuits (see discussion above), some states give employers who provide this information immunity. This means that the former employee cannot sue the employer for giving out the information as long as the employer acted in good faith.

Some states have laws, sometimes known as service letter laws, that require employers to provide former employees with letters describing certain aspects of their employment (typically, their work histories, pay rates, or reasons for their termination). These laws vary greatly from state to state and are summarized in the chart at the end of this chapter.

CAUTION

You don't get it both ways. When asking a former employer for a service letter, you are asking for the truth, the whole truth, and nothing but the truth as to why you were fired. But reasons for firing are subjective. And, chances are, you may not like what you read. As noted above, a number of states specifically protect employers from being sued for defamation because of what they have written in service letters. Most laws require a former employer to make the statement "in good faith" in order to take advantage of this protection.

Requesting an Explanation

If you live in a state that has a service letter law requiring explanations of dismissals, and your employer does not provide you with one, request one in writing. Use the following sample letter as a starting point for drafting your request.

Did They Say Merge or Squeeze Out?

In uncertain economic times, many formerly hardy employers are forced to scuttle about for funds. Some pressed companies decide that the best route out of their woes is to restructure the business completely. Many of them opt to merge with or acquire other companies. This can leave all employees involved unsure of their rights and the security of their jobs.

The law is lurching to keep up with these corporate gyrations, too. Legal questions are just now beginning to emerge that may help shape employees' rights during mergers and acquisitions.

A few hot spots are already clear.

Imperiled personnel information. When two companies merge, the negotiation process leaves all the transitory employees vulnerable: Their salaries are disclosed to potential buying companies, and their personnel files are often laid bare as part of full disclosure before the deal gets closed.

Lost negotiation rights. Employees who are left over after a merger are most often handed a take-it-or-leave-it package: They can accept the position available at the reconstituted company, or they can walk. The deal their employer strikes may rob them of the chance to negotiate a severance package.

Noncompete rights and wrongs. A number of employees sign noncompete agreements when they come on board, in which they typically agree not to go into the same type of business within a certain geographical region for a specified number of years. This is to prevent workers from running off with trade secrets and established clients by setting up a competing business. (In Chapter 10, see "Agreements Not to Compete.") But, as more of the specialized companies merge to become conglomerates, this will mean that employees who quit or are fired will have fewer places to look for work.

Sample Letter

June 10, 20xx

Ellen Ullentine
President
Tasteless Frozen Pizzas, Inc.
123 Main Street
Anywhere, MO 54321

Dear Ms. Ullentine:

As required by Missouri Statutes Section 290.140, I request from you a letter stating the length of my employment with Tasteless Frozen Pizzas, Inc., the nature of my work there, and the reason I was dismissed from employment.

Please note that this law requires you to provide me with such a letter within 45 days of when you receive this request.

Sincerely,

Paul Smith

Paul Smith
321 Front Street
Anywhere, MO 54321
234-555-6666

Some laws specify a time limit for requesting service letters. But, if possible, you should make your request within a day or two of your dismissal to make sure that you meet any such deadlines and to prevent the passage of time from affecting people's memories. Send your request for a service letter by certified mail so that you can prove, if necessary, that you made your request within any time limits specified.

States Without Laws or Explanations

If you live in a state that does not have a service letter law, your employer might not offer you any written explanation for your firing. In that case, ask the person who officially informs you of your firing for a written explanation of the company's decision to dismiss you. Be firm but polite; keep in mind that having to fire someone is an extremely stressful assignment for even the most experienced managers.

Companies usually want dismissed employees out of their buildings and away from their remaining employees as quickly as possible to prevent vengeful sabotage or the spreading of anticompany sentiment. Therefore, a person being fired might have some negotiating power by merely sitting in place in front of the person doing the firing, quietly insisting on written documentation until the request is satisfied. Remember, however, that in some companies, using your posterior as a negotiating tool, can get you escorted out forcibly by the corporate security force or local police.

Letters of Understanding

If you have done everything within the limits of civility and your employer still refuses to give you written documentation of the reasons for your dismissal, you may be in for a wait—and some extra work—before you get it. If your state is among the majority that have no laws requiring such documentation, there is not much else you can do to force the issue at the time of your dismissal. Later, you may obtain documentation through some of the laws granting employees access to their personnel files (In Chapter 5, see "Your Personnel Records"), or by filing a wrongful discharge lawsuit (see "Taking Action Against Your Dismissal," below) and demanding the company's internal documents concerning your employment during the course of the lawsuit.

But, before that, you might want to write a letter of understanding to the person who fired you, like the sample letter, below. This is especially important if you received some mixed messages upon being fired. Of course, it is to your advantage to get your employer to specify the reason for your firing that makes you seem the least culpable and the most attractive to prospective employers.

Although you should mail your letter of understanding promptly, it is usually best to let it sit for a day or two after writing it. Then, read it over again to make sure you have kept it businesslike and to the point. Getting fired is a very emotional event, one that often generates more than a little anger and desire for revenge in even the most saintly people.

Correspondence between you and your former employer may eventually become the basis of future negotiations or even courtroom evidence, and you do not want its credibility to be tainted by ink from a poison pen.

Send your letter of understanding by certified mail so that you will be able to prove that the company received it. Using certified mail in this case may also help drive home to your former employer that you are serious about enforcing your rights concerning your dismissal.

Sample Letter

August 2, 20xx

Aggie Supervisor
XYZ Company
2222 Lake Street
Anytown, CA 12345

Dear Ms. Supervisor:

I'm writing to clarify the reasons for my dismissal from employment at XYZ Company on July 29, 20xx.

My understanding is that I was dismissed because there was a sharp decline in the market for our product, seamless rolled rings, due to the recent cutback in government military spending.

If you feel that my understanding is incorrect, please advise me in writing by August 16, 20xx.

Sincerely,
John Employee
John Employee
123 Any Street
Anytown, CA 12345
234-555-6666

If the company responds to your letter, you have obtained at least one piece of documentation of its reason for firing you. If the company does not respond to your letter after a month or so, you can probably assume that the reason stated in your letter of understanding won't be refuted by your former employer.

Additional Documentation

Other important forms of documentation for your firing may come your way in the weeks following your dismissal. For example, if you file a claim for unemployment compensation, your former employer might respond to that claim. That response will eventually be translated into a document that the local unemployment insurance office will provide to you. (See Chapter 11.)

Store all such documents in a file folder, a shoebox, or some safe place where they will not get lost or destroyed.

Waiving Your Right to Sue

In some companies, the firing process may work like this: Someone from human resources hands you a formal written notice that you are fired. You are then asked to sign a statement indicating that you have read the documents and that you accept what is written in them. You are given a check for a few extra months of severance pay, although this is beyond the company's legal obligations. You will then be told that the check will be released to you immediately if you sign a waiver of any rights to take legal action against the company as a result of your dismissal.

This method of firing can seem cruel or unfair. But, in the past, it was effective for some companies in discouraging wrongful termination lawsuits.

It is no longer a foolproof tactic. An increasing number of employees who have signed these types of waivers have later succeeded in having the courts throw out the waivers by arguing, for example, that the waivers were signed under duress. Whether signing such a waiver will prevent you from suing your former employer depends on the circumstances of each individual case. However, courts will often uphold waivers when they are written in clear terms and the employee was given a reasonable amount of time to consider the agreement and have it reviewed by an attorney.

Going along with the firing will typically mean that you get immediate severance pay. However, if you have doubts about the validity of your dismissal, withhold your signature on any waiver of your right to sue while you think over the company's offer, obtain more information, and perhaps talk to a lawyer. (See Chapter 17.) You take the chance of not getting the money that the company waves in front of you, but you will reduce the risk of buyer's remorse.

CAUTION

Beware of the early retirement waiver. If you are asked to sign a waiver of your right to sue in return for participation in an early retirement program offered by your former employer, the Older Workers Benefit Protection Act may give you the right to consider the company's offer for 45 days before you accept or reject it, and seven more days to revoke a decision to accept the company's offer. (In Chapter 7, see "The Older Workers Benefit Protection Act.")

Taking Action Against Your Dismissal

Once you become familiar with how employee dismissals are successfully challenged, compare those legal strategies to your firing and decide:

- which legal principle used to challenge a job loss best fits your situation
- whether you are willing to expend the effort, money, and time it usually takes to fight a firing, and
- whether or not you will need additional legal help to challenge your firing.

Many employment lawyers offer an initial consultation for free or a relatively small fee. This is a valuable opportunity to get some advice on whether you have any legal claims, how likely you are to win, and how much you might receive. After meeting with a couple of lawyers, it will probably be clear to you whether your case is worth pursuing.

(For more on finding and hiring a lawyer, see Chapter 17.)

Plant Closings

Sometimes, a job is lost through no fault of the employer or the employee; economics or changing marketplace demands can simply make a job superfluous or extinct. Even in such situations, however, plant closing laws may give employees some rights as the workplace doors close.

The statutes typically known as plant closing laws apply only to mass layoffs of employees. Also, keep in mind that neither the federal plant closing law nor the state and local laws in the same category actually forbid closing worksites and dismissing the people who work there. All these laws really do is require that companies give employees a little advance notice that their jobs are going to go away, like it or not.

Federal Law

The federal plant closing law—the Worker Adjustment and Retraining Notification, or WARN, Act—applies to employers with 100 or more employees, not including those who work less than 20 hours per week or that have worked fewer than six out of the last 12 months. The law requires covered employers to provide 60 days' written notice to employees before a plant closing or mass layoff, defined as follows:

- **Plant closing.** The permanent or temporary shutdown of a single job site, or one or more facilities in a job site, that would result in employment loss for 50 or more employees during any 30-day period.
- **Mass layoff.** A reduction in force that results in employment loss at a single site of employment during a 30-day period of at least 500 employees, or between 50 and 499 employees if they make up at least one-third of the workforce.

Any layoffs or plant closings that happen in a 90-day period are considered one event for purposes of determining the above thresholds. This is to prevent employers from evading the WARN Act requirements by dividing layoffs into smaller groups.

Employers are also required to provide 60 days' written notice to the chief local elected official, such as the mayor of the city in which the cut will take place, and to the Dislocated Worker Unit of the state in which the cut will occur. The agency designated as the Dislocated Worker Unit varies from state to state, but your state's labor department should be able to direct you to the agency responsible for assisting workers who lose their jobs in mass dismissals. (See the appendix for contact information.)

Exceptions

Employers are not required to provide notice if:
- the plant closing or mass layoff is due to a strike or lockout, or

- the employees affected were working at a temporary facility or on a temporary project, and they were told that when they were hired.

Employers must give as much notice as is practicable under the following circumstances:
- the plant closing or mass layoff is due to a natural disaster
- the plant closing or mass layoff is caused by business circumstances that were not reasonably foreseeable 60 days in advance, or
- the employer was seeking new capital or business to keep the plant open and reasonably believed that giving notice would have ruined the opportunity.

Penalties for Violations

Obviously, the plant closing law has almost as many holes as fabric. But employers that manage to violate it despite all the exceptions can be made to pay the following penalties:
- back pay to each employee affected by the violation, up to a maximum of 60 days of pay
- reimbursement of the employees' benefit costs that would have been paid by the company had the illegal staff cut not occurred
- a fine of up to $500 per day for each day of the violation, up to a maximum of $30,000 (this fine is paid to the state, not to the workers who were laid off), and
- any attorneys' fees incurred.

This last item—requiring that legal fees be paid—is important because if you have received your walking papers as part of a mass firing that violates the federal plant closing law, you and your coworkers might have no recourse but to file a lawsuit to enforce your rights. Unlike other employment laws, the WARN Act does not designate a federal agency to accept and investigate violations of the law. However, some state agencies might investigate complaints based on violation of similar state laws.

Help From Your Uncle Sam

Before you hire a lawyer to take action under the federal plant closing law, you may want to write or call the highest elected official (such as the mayor) of the municipality where the staff cut took place and ask him or her to pursue your complaint. The WARN Act specifies that a unit of the aggrieved local government may sue the employer involved in the federal district court where the incident occurred or in any district where the employer does business.

In general, governmental bodies are not very aggressive in pursuing complaints against businesses. But, because large-scale staff cutting may be a high-profile political issue, your local mayor might surprise you by suddenly becoming your legal advocate.

CAUTION

The math may be tricky. Counting the days may be more difficult than you would assume. Several courts have ruled that back pay was based on workdays in the 60-day notice period rather than calendar days.

State Plant Closing Laws

A growing number of states have their own plant closing laws. (See the "State Laws on Mass Layoffs and Plant Closings" chart at the end of this chapter.) Even a few cities have laws restricting companies that order mass dismissals.

A few of the state plant closing laws even require the employer to pay some severance to the affected employees. For example, Hawaii's version requires an employer, under certain conditions, to make up the difference between a worker's regular pay and the unemployment compensation the worker will receive for up to four weeks after the staff cut. Employers that shirk this legal duty must pay a high price: three months of compensation to every former worker.

State Laws on Information From Former Employers

Alaska

Alaska Stat. § 09.65.160

Information that may be disclosed:
- job performance

Who may request or receive information:
- prospective employer
- the former or current employee

Employer immune from liability unless:
- Employer knowingly or intentionally discloses information that is false or misleading or that violates employee's civil rights.

Arizona

Ariz. Rev. Stat. Ann. § 23-1361

Information that may be disclosed:
- job performance
- reasons for termination
- performance evaluation
- professional conduct

Who may request or receive information:
- prospective employer
- the former or current employee

Copy to employee required:
- Copy of disclosures must be sent to employee's last known address.

Employer immune from liability:
- employer with fewer than 100 employees who provides only information listed above
- employer with at least 100 employees who has a regular practice of providing information listed above upon request of a prospective employer

Employer immune from liability unless:
- Information is intentionally misleading.
- Employer provided information knowing it was false or not caring if it was true or false.

Arkansas

Ark. Code Ann. § 11-3-204

Information that may be disclosed:
- dates and duration of employment
- current pay rate and pay history
- job description and job duties
- last written performance evaluation
- attendance information
- results of drug or alcohol tests administered within one year before the request
- threats of violence, harassing acts, or threatening conduct toward another employee or related to the workplace
- the reasons for termination, including whether it was voluntary or involuntary
- whether the employee is eligible for rehire

Who may request or receive information:
- prospective employer (employee must provide written consent)
- the former or current employee

Employer immune from liability unless:
- Employer disclosed information knowing it was false or not caring if it was true or false.
- Information was provided with the intent to discriminate or retaliate against an employee for exercising a federal or state right or for acting in accordance with the public policy of the state.

Other provisions:
- Employee consent required before employer can release information.
- Consent must follow required format and must be signed and dated.
- If the employee secures new employment for six months or more, the consent is no longer valid.

State Laws on Information From Former Employers (continued)

- If the employee secures new employment, but works there for less than six months, the consent is valid for another six months.

California

Cal. Civ. Code § 47(c); Cal. Lab. Code §§ 1053, 1055

Information that may be disclosed:
- job performance
- reasons for termination or separation
- knowledge, qualifications, skills, or abilities based upon credible evidence
- eligibility for rehire

Who may request or receive information:
- prospective employer

Employer required to write letter:
- public utility companies only

Employer immune from liability unless:
- Information was known to be false or was disclosed with reckless disregard for its truth or falsity.

Colorado

Colo. Rev. Stat. § 8-2-114

Information that may be disclosed:
- job history
- job performance, including work-related skills, abilities, and habits
- reasons for separation
- eligibility for rehire

Who may request or receive information:
- prospective employer
- the former or current employee

Copy to employee required:
- Upon request, a copy must be sent to employee's last known address.
- Employee may obtain a copy in person at the employer's place of business during normal business hours.

- Employer may charge reproduction costs if multiple copies are required.

Employer immune from liability unless:
- Information disclosed was false, and employer knew or reasonably should have known it was false.

Connecticut

Conn. Gen. Stat. Ann. § 31-51

Information that may be disclosed:
- "truthful statement of any facts"

Who may request or receive information:
- prospective employer
- the former or current employee

Delaware

Del. Code Ann. tit. 19, §§ 708 to 709

Information that may be disclosed:

All employers:
- job performance
- performance evaluation or opinion
- work-related characteristics
- violations of law

Health or child care employers:
- reasons for termination or separation
- length of employment, pay level, and history
- job description and duties
- substantiated incidents of abuse, neglect, violence, or threats of violence
- disciplinary actions

Who may request or receive information:
- prospective employer (health or child care employers must provide signed statement from prospective applicant authorizing former employer to release information)

Employer required to write letter:
- letter required for employment in health care and child care facilities

State Laws on Information From Former Employers (continued)

- letter must follow required format
- employer must have written consent from employee
- employer must send letter within 10 days of receiving request

Employer immune from liability unless:

- Information was known to be false, was deliberately misleading, or was disclosed without caring whether it was true.
- Information was confidential or disclosed in violation of a nondisclosure agreement.

Florida

Fla. Stat. Ann. §§ 435.10, 655.51, 768.095

Information that may be disclosed:

Employers that require background checks:

- reasons for termination or separation
- disciplinary matters

Banks and financial institutions:

- violation of an industry-related law or regulation, which has been reported to appropriate enforcing authority

Who may request or receive information:

- prospective employer
- the former or current employee

Employer required to write letter:

- only employers that require background checks

Employer immune from liability unless:

- Information is known to be false or is disclosed without caring whether it is true.
- Disclosure violates employee's civil rights.

Georgia

Ga. Code Ann. § 34-1-4

Information that may be disclosed:

- job performance
- violations of state law
- ability (or lack of ability) to perform job duties

Who may request or receive information:

- prospective employer
- the former or current employee

Employer immune from liability unless:

- Information was disclosed in violation of a nondisclosure agreement.
- Information was confidential according to federal, state, or local law or regulations.
- Employer didn't act in good faith in disclosing information.

Hawaii

Haw. Rev. Stat. § 663-1.95

Information that may be disclosed:

- job performance

Who may request or receive information:

- prospective employer

Employer immune from liability unless:

- Information disclosed was knowingly false or misleading.

Idaho

Idaho Code § 44-201(2)

Information that may be disclosed:

- job performance
- performance evaluation or opinion
- professional conduct

Employer immune from liability unless:

- Information is deliberately misleading, known to be false, or provided with reckless disregard for its truth or falsity.

Illinois

745 Ill. Comp. Stat. § 46/10

Information that may be disclosed:

- job performance

Who may request or receive information:

- prospective employer

State Laws on Information From Former Employers (continued)

Employer immune from liability:

- Information is truthful, or employer believed, in good faith, that it was.

Employer immune from liability unless:

- Information is knowingly false or in violation of a civil right.

Indiana

Ind. Code Ann. §§ 22-5-3-1(b),(c), 22-6-3-1

Information that may be disclosed:

- information about a current or former employee

Who may request or receive information:

- the former or current employee (must be in writing)

Copy to employee required:

- Prospective employer must provide copy of any written communications from current or former employers that may affect hiring decision.
- Prospective employee must make request in writing within 30 days of applying for employment.

Employer required to write letter:

- Must have written request from employee.
- Must state nature, character, and length of employment and reason, if any, for separation.
- Employers that don't require written recommendations do not have to provide them.

Employer immune from liability unless:

- Information was known to be false.

Iowa

Iowa Code § 91B.2

Information that may be disclosed:

- work-related information

Who may request or receive information:

- prospective employer
- the former or current employee

Employer immune from liability unless:

- Information violates employee's civil rights.
- Information is not relevant to inquiry being made.
- Information is knowingly provided to a person who has no legitimate interest in receiving it.
- Information is provided maliciously.
- Information is provided with no good faith belief that it is true.

Kansas

Kan. Stat. Ann. §§ 44-119a, 44-808(3)

Information that may be disclosed:

Does not have to be in writing:

- dates of employment
- pay level
- wage history
- job description and duties

Must be in writing:

- performance evaluation or opinion (written evaluation conducted prior to employee's separation)
- reasons for termination or separation

Who may request or receive information:

- prospective employer (written request required for performance evaluation and reasons for termination or separation)
- former or current employee (request must be in writing)

Copy to employee required:

- Employee must be given copy of performance evaluations and reasons for separation upon request.

State Laws on Information From Former Employers (continued)

Employer required to write letter:
- Must give former employee a service letter stating the length of employment, job classification, and rate of pay, upon written request.

Employer immune from liability:
- employer who provides information as it is specified in the law

Kentucky
Ky. Rev. Stat. Ann. § 411.225

Information that may be disclosed:
- job performance
- performance evaluation
- professional conduct

Who may request or receive information:
- prospective employer
- the former or current employee

Employer immune from liability unless:
- Employer knows information is false or provides it with reckless disregard as to its truth or falsity.
- Information is intentionally misleading.
- Providing the information is an illegal discriminatory act under state law.

Louisiana
La. Rev. Stat. Ann. § 23:291

Information that may be disclosed:
- accurate information on reasons for employee's separation and employee's job performance, including: attendance
- attitude
- awards
- demotions
- job duties
- effort
- evaluations

- knowledge
- skills
- promotions
- disciplinary actions

Who may request or receive information:
- prospective employer
- the former or current employee

Employer immune from liability:
- Under certain conditions if employer has conducted a background check.

Employer immune from liability unless:
- Information is knowingly false and deliberately misleading.

Maine
Me. Rev. Stat. Ann. tit. 26, §§ 598, 630

Information that may be disclosed:
- job performance
- work record

Who may request or receive information:
- prospective employer

Employer required to write letter:
- Employer must provide a discharged employee with a written statement of the reasons for termination within 15 days of receiving employee's written request.

Employer immune from liability unless:
- Employer knowingly discloses false or deliberately misleading information with malicious intent.

Maryland
Md. Code Ann. [Cts. & Jud. Proc.] § 5-423

Information that may be disclosed:
- job performance
- reasons for termination or separation
- information disclosed in a report or other document required by law or regulation

State Laws on Information From Former Employers (continued)

Who may request or receive information:
- prospective employer
- the former or current employee
- federal, state, or industry regulatory authority

Employer immune from liability unless:
- Employer intended to harm or defame employee.
- Employer intentionally disclosed false information, or disclosed without caring if it was false.

Massachusetts

Mass. Gen. Laws ch. 111, § 72L 1/2

Information that may be disclosed:
(applies only to hospitals, convalescent or nursing homes, home health agencies, and hospice programs)
- reasons for termination or separation
- length of employment, pay level, and history

Employer immune from liability unless:
- Information disclosed was false, and employer knew it was false.

Michigan

Mich. Comp. Laws §§ 423.452, 423.506 to 423.507

Information that may be disclosed:
- job performance information that is documented in personnel file

Who may request or receive information:
- prospective employer
- the former or current employee

Employer immune from liability unless:
- Employer knew that information was false or misleading.
- Employer disclosed information without caring if it was true or false.
- Disclosure was specifically prohibited by a state or federal statute.

Other provisions:
- Employer may not disclose any disciplinary action or letter of reprimand that is more than 4 years old to a third party.
- Employer must notify employee by first class mail on or before the day of disclosure of disciplinary records (does not apply if employee waived notification in a signed job application with another employer).

Minnesota

Minn. Stat. Ann. §§ 181.933, 181.967

Information that may be disclosed:
- dates of employment
- compensation history
- job description and job duties
- any education and training provided by the employer
- any acts of violence, harassment, theft, or illegal conduct documented in the employee's personnel records that led to the employee's discipline or resignation, along with the employee's written response, if any (this information may be disclosed only in writing)

If employee provides written authorization, employer may also disclose:
- written evaluations, along with the employee's written response (if any)
- written warnings and other disciplinary actions that took place within five years of the employee's authorization, along with the employee's written response (if any), and written reasons for the employee's separation from employment

Who may request or receive information:
- prospective employer
- former or current employee

State Laws on Information From Former Employers (continued)

Copy to employee required:
- Employer who provides written evaluations, written warnings, written reasons for employee's separation, or information on acts of violence, harassment, theft, or illegal conduct must send a copy to the employee's last known address.

Employer required to write a letter:
- Must provide a written statement of the reasons for termination within 10 working days of receiving employee's request.
- Employee must make request in writing within 15 working days of being discharged.

Employer immune from liability:
- Employer that provides information allowed by law may be sued only if the information was false and defamatory, and the employer knew or should have known that the information was false and acted with malicious intent to injure the employee.
- Employer can't be sued for libel, slander, or defamation for sending employee written statement of reasons for termination.

Missouri

Mo. Rev. Stat. §§ 290.140, 290.152

Information that may be disclosed:
- reasons for termination or separation
- length of employment, pay level, and history
- job description and duties

Who may request or receive information:
- prospective employer (request must be in writing)

Copy to employee required:
- Employer must send copy to employee's last known address.
- Employee may request copy of letter up to one year after it was sent to prospective employer.

Employer required to write letter:
- Only employers with 7 or more employees, and employees with at least 90 days of service.
- Must state the nature and length of employment and reason, if any, for separation.
- Employee must make request by certified mail within one year after separation.
- Employer must reply within 45 days of receiving request.

Employer immune from liability unless:
- Information provided was false, and employer either knew it was false or provided it with reckless disregard as to its truth or falsity. Employer is protected from liability only if it provides information in writing.

Other provisions:
- All information disclosed must be in writing and must be consistent with service letter.

Montana

Mont. Code Ann. §§ 39-2-801, 39-2-802

Information that may be disclosed:
- reasons for termination or separation

Who may request or receive information:
- prospective employer

Employer required to write letter:
- Must give discharged employee a written statement of reasons for discharge, upon request.
- If employer doesn't respond to request within a reasonable time, may not disclose reasons to another person.

Nebraska

Neb. Rev. Stat. §§ 48-209 to 48-211

Employer required to write letter:
- Law applies only to public service corporations, contractors working for public service corporations, and contractors doing

State Laws on Information From Former Employers (continued)

business with the state: upon request from employee, must provide service letter that states length of employment, nature of work, and reasons employee quit or was discharged.
- Letter must follow prescribed format for paper and signature.

Nevada

Nev. Rev. Stat. Ann. §§ 41.755, 613.210(4)

Information that may be disclosed:
- the employee's ability to perform the job
- the employee's diligence, skill, or reliability in carrying out the job's duties, or
- any illegal act or wrong the employee committed

Who may request or receive information:
- former or current employee

Employer required to write letter:
- must provide a written statement listing reasons for separation and any meritorious service employee may have performed, upon request of an employee who leaves or is discharged
- statement not required unless employee has worked for at least 60 days
- employee entitled to only one statement

Employer immune from liability unless:
- Employer acted with malice or ill will.
- Employer disclosed information that the employer believed was inaccurate or had no reasonable grounds to believe was accurate.
- Employer recklessly or intentionally disclosed inaccurate information.
- Employer intentionally disclosed misleading information.
- Employer disclosed information in violation of federal or state law or in violation of an agreement with the employee.

New Mexico

N.M. Stat. Ann. § 50-12-1

Information that may be disclosed:
- job performance

Who may request or receive information:
- no person specified ("when requested to provide a reference ...")

Employer immune from liability unless:
- Information disclosed was known to be false or was deliberately misleading.
- Disclosure was made with malicious intent or violated former employee's civil rights.

North Carolina

N.C. Gen. Stat. § 1-539.12

Information that may be disclosed:
- job performance or history
- reasons for termination or separation
- suitability for reemployment
- job-related skills, abilities, or traits

Who may request or receive information:
- prospective employer
- the former or current employee

Employer immune from liability unless:
- Information disclosed was false, and employer knew or reasonably should have known it was false.

North Dakota

N.D. Cent. Code § 34-02-18

Information that may be disclosed:
- job performance
- length of employment, pay level, and wage history
- job description and duties

Who may request or receive information:
- prospective employer

State Laws on Information From Former Employers (continued)

Employer immune from liability unless:

- Employer who provides information only on employee's length of employment, pay level, wage history, and job description and duties is immune unless providing the information violated a nondisclosure agreement or other legal confidentiality requirement.
- Employer who provides information on job performance may also be sued if the information was knowingly false, deliberately misleading, provided with reckless disregard as to its truth or falsity, or provided with a malicious purpose.

Ohio

Ohio Rev. Code Ann. § 4113.71

Information that may be disclosed:

- job performance

Who may request or receive information:

- prospective employer
- the former or current employee

Employer immune from liability unless:

- Disclosed information knowing that it was false or with the deliberate intent to mislead the prospective employer or another person.
- Information was disclosed in bad faith or with a malicious purpose.
- Disclosure constitutes an unlawful or discriminatory practice.

Oklahoma

Okla. Stat. Ann. tit. 40, §§ 61, 171

Information that may be disclosed:

- job performance

Who may request or receive information:

- prospective employer (must have consent of employee)
- the former or current employee

Employer required to write letter:

- Law applies only to public service corporations and contractors who work for them.
- Upon request from employee, must provide letter that states length of employment, nature of work, and reasons employee quit or was discharged.
- Letter must follow prescribed format for paper and signature.

Employer immune from liability unless:

- Information was false, and employer knew it was false, acted maliciously, or acted with reckless disregard as to its truth or falsity.

Oregon

Ore. Rev. Stat. § 30.178

Information that may be disclosed:

- job performance

Who may request or receive information:

- prospective employer
- the former or current employee

Employer immune from liability unless:

- Information was knowingly false or deliberately misleading.
- Information was disclosed with malicious intent.
- Disclosure violated a civil right of the former employee.

Pennsylvania

42 Pa. Cons. Stat. Ann. § 8340.1

Information that may be disclosed:

- job performance

Who may request or receive information:

- prospective employer
- the former or current employee

Employer immune from liability unless:

- knew the information was false or should have known it was false, had the employer

State Laws on Information From Former Employers (continued)

exercised due diligence
- provided information that was deliberately misleading
- provided information that was false with reckless disregard as to whether it was true or false, or
- violated the employee's contract, statutory, common law, or civil rights

Rhode Island

R.I. Gen. Laws § 28-6.4-1(c)

Information that may be disclosed:
- job performance

Who may request or receive information:
- prospective employer
- the former or current employee

Employer immune from liability unless:
- Information was knowingly false or deliberately misleading.
- Information was in violation of current or former employee's civil rights under the employment discrimination laws in effect at time of disclosure.
- Information was disclosed for a malicious purpose.

South Carolina

S.C. Code Ann. § 41-1-65

Information that may be disclosed:
- length of employment, pay level, and wage history
- the employee's written performance evaluations
- official personnel documents that state the reasons for the employee's termination
- whether the employment relationship was terminated voluntarily or involuntarily, and the reasons for that termination

- information about the employee's job performance, including attendance, attitudes, awards, demotions, duties, effort, evaluation, knowledge, skills, promotions, and disciplinary actions

Who may request or receive information:
- prospective employer (written request required for all information except dates of employment and wage history)
- the former or current employee

Copy to employee required:
- Employee must be allowed access to any written information sent to prospective employer.

Employer immune from liability unless:
- Employer knowingly or recklessly releases or discloses false information.

Other provisions:
- All disclosures other than length of employment, pay level, and wage history must be in writing for employer to be entitled to immunity.

South Dakota

S.D. Codified Laws Ann. § 60-4-12

Information that may be disclosed:
- job performance (must be in writing)

Who may request or receive information:
- prospective employer (request must be in writing)
- the former or current employee (request must be in writing)

Copy to employee required:
- upon employee's written request

Employer immune from liability unless:
- Employer knowingly, intentionally, or carelessly disclosed false or deliberately misleading information.

State Laws on Information From Former Employers (continued)

- Information is subject to a nondisclosure agreement or is confidential according to federal or state law.

Tennessee

Tenn. Code Ann. § 50-1-105

Information that may be disclosed:
- job performance

Who may request or receive information:
- prospective employer
- the former or current employee

Employer immune from liability unless:
- Information is knowingly false, deliberately misleading, or disclosed for malicious reasons.
- Employer disclosed information regardless of whether it was false or defamatory.
- Disclosure is in violation of employee's civil rights according to current employment discrimination laws.

Texas

Tex. Lab. Code Ann. §§ 52.031(d), 103.001 to 103.004; Tex. Civ. Stat. Ann. Art. 5196

Information that may be disclosed:
- reasons for termination or separation (must be in writing)
- job performance
- attendance, attitudes, effort, knowledge, behavior, and skills

Who may request or receive information:
- prospective employer
- the former or current employee

Copy to employee required:
- Within 10 days of receiving employee's request, employer must send copy of written disclosure or true statement of verbal disclosure, along with names of people to whom information was given.

- Employer may not disclose reasons for employee's discharge to any other person without sending employee a copy, unless employee specifically requests disclosure.

Employer required to write letter:
- Employee must make request in writing.
- Employer must respond within 10 days of receiving employee's request.
- Discharged employee must be given a written statement of reasons for termination.
- Employee who quits must be given a written statement that includes all job titles and dates, states that separation was voluntary, and indicates whether employee's performance was satisfactory.
- Employee entitled to another copy of statement if original is lost or unavailable.

Employer immune from liability unless:
- Employer knew the information was false (this means that the employer had information about the employee demonstrating the falsity of the reference).
- The employer disclosed the information in reckless disregard for its truth or falsity.
- The employer disclosed the information maliciously.

Utah

Utah Code Ann. § 34-42-1

Information that may be disclosed:
- job performance

Who may request or receive information:
- prospective employer
- the former or current employee

Employer immune from liability unless:
- There is clear and convincing evidence that employer disclosed information with the intent to mislead, knowing it was false, or not caring if it was true or false.

State Laws on Information From Former Employers (continued)

Virginia

Va. Code Ann. § 8.01-46.1

Information that may be disclosed:

- the employee's professional conduct, including the ethical standards governing the employee's profession or the standards of conduct imposed by the employer
- the employee's job performance, including ability, attendance, awards, demotions, duties, effort, evaluations, knowledge, skills, promotions, productivity, and discipline
- the reasons for the employee's separation from employment

Who may request or receive information:

- prospective employer

Employer immune from liability unless:

- Employer disclosed information deliberately intending to mislead, knowing it was false, or not caring if it was true or false.

Washington

Wash. Rev. Code § 4.24.730; Wash. Admin. Code § 296-126-050

Information that may be disclosed:

- the employee's ability to perform the job
- the employee's diligence, skill, or reliability in performing the job's duties
- any illegal or wrongful act the employee committed relating to the job

Who may request or receive information:

- prospective employer

Copy to employee required:

- Employer must keep written records of all prospective employers to whom it has provided reference information for at least two years.
- Employee has the right to inspect these records on request.

Employer required to write letter:

- Within 10 business days of receiving written request, employer must give former employee a signed statement of reasons for and date of termination.

Employer immune from liability unless:

- Employer provided information with the intent to mislead, knowing it was false, or with reckless disregard for its truth or falsity.

West Virginia

W.Va. Code § 55-7-18a

Information that may be disclosed:

- Employer may provide job-related information that might reasonably be considered adverse about an employee and information for the purpose of evaluating the employee's suitability for employment, including:
  - education
  - training
  - experience
  - qualifications
  - conduct
  - job performance
- Information must be provided in writing

Who may request or receive information:

- prospective employer

Copy to employee required:

- Employee must receive copy of information provided to prospective employers. If employer provides incorrect information, it must, on employee's request, provide corrected information to every prospective employer that received the incorrect information.

State Laws on Information From Former Employers (continued)

Employer immune from liability unless:
- Employee can prove, by clear and convincing evidence, that employer provided information:
  - knowing that it was false
  - with reckless disregard for its truth or falsity
  - with the intent to mislead
  - with a malicious purpose
  - in violation of the law or a nondisclosure agreement.

Wisconsin

Wis. Stat. Ann. §§ 134.02(2)(a), 895.487

Information that may be disclosed:
- job performance
- qualifications
- any statement employer and employee have negotiated as part of an agreement to end the employment relationship

Who may request or receive information:
- prospective employer
- the former or current employee

Employer immune from liability unless:
- Employer knowingly provided false information in the reference.
- Employer made the reference maliciously.
- Reference was in violation of employee's civil rights.

Wyoming

Wyo. Stat. § 27-1-113

Information that may be disclosed:
- job performance

Who may request or receive information:
- prospective employer

Employer immune from liability unless:
- Information was knowingly false or deliberately misleading.
- Information was disclosed for a malicious purpose.

State Laws on Mass Layoffs and Plant Closings

California

Cal. Lab. Code §§ 1400 to 1408

Covered Employers: Industrial or commercial facility that employs at least 75 employees.

When law applies: Mass layoff (of at least 50 employees); relocation 100 or more miles away; or closing of industrial or commercial facility with at least 75 employees.

Notification requirements: Employer must give at least 60 days' advance notice, in writing, before mass layoff, relocation, or closing of facility. Notice must include the elements required by the federal WARN Act and must be provided to affected employees, Employment Development Department, local workforce investment board, and chief elected official of each city or county where job losses occur. Employer that fails to give notice to employees is liable for back pay and benefits for the period of the violation, up to 60 days or one-half the length of the employee's tenure with the company, whichever is shorter.

Exceptions: Notice not required if job loss due to physical calamity or act of war; or if employer was actively seeking capital that would have avoided or postponed job losses when notice should have been given.

Connecticut

Conn. Gen. Stat. Ann. §§ 31-51n, 31-51o

Covered Employers: Industrial, commercial, or business facility with 100 or more employees at any time during the last 12 months.

When law applies: Permanent shutdown of facility or relocation of facility out of state.

Severance requirements: Employer must pay for existing group health insurance coverage for terminated employee and dependents for 120 days or until employee is eligible for other group coverage, whichever comes first.

Exceptions: Notice not required if facility closure is due to bankruptcy or natural disaster.

District of Columbia

D.C. Code Ann. §§ 21-101 to 32-103

Covered Employers: Contractors and subcontractors who employ 25 or more nonprofessionals as food service, health service, security, janitorial, or building maintenance workers.

When law applies: When a new contractor takes over a service contract.

Severance requirements: Within 10 days after new contract is awarded, previous contractor must give new contractor names of all employees. New contractor must retain all employees who have worked for the past 8 months for a 90-day transition period. If fewer employees are needed, the new contractor must retain by seniority within job classifications; otherwise, employees may not be fired without cause during the transition period. After transition period ends, new contractor must give written performance evaluations and retain all employees with satisfactory performance. Contractor whose contract is not renewed and is awarded a similar contract within 30 days must hire at least half of the employees from the former site(s).

Hawaii

Haw. Rev. Stat §§ 394B-1 to 394B-13

Covered Employers: Industrial, commercial, or other business entity with at least 50 employees at any time during the last 12 months.

When law applies: Permanent or partial closing of business; relocation of all or substantial portion of business operations out of state.

State Laws on Mass Layoffs and Plant Closings (continued)

Severance requirements: Employer must pay dislocated worker allowance for 4 weeks to supplement unemployment compensation; amount is the difference between the employee's former weekly wage and the employee's weekly unemployment benefit. Employer who does not pay severance is liable to each employee for 3 months of compensation.

Notification requirements: Employer must give notice to employees 60 days in advance of closing or relocation. Employer who fails to provide notice is liable to each employee for back pay and benefits for the period of the violation, up to 60 days.

Illinois

820 Ill. Comp. Stat. §§ 65/1 to 65/55

Covered Employers: Any business enterprise that employs at least 75 full-time employees or at least 75 employees who work an aggregate of 4,000 hours a week (not including overtime).

When law applies: Mass layoff (of at least 250 employees or at least 25 employees who make up 33% or more of the workforce); relocation; or plant closing (shutdown of a site or operating unit resulting in job loss for at least 50 full-time employees).

Notification requirements: Employer must give at least 60 days' written notice to affected employees, their representatives, the Department of Commerce & Economic Opportunity, and the chief elected official of each municipal and county government where job losses occur. Employer that doesn't give notice is liable for back pay and benefits for the period of the violation, up to 60 days or one-half the length of the employee's tenure with the company, whichever is shorter.

Exceptions: Notice not required if job loss due to completion of temporary project or closure of temporary facility; unforeseen circumstances; strike or lockout; physical calamity; or war; or if employer was seeking capital in good faith that would have avoided or postponed job losses when notice should have been given.

Iowa

Iowa Code §§ 84C.1 to 84C.5

Covered Employers: Employers with at least 25 full-time employees.

When law applies: Business closing (permanent or temporary shutdown) or mass layoff that will affect 25 or more full-time employees.

Notification requirements: Employer must give 30 days' notice or amount of notice required by collective bargaining agreement. Employer may pay wages in lieu of notice.

Exceptions: Notice not required if job loss due to strike or lockout; unforeseeable business circumstances; or natural disaster; or if employer was seeking capital in good faith that would have avoided or postponed job loss when notice should have been given.

Maine

Me. Rev. Stat. Ann. tit. 26, § 625-B

Covered Employers: Employers with at least 100 employees at any time during the last 12 months.

When law applies: Closing, discontinuation or relocation of business operations at least 100 miles distant; mass layoff (job loss for at least 500 employees or at least 50 employees, if they represent at least 33% of the workforce).

Severance requirements: Employer must give one week of severance pay for each year of

State Laws on Mass Layoffs and Plant Closings (continued)

employment and partial pay for any partial year of employment to all employees who have worked for at least 3 years.

Notification requirements: Employer must give employees at least 60 days' notice, in writing, before relocating or closing. Employer must also notify the director of the Bureau of Labor Standards and municipal officials where plant is located. Employers initiating mass layoffs must report to the director, within 7 days, the expected duration of the layoff, and whether the layoff is definite or indefinite.

Exceptions: No fine for failure to give notice if closing is due to physical calamity or final order by the government, or if unforeseen circumstances prevent giving notice.

Maryland

Md. Code Ann. [Lab. & Empl.] §§ 11-301 to 11-304; Md. Code Regs. tit. 9 § .09.33.02.04

Covered Employers: Employers with at least 50 employees that have been in business for at least one year.

When law applies: Shutdown of workplace or portion of operations resulting in layoffs of at least 25% of the workforce or 15 employees, whichever is greater, over any 3-month period.

Severance Requirements: Employers are encouraged to follow Department of Labor voluntary guidelines for severance pay, continuation of benefits, and notification.

Notification requirements: Employers should provide 90 days' notice whenever possible.

Exemptions: Notice not required if job loss is due to bankruptcy; seasonal factors common to industry; labor disputes; or the closure of a construction site or temporary workplace.

New Hampshire

N.H. Rev. Stat. Ann. §§ 275-F:1 to 275-F:12

Covered Employers: Employers with at least 100 full-time employees or at least 100 employees who work a total of at least 3,000 hours per week.

When law applies: Plant closing (shutdown of a single employment site, facility, or operating unit resulting in job loss for at least 50 full-time employees); mass layoff (job loss for at least 250 full-time employees or at least 25 employees, if they represent at least 33% of the workforce).

Notification requirements: Employer must give 60 days' notice of plant closing or mass layoff to affected employees, their representatives, the state labor commissioner and attorney general, and the chief elected official of each municipality where job losses occur.

Exemptions: Notice is not required if job loss due to shutdown of a temporary facility; physical calamity; natural disaster; act of war; or strike or lockout. Notice is also not required if need for notice was not reasonably foreseeable or if the company was actively seeking capital, in good faith, that would have postponed or avoided job loss when notice should have been given.

New Jersey

N.J. Stat. Ann. §§ 34:21-1 to 34:21-7

Covered Employers: Employers that have operated a business establishment for at least 3 years.

When law applies: Mass layoff (at least 500 full-time employees or at least 50 full-time employees that represent at least one-third of the full-time employees at that establishment); termination or relocation of operations resulting in job loss for at least 50 full-time employees.

State Laws on Mass Layoffs and Plant Closings (continued)

Severance Requirements: Employer that does not provide at least 60 days' notice must pay laid-off full-time employees one week of severance for each year of employment.

Notification requirements: Employers with 100 or more employees must provide 60 days' notice or such notice as is required by the federal WARN Act. Notice must be given to affected employees, their collective bargaining units, the commissioner of Labor and Workforce Development, and the chief elected official of each municipality where job losses occur.

New York

N.Y. Lab. Law §§ 860 to 860-i

Covered Employers: Employers with at least 50 employees.

When law applies: Plant closing (permanent or temporary shutdown of single site, facility, or operating unit that results in job loss for at least 25 full-time employees in a 30-day period); mass layoff (reduction in force at a single site that results in job loss for at least 25 full-time employees representing at least 33% of the employer's workforce or at least 250 full-time employees in a 30-day period); relocation (moving employer's entire operation at least 50 miles away).

Notification requirements: Employer must give notice at least 90 days before a mass layoff, plant closing, or relocation to affected employees, their representatives, the department of labor, and local workforce investment boards where job losses occur. Employer that fails to give required notice to employees is liable for back pay and lost benefits for up to 60 days.

Exceptions: Notice not required if job loss due to physical calamity or act of terrorism or war; closure of a temporary facility; natural disaster;

or strike or lockout. Notice is also not required if job losses were not reasonably foreseeable or if employer was actively seeking capital that would avoid or postpone job losses when notice should have been given.

Tennessee

Tenn. Code Ann. §§ 50-1-601 to 50-1-604

Covered Employers: Employers with 50 to 99 full-time employees within the state.

When law applies: Closing, modernization, relocation, or new management policy of a workplace or portion of operations that permanently or indefinitely lays off 50 or more employees during any 3-month period.

Notification requirements: Employer must notify employees who will lose their jobs, then the commissioner of Labor and Workforce Development.

Exceptions: Notice not required if job loss due to closure of construction site; labor disputes; or seasonal factors common to industry.

Vermont

Vt. Stat. Ann tit. 21 §§ 411 to 418

Covered Employers: Employers with 50 or more full-time employees; employers with 50 or more part-time employees each working at least 1,040 hours per year; or employers with a combination of 50 or more full-time employees and part-time employees each working at least 1,040 hours per year.

When law applies: Mass layoff (permanent layoff of 50 or more employees at one or more worksites in a 90-day period); business closing (permanent shutdown of a facility, permanent cessation of operations at one or more worksites that results in layoff of 50 or more employees in a

State Laws on Mass Layoffs and Plant Closings (continued)

90-day period, or the cessation of operations not scheduled to resume within 90 days that affects 50 or more employees).

Severance Requirements: If employer fails to give notice, it must pay each employee up to ten days' severance pay—and up to one month of continuing medical and dental coverage.

Notification requirements: Employer must give at least 30 days' notice to affected employees, municipal government, and employees' collective bargaining representatives. Employer must provide 45 days' notice to the Agency of Commerce and Community Development and the Vermont Department of Labor.

Exceptions: Compliance not required: when closing or mass layoff is caused by strike or lockout, by business circumstances that were not reasonably foreseeable, by disaster beyond the control of the employer, or due to the conclusion of seasonal employment or a particular project; when affected employees were hired with the understanding that their employment was limited to the duration of the season or project; or when the employer is actively trying to secure funds to avoid a closing or mass layoff and it reasonably believes that giving notice would have precluded securing such funds.

Wisconsin

Wis. Stat. Ann. §§ 106.15; 109.07

Covered Employers: Employers with at least 50 employees in the state.

When law applies: Business closing (permanent or temporary shutdown of an employment site, facility, or operating unit(s) at one site or within one town that affects 25 or more full-time employees); mass layoff (reduction in force that affects at least 25% or at least 25 full-time employees, whichever is greater, or at least 500 employees). Employees include only those who have worked at least 6 of the last 12 months and work at least 20 hours a week.

Notification requirements: Employer must give at least 60 days' written notice to affected employees, their collective bargaining representatives, the Dislocated Worker Committee in the Department of Workforce Development, and the highest official in the municipality where job losses occur. Employer who fails to give required notice to employees is liable for up to 60 days of back pay and lost benefits.

Exceptions: Notice not required if job loss due to sale of company, if buyer agrees to hire affected employees with no more than 6-month break in employment; end of seasonal or temporary work; unforeseeable business circumstances; or disaster.

After a Job Loss

I f you have lost your job or think you may soon lose it, do not despair. There are some laws that may protect you against suddenly joining the ranks of the unemployed without money or other help to ease the impact.

Depending on your situation, you might have the legal right to:

- all money you have earned, plus accrued vacation pay
- severance pay
- a truthful reference from your former employer to help in future job hunting, or
- continuing coverage under your former employer's group health plan.

This chapter also outlines state income replacement programs that may be available to you. And it explains how and whether to take action if you feel your former employer's bad actions are preventing you from getting a new job and moving on.

Your Final Paycheck

Most state laws specify when a final paycheck must be issued to employees who are fired or resign, and some of those laws require your employer to pay you in fairly short order. (See the chart "State Laws That Control Final Paychecks," at the end of this chapter.) For example, the laws in several states require that an employee who is fired be paid that same day. The chart also indicates which states require

employers to include accrued vacation pay in the final paycheck.

CAUTION

If you have a contract, different rules might apply. If you are one of the rare breed who has an employment contract (in Chapter 9, see "When a Firing May Be Illegal") you may be specifically excluded from the protections of these laws. Your rights to pay are dictated by the terms of the employment contract you signed.

Severance Pay

Many people assume that when they leave a job, they have a legal right to severance pay. This is yet another bit of workplace lore that builds false hope in the newly unemployed.

Many employers do offer severance in the form of a month's salary or more to employees who are laid off or let go for some reason other than misconduct. The old rule of thumb was that where severance was offered, a reasonable amount was one month of pay for every year of service. These days, one or two weeks' pay for each year of service is common.

And severance often comes with an additional price tag, as more companies demand that departing employees sign broad severance agreements before getting a red cent. The agreements typically include provisions requiring a former employee to waive the right to file a number of legal claims against the company. And, increasingly, severance agreements include confidentiality and "nondisparagement" clauses, aimed at preventing former employees from complaining about the company to other employees, talking to the media about negative experiences while on the job, and even telling people how much money the company gave them in severance.

Some employment experts are quick to disparage such so-called nondisparagement clauses, fearing that disgruntled workers are being unjustly paid to zip their lips rather than shed light on larger workplace wrongs.

There is no grand guidance on the issue. If presented with the option of either signing a nondisparagement clause and getting a hefty severance sum or keeping the right to vent and getting nothing, you are the only one who can evaluate which is more important.

But keep in mind that no law requires an employer to pay severance. Whether it is given at all now varies drastically from employer to employer, region to region, and industry to industry.

However, an employer may be legally obligated to pay you some severance if you had good reason to believe you had it coming, as evidenced by:

- a written contract stating that severance will be paid
- a promise or policy that employees would receive severance pay as documented in an employee handbook

- a history of the company paying severance to other employees in your position, or
- an oral promise that the employer would pay you severance (although you may run into difficulties proving the promise was made).

If your employer refuses to pay you severance or offers an amount that you find unacceptable, you have nothing to lose by asking for more. Request a meeting with a company representative to discuss the issue. Remain calm and polite; do not threaten. Explain why you need the money: to support yourself or your family while finding another job is the usual reason. In the last few years, employers' building fear of lawsuits has meant that more of them are willing to grant severance pay to departing employees, although strapped finances may mean smaller overall pay-outs.

If you meet with no success, take another hard look at the legal reasons listed above that may entitle you to severance pay. If you feel you may have a valid claim, collect as much evidence as you can to back up your position. (See "Getting Documentation" in Chapter 9.)

Then think again. A breach of contract action, which is what you can bring against an employer that has reneged on a promise to pay severance, will likely require the help of an attorney. If the amount involved is not substantial, you could be facing more in legal fees than you would stand to gain by collecting the severance money. If you consult with an attorney about handling your case, that calculation should be one of the first questions you ask. (In Chapter 17, see "Hiring a Lawyer.")

Getting References

As soon as you feel ready, put your best foot forward and prepare for a new job. For many, that means glancing backward to secure references from past employers.

Sometimes, that task is not as simple as it sounds. Employers contacted for references about former employees often find themselves caught between the desire to be truthful and the fear that if they say anything unflattering, they will be sued.

These days, conventional legal wisdom cautions employers to stick to the barest bones. Many companies have steel-clad policies to supply only the dates of employment, job title, and amount of final salary to prospective employers.

So when seeking references from a former employer, you may run into resistance. But depending on where you live, your efforts may also be helped or hampered by a state law that spells out information that may be disclosed by a former employer. Be sure to check those requirements and point to them if they are in your favor. (In Chapter 9, see "State Laws on Information From Former Employers.")

Some cautious companies require employees who leave to sign releases allowing the companies to give reference information in the future; in some states, the law requires this. Before providing a job reference, some cautious companies require former employees to sign a release giving up the right to sue the company for anything it reveals. Some state laws also protect employers from defamation lawsuits as long as they acted in good faith in giving the reference. (See "Defamation" in Chapter 9.)

The broad warning for employers giving references is that they should give out only easily documented facts, such as your attendance record or production record.

But this closed approach seems to unfairly penalize prize employees, who may depend on good references to snag their next jobs. And many employers that think that an employee has done a poor job or has blatantly violated company rules feel that they have a responsibility to let prospective employers know about the problem. There is nothing inherently illegal about this, unless you can prove that an employer told a bald-faced lie about you (for example, that you raided the company till when you did not). However, gathering proof of an intentional lie is nearly impossible. And a seemingly noncommittal "no comment" in response to a prospective employer's probe about your job performance may be the most damaging of all, yet it can't serve as the basis of a defamation lawsuit.

If you suspect your former employer might give a negative review of your work, it is best to have a strategy worked out ahead of time. Try to secure a letter of recommendation from someone in the company who would praise your work. Perhaps you can persuade your employer to keep certain employment matters confidential, such as the reason for your dismissal. If not, it's probably best not to list the employer as a reference. But have a ready reason to explain the circumstances that has no acrimonious ring to it. For example, you might explain that it was time for you to move on to new challenges.

Collecting Fringe Benefits

Employers are generally not required by law to provide workplace benefits, formerly known by the quaint title of "fringe benefits." However, most employers do provide some fringe benefits, at least to full-time employees. Common workplace benefits include retirement plans, group health insurance, and paid days off for vacations, holidays, personal reasons, and medical leave. (See Chapters 2, 3, and 4 for a more in-depth discussion of these topics.)

If your employer does have a policy of offering some or all of these job benefits, it cannot discriminate in offering them. The question that most often arises about these discretionary benefits when employees quit or are fired from a job is whether they are entitled to be paid for time that was accrued—or earned and owing—but not taken.

There is no easy answer.

First of all, just as the benefits are discretionary with each employer, so is the policy of how and when they accrue. Employers are free to apply conditions on fringe benefits. For example, it is perfectly legal for employers to require a certain length of employment—six months or a year are common—before an employee is entitled to any fringe benefits. It is perfectly legal for employers to prorate—or deny—fringe benefits for part-time employees.

Getting the Benefits You Are Due

In evaluating whether your former employer has given you all accrued fringe benefits you are due, you have two allies: documentation and history. First, search for any written policy on benefit accrual in an employee manual, personnel package, or company memo. If the rights have been promised to you, you can enforce them just like any other contract. If the promise is in writing, you have an even better chance of succeeding.

Look, too, to how other employees were treated in the recent past. If it has become company custom to pay employees accrued fringe benefits when they leave, you may be legally entitled to them, too. You must compare apples with apples. Look to other employees who worked in jobs similar to yours.

Finding out what others were paid when they left may take some brave sleuthing on your part: You may have to hunt down past employees and ask them some uncomfortable questions, point blank. But the effort may be worth it. If other former workers with jobs similar to yours were given benefits you were denied, you may be able to claim that your employer discriminated against you when it denied them. (See Chapter 7.)

Continuing Health Care Coverage

Most workplace disputes and misunder-standings over fringe benefits concern health care coverage. A federal law called the Consolidated Omnibus Budget Reconcilia-tion Act, or COBRA, offers some protection. Under COBRA, employers with 20 or more employees must offer former employees the option of continuing their coverage under the company's group health care insurance plan at the workers' own expense. Family coverage is included.

In general, COBRA gives an employee who quits or is dismissed for reasons other than gross misconduct the right to continue group health care coverage for 18 months. In some other circumstances, such as the death of the employee, that employee's dependents can continue coverage for up to 36 months. (In Chapter 3, see "Coverage for Former Employees.")

Outplacement Programs

Each year, thousands of workers are permanently dismissed by corporations that are shrinking or dying. And, as they bid adieu, many former employers—about 70%, according to a recent tally—offer out-placement services to workers to help ease the sting of being out of work.

Outplacement services are not employment agencies. They do not find a new job for you, but they do help and encourage you in finding one for yourself.

Although some outplacement firms offer packages of services that can be purchased by individuals, outplacement counselors are most often brought in and paid for by employers that want to diminish their risks of being sued for wrongful discharge. Outplacement benefits have even been negotiated into union contracts.

The theory underlying the popularity of outplacement in the corporate world is that fired employees who move quickly and smoothly into a new job typically do not sustain grudges against the company that fired them. Nor do they experience the kind of financial problems that can inspire job-related lawsuits. If a person goes through outplacement, cannot find a replacement job, and decides to file a wrongful discharge lawsuit, the company can show a court that it has done all it can to limit the financial damage done to the employee by the firing.

The quality of outplacement services varies, depending on how much your employer is willing to invest. A good program might provide in-person group workshops and one-on-one coaching, assistance with creating a résumé and cover letter, help with interview prep, and even office space equipped with a phone and computer. A cheaper program might only offer access to job postings, online webinars, and a small amount of one-on-one phone counseling. There is no standard duration of outplacement services; they might last for a couple of months or for a year or more.

Two Wrongs May Mean No Rights

Many jobseekers inflate their résumés by exaggerating their experience or credentials. A 2014 survey by CareerBuilder revealed that 58% of responding employers had caught a lie on a résumé. The most common falsifications were about job skills, dates of employment, job duties, job titles, academic degrees, and dates of employment.

Employers have always been free to fire employees who lie about a significant qualification. Now they may be able to use this misinformation to defend against lawsuits for wrongful termination or discrimination. Courts reason, in essence, that employees who lied to get a job cannot later come to court and claim that the employer did them wrong.

The tactic even has a name: the after-acquired evidence theory. Conduct that has been held sufficiently serious to be admitted as after-acquired evidence has included:

- 150 instances of falsifying company records
- failing to list a previous employer on a résumé
- failing to admit being terminated for cheating on timecards
- failing to reveal a prior conviction for a felony
- lying about education and experience on a job application
- fabricating a college degree during an interview, and
- removing and copying the company's confidential financial statements.

If you did lie on your job application or résumé, however, you may not be completely out of luck. Your employer can use the misinformation as a defense only if it was truly related to your job duties or performance. The employer must be able to show that you would have been fired—or not hired in the first place—if it had known the truth. Proving this type of second-guessing may not be easy.

An employer cannot force you to partici-pate in an outplacement program. However, some large employers will continue to pay your salary and benefits for at least a few weeks or months after you are fired on the condition that you actively participate in the outplacement services provided. If you drop out, you are on your own financially.

Your refusal to participate in an outplace-ment program might also weaken any lawsuit you might later file against your former employer, because you could be depicted as contributing to your wage loss. Your participation in outplacement might, on the other hand, provide additional verification that you have done everything you can to avoid financial loss.

Replacing Your Income

When your employment is interrupted, it is important to act quickly to replace as much of your income as you can. Each day that passes without money earned puts you and those who rely on you for financial support in greater risk of running into money troubles. And applying for the wrong income replacement program can waste many more precious days, weeks, or even months.

Here is a brief breakdown of what is covered by each of the three major income replacement programs:

- **Unemployment insurance.** This program provides some financial help if you lose your job, temporarily or permanently,

through no fault of your own. (See Chapter 11.)
- **Workers' compensation.** When you cannot work because of a work-related injury or illness, this is the program that is most likely to provide you with replacement income promptly. (See Chapter 12.)
- **Social Security disability insurance.** This is intended to provide income to adults who cannot work for at least 12 months due to a disability. Unlike the workers' compensation program, it does not require that your disability be caused by a workplace injury or illness. (See Chapter 13.)

Once you have decided which of these programs fits your situation, read the more detailed description of that program in the chapters noted, and then apply for the appropriate benefits without delay.

Dual Payments for Disabled Workers

Some employees qualify for benefits under both workers' compensation and Social Security disability insurance. There is nothing illegal about collecting from both at the same time if the claims you file are valid.

However, if you qualify for benefits from both programs, the total benefits you receive from both programs cannot equal more than 80% of your average earnings prior to becoming disabled.

Although the government insurance programs covering unemployment, workplace injuries, and permanent disability are the most substantial sources of replacement income for people who are out of work, there are other options.

Private Disability Insurance

While you were working, you or your employer may have been paying into a private disability insurance program. If you were paying for it through payroll withholdings, or if all the premiums were being paid by your employer, you may have forgotten that you even have this coverage.

Coverage and eligibility for benefits differ among policies and companies. Review the employee policy manual or packet that your employer gave you when you took the job to see whether any private disability coverage is described there. If not, the people who handle benefits for your employer should be able to help you determine whether you have such coverage.

State Disability Programs

A handful of states—including California, Hawaii, New Jersey, New York, and Rhode Island—offer short-term disability benefits as part of a state-run program. Typical program requirements mandate that you submit your medical records and show that you requested a leave of absence from your employer. Some may also require proof that you intend to return to your job when you recover. Call your state unemployment insurance agency to determine whether your state offers this kind of benefit. (See Chapter 11.)

Withdrawals From Retirement Plans

Some retirement plans allow withdrawals prior to retirement for emergency purposes. The administrator of your plan can advise you on whether you have this option. (For more on pensions, see "Private Pensions" in Chapter 14.)

Food Stamps

Although many people incorrectly think that the federal food stamp program is a form of welfare, it is actually financed by the U.S. Department of Agriculture as a way of increasing the demand for food products. You do not have to be receiving welfare to qualify for food stamps. If your income is eliminated or significantly reduced for several months because you are not working, you might be eligible.

To learn more, visit the USDA's Food and Nutrition Service website at www.fns.usda. gov/snap/eligibility.

Veterans' Benefits

There are programs that provide income to veterans of the U.S. military who become unable to work because of a disability, even if that disability is not a result of military service. Additional specialized laws also provide veterans returning from service with the right to return to their jobs without losing seniority or benefits.

Your local Department of Veterans Affairs office can give you details. Regional offices are listed on the VA's website at http://benefits.va.gov.

Supplemental Security Income

Usually known as SSI, this program provides money to people who are unable to work and who have low incomes and very few assets. Unlike Social Security disability insurance, it does not require you to have worked under and paid into the Social Security program. If the circumstances surrounding your inability to earn income are so unusual that you have fallen between the cracks of the larger programs, SSI may be the one program that provides you with some income.

You can get details and file a claim at your local Social Security Administration office. For information and contact details, visit www.ssa.gov/ssi.

Disaster Unemployment Assistance

Disaster Unemployment Assistance (DUA), also referred to as Disaster Relief and Emergency Assistance, is a federal program that provides temporary financial assistance to individuals unemployed as result of a major disaster declared by the president.

Common disastrous causes are severe storms, flooding, wildfires, and earthquakes. For a current list of the declared disasters, see the Federal Emergency Management Agency's website at www.fema.gov/disasters.

To qualify for DUA, you must meet two major requirements. You must be out of work as a "direct result" of a major disaster. And you must not qualify for regular unemployment insurance (UI) from any state. Once found to be eligible for DUA, workers must actively look for work and accept suitable work offered them, unless the state opts to temporarily suspend its work search requirements for some workers.

In addition, a person must show that for every week he or she is collecting DUA, his or her unemployment continues to be the direct result of the disaster, not other factors.

Agreements Not to Compete

A growing number of employers are straining to expand their control beyond the office by asking employees to sign noncompete agreements promising that they will not work for a direct competitor or start a competing business.

These concerns are more understandable and more often enforced where workers have access to sensitive business information or trade secrets. A trade secret is information that gives a company a competitive advantage because it is not generally known and cannot be readily learned by other people who could benefit from it. It can be a formula, pattern, compilation, program, device, method, technique, or process that an employer has made reasonable efforts to keep secret.

Next Time, I'll Know Better

When initially faced with signing a non-compete agreement, your best option might be to negotiate some of the finer print with your employer.

Here are a few pointers for crafting your arguments:

- If you are promoted to a new job that carries with it a new request to sign a noncompete agreement, it is not too cheeky to ask for money to compensate you for signing. Keep in mind, though, that this will almost certainly prevent you from later claiming that the clause should not be enforced against you. Courts will likely point to your fattened wallet and conclude that it would be unfair for you to undo your promise after profiting from it.
- If presented with a noncompete clause, demand that it take effect only if you leave the job voluntarily. This may make a job search less daunting for an employee who is fired or laid off.
- Ask for the prohibited actions to be clearly specified. Many employers, for example, will fear competition with only one or two specific companies—and will readily name their names in your agreement. This gives you needed specificity and a larger pool of potential future employers.

When employees with access to trade secrets leave—because they either quit or have been fired—their former employers might be concerned that they will use the information to their personal advantages. For example, a former employee might open a competing business or go to work for a competitor and unwittingly or wittingly divulge hard-won keys to success.

Whether a judge will enforce a noncompete agreement is always an iffy question. The legal system puts a high value on a person's right to earn a living. California, for example, has taken a hard-line stance against noncompetes: A state statute makes them illegal, except in very narrow circumstances.

But the rule in most states is that noncompetes will be enforced only if they're reasonable. A covenant may be held unreasonable —and therefore invalid—if it:

- lasts for too long a time
- covers too wide a geographic area
- is too broad in the types of business it prohibits, or
- imposes an undue hardship on the worker.

The biggest and most often raised bone of contention with noncompete agreements is how long they last: that is, for how long can an employee be restrained from competing in a similar business. While there is no dyed-in-the-wool guidance on what will and will not pass muster, courts and legislatures are beginning to set out some bounds as to what is reasonable. A good example is Florida's statute (Fla. Stat. Ann. § 542.335), which sets out specific guidance as to the reasonable length of a noncompete agreement, depending on the situation. When an agreement aims to protect a company's trade secrets, a Florida court will presume a five-year term to be reasonable and a ten-year term to be unreasonable. However, in other states, the upper term limit might be closer to one or two years.

A covenant may also be held unreasonable if the information revealed to the worker isn't all that sensitive, on grounds that the restriction doesn't serve a valid business purpose.

Judges are more likely to enforce restrictive covenants against high-level managers who truly are given inside information, on the theory that such former employees are in a position to do real harm.

Even if a company isn't able to enforce a noncompete against an employee, it can ask a judge to stop a former employee from using its trade secrets in a new or competing business. Revealing or using a company's trade secrets is illegal, even if you haven't signed a confidentiality agreement. However, to win a trade secret misappropriation case, the employer must show that what the employee took or used is truly a trade secret. For example, an employer cannot stop a former employee from using general knowledge and skills learned on the job. However, it likely can stop the employee from using the company's valuable customer list that it spent years developing and that includes information not generally available to the public.

Blacklisting

As archaic and barbaric as it may seem, there are still some companies, labor unions, and people working within them that are not content to merely fire you or force you out of your job. They seem unwilling to rest until they have squelched all hope that you will ever work again.

The danger of losing a defamation lawsuit does not seem to dissuade some vengeful people from trying to put former employees on a list of people that no one else will hire. So some states have passed laws that expressly allow former employees to take legal action—criminal, civil, or both—against those who try to sabotage their efforts to secure new employment.

Although, in many cases, you could sue for defamation instead, the advantage of using the blacklisting statute is that you do not have to prove that you were harmed, often a difficult task at trial. (In Chapter 9, see "Defamation.")

The mere fact that you have to work hard at finding a new job usually is not sufficient evidence to suggest blacklisting. But a strong signal would be a series of situations in which potential new employers seem to be on the verge of hiring you, then suddenly lose all interest. This indicates that, when a prospective employer checks your references just before hiring you, the blacklister is tipped off to where you have applied for work and is able to ding you.

To find out if your state has a blacklisting law, contact your state labor department. (See the appendix for more information.)

State Laws That Control Final Paychecks

Note: States that are not listed do not have laws specifically controlling final paychecks. Contact your state department of labor for more information. (See appendix for contact list.)

Alaska

Alaska Stat. § 23.05.140(b)

Paycheck due when employee is fired: Within 3 working days after termination.

Paycheck due when employee quits: Next regular payday at least 3 days after employee gives notice.

Unused vacation pay due: Only if agreed to by employer or required by company policy or practice.

Arizona

Ariz. Rev. Stat. §§ 23-350, 23-353

Paycheck due when employee is fired: Next payday or within 7 working days, whichever is sooner.

Paycheck due when employee quits: Next regular payday or by mail at employee's request.

Unused vacation pay due: No provision.

Arkansas

Ark. Code Ann. § 11-4-405

Paycheck due when employee is fired: Upon request, within 7 days of discharge; otherwise, next regular payday.

Paycheck due when employee quits: No provision.

Unused vacation pay due: No provision.

Special employment situations: Railroad or railroad construction: day of discharge.

California

Cal. Lab. Code §§ 201 to 202, 227.3

Paycheck due when employee is fired: Immediately.

Paycheck due when employee quits: Immediately if employee has given 72 hours' notice; otherwise, within 72 hours.

Unused vacation pay due: Yes.

Special employment situations: Motion picture business: next payday.

Oil drilling industry: within 24 hours (excluding weekends and holidays) of termination.

Seasonal agricultural workers: within 72 hours of termination.

Colorado

Colo. Rev. Stat. § 8-4-109

Paycheck due when employee is fired: Immediately. (Within 6 hours of start of next workday, if payroll unit is closed; 24 hours if unit is off-site.) When paycheck is not due immediately, employer may make the check available at the worksite, the employer's local office, or the employee's last-known mailing address.

Paycheck due when employee quits: Next payday.

Unused vacation pay due: Yes.

Connecticut

Conn. Gen. Stat. Ann. §§ 31-71c, 31-76k

Paycheck due when employee is fired: Next business day after discharge.

Paycheck due when employee quits: Next payday.

Unused vacation pay due: Only if policy or collective bargaining agreement requires payment on termination.

State Laws That Control Final Paychecks (continued)

Delaware

Del. Code Ann. tit. 19, § 1103

Paycheck due when employee is fired: Next payday.

Paycheck due when employee quits: Next payday.

Unused vacation pay due: Only if required by employer policy or agreement, in which case vacation must be paid within 30 days after it becomes due.

District of Columbia

D.C. Code Ann. §§ 32-1301, 32-1303

Paycheck due when employee is fired: Next business day unless employee handles money, in which case employer has 4 days.

Paycheck due when employee quits: Next payday or 7 days after quitting, whichever is sooner.

Unused vacation pay due: Yes, unless there is an agreement to the contrary.

Hawaii

Haw. Rev. Stat. § 388-3

Paycheck due when employee is fired: Immediately or next business day, if timing or conditions prevent immediate payment.

Paycheck due when employee quits: Next payday or immediately, if employee gives one pay period's notice.

Unused vacation pay due: No.

Idaho

Idaho Code §§ 45-606, 45-617

Paycheck due when employee is fired: Next payday or within 10 days (excluding weekends and holidays), whichever is sooner. If employee makes written request for earlier payment, within 48 hours of receipt of request (excluding weekends and holidays).

Paycheck due when employee quits: Next payday or within 10 days (excluding weekends and holidays), whichever is sooner. If employee makes written request for earlier payment, within 48 hours of receipt of request (excluding weekends and holidays).

Unused vacation pay due: No provision.

Illinois

820 Ill. Comp. Stat. § 115/5

Paycheck due when employee is fired: At time of separation if possible, but no later than next payday. Employer must comply with employee's written request to mail final paycheck.

Paycheck due when employee quits: At time of separation if possible, but no later than next payday. Employer must comply with employee's written request to mail final paycheck.

Unused vacation pay due: Yes.

Indiana

Ind. Code Ann. §§ 22-2-5-1, 22-2-9-1, 22-2-9-2

Paycheck due when employee is fired: Next payday.

Paycheck due when employee quits: Next payday. (If employee has not left address, (1) 10 business days after employee demands wages or (2) when employee provides address where check may be mailed.)

Unused vacation pay due: If employer agrees to vacation pay, absent an agreement to the contrary, employer must pay out accrued unused vacation upon termination.

Special employment situations: Does not apply to railroad employees.

State Laws That Control Final Paychecks (continued)

Iowa

Iowa Code §§ 91A.2(7)(b), 91A.4

Paycheck due when employee is fired: Next payday.

Paycheck due when employee quits: Next payday.

Unused vacation pay due: Yes.

Special employment situations: If employee is owed commission, employer has 30 days to pay.

Kansas

Kan. Stat. Ann. § 44-315

Paycheck due when employee is fired: Next payday.

Paycheck due when employee quits: Next payday.

Unused vacation pay due: Only if required by employer's policies or practice.

Kentucky

Ky. Rev. Stat. Ann. §§ 337.010, 337.055

Paycheck due when employee is fired: Next payday or within 14 days, whichever is later.

Paycheck due when employee quits: Next payday or within 14 days, whichever is later.

Unused vacation pay due: Yes.

Louisiana

La. Rev. Stat. Ann. § 23:631

Paycheck due when employee is fired: Next payday or within 15 days, whichever is earlier.

Paycheck due when employee quits: Next payday or within 15 days, whichever is earlier.

Unused vacation pay due: Yes.

Maine

Me. Rev. Stat. Ann. tit. 26, § 626

Paycheck due when employee is fired: Next payday.

Paycheck due when employee quits: Next payday.

Unused vacation pay due: Yes, accrued vacation is considered wages and must be paid out upon termination.

Special employment situations: Employer must pay employees all wages due within two weeks of the sale of a business.

Maryland

Md. Code Ann., [Lab. & Empl.] § 3-505

Paycheck due when employee is fired: Next scheduled payday.

Paycheck due when employee quits: Next scheduled payday.

Unused vacation pay due: Yes.

Massachusetts

Mass. Gen. Laws ch. 149, § 148

Paycheck due when employee is fired: Day of discharge.

Paycheck due when employee quits: Next payday. If no scheduled payday, then following Saturday.

Unused vacation pay due: Yes.

Michigan

Mich. Comp. Laws §§ 408.471 to 408.475; Mich. Admin. Code § 408.9007

Paycheck due when employee is fired: Next payday.

Paycheck due when employee quits: Next payday.

Unused vacation pay due: Only if required by written policy or contract.

Special employment situations: Hand-harvesters of crops: within one working day of termination.

State Laws That Control Final Paychecks (continued)

Minnesota

Minn. Stat. Ann. §§ 181.13, 181.14, 181.74

Paycheck due when employee is fired: Within 24 hours.

Paycheck due when employee quits: Next regular payday. If next payday is less than 5 days after employee's last day, employer may delay payment until payday after that. But in no event may payment exceed 20 days from employee's last day.

Unused vacation pay due: Only if required by written policy or contract.

Special employment situations: If employee was responsible for collecting or handling money or property, employer has 10 days after termination or resignation to audit and adjust employee accounts before making payment.

Commissions must be paid to sales employees within 3 days if employee is fired or quits with at least 5 days' notice. Otherwise, commissions must be paid within 6 days.

Migrant agricultural workers who resign: within 5 days.

Missouri

Mo. Rev. Stat. § 290.110

Paycheck due when employee is fired: Day of discharge.

Paycheck due when employee quits: No provision.

Unused vacation pay due: No.

Special employment situations: Requirements do not apply if employee is paid primarily based on commission and an audit is necessary or customary to determine the amount due.

Montana

Mont. Code Ann. § 39-3-205; Mont. Admin. Code § 24.16.7521

Paycheck due when employee is fired: Immediately if fired for cause or laid off (unless there is a written policy extending time to earlier of next payday or 15 days).

Paycheck due when employee quits: Next payday or within 15 days, whichever comes first.

Unused vacation pay due: Yes.

Nebraska

Neb. Rev. Stat. §§ 48-1229 to 48-1230

Paycheck due when employee is fired: Next payday or within 2 weeks, whichever is earlier.

Paycheck due when employee quits: Next payday or within 2 weeks, whichever is earlier.

Unused vacation pay due: Only if required by agreement.

Special employment situations: Commissions due on next payday following receipt.

Nevada

Nev. Rev. Stat. Ann. §§ 608.020, 608.030

Paycheck due when employee is fired: Immediately.

Paycheck due when employee quits: Next payday or within 7 days, whichever is earlier.

Unused vacation pay due: No.

New Hampshire

N.H. Rev. Stat. Ann. §§ 275:43(v), 275:44

Paycheck due when employee is fired: Within 72 hours. If laid off, next payday.

Paycheck due when employee quits: Next payday, or within 72 hours if employee gives one pay period's notice.

Unused vacation pay due: Yes.

New Jersey

N.J. Stat. Ann. § 34:11-4.3

State Laws That Control Final Paychecks (continued)

Paycheck due when employee is fired: Next payday.

Paycheck due when employee quits: Next payday.

Unused vacation pay due: Only if required by policy.

New Mexico

N.M. Stat. Ann. §§ 50-4-4, 50-4-5

Paycheck due when employee is fired: Within 5 days. 10 days for commission or piece-based workers. § 50-4-4(A).

Paycheck due when employee quits: Next payday.

Unused vacation pay due: No provision.

Special employment situations: If paid by task or commission, 10 days after discharge.

New York

N.Y. Lab. Law §§ 191(3), 198-c(2)

Paycheck due when employee is fired: Next payday.

Paycheck due when employee quits: Next payday.

Unused vacation pay due: Yes, unless employer has a contrary policy.

North Carolina

N.C. Gen. Stat. §§ 95-25.7, 95-25.12

Paycheck due when employee is fired: Next payday.

Paycheck due when employee quits: Next payday.

Unused vacation pay due: Yes, unless employer has a contrary policy.

Special employment situations: If paid by commission or bonus, on next payday after amount calculated.

North Dakota

N.D. Cent. Code § 34-14-03; N.D. Admin. Code § 46-02-07-02(12)

Paycheck due when employee is fired: Next payday.

Paycheck due when employee quits: Next payday.

Unused vacation pay due: Yes. However, if an employer provides written notice at the time of hire, employer need not pay out vacation that has been awarded, but not yet earned. And, if an employee quits with less than 5 days' notice, employer may withhold accrued vacation, as long as the employer gave written notice of the limitation at the time of hire and the employee was employed for less than one year.

Ohio

Ohio Rev. Code Ann. § 4113.15

Paycheck due when employee is fired: First of month for wages earned in first half of prior month; 15th of month for wages earned in second half of prior month.

Paycheck due when employee quits: First of month for wages earned in first half of prior month; 15th of month for wages earned in second half of prior month.

Unused vacation pay due: Yes, if company has policy or practice of making such payments.

Oklahoma

Okla. Stat. Ann. tit. 40, §§ 165.1(4), 165.3

Paycheck due when employee is fired: Next payday.

Paycheck due when employee quits: Next payday.

Unused vacation pay due: Yes.

State Laws That Control Final Paychecks (continued)

Oregon

Ore. Rev. Stat. §§ 652.140, 652.145

Paycheck due when employee is fired: End of first business day after termination.

Paycheck due when employee quits: Immediately, with 48 hours' notice (excluding weekends & holidays); without notice, within 5 business days or next payday, whichever comes first (must be within 5 days if employee submits time records to determine wages due).

Unused vacation pay due: Only if required by policy.

Special employment situations: Seasonal farmworkers: fired or quitting with 48 hours' notice, immediately; quitting without notice, within 48 hours or next payday, whichever comes first. If the termination occurs at the end of harvest season, the employer is a farmworker camp operator, and the farmworker is provided housing at no cost until wages are paid, employer must pay by noon on the day after termination.

Pennsylvania

43 Pa. Cons. Stat. Ann. §§ 260.2a, 260.5

Paycheck due when employee is fired: Next payday.

Paycheck due when employee quits: Next payday.

Unused vacation pay due: Only if required by policy or contract.

Rhode Island

R.I. Gen. Laws § 28-14-4

Paycheck due when employee is fired: Next payday. Paycheck is due within 24 hours if employer liquidates, merges, or disposes of the business, or moves it out of state.

Paycheck due when employee quits: Next payday.

Unused vacation pay due: Yes, if employee has worked for one full year and the company has verbally or in writing awarded vacation.

South Carolina

S.C. Code Ann. §§ 41-10-10(2), 41-10-50

Paycheck due when employee is fired: Within 48 hours or next payday, but not more than 30 days.

Paycheck due when employee quits: No provision.

Unused vacation pay due: Only if required by policy or contract.

South Dakota

S.D. Codified Laws Ann. §§ 60-11-10, 60-11-11, 60-11-14

Paycheck due when employee is fired: Next payday (or until employee returns employer's property).

Paycheck due when employee quits: Next payday (or until employee returns employer's property).

Unused vacation pay due: No.

Tennessee

Tenn. Code Ann. § 50-2-103

Paycheck due when employee is fired: Next payday or within 21 days, whichever is later.

Paycheck due when employee quits: Next payday or within 21 days, whichever is later.

Unused vacation pay due: Only if required by policy or contract.

Special employment situations: Applies to employers with 5 or more employees.

Texas

Tex. Lab. Code Ann. §§ 61.001, 61.014

Paycheck due when employee is fired: Within 6 days.

Paycheck due when employee quits: Next payday.

Unused vacation pay due: Only if required by policy or contract.

State Laws That Control Final Paychecks (continued)

Utah
Utah Code Ann. §§ 34-28-5; Utah Admin. Code § 610-3

Paycheck due when employee is fired: Within 24 hours.

Paycheck due when employee quits: Next payday.

Unused vacation pay due: Only if required by policy or contract.

Special employment situations: Requirements do not apply to commissioned sales employees if audit is necessary to determine the amount due..

Vermont
Vt. Stat. Ann. tit. 21, § 342(c)

Paycheck due when employee is fired: Within 72 hours.

Paycheck due when employee quits: Next regular payday or next Friday, if there is no regular payday.

Unused vacation pay due: No provision.

Virginia
Va. Code Ann. § 40.1-29(A.1)

Paycheck due when employee is fired: Next payday.

Paycheck due when employee quits: Next payday.

Unused vacation pay due: Only if agreed to in a written statement.

Washington
Wash. Rev. Code Ann. § 49.48.010

Paycheck due when employee is fired: End of pay period.

Paycheck due when employee quits: End of pay period.

Unused vacation pay due: No provision.

West Virginia
W.Va. Code §§ 21-5-1, 21-5-4

Paycheck due when employee is fired: Next regular payday.

Paycheck due when employee quits: Next regular payday.

Unused vacation pay due: Only if required by policy or contract.

Wisconsin
Wis. Stat. Ann. §§ 109.01(3), 109.03

Paycheck due when employee is fired: Next payday or within 1 month, whichever is earlier. If termination is due to merger, relocation, or liquidation of business, within 24 hours.

Paycheck due when employee quits: Next payday.

Unused vacation pay due: Yes.

Special employment situations: Does not apply to managers, executives, or sales agents working on commission basis.

Wyoming
Wyo. Stat. Ann. §§ 27-4-104, 27-4-501, 27-4-507(c)

Paycheck due when employee is fired: Next regular payday.

Paycheck due when employee quits: Next regular payday.

Unused vacation pay due: No, if employer's policies state that vacation is forfeited upon termination of employment and the employee acknowledged the policy in writing.

Special employment situations: Requirements do not apply to commissioned sales employees if audit is necessary to determine the amount due.

Unemployment

Unemployment insurance, often called UI or unemployment compensation, is intended to provide you with financial support when you are out of work.

Unemployment insurance programs are run jointly by the federal government and the states and are paid for primarily by a tax on employers. There are differences among the states in how the programs are administered, who is eligible to receive benefits, and, perhaps most important, how much is available in benefits.

This chapter discusses unemployment insurance in general and explains some specific state nuances. For more information on your state's program, check with your state's unemployment insurance office or employment security division, usually part of the state department of labor.

Who Is Covered

Unemployment insurance covers nearly 97% of the workforce, including part-timers and temporary workers. To be covered, you must meet a number of qualifications:

- You must have worked as an employee for a certain number of hours and/or earned a minimum amount in wages before becoming unemployed. In most states, you must have been employed for at least six months during the year before your job loss. The amount you are required to have earned to qualify for unemployment insurance benefits varies by state and is frequently changed to reflect inflation and the cost of living.

- You must be a U.S. citizen or have the documents required by the U.S. Citizenship and Immigration Services to legally work in the United States. (See Chapter 16.)

- You must be available for work. For example, you won't be eligible if you can't work because you lack transportation or child care.

- You must be physically and mentally able to work. The requirement that workers must be physically able to work can be confusing when applied to pregnant women. In general, the courts have ruled that unemployment insurance benefits cannot be denied simply because an employee is pregnant, but can be denied if the pregnancy makes the employee physically unable to perform her normal job or one similar to it.

Workers who are physically unable to perform their job might, however, be eligible for financial help through another program, such as workers' comp, Social Security Disability, or a state temporary disability program.

Being Disqualified for Benefits

A few categories of employees are specifically ineligible to receive unemployment insurance benefits. And a great many more employees are disqualified because of their own behavior or actions, such as quitting a job without sufficient grounds or being fired for misconduct.

Employees Excluded

The categories of employees not covered by unemployment insurance usually include people employed by small farms, those who are paid only through commissions, casual domestic workers and babysitters, newspaper carriers under age 18, children employed by their parents, adults employed by their spouses or their children, employees of religious organizations, some corporate officers, and elected officials.

Disqualifying Behavior

Even if you are covered by unemployment insurance, you will be disqualified from receiving benefits for certain reasons. The most common reasons are:

- **Fired for misconduct.** If you were fired for misconduct, you will not eligible for unemployment benefits. The definition of "misconduct" varies widely from state to state. In most states, misconduct includes being intoxicated on the job, being chronically late or absent without a good reason, committing theft or another crime, insubordination, and other relatively serious violations of

the law or workplace rules. However, some states take a harder line and disqualify employees even for minor violations of workplace rules. In general, though, you will still be able to receive unemployment benefits if you were fired for being a poor fit, for a good faith error in judgment, or for not being able to meet workplace standards despite your best efforts.

- **Quit without good cause.** If you quit your job without good cause, you will not be eligible to receive unemployment benefits. States define "good cause" differently. Some common examples of good cause include quitting: due to workplace harassment or unsafe working conditions that your employer refused to correct; due to reasons related to domestic violence; to relocate with a spouse in the military; because your employer misled you about your wages or significantly changed your working arrangement; or because your employer relocated and the commute would have been unreasonable. In some states, other personal reasons will qualify as good cause, such as quitting to relocate with a nonmilitary spouse or to take care of an ill immediate family member.

- **Insufficient work search efforts.** To receive unemployment benefits, you must be actively searching for work and accept a suitable job offer if you receive one.

The requirements depend on what state you live in, but in general, you will be expected to make a certain number of job contacts each week and keep records of your efforts. If you turn down a suitable job offer, your unemployment benefits will end. Whether a job is suitable depends on several factors, including your qualifications and work experience, the length of the commute, the pay, and how long you've been unemployed.

Because state rules on these issues vary considerably, you should do a little research on your eligibility for benefits before you leave your job. State tolerances and requirements change over time and with economic winds. Filing for unemployment benefits often requires perseverance, time, wading through paperwork, and waiting in lines to speak with—and sometimes be put off by—unemployment office personnel. But you have little to lose by filing a claim you consider to be valid and hoping for a favorable decision.

Independent Contractors: A Gray Area

Independent contractors are not usually eligible for unemployment insurance. But, in some cases, workers who were treated as independent contractors by companies actually should have been classified as employees—and therefore are eligible for unemployment benefits. If you have questions about your legal work status, contact your local department of labor. (See the appendix for specifics.)

In fact, the legal controls are somewhat relaxed in allowing independent contractors to be covered by unemployment benefits. If your employment status is somewhat uncertain, you may need to provide proof that you qualified as an employee of a company rather than as an independent contractor.

Persuasive proof would be evidence showing any of the following:

- Your work was supervised by employees of the company.
- Your work was considered a normal part of the company's course of business—for example, an integral part of the quarterly financial review, rather than a one-time consulting job.
- You worked in the company office, rather than from your own home, workshop, or studio.
- You used company-owned equipment—computers, machining tools, construction equipment—to get the work done.
- You received detailed instructions on how to perform the work.
- You were on the company's payroll.

Calculating Your Benefits

Each state sets its own maximum and minimum limits on the amount of benefits you can collect. Whether you are entitled to the high end or the low end of the benefit range depends on how much money you earned in your last position.

You must meet the state requirements for wages earned or time worked (or both) during a one-year period referred to as a base period. In most states, this is the first four out of the last five calendar quarters completed just before you file your claim, In general, benefits are based on a percentage of your earnings during this time. Under

---

Severance Pay: It May Not Compute

As protection against wrongful discharge lawsuits, employers increasingly offer an unearned severance payment—usually several weeks' worth of the employee's normal pay—to get an employee to quit a job rather than be fired. (In Chapter 9, see "Waiving Your Right to Sue.") In such situations, severance pay can delay the start of unemployment insurance benefits or even make a worker ineligible for them.

EXAMPLE: Raj worked for a company that wanted to economize by cutting 500 employees. He accepted the company's offer of six months' severance pay—four months more than the two months' severance pay he had earned through the benefits program—in return for a signed statement that he had not been dismissed but had volunteered to quit his job.

When Raj filed a claim for unemployment insurance benefits, he was shocked and disappointed when it was denied. His former employer contested the claim, arguing that Raj had made a decision to quit voluntarily.

Raj appealed the denial of his claim, and he won because he proved that he was coerced into quitting. But the appeal office also ruled that Raj could not begin collecting unemployment insurance benefits until the four months covered by the unearned severance package had expired.

Regulations and rulings covering the effect that severance pay has on unemployment insurance vary greatly from state to state. In some cases, groups of workers who have been cut from company payrolls through offers of severance packages have created enough political pressure to have the rules in their state changed in their favor.

If you quit your job in exchange for severance pay, protect your rights by filing a claim for unemployment insurance benefits. If that claim is denied, you will then have the right to explain during the appeals process what really happened or to benefit from any changes in your state's unemployment insurance rules covering severance pay.

most state formulas, unemployment benefits are around one-half of your average weekly wages, up to a maximum set by state law. States have different maximums, with the lowest around $240 per week and the highest around $770 per week.

To find out your state's current benefit scheme, contact your state unemployment agency. Many of the state agency websites even have helpful calculators that you can use to estimate your benefit amount.

Part-Time Work: Throwing It Into the Mix

Unemployment benefits are based on the amount you used to earn. If your former job was part time, you still might be eligible to collect unemployment benefits if you lose that job. This is true even if you hold down several part-time jobs, and lose only one of them. Keep in mind, however, that the amount to which you are entitled in unemployment benefits will be offset by the amount you still earn and any amounts you receive from workers' compensation and other sources.

The same is true if you secure a part-time job after losing other work. Your unemployment benefits will typically be reduced by the amount of income you earn in the new part-time job. However, to encourage part-time work, many states also allow you to earn a certain amount in wages before your benefits will be reduced. For example, the first 25% of your part-time wages might not count against your weekly benefit amount.

Under normal circumstances, unemployment insurance benefits are usually paid for only 26 weeks. However, this period might be extended during periods of high unemployment.

State Unemployment Insurance Agencies

You can find links and contact information for every state's unemployment agency, including a link to the online filing service (if the state has one), at www.servicelocator.org/OWSLinks.asp. This is the Career One Stop site sponsored by the federal Department of Labor's Employment and Training Administration.

Filing a Claim

Claims for unemployment insurance benefits are accepted and paid by the states through thousands of offices throughout the country. Tales of difficult dealings with the unemployment office are common—long waits, surly office workers, piles of paperwork—all coming your way at what is likely to be an emotionally shaky time for you. Keep in mind that you are merely pursuing your legal right. And cloak yourself with the mantle of patience.

In many states, you can apply for unemployment benefits over the telephone, online, or by mailing or faxing a form; you need not apply in person. In most states, there is a waiting period of one week between the time you file for unemployment benefits and the time you can collect them. But it is a good idea to contact the nearest unemployment office as soon after you lose your job as possible. You can then supply all required information, complete the necessary paperwork, and convince agency representatives to begin investigating your claim, all the initial steps needed to get the bureaucratic ball rolling.

The Taxman Will Cometh

Unlike workers' compensation benefits (discussed in Chapter 12), unemployment insurance benefits are taxed as income. Because the benefit amounts paid are often below the taxable annual earning level, however, many states will not take the automatic step of deducting any taxes from your unemployment benefit check.

However, the state will—almost unfailingly—report the unemployment benefit amount you were paid to the Internal Revenue Service and to your state taxing authority.

If you receive unemployment benefits during a year in which you get a new job, you may want to increase the amount your employer withholds in taxes from your paycheck. Otherwise, you may be unpleasantly surprised at tax time when you either owe more tax or receive less of a refund than anticipated.

Required Documentation

Your claim will get processed more quickly if you bring the proper documentation when you visit the local office or have it handy if you are able to apply online or over the telephone. You will need:

- recent pay stubs and other wage records, such as the W-2 form on which your employer reports your income to the Internal Revenue Service
- your Social Security card, or another document that shows your Social Security number, and
- any documentation you have that proves you are unemployed, such as a layoff or dismissal notice from your employer, and your employer's unemployment insurance account number, if you know it. (For more on how to document a job loss, see "Getting Documentation" in Chapter 9.)

Typically, the unemployment insurance claims office will require some type of orientation, ranging from reading simple explanatory pamphlets to watching sophisticated video productions or attending live group seminars.

The Investigation

Once you have handed in your completed forms, the rituals that follow vary somewhat from state to state. You may be interviewed the same day, told to come back for an interview, or simply sent a check in the mail. If a second visit is required, be sure to take your employment document collection with you.

Whatever the procedure is in your locale, the goal of the unemployment insurance claim filing process is to determine whether you are entitled to benefits and what the amount of those benefits should be. The interviewer will likely concentrate on why you left your last job. Keep your explanations helpful but as brief and objective as possible.

In some states, you might be approved to receive benefits immediately. If your employer later challenges the award, you should continue to get those benefits during the time the appeal is processed.

But, in most states, the clerks at the unemployment insurance office will use your first interview to launch an investigation of your claim by sending inquiries to your former employer. The employer then must respond, either verifying or disputing your version of the circumstances surrounding your unemployment, the wages you received, and other relevant information. The process usually takes at least a few weeks, and sometimes more.

While waiting for your claim to go through this verification process, you will probably be required to visit the unemployment insurance office once each week or two or sign a statement that will be mailed to you affirming that you still meet all the legal requirements of the program, including that you are looking for a new job. It is important to comply with this reporting requirement even before receiving unemployment insurance checks. If you have not yet received a cent in unemployment benefits, once your claim is verified, you will usually be paid after the fact for all the weeks for which you did qualify.

If your claim is approved, you will typically receive your unemployment benefits every two weeks by check, state-issued debit card, or direct deposit.

What to Say, and What Not to Say

When completing your unemployment forms, one of the first questions posed will be something like: Explain in your own words the reason for leaving your last job. You will see first that there is little room for long-worded explanations. Take the clue and keep your responses simple and noncommittal.

Unless you were clearly dismissed from your job because of something you did wrong, avoid using the word "fired" in filling out any forms or answering any interview questions at the unemployment insurance office. There are many unspecified words thrown around concerning the end of employment, but "fired" is the one most often taken to mean that you did something wrong and were dismissed because of it.

If you lost your job because business was slow, note that you were laid off. "Laid off" is an equally vague term, but it is less likely to raise questions about the validity of your claim.

If you were discharged by your employer, take pains to note: "Discharged without any misconduct" or "Quit for good cause personal reason." Leave out any qualifying details, such as: "My supervisor never liked me from the first day I walked in, so naturally I was the first to be laid off."

Where to File If You Move

If you become unemployed in one state and then move to another, you can file your claim in your new state. However, your benefits will be determined by the rules of your former state. Although your new state administers your claim, the cost of your benefits is charged back to the state in which you became unemployed. A move will also add time to processing your claim, usually increasing the delay by several weeks.

Keep in mind that, even when you relocate, you still must meet all the requirements of the unemployment insurance program to qualify for benefits. Your new location must be one to which you were required to move by family circumstances or in which it is logical for you to expect to find a new job. For example, you cannot decide to move to a small seacoast town with virtually no business activity because you like the countryside there, quit your old job for no other reason, then expect to be eligible for unemployment insurance when you get to your new home and cannot find work.

Continuing Your Benefits

Once you have qualified for unemployment insurance benefits, you are not free to simply sit back and welcome the checks each week. You must continue to comply with the state program's rules and rituals to keep them coming.

This usually means filing a claim each week or two verifying that you remain unemployed but available for work, that you remain physically able to work, and that you are actively looking for work. You will typically be asked to certify that you continue to meet these requirements; it is usually a criminal offense to lie in any of your answers. In most states, you can file your weekly claims online or by phone.

In some states, you will also be asked to provide a work search log, showing how many job contacts you made for the week.

The unemployment insurance agency won't require you to take a job that varies too much from your normal field of work and your normal wage level, at least not at first. But these ranges are subject to interpretation, so exercise care in deciding where to apply for a new job. Some unemployment insurance offices maintain and post listings of jobs that are available locally. At first, apply only for jobs that are similar to your normal type of work and wage levels so that you will not run the risk of having your unemployment insurance claim discontinued because you refused to accept suitable employment. But, the longer you are unemployed, the more you will be expected to widen your search and accept a job with different duties or that pays less.

Appealing Benefit Decisions

If your claim is approved, your former employer will have the right to appeal it. If you are denied benefits, you are legally entitled to appeal the decision.

If Your Employer Appeals

Some former employees begin to collect unemployment insurance benefits to which they are not legally entitled, and the employer justifiably appeals the decision.

However, some employers have an outrageous policy of appealing all unemployment insurance claims filed against them. Typically, they use tactics such as claiming that workers quit when, in fact, they were fired because business became slow.

These employers often hire lawyers or agencies that specialize in frustrating unemployment insurance claims, fighting employees' claims until the employees find new jobs and drop their complaints. Money is usually their motivation: The more unemployment claims filed against

---

Representing Yourself

If you can clearly document the reasons that you are unemployed and present them in an organized manner, you can do a good job of representing yourself in all but the most complex situations. At this level, the appeal process is intended to resolve disputes rather than to take on the look of a formal court action, so don't be afraid to ask questions at the unemployment insurance office or at your hearing.

Well before the hearing is scheduled to begin, write down the reasons that you feel you are entitled to unemployment insurance benefits in as few words as possible; then practice presenting those reasons to a friend or family member. Do not give in to the human temptation to use the hearing as an opportunity to insult or get revenge on your former employer.

Do a thorough and thoughtful job of researching, organizing, documenting, and presenting your case. Keep your argument focused at the hearing, because it is at this level that you are most likely to win a decision that will quickly start your benefit checks flowing. (For details of how to document your job loss, see "Getting Documentation" in Chapter 9.)

If you win this appeal, you will soon begin receiving benefits, typically including back payments from the date on which you first became eligible.

Both you and your former employer will have the option of appealing the judge's ruling to the state courts. However, only a tiny percentage of unemployment insurance cases continue up into the state courts or higher. Those that do typically require help from a lawyer. (In Chapter 17, see "Hiring a Lawyer.")

a company, the higher the company's unemployment premiums.

If your claim is approved but your employer appeals it, you will be notified of that appeal in writing. In general, an appeal by your former employer will be conducted in the same way as your appeal of a denied claim.

You will be able to continue collecting your benefits until a decision is issued on your former employer's appeal. You might, however, be required to repay all or part of the benefits if your ex-employer wins the appeal. Typically, your ability to repay is the deciding factor in such circumstances.

Appealing a Denied Claim

If your claim is denied, you will be notified in writing of the reasons for that decision and the procedure and time limits for filing an appeal. Depending on your state, you will have from one to four weeks to file an appeal after the notice of denial is mailed to you.

A hearing will likely be scheduled within a few weeks after you advise the unemployment insurance office of your intention to appeal its decision. You will have the option of representing yourself or hiring a lawyer for help. If you want a lawyer but cannot afford one, check with your local Legal Aid Society or a clinic at a nearby law school to see if someone there can represent you. (See the appendix for additional contacts for legal help.)

Your former employer also has the option of being represented by a lawyer or an agency that specializes in challenging unemployment insurance claims. Typically, the appeal hearing will be conducted informally before a hearing examiner, referee, or administrative law judge. At the hearing, you and your former employer will be allowed to bring witnesses, such as coworkers and medical experts. Most of the formal rules of evidence that apply to formal courtroom proceedings will not apply or will be only loosely enforced. In some states, unemployment appeal hearings are routinely conducted over the phone.

> **CAUTION**
>
> **Keep an eye on the deadline.** Most states have strict rules about the time limits within which appeals must be filed. You should find the appeal limit clearly marked on the notice of the determination or ruling. Late appeals will be accepted only if you can show that you have extremely good cause for being late: that unanticipated circumstances beyond your control caused your tardiness. Excuses such as you forgot or did not note the filing due date will not pass legal muster.

> **RESOURCE**
>
> **Want more information on UI appeals?** Many unemployment insurance appeals boards publish pamphlets or other publications explaining the state's appeal process. These publications vary in comprehensiveness and helpfulness. But, if you plan to appeal, it is certainly worth your while to contact the local UI office or visit its website and find out whether a publication is available. ●

Workers' Compensation

The workers' compensation system provides some replacement income and medical expense coverage to employees who are injured or become ill as a result of their jobs. Financial benefits may also be paid to a worker's dependents, if the worker passes away due to a work-related injury or illness. In most circumstances, workers' compensation protects employers from being sued for those injuries or deaths in court.

The benefits paid by workers' compensation are relatively modest. The system is financed primarily by insurance premiums paid by employers. In most states, larger employers may opt to self-insure (that is, they can pay any claims themselves). However, the majority of employers are required to purchase workers' comp insurance from a private insurer or through a state-run program.

Contrary to popular misconception, filing a workers' comp claim does not involve suing the employer. Unless the employer has committed some serious wrong or is illegally uninsured or underinsured, filing for workers' comp is more like submitting a claim to a car insurer following an accident.

The purpose of the workers' comp system is to allow employers and employees to settle their potential differences over money and liability privately and quickly. Injured employees are compensated for the costs of workplace injuries and illnesses. In return, employers can run their businesses free from the threat of negligence lawsuits filed by their employees. In reality, however, the system is fraught with difficulties: high premiums

for employers and grindingly slow claim processing and limited benefits for injured employees. Doctors and lawyers are often thrown into the fray to make the system more costly and complicated.

Other Laws on Work-Related Illness and Injury

Workers' compensation covers some aspects of work-related injuries, illnesses, and deaths. But injured workers should be aware of other laws that might give them rights or entitle them to compensation. Some laws work in tandem, providing individuals with different options; some provide the exclusive remedy for a workplace wrong:

- Social Security disability insurance provides some income for people who are unable to work because of a physical or mental disability. (See Chapter 13.)
- The Americans with Disabilities Act prohibits discrimination against workers who have physical or mental impairments. (See Chapter 7.)
- The Family and Medical Leave Act allows an employee to take up to 12 weeks of unpaid leave in a year due to a serious health condition that makes the employee unable to do his or her job. (See Chapter 4.)

Other lawsuits for injuries or job loss may help redress some additional workplace injuries, particularly where workers have lost their jobs. For example, a worker who is fired for filing a workers' comp claim might be able to sue for wrongful termination.

Similar to unemployment insurance (discussed in Chapter 11), the workers' compensation system is administered by the states. The laws and court decisions governing workers' comp follow a pattern throughout the country but vary significantly from state to state on everything from eligibility for benefits to the proper process for filing claims.

Who Is Covered

In almost every state, workers' compensation insurance coverage is mandatory. Many states require all private employers to have workers' comp insurance. However, in some states, smaller employers—typically those with fewer than five employees—are not required to have coverage. Texas is the only state that makes workers' comp insurance optional for employers. However, an employer that chooses not to have coverage may be sued by an injured worker in court for their full range of damages.

In general, anyone who qualifies as a part-time or full-time employee is covered by workers' compensation insurance. There are a few exceptions to this rule—notably harbor workers, seafarers, railroad employees, and federal employees—all of whom must file lawsuits to get payment for their injuries rather than going through the workers' comp system.

But coverage details vary from state to state, so certain categories of employees may be excluded from coverage in some locales. For example, many states exclude volunteers, farmworkers, federal employees, and domestic workers from coverage.

Workers who are not covered by workers' comp but who suffer work-related illnesses or injuries are usually relegated to getting compensation from their employers through:

- a company-backed policy, such as paid time off for sick days
- a settlement reached through arbitration or mediation (see Chapter 17), or
- a lawsuit filed against an employer or former employer (for negligence or breach of contract, for example).

Many states require employers to post an explanation of workers' compensation coverage in a prominent place within the work area. If your employer keeps such a notice on your workplace bulletin board, you are probably covered. If you are unsure whether your employer is covered, your state workers' compensation agency should tell you. You can find a list of state workers' compensation agencies at the website of the federal Department of Labor, www.dol.gov. Select "Workers' Compensation" from the list of topics, then click the link for "state workers' compensation board."

If your employer has failed to secure workers' comp insurance that is required by law, you can typically file a lawsuit against the employer in court or file a claim against a state uninsured employer fund. These funds pay out workers' comp benefits to injured workers who would have been covered under an employer's workers' comp policy, had it secured one.

> ⓘ **CAUTION**
>
> **Independent contractors lose out.**
> Independent contractors are not covered under the workers' comp systems in most states. However, workers who are categorized as independent contractors by their employers may in reality be employees. If you are unclear about your status as a worker, file a workers' comp claim for your injuries anyway. It will then be up to your employer to prove that you are not eligible because you qualify legally as an independent contractor rather than an employee. If you are truly an independent contractor, you can still sue for your injuries, but you will need to prove that the company was somehow at fault for causing them.

Conditions Covered

Workers' compensation provides a claim and benefit system for workers who become ill, are injured, or die on the job.

Injuries

To be covered by workers' compensation, an injury need not be caused by a sudden accident such as a fall. Equally common are claims for injuries due to repeated physical motions, such as backstrain from lifting heavy boxes. Also covered may be a physical condition that was aggravated by workplace conditions, such as emphysema made worse by airborne chemicals. And, in some cases, workers can be compensated for the effects of psychological injuries caused by the job.

With a few exceptions, any injury that occurs in connection with work is covered. The legal boundary is that employees are protected by workers' comp as long as the injury happened "in the course of employment." For example, a computer repair technician would be covered by workers' comp while making service calls on customers, but not while commuting to and from work or going to a purely social dinner later that evening.

From the employee's standpoint, workers' comp is a no-fault system. It does not matter whether a worker was careless when injured, although claims from employees hurt while drunk or fighting have traditionally been rejected as outside the bounds of "work-related activity." Some states restrict coverage for injuries caused by employees' own "willful misconduct," a term given differing spins by different courts. And a number of states expressly restrict or deny benefits when an employee's claim is based on injuries caused by illegal drug use.

Injuries that can be shown to have been intentionally self-inflicted by the employee, or to have been caused by substance abuse, generally are not covered. However, courts have often sided with the injured worker when such cases are disputed, ruling that the injury is covered as long as the employee's behavior was not the only thing that caused the injury. Another questionable area is injuries caused by a coworker's violent behavior (although the workers' comp laws in a few states, including California, specifically cover them).

Avoiding Injuries Caused by Repetitive Motion

In a typical year, more than six million work-related injuries and illnesses occur in the United States. The most rapidly growing category of workplace injuries is caused by repetitive motions of the body. These occupational pains go by many names and acronyms: repetitive stress injuries (RSIs), cumulative trauma disorders (CTDs), and repeated motion injuries (RMIs), to name a few.

When they primarily afflict the wrists, hands, and forearms, these injuries are called carpal tunnel syndrome: the bane of office workers who spend their days in front of computer terminals. Many other parts of the body are susceptible to injury when used repeatedly to perform motions beyond the specifications for which nature designed them. Our bodies were simply not made to withstand the demands of making the same motion thousands of times in a short time period, especially if we don't want to. A recent study found that employees who were dissatisfied with their jobs were most likely to develop repetitive stress injuries.

Typical symptoms of repetitive stress injuries include swelling and redness near bone joints; extreme sensitivity to movement and external touch; pain, both sharp and dull, in the overused area that may radiate into other parts of the limb, abdomen, head, or back; and numbness of the affected body part or those near it. If detected early, injuries caused by repeated motions can often be cured by a short period of rest, light medication, and rehabilitative exercise. The most serious cases, however, can escalate to lifelong physical disabilities.

Work-related cumulative motion injuries are typically covered by workers' compensation insurance. But the best workers' compensation claim is the one that you never have to file, so here are a few of the steps that health experts recommend to avoid these injuries:

- Take frequent, short breaks from repetitive, physically stressful work whenever possible. This allows your muscles and joints to recover a bit from unnatural tensions that may result from your work.

- Do gentle stretching exercises at work regularly, paying particular attention to the parts of your body that you use most often. This reduces the muscle tightening that contributes to the problem.

- Watch for early symptoms, such as stiffness or other discomfort in heavily used body parts. Complete recovery is much more likely if the symptoms are recognized early.

- Redesign your work tools or your work position and movements or ask your employer for help doing so. Good redesign examples are wrist rests for use with personal computer keyboards and ergonomic office furniture.

- Remember that heart-pounding physical exertion is not necessary for dangerous body stress to occur. Just as you can wake up with a sore shoulder after sleeping all night, you can suffer a muscle or tendon injury even in jobs that involve very limited exertion. (For more on preventing workplace injuries, see "Enforcing OSHA Rights" in Chapter 6.)

The legal definition of when you are working, for workers' compensation purposes, also has expanded in recent years to cover a greater number of injuries. For example, employees who were injured playing baseball or football on a company-affiliated team have been allowed to collect workers' compensation benefits for those injuries.

Illnesses

An illness becomes an occupational illness—and is covered under the workers' compensation system—when the nature of a job increases the worker's chances of suffering from that disease. In fact, in some states, certain illnesses (such as heart attacks and hernias) are presumed to be covered for high-stress jobs such as police work and firefighting. There must, however, be a clear connection between the job and the illness. Also, in examining a claim, investigators will look into nonwork factors—such as diet, exercise, smoking and drinking habits, and hobbies—that might have contributed to a particular condition.

Illnesses that are the gradual result of work of stressful work conditions—for example, emotional illness and stress-related digestive problems—increasingly are being recognized by the courts as covered by workers' compensation insurance. Perhaps not coincidentally, such stress injury claims are on the rise, too.

The American medical profession, traditionally slow to acknowledge the interworkings of mind and body, is starting to recognize the effects of job-related stress on general health. According to the American Institute for Preventive Medicine, stress is at the root of nearly two-thirds of all office visits and plays a major role in heart disease and cancer.

Some states allow employees to recover compensation for stress-based injuries, at least when there is a diagnosed medical condition. However, these claims are typically subject to stricter requirements and are more difficult to prove. In general, you are more likely to receive compensation for a mental or emotional injury where:

- you have physical manifestations of the mental or emotional injury, such as high blood pressure or hair loss
- the mental injury was caused by or related to a physical injury (for example, depression caused by chronic pain from a work-related injury), or
- the mental injury is clearly related to an on-the-job incident (for example, developing PTSD after a robbery at the workplace).

Deaths

Dependents—usually a spouse, children, or other close family members—of a worker who is killed on the job or dies as a result of a work injury or illness are almost always eligible to collect workers' compensation benefits.

Even if an employee is found dead in the workplace, no one witnessed the death, and no cause of death is obvious, the death is usually covered by workers' compensation. The possibilities of suicide or murder are usually ignored by courts unless there is strong evidence that the death qualifies as one or the other.

The Right to Medical Care

When you are injured at work, the workers' comp system usually entitles you to receive immediate medical care.

Treating Physician

Whether you have the right to be treated by your regular doctor depends on your state's law. In some states, the injured worker has the right to select the treating doctor. In other states, the employer has the right to select the treating doctor. It's also common for employers to set up managed care organizations to treat injured workers; in that case, the worker typically must select a doctor from within the network. However, some states allow workers to switch to a doctor of their own choosing after a certain period of time (for example, 30 days). The rules on selecting and changing treating doctors through workers' comp vary greatly from state to state. To learn more, visit the website of your state's workers' compensation agency.

Continuing Treatment

The insurance company is responsible for paying for all reasonable and necessary treatment related to your work injury. Treatment related to your injury should be paid for life, but you can trade away future medical payments for cash when you settle your case.

If you are uncertain about whether settling makes good financial sense for you—especially if your work-related illness or injury is severe—you should consult with an experienced workers' comp attorney. (In Chapter 17, see "Hiring a Lawyer.")

Filing a Workers' Compensation Claim

Get immediate medical care if your injury requires it. You must then inform your employer of your injury as soon as possible. This is a tricky part of processing a workers' comp claim because states have wildly different deadlines for notifying your employer. In many states, the time limit is between 30 and 90 days. However, several states require notice in a much shorter time frame, sometimes within just a few days.

In the unlikely event that your employer refuses to cooperate with you in filing a workers' compensation claim, a call to your local workers' compensation office will usually remedy the situation.

Typically, your employer will have claim forms for you to fill out and submit. It then becomes your employer's responsibility to submit the paperwork to the proper insurance carrier. Depending on state law, you—rather than your employer—might need to file a separate claim with your state's workers' compensation agency. There is a time limit on this, too; typically, you must file a claim within a year or two after the injury. Similar time limits typically apply if you want to appeal the denial of a workers' comp claim.

If your claim is not disputed by your employer or its insurance carrier, it will be approved and an adjuster for the insurance company will typically contact you or your employer with instructions on next steps. But be prepared; things do not always go smoothly. Insurance companies and employers often challenge claims in order to keep costs low. The best way you can counteract such disputes is by producing good documentation, including complete medical records, of your injury and treatment.

If your injury is not permanent and does not cause you to take time off work, getting payment for your medical bills will probably be the extent of your claim, and there won't be much else for you to do. If you are temporarily unable to work because of your injury, you will also begin receiving checks to cover your wage loss. Checks typically start within a couple weeks after your claim

is approved. Your employer will notify the insurance company to stop sending you wage-replacement checks as soon as you recover and return to work.

Calculating Benefits

Your workers' compensation benefits may take several forms. The following are the most common, although some states may provide additional benefits.

Costs of Medical Care

The bills for your medical care will be paid, as long as you see an authorized provider. Theoretically, at least, there is typically no limitation on medical coverage for illnesses and injuries that are covered. Medical coverage includes costs of:

- doctors
- hospitals
- nursing services, including home care
- physical therapy
- dentists
- chiropractors, and
- prosthetic devices.

Temporary Disability

This is the most common disability compensation paid under workers' compensation, awarded if you are unable to work while receiving medical treatment for your injuries.

You will receive tax-free temporary disability payments to make up for your wage loss. If you cannot work at all, you will typically be paid two-thirds of your average wages, with state-set minimums and maximums. If you're able to work during this time, but you're earning less because you had to cut your hours or accept light-duty work, you can receive partial benefits. In many states, these benefits are two-thirds of the difference in your earnings.

In most states, workers become eligible for wage loss replacement benefits as soon as their injury causes them to miss a few days of work. The number of days required to qualify varies by state. Some states allow the payments to be paid retroactively to the first day of wage loss if the injury keeps the employee out of work for an extended period.

Permanent Disability

At a certain point, your doctor will find that your condition has plateaued and that you're not likely to improve with further treatment. This stage is often called reaching "maximum medical improvement." Your doctor will issue a report, stating whether you continue to have any permanent limitations as a result of your work injury. Based on this report, you will receive a permanent disability rating that translates to a monetary award.

- **Permanent total disability.** Workers who are permanently and totally disabled are not expected to be able to work again. These employees will usually receive benefits at their temporary disability rates for the rest of their lives.
- **Permanent partial disability.** Workers who are still able to perform some type of work, even if it's not their normal job, fall under the permanent partial disability (PPD) category. The methods for calculating a PPD award vary greatly from state to state. Many states have a "schedule" of injuries, listing certain body parts and a corresponding amount of compensation—either stated as a lump sum or a number of weeks of payment. These awards are usually available regardless of whether the worker suffers any wage loss from the permanent disability. If the body part is not listed on a schedule, or if the state doesn't have a schedule of injuries, PPD benefits are typically based on a calculation that takes into account the degree of the impairment, the employee's loss of wages, or both.

Vocational Rehabilitation

If you have a permanent disability that prevents you from returning to your job, but you can still perform some type of work, you might be eligible for vocational rehabilitation benefits. These are services—such as schooling, training, career counseling, or other resources—designed to help you find a job in a new line of work.

Death Benefits

Weekly compensation benefits are paid to surviving dependents (usually children and spouses) of workers who are killed in the course of employment or as the result of a work-related injury or occupational disease. The amounts paid typically equal about two thirds of the deceased worker's weekly salary. About a third of the states limit the total amount of the death award given; a few states limit the number of weeks or years survivors may receive death benefits.

Complex Cases Require Expertise

If your workers' compensation claim is denied, you have the right to appeal it at several levels. If your work-related injury is a permanent or long-term one, then pursuing your claim for workers' compensation benefits to its fullest extent will likely be a complicated task.

If your claim falls into these categories, you will probably need to hire a lawyer who specializes in workers' compensation cases. (In Chapter 17, see "Hiring a Lawyer.")

Death benefits to surviving spouses usually come to an end if they remarry; some states provide for a lump sum to a former spouse upon remarriage. Death benefits for surviving children usually end when they reach age 18 (or somewhat later for full-time students).

In addition, if an employee dies from a workplace accident, the employee's family or estate can receive burial expenses up to an amount specified by law in the state where the accident occurred.

Related Lawsuits for Work Injuries

The workers' compensation system is often the exclusive remedy against an employer for work-related injuries and illness. But, in some situations, an injured worker will have the option of filing a lawsuit against another responsible person or company in addition to filing a claim for workers' compensation. For example, an injured worker might sue the manufacturer of a defective machine for negligence.

Employers that fail to maintain the workers' compensation coverage required in their state or otherwise violate the laws of the workers' compensation system generally can be sued over work-related injuries. You will probably need to hire a lawyer to help with this type of lawsuit. (In Chapter 17, see "Hiring a Lawyer.")

Many states also allow employees to sue employers that fired them in retaliation for filing a workers' compensation claim or for testifying on someone else's behalf in a workers' compensation case. ●

Social Security Disability Insurance

Social Security disability insurance (SSDI) is one component of the federal Social Security system. The benefits it provides are intended to prevent people from becoming paupers because injury or illness has left them completely unable to earn a living. This is something that happens to a surprisingly large portion of the population. In fact, according to the Social Security Administration, a 20-year-old worker has a 25% chance of becoming disabled before retirement age. And more than ten million people currently draw Social Security disability benefits.

When you and your employer pay into the Social Security program, you are buying long-term disability insurance coverage. Once you have paid into the program for a period specified by the government, you are eligible for benefits should you become unable to earn a living.

Disability program payments are not intended to cover temporary, short-term, or partial disability. The benefits were sanctioned by Congress with the assumption that working families have other support resources during short-term disabilities, such as workers' compensation, insurance, savings, and investment income.

RESOURCE

Need to know more about SSDI? For a complete explanation of the Social Security system and more detail on filing and appealing Social Security disability insurance claims, see *Nolo's Guide to Social Security Disability: Getting & Keeping Your Benefits*, by David Morton (Nolo).

Workers' Comp and Social Security: Separate and Unequal

In contrast to the workers' compensation program (see Chapter 12), the Social Security disability insurance system does not recognize degrees of wage-earning capability. Under Social Security eligibility rules, you are either able to work (in which case you do not qualify for its benefits) or you are not able to work (in which case you may qualify). Also, unlike workers' comp eligibility requirements, a disability need not be work-related to be covered under the Social Security benefit system.

However, if you receive workers' comp payments, your Social Security benefit may be reduced. The law states that the sum of all your disability payments cannot exceed 80% of your earnings averaged over a period of time shortly before you became disabled. (See "Other Disability Benefits," below.)

Who Is Covered

Workers must pass two different earnings tests to qualify for Social Security disability benefits: a "duration of work" test and a "recent work" test.

Examples of Work Needed for the Duration of Work Test	
If you become disabled...	**Then you generally need**
Before age 28	1.5 years of work
Age 30	2 years
Age 34	3 years
Age 38	4 years
Age 42	5 years
Age 44	5.5 years
Age 46	6 years
Age 48	6.5 years
Age 50	7 years
Age 52	7.5 years
Age 54	8 years
Age 56	8.5 years
Age 58	9 years
Age 60	9.5 years

Duration of work test. This test reviews your work history to make sure that you paid into the Social Security system for a sufficient period throughout your working life so that you can now collect benefits.

The table above shows examples of how much work you need to meet the duration of work test if you become disabled at various ages.

CAUTION

Special rules apply to blind individuals. Certain blind workers have to meet only the duration of work test. In addition, a number of other waivers and rules may apply. For more information, see *If You Are Blind or Have Low Vision—How We Can Help*, Publication No. 05-10052, available for a free download at www.ssa.gov.

Recent work test. This test mandates that you must have worked approximately five out of ten years before your disability totally removed you from the workforce. Special rules apply to workers under age 31: In general, they must have worked roughly half of the time since turning 21. See the chart below for details.

The calendar quarters are:

First quarter: January 1 through March 31
Second quarter: April 1 through June 30
Third quarter: July 1 through September 30
Fourth quarter: October 1 through December 31.

Certain members of your family may also qualify for benefits, including:

- your spouse, if he or she is 62 or older
- your spouse, at any age who is caring for your child who is younger than age 16 or disabled

- your unmarried child, including an adopted child, or, in some cases, a stepchild or grandchild; the child must be under age 18 or under age 19 if still in high school; and
- your unmarried child, age 18 or older, if he or she has a disability that started before age 22 and whose disability also meets the definition of disability for adults discussed below.

Rules for Work Needed for the Recent Work Test	
If you become disabled...	**Then you generally need**
In or before the quarter you turn 24	1.5 years of work during the three-year period ending with the quarter your disability began
In the quarter after you turn 24 but before the quarter you turn 31	Work during half the time for the period beginning with the quarter after you turned 21 and ending with the quarter you became disabled Example: If you become disabled in the quarter you turned 27, then you would need three years of work out of the six-year period ending with the quarter you became disabled.
In the quarter you turn 31 or later	Work during five years out of the 10-year period ending with the quarter your disability began

A former spouse age 62 or older may also qualify for benefits based on your earnings if he or she was married to you for at least ten years and is not currently married. The money paid to a divorced spouse does not reduce your benefit or any benefits due to a current spouse or children.

Disabilities Covered

Many injuries and illnesses are obviously disabling. There are others, however, such as chronic illnesses that become acute with age, or residual conditions that deteriorate over time, which become disabling even though they were not initially too severe. For example, a worker may have had a previous injury that is aggravated through the years to the point where work is extremely difficult or impossible. He or she may become eligible for disability benefits even though the original illness or injury was not disabling.

Because Social Security disability is a government program, its features include a grand amount of qualifying rules and regulations. To receive Social Security disability benefits all of the following must be true:

- You must have a physical or mental impairment.
- The impairment must prevent you from doing any substantial gainful work.
- The disability must be expected to last, or have lasted, at least 12 months, or must be expected to result in death.

Of course, many of these terms are subject to different interpretations. There are guidelines developed by Social Security and the courts regarding qualifications for disability. But proving a disability is often a difficult task. In preparing your claim for a disability, examine these guidelines carefully, discuss the matter with your doctor or doctors, and plan your claim accordingly.

Physical or Mental Impairments

The basic rule regarding disability is that the condition preventing you from working must be a medical one, which can be discovered and described by doctors. To prove this, when you file your disability claim, you should bring letters from doctors, or from hospitals or clinics where you have been treated, describing the medical condition that prevents you from doing any substantial gainful work. The letters should also state that your disability is expected to last for 12 months or to result in your death.

Substantial Gainful Work

Social Security will first consider whether your condition prevents you from doing the job you had at the time you became disabled, or the last job you had before becoming disabled. If your disability prevents you from performing your usual job, Social Security will next decide whether you are able to do any other kind of substantial gainful work. For 2018, this is defined as any job that pays $1,180 per month or more.

Your age, education, training, and work experience will be considered in making this determination, as will the practicality of learning new job skills for another line of work. Social Security will evaluate whether you are able to perform any kind of work for pay, whether or not there are actually any such jobs available in your area. However, it is up to Social Security to prove that there is gainful employment you can perform. You need not prove there is no work you can do.

EXAMPLE: Arnold has been a longshoreman for 40 of his 58 years. Weakened by an early injury, Arnold's back has grown slowly but steadily worse over the past decade, causing him to miss several months of work in the past two years. His doctor has told him that his back will not get better, and Arnold decides to apply for disability benefits.

As Arnold's back prevents him from standing for long periods of time and restricts the movement of his arms, Social Security determines he is unable to do any physical labor. The next question would be whether he is able to do any other kind of work. It is possible that his back pain would prevent him from doing even a desk job; if Arnold proved this to Social Security through his doctor or by trying and being unable to do a desk job, he would probably get his disability payments. On the other hand, if his back wasn't quite that bad, he might be forced to at least try other work.

Disability Must Be Lasting

No matter how serious or completely disabling your illness or injury is, you will not qualify for disability benefits unless your condition has lasted, or is expected to last, for 12 months. During this time, you must be unable to perform substantial gainful work. The disability will also qualify if it is expected to result in your death. Even though the disability must be expected to last 12 months, you do not have to wait for 12 months to apply.

As soon as the condition is disabling and a doctor can predict that it is expected to last a year, you may qualify for disability benefits. And if, after you begin receiving benefits, it turns out that your disability does not last 12 months, Social Security cannot ask for its money back. You are not penalized for recovering sooner than expected, as long as the original expectation that the illness would last 12 months was a legitimate one.

Filing a Social Security Claim

It is extremely important to file your claim for Social Security disability benefits as soon as you become disabled, because there is a waiting period of five months after you file before you can begin receiving payments. The Social Security Administration imposes this waiting period to ensure that your disability is a lasting one, as required. If you wait a long time to file, you will be disappointed to learn that back payments are limited to the 12 months before the date on which you file.

You may file a claim by calling the Social Security Administration at 1-800-772-1213. The SSA will set up an appointment for you to be interviewed by phone or in person at a local SSA office. For many years, this was the only method for filing a disability claim. However, the SSA now also accepts online claims at https://secure.ssa.gov/iClaim/dib.

Documentation Required

Depending on how you apply, you might need to provide the following information and documents:

- medical information: names, addresses and phone numbers of all doctors, hospitals, and clinics; patient ID numbers; dates you were seen; names of medicines you are taking; and medical records
- an original or certified copy of your birth certificate; if you were born in another country, proof of U.S. citizenship or legal residency
- if you were in the military service, the original or a certified copy of your military discharge papers (Form DD 214) for all periods of active duty
- if you worked, your W-2 form from last year, or if you were self-employed, your federal tax return (IRS 1040 and Schedules C and SE)
- workers' compensation information, including date of injury, claim number, and proof of payment amounts
- Social Security numbers for yourself, your spouse, and minor children

Are You Disabled? How the Social Security Administration Decides

To decide whether you are disabled and eligible to receive benefits, the Social Security Administration uses a step-by-step process involving five questions.

Step 1: Are you working?

If you are working and your earnings average more than $1,180 a month—the base amount set by Social Security for 2018—you generally cannot be considered disabled. If you are not working, go to Step 2.

Step 2: Is your condition severe?

Your condition must interfere with basic work-related activities—such as walking, lifting, and sitting—for your claim to be considered. If it does not, the Social Security Administration will find that you are not disabled. If your condition does interfere with basic work-related activities, go to Step 3.

Step 3: Is your disability found in the list of disabling conditions?

The Social Security Administration maintains a list of medical conditions that are so severe they automatically mean that you are disabled. If your condition is not on the list, the Social Security Administration will have to decide if it is of equal severity to a medical condition that is listed. (See www.ssa.gov/disability/professionals/bluebook/AdultListings.htm.) If it is, the Social Security Administration will find that you are disabled. If it is not, go to Step 4.

Step 4: Can you do the work you did previously?

If your condition is severe but not at the same or equal level of severity as a medical condition on the list, then the Social Security Administration must determine if your condition interferes with your ability to do the work you did previously. If it does not, your claim will be denied. If it does, proceed to Step 5.

Step 5: Can you do any other type of work?

If you cannot do the work you did in the past, the Social Security Administration will see if you are able to do other work. The Social Security Administration considers your medical conditions and your age, education, skills, and past work experience. If you cannot adjust to other work, your claim will be approved. If you can adjust to other work, your claim will be denied.

Source: Social Security Administration, *Disability Planner*, www.ssa.gov.

- your checking or savings account number, if you have them
- name, address, and phone number of a person to contact if the agency is unable to get in touch with you, and
- kinds of jobs and dates you worked in the 15 years before you became unable to work.

Admittedly, this is a fairly comprehensive list. Do the best you can. Do not put off applying or cancel a planned visit to the Social Security office if you don't have it all in hand.

If you have dependents who may be eligible for benefits under your Social Security disability insurance claim, you will have to present similar documentation for them when you file your claim.

The Social Security Administration will investigate your claim. It will pay for any examinations and reports it requires to verify your claim. The Social Security staff will also help you with the paperwork and procedures required for payment if needed.

The results of those examinations and reports will usually be sent to your state's vocational rehabilitation agency, which is responsible for determining whether or not you are considered sufficiently disabled to qualify for benefits. In some cases, the vocational rehabilitation office will conduct its own examination, tests, and personal interviews before giving the Social Security Administration a decision on your case.

The Social Security Administration provides emergency funds for disabled people who need financial help during the long

waiting period while their claims are being processed. The Social Security employees handling your claim can give you details on how to apply.

Calculating Benefits

Like other Social Security benefits, the amount of your monthly disability check is determined by your age and earnings record. The amount of your benefits will be based upon your average earnings for all the years you have been working, not just on the salary you were making most recently. Although the amount may be substantial, it alone will not equal your preinjury income.

Monthly payments for individuals qualifying for disability benefits average about $1,197. The average disability payment for a disabled worker, spouse, and child(ren) is $2,051 per month in 2018.

Some people—generally only those with high total incomes—may have to pay federal income taxes on their Social Security disability benefits. At the end of the year, you will receive a Social Security Benefit Statement showing the amount of benefits you received.

 RESOURCE

Want to know more about your tax obligations? Contact the Internal Revenue Service's toll-free number for forms and publications, 800-829-3676, and ask for IRS Publication 907, *Tax Highlights for Persons With Disabilities*. You can also download the publication from the IRS website at www.irs.gov.

Trial Runs at Returning to Work

SSDI is more friendly than other income-replacement programs because it allows you to try going back to work without canceling your claim. You can participate in a total of nine months of trial work without losing any benefits. The nine months need not be consecutive or in one job. Of course, you must still technically qualify as disabled to take advantage of this trial period.

You could, for example, continue to receive Social Security disability checks while trying different jobs for a week or two every few months, until you find one you can do with your disability. Any months in which you earn $850 or less (in 2018)—or spend less than 80 hours in self-employment—do not count as trial months.

After a trial work period, Social Security will review your case to see whether you have become able to work gainfully. If you succeed in returning to work after qualifying for Social Security disability benefits, the checks will keep coming for two months after your period of disability has ended, to help ease your transition back into the workforce.

Your monthly check will be based entirely on your earnings record, with no consideration given to a minimum amount you may need to survive. If you receive only a small disability benefit, however, and you do not have a large amount of savings or other assets, you may be eligible for some other benefits in addition to your Social Security disability benefits. (See "Collecting Other Benefits," below.)

Help With Estimating Benefits

The Social Security Administration provides a comprehensive website at www.ssa.gov that includes calculators that you can use to estimate your potential benefit amounts using different retirement dates and levels of future earnings.

The calculators will also show your disability and survivor benefit amounts if you should become disabled or die. There are three types of benefits calculators available:

- A quick calculator: This gives you a simple, rough estimate based on your date of birth and this year's earnings.
- An online calculator: You can input your date of birth and your complete earnings history to get a benefit estimate. You may project your future earnings until your retirement date.
- A detailed calculator: This calculator provides the most precise estimates. It must be downloaded and installed on your computer before you can use it.

All of these helpful calculators are available on the Social Security Administration's website at: www.ssa.gov/planners/calculators.

Periodic Reviews

Social Security will review your case periodically —or at least once every three years— to determine whether, in its opinion, your condition has improved enough for you to go back to work. From time to time, therefore, Social Security may ask for updated medical evidence from your doctor or may even require that you be examined by another doctor or undergo additional medical tests arranged and paid for by Social Security.

You must cooperate with these periodic reviews or run the risk of losing your disability benefits. You have the right, however, to insist on being given enough time to gather necessary information from your doctor, and enough notice to meet the appointment for the examination or test. If you are unable to keep an appointment scheduled for you by the Social Security office, do not hesitate to ask for a rescheduling.

Appealing a Denied Claim

The greatest number of Social Security disability claims are denied because an individual is deemed to be able to do some kind of work, in spite of a disability. If your claim is denied, there are four levels of appeal available to you. At each step of the appeal process, you have 60 days from the date of the previous decision to take action to move up to the next appeal level.

With the exception of the fourth option, filing a lawsuit in federal court, the staff at the Social Security Administration office will supply you with the proper forms for pursuing an appeal and will assist you in completing them. You can also find the forms you need online at www.ssa.gov.

Request for reconsideration. After your claim is denied, you can ask to see the Social Security Administration's files concerning your claim, then submit corrections or additional information that you hope will cause the agency to reconsider your claim and approve it.

Administrative hearing. You can request a hearing by an administrative law judge who has never looked at your case before. You can ask to have the judge issue a ruling based on the evidence you have already submitted, or you can ask the judge to rule without a hearing after considering additional written evidence. You can also request a hearing at which new or more detailed evidence can be presented. These hearings are usually informal and held at a local SSA office.

Review by appeals council. If the judge doesn't find in your favor, you can ask to have the Social Security Appeals Council, based in Washington, DC, consider your claim. If the council decides to hear your appeal, you can submit a written argument in support of your evidence. Or you can elect to appear before the council to argue your case.

Federal court. If you do not win approval of your claim at any of the previous levels, or if the appeals council refuses to hear your appeal, you can file a lawsuit in federal court to try to get the courts to order the Social Security Administration to approve your claim. You will probably have to hire a lawyer to help you at this appeal level. (In Chapter 17, see "Hiring a Lawyer.")

 TIP

If at first you don't succeed, try again. Some disabilities experts estimate that only about 35% of all Social Security disability claims are approved the first time they are submitted. Another 13% of applicants win benefits after appealing.

Collecting Other Benefits

Since disability payments are often not enough to live on, it will be important for you to collect all other benefits to which you may be entitled and even try to supplement your income by working a little, if you are able.

Earned Income

If you earn any regular income, you might not be considered disabled any longer, and you could lose your disability eligibility altogether. You are only officially disabled if you are unable to perform any substantial gainful work.

However, Social Security usually permits you to earn up to about $1,180 per month (in 2018) before you will be considered to be performing substantial gainful work. But this income limit is not an absolute rule; other facts will be considered, including your work duties, the number of hours you work, and, if you are self-employed, the extent to which you run or manage your own business. In deciding how much you are earning, the Social Security office can deduct from your income the amounts of any disability-related work expenses, such as medical devices or equipment—a wheelchair, for example—attendant care, drugs, or services you require to be able to work.

Other Social Security Benefits

You are not permitted to collect more than one Social Security benefit at a time. If you are eligible for more than one monthly benefit—disability and retirement, for example, or disability based on your own work record and also as the disabled spouse of a retired worker—you will receive the higher of the two benefit amounts, but not both.

For the purposes of this rule, though, Supplemental Security Income (SSI)—a program jointly run by federal and state governments to guarantee a minimum income to elderly, blind, and disabled people—is not considered a Social Security benefit. You may collect SSI in addition to Social Security retirement or disability benefits.

Other Disability Benefits

You are permitted to collect Social Security disability payments and, at the same time, private disability payments from an insurance policy or coverage from your employer. You may also receive Department of Veterans Affairs disability coverage at the same time as Social Security disability benefits.

You may collect workers' compensation benefits at the same time as Social Security disability benefits. However, the total of your disability and workers' compensation payments cannot be greater than 80% of what your average wages were before you became disabled. If they are, your disability benefits (or, in some states, your workers' comp benefits) will be reduced to the point where the total of both benefits is 80% of your earnings before you became disabled. If you are still receiving Social Security disability benefits when your workers' compensation benefits run out, you can again start receiving the full amount of your Social Security benefits.

> **EXAMPLE:** Minnie became disabled while working for the telephone company in the computer analysis department. At that time, she was making $1,400 a month. Her Social Security disability benefits were $560 a month; she also applied for and began receiving workers' compensation benefits of $625 a month. Because the total of the two benefits was more than 80% of her prior salary (80% of $1,400 is $1,120, and she would be getting $1,185), her disability benefits were reduced by the extra $65 down to $495 a month.
>
> If Minnie were still disabled when her workers' compensation benefits ran out, her Social Security disability benefits would go back up to $560 a month, plus whatever cost of living increases had been granted in the meantime. If Minnie also had private insurance that paid disability benefits, she could receive those benefits as well.

Medicare

After you have been collecting disability benefits for 24 months—not necessarily consecutive months—you become eligible for Medicare coverage even if you are not old enough to be covered by Medicare under the regular rules of the program. Medicare Part A hospitalization coverage is free after you pay a deductible. Like everyone else, though, you must pay a monthly premium if you want to be covered by Medicare Part B medical insurance that partially covers doctor bills, lab work, outpatient clinic care, and some drugs and medical supplies.

For more information on Medicare, go to the Medicare website at www.mcdicare.gov.

Retirement Plans

No law requires private employers to offer their employees retirement plans. In fact, only about half of the workers in this country's private workforce are employed by companies that have some kind of pension plan.

Those employers that do offer pension plans are not required to pay any minimum amount of money. In fact, many individuals who invested in saving for their futures are disappointed and disillusioned to learn that their retirement plans simply do not deliver what they promised.

The old standby, Social Security—the government's income system for people 55 and over created by the passage of the Social Security Act in 1935—was not meant to be a pension program as much as insurance against extreme poverty in the later years of life. Although Social Security benefit checks for retirees have increased some in recent years, they still do not provide enough income for most people to maintain their preretirement lifestyles. Consequently, many people rely on some form of private pension—however small—to enhance their incomes after they retire.

This chapter cannot begin to cover all aspects of pension law, which has evolved into a complex morass of legal exceptions, exemptions, and loopholes and is controlled by the terms of individual pension plans. It discusses the most important laws concerning your right to collect the pension benefits you have earned and provides resources for more help.

Social Security Retirement Benefits

There are many ins and outs to the Social Security retirement benefit system. Typically, your benefits depend on factors such as the type of job you hold, the length of time you work, and the age at which you retire.

 RESOURCE

Need more information about Social Security? For more information on Social Security programs and benefits and how to file for them, see *Social Security, Medicare, & Government Pensions: Get the Most Out of Your Retirement & Medical Benefits*, by Joseph L. Matthews (Nolo).

Who Is Qualified

As with other Social Security benefits, you will be eligible for retirement benefits only if you have accumulated enough work credits. Work credits are measured in quarters (January through March, April through June, and so on) in which you earned more than the required amount of money. People born in or after 1929 must have 40 work credits.

In addition, certain dependents of retired workers are eligible for monthly benefits if the worker has amassed enough work credits to qualify for benefits. Dependents who may qualify for these derivative benefits include:

- a spouse age 62 or older

- a spouse younger than 62 who cares for the worker's young or disabled children
- a divorced spouse age 62 or older, if the marriage lasted at least ten years and if at least two years have passed since the divorce
- children up to age 18 or age 19 for full-time high school students, and
- disabled children.

Calculating Your Benefits

Note that when the term "retire" is used by the Social Security Administration, it only refers to the date when you claim your retirement benefits. It does not necessarily mean you have reached a particular age or that you have stopped working.

The average benefit for a person who retires is about $1,404 per month in 2018—a figure that changes based on the total amount of all benefits paid and the number of people receiving them. Whatever the amount of your retirement benefit, you will receive an automatic cost of living increase on January 1 of each year. This increase is tied to the rise in the Consumer Price Index, which measures the cost of basic goods and services.

Even if you have not worked for many years and you did not make much money in the years you did work, check your earnings record. You might be surprised to find you have quite a few quarters of credit from years gone by.

If you want to estimate the amount of Social Security benefits you are entitled to receive after you have retired from your job,

complete and submit the Social Security Administration's Form SSA-7004, *Request for Social Security Statement*. You can obtain one from the Social Security Administration office closest to you or download one at www.ssa.gov.

Taxes on Your Benefits

Most Social Security retirement benefits are not considered taxable income by the Internal Revenue Service, although you do have to pay income tax on any interest you earn from saving your benefits. But, if your adjusted gross annual income—from a part-time job, for example—plus one-half of your year's Social Security benefits adds up to $25,000 or more, then you must pay income tax on a portion of your Social Security benefits.

In January of each year, you will receive a statement from the Social Security Administration showing the amount of benefits you received in the previous year and an IRS form explaining how to report this income, if necessary.

Timing Your Retirement

You can start your Social Security retirement benefits as early as age 62, but, if you do decide to jump that gun, the benefit amount you receive will be less than your full retirement benefit amount. If you start your benefits early, they will be permanently reduced based on the number of months before you reach what Social Security defines as your full retirement age.

What is considered full or normal retirement age has traditionally been age 65. However, beginning with people born in 1938 or later, that age will gradually increase until it reaches 67 for people born in 1960 and later. For example, if you were born in 1955, the SSA currently clocks your full retirement age as 66 years and two months.

On the opposite side of the scale, however, a good many people these days are opting to continue working full time beyond retirement age. These industrious souls can increase their Social Security benefit in two ways:

- Each additional year a person works adds another year of earnings to their Social Security record. Higher lifetime earnings may result in higher benefits at retirement.
- In addition, a person's benefit will be increased by a certain percentage if he or she delays retirement. These increases, called delayed retirement credits, will be added automatically from the time one reaches full retirement age until that individual starts taking benefits or reaches age 70.

Private Pensions

Pension plans became popular during the Second World War, when there were more jobs than workers. Employers used fringe benefits such as pensions to attract and keep workers without violating the wartime wage freeze rules. Since the early 1950s, unions and employers have both recognized pension plans as crucial elements in labor negotiations.

But, until the mid-1970s, having a pension plan and actually collecting a pension benefit check were two different things. Many people were promised a pension as part of the terms of their employment, and many workers contributed to pension funds through payroll deductions, but relatively few actually received much in the way of benefits at retirement. There were several reasons for the failure of pensions to deliver what they promised: People changed jobs and had to leave their pension rights behind; workers were not-so-mysteriously let go just before they reached retirement age; and pension plans, or whole companies, went out of business.

Legal Controls on Pensions

Since the passage of a federal law, the Employee Retirement Income Security Act of 1974 (ERISA), at least some of the worst sorts of disappearing pension acts have been halted. ERISA sets minimum standards for pension plans, guaranteeing that pension rights cannot be unfairly denied or taken from a worker. ERISA also provides some protection for workers if certain types of pension plans cannot pay all the benefits to which workers are entitled. But, while ERISA provides the protection of federal law for certain pension rights, its scope is limited.

The Incredible Shrinking Pension Check

Inflation is an old enemy of your right to receive a decent retirement pension. The figures an employer shows you as your potential pension benefit may seem decent when you are hired, and may even pay a reasonable amount when you first retire. But, because few private pension plans are indexed to the rising cost of living, the amount you receive when you retire will seem smaller and smaller as inflation cuts into the value of your pension dollar. In other words, the cost of living will go up, but your pension check will not. Unfortunately, ERISA does not require pension plans to respond to inflation's bite into your retirement benefits.

Eligibility for Pension Coverage

There is no law that requires an employer to offer a pension plan. However, if a company chooses to do so, ERISA requires that the pension plan spell out who is eligible for coverage. Pension plans do not have to include all workers, but they cannot be structured to benefit only the top executives or discriminate based on a protected characteristic. The plan administrator for your company's pension program can tell you whether you are eligible to participate.

If you are eligible to participate in your employer's pension program, the administrator must provide you with several documents to help you understand the plan:

- **A summary plan description.** Explains the basics of how your plan operates. ERISA requires that you be given the summary plan within 90 days after you begin participating in a pension plan, as well as any updates issued.

  This document will also tell you the formula for vesting in the plan (if it is a plan that includes vesting), the formula for determining your defined benefits or the defined contributions that your employer will make to the plan, and whether or not your pension is insured by the Pension Benefit Guaranty Corporation or PBGC. (See "Mismanaged Plans," below.)

- **A summary annual report.** A yearly accounting of your pension plan's financial condition and operations.

- **Survivor coverage data.** A statement of how much your plan would pay to any surviving spouse should you die first.

Your plan administrator is also required to provide you with a detailed, individual statement of the pension benefits you have earned, but only if you request it in writing or are going to stop participating in the plan because, for example, you change employers. Note, however, that ERISA gives you the right to only one such statement from your plan per year.

Early Retirement and Pension Benefits

Each pension plan has its own rules on the minimum age for claiming benefits. Most private pension plans still consider 65 to be the normal retirement age. However, some private pensions also offer the option of retiring early, usually at age 55. If you elect early retirement, however, expect your benefit checks to be much smaller than they would be if you had waited until the regular retirement age.

Many corporations now use the early retirement option of their pension plans to cut staff. By making a temporary offer to increase the benefits available to those who opt to retire early, these corporations create an incentive for employees to voluntarily leave the company's payroll before turning age 65. Sometimes companies make the early retirement offer even more attractive by throwing in a few months of extra severance pay.

Some early retirement offers are very lucrative and some are not. Before accepting one, study the details carefully, keeping in mind that the offer you accept may have to serve as your primary income for the rest of your life.

Because pension law is so specialized and complex, you may also consider consulting a lawyer who specializes in it if the terms of your employer's early retirement offer are not clear. (See Chapter 17, "Hiring a Lawyer.")

When Retirement Does Not Mean Retirement

If your benefits have vested when you reach the retirement age established by your pension plan—usually 65—you are free to leave a job with the employer that pays your pension and work for someone else, or open your own business, while collecting your full pension.

However, if you return to work for the employer that is paying your pension benefits, ERISA permits the employer to suspend payment of your pension for as long as you continue working for that employer. Some workers are covered by a multiemployer pension plan, such as those through an industry-wide union contract. If you are covered by this type of plan, your pension benefits can be suspended if you return to work for a different employer whose employees are covered by the same plan.

Filing for Benefits

Although ERISA does not spell out one uniform claim procedure for all pension plans, it does establish some rules that must be followed when you retire and want to claim your benefits. All pension plans must have an established claim procedure, and all participants in the plan must be given a summary of the plan that explains it clearly.

Pension Terms Defined

Jargon dominates the pension industry. The following definitions will get you on the road to understanding pension rights and wrongs.

Defined benefit plan. The employer promises to pay the employee a fixed amount of money, usually monthly, after the employee retires. Although a defined benefit plan is what usually comes to mind when people think about pensions, this plan has become less common than the defined contribution type.

Defined contribution plan. The employee, and sometimes the employer, contribute to the employee's retirement account. However, the employee is not guaranteed a specific amount of income after retirement. The size of the monthly pension check you receive after retirement varies according to the interest rate paid on your pension account and other economic factors.

Defined contribution plans can take several different forms, including 401(k) plans, through which your employer and you can contribute jointly to retirement savings. (See "401(k) Deferred Compensation Plans," below.) Defined contribution pension plans are individual savings accounts that usually have some tax advantages—but also some limitations on withdrawals and reinvestment—that regular savings accounts do not have.

Integrated plan. When a pension plan is integrated with Social Security, the actual monthly or yearly pension benefit is reduced by some—or all—of your Social Security check. This approach allows employers that sponsor their own pension plans to take credit for the fact that their FICA contributions on behalf of lower-income workers buy proportionately more generous benefits than their contributions for higher-income workers. Pension benefits are thereby lowered for all workers, and total retirement benefits—that is, pensions plus Social Security—replace a more uniform percentage of final pay for all employees. Both defined benefit and defined contribution plans may operate as integrated plans.

Employee Retirement Income Security Act (ERISA). Administered by the U.S. Department of Labor, the Internal Revenue Service, and the Securities and Exchange Commission, ERISA sets minimum standards for pensions and attempts to guarantee that pension rights cannot be unfairly taken from or denied to workers.

Pension Benefit Guaranty Corporation. An organization that insures many defined benefit plans in the United States, the PBGC is half private and half public. It is supposed to be funded by insurance premiums paid by the pension plans it covers, but it regularly turns to the federal government for money when it runs short.

Plan administrator. The person or organization with the legal authority and responsibility for managing your pension program.

Vesting. Getting a legal right to collect from a benefit program. Some pension plans require you to work a certain number of years for a company before you have a right to a pension. Once you are vested, you continue to have rights to the pension plan even if you no longer work there.

Once you file a claim, the pension plan typically has 90 days to make a decision. The decision must state specific reasons that any claimed benefits were denied and must explain the basis for determining the benefits that are granted.

From the date you receive a written decision on your pension claim, you have 60 days to file a written appeal of the decision. The rules on where and how this appeal should be filed must be explained in the plan summary. In presenting your appeal, the claim procedures must permit you to examine the plan's files and records and to submit evidence of your own. ERISA does not, however, require the pension plan to actually give you a hearing regarding your appeal. Within 60 days after you file your appeal, the pension plan administrators must file a written decision on your appeal. If your claim is still denied, in whole or in part, you then have a right to press your claim in either state or federal court.

Appealing a Denial of Benefits

Each pension plan has its own system for appeals. If your pension plan denies you benefits to which you are entitled, its administrator is required to tell you how to appeal that decision. You will have at least 60 days to request such an appeal, and the group that reviews your appeal will have 60 days to make a decision—or 120 days if it notifies you in writing that it needs more

time. ERISA requires that you be given plain-English explanation of the decision on your appeal.

If your appeal is denied, you may file a lawsuit in court to enforce any rule or provision of the ERISA law or of a pension plan covered by ERISA rules. In particular, you may file a federal court lawsuit under ERISA to:

- recover benefits that have been unfairly denied
- challenge a ruling by the pension plan that would affect your future benefits, such as a ruling regarding eligibility, accrual, or vesting
- force the plan to provide information required by ERISA
- correct improper management of the plan or its funds, and
- protect any other right established by the rules of your particular pension plan or by ERISA itself.

You may also contact the Employee Benefits Security Administration (EBSA) for assistance at www.dol.gov/ebsa, if you believe the pension administrator violated ERISA in its handling of your claim.

Terminated Plans

Your employer may simply decide to terminate your plan, even if it is financially sound. Many companies do just that every year, mostly in the name of cutting back on corporate costs. If your employer terminates your pension plan, your plan administrator is required to notify you of the approaching termination, in writing, at least 60 days before the plan ends.

If the termination is a standard one, that means that your plan has enough assets to cover its obligations. Your plan administrator is required to tell you how the plan's money will be paid out and what your options are during the payout period.

If the termination happens under distress, the Pension Benefit Guaranty Corporation might become responsible for paying your pension benefits. (See "Mismanaged Plans," below.) If your plan is not insured by the PBGC and it is terminated, your pension rights may be reduced or lost entirely.

Mismanaged Plans

In recent history, a number of pension funds have gone broke because of mismanagement, fraud, or overextended resources. The future is likely to bring an increasing number of pension plan failures. Under ERISA, there is some insurance against pension fund collapses. ERISA established the Pension Benefit Guaranty Corporation, a public, nonprofit insurance fund, to provide protection against bankrupt pension funds. Should a pension fund be unable to pay all its obligations to retirees, the PBGC may, under certain conditions, pick up the slack and pay much of the pension fund's unfulfilled obligations.

However, the PBGC does not cover all types of pension plans and does not guarantee all pension benefits of the plans it does cover. Only defined benefit plans are covered—through insurance premiums they pay to the PBGC—and only vested benefits are protected by the insurance. Also, PBGC insurance normally covers only retirement pension benefits; other benefits, such as disability, health coverage, and death benefits, are not usually covered.

If you have a question about termination of benefits because of the failure of your pension plan, contact the Pension Benefit Guaranty Corporation, www.pbgc.gov.

If you think you can prove that the people managing your pension plan are not handling your pension money in your best interests— for example, they are making questionable investments—ERISA gives you the right to file a lawsuit against them in court. You will probably need to hire a lawyer to help you with this type of lawsuit. (In Chapter 17, see "Hiring a Lawyer.")

RESOURCE

Want more details on your rights to receive benefits from a private pension plan? See the information published by the American Association of Retired Persons (AARP), www.aarp.org.

Another organization that offers a number of publications relating to pensions is the Pension Rights Center, www.pensionrights.org.

401(k) Deferred Compensation Plans

Many employers that offer retirement benefits do so through a 401(k) deferred compensation plan; the name is taken from the number of an IRS regulation that provides the plan with its tax-deferred status. A 401(k) plan is a deferred compensation program in which employees invest part of their wages, sometimes with added employer contributions, to save on taxes. They are not actually pension programs that establish a right to retirement benefits. Instead, they are a type of investment plan. This section explains the basics of 401(k) plans.

Structure of 401(k) Plans

In a 401(k) plan, an employee contributes part of his or her salary to one of several retirement investment accounts set up by the employer and administered by a bank, brokerage, or other financial institution.

Depending on the rules of the particular plan, the employer often makes a contribution in addition to the amount the employee sets aside. However, unlike traditional pension plans, the employer has no obligation to contribute anything and can change the contribution amounts from year to year.

These plans are cheaper for the employer than more traditional pension plans, because employees make the primary contributions from their salaries, the employer has no fixed obligation to contribute, and, when the employer does contribute, it does so as a tax-deductible business expense.

Investment Choices

401(k) plans do not require either the employee or the employer to contribute any set amount each year. The IRS limits how much an employee can contribute each year. The maximum permissible contribution amount goes up each year with the rise in the cost of living. Many employers contribute a percentage of the employee's contribution. However, an increasing number of employers offer 401(k)s with no employer contributions.

Tax Advantages of 401(k) Plans

A 401(k) plan has two tax advantages for the employee.

First, income taxes on the amount of wages invested in the plan are not paid in the year you earn them but are deferred until you withdraw the money from the plan after retirement. Most people have significantly lower income tax brackets after they stop working, so the total tax paid on the income is lower.

Second, taxes on income earned by the investments of the 401(k) plan are likewise deferred until the money is withdrawn after retirement.

A 401(k) plan usually offers the employee a choice among different investments for the deferred income. Some plans offer a selection of preapproved savings accounts, money market funds, stocks and bonds, and mutual funds. Other plans permit employees to select their own investment funds or even to buy individual stock shares on the open market. However, there are usually some limits on the number of investments offered and on the frequency and number of changes in investments that can be made in a given period of time.

CAUTION

401(k) investments may be risky. Along with a choice of investments for the employee comes the risk of poor returns. Unlike traditional pension plans that sink or swim on the total pension fund's portfolio and are backed up by the government's Pension Benefit Guaranty Corporation, the amount of an employee's 401(k) plan fund at retirement depends entirely on how well the plan's individual investments do over the years. An employee who makes particularly risky investments could wind up with less in 401(k) funds than he or she invested.

Withdrawing Money

One of the advantages of most 401(k) plans is that they permit you to withdraw your deferred compensation earlier than pension plans. Most 401(k) plans permit withdrawal without any tax penalty at age 59½, or at age 55 if you have stopped working. Funds may be withdrawn in a lump sum or in monthly allotments. Money that remains in the account, including future earnings, will

not be taxed until withdrawal. 401(k) plans also allow your beneficiaries to withdraw the 401(k) funds without tax penalty if you die at any age.

If you withdraw funds before the age permitted by the rules of your plan, you will pay a 10% penalty on the amount withdrawn, plus all income taxes at your current tax rate. And IRS rules require that you begin withdrawing funds by age 70½ at the latest. The amount you must withdraw to avoid a tax penalty is determined by the IRS based on your age and the year you were born. The administrator of your plan can tell you your minimum withdrawal amount.

Some 401(k) plans also permit you to withdraw funds without penalty if needed for a family emergency, such as for medical expenses or for investment in a home. And, in some plans, you can take out a loan from your own 401(k) funds, up to 50% of the total in the account or $50,000, whichever is less, if you have sufficient collateral and you repay it within five years. There are strict rules applying to such withdrawals and loans. Check with your 401(k) plan administrator or a financial adviser.

RESOURCE

Need more information on withdrawals from a retirement plan? For an explanation of how to take money out of your retirement plan, see *IRAs, 401(k)s, & Other Retirement Plans: Strategies for Taking Your Money Out,* by Twila Slesnick and John C. Suttle (Nolo).

Ten Warning Signs of 401(k) Fraud

Increasingly, employees are asked to make voluntary or mandatory contributions to pension and other benefit plans. This is particularly true for 401(k) savings plans, which allow you to deduct from your paycheck a portion of pretax income every year, invest it, and pay no taxes on those contributions until the money is withdrawn at retirement. But as these plans have become more common, so have incidents of 401(k) fraud.

An antifraud campaign by the Department of Labor uncovered a number of employers that abused employee contributions by either using the money for corporate purposes or holding on to the money too long.

Here are ten warning signs that your pension contributions are being misused:

1. Your 401(k) or individual account statement is consistently late or comes at irregular intervals.

2. Your account balance does not appear to be accurate.

3. Your employer failed to transmit your contribution to the plan in the time it was required to do so.

4. There is a significant drop in account balance that cannot be explained by normal market ups and downs.

5. Your 401(k) or individual account statement shows your contribution from your paycheck was not made.

6. Investments listed on your statement are not what you authorized.

7. Former employees are having trouble getting their benefits paid on time or in the correct amounts.

8. Unusual transactions, such as a loan to the employer, a corporate officer, or one of the plan trustees, are made to the account.

9. There are frequent and unexplained changes in investment managers or consultants.

10. Your employer has recently experienced severe financial difficulty.

Source: U.S. Department of Labor, Employee Benefits Security Administration.

Labor Unions

Labor unions are organizations that deal with employers on behalf of a group of employees. Their best-known role is negotiating group employment contracts for members that spell out workplace essentials such as mandatory procedures for discipline and firing. But unions also often perform other workplace chores such as lobbying for legislation that benefits their members and sponsoring skill training programs.

Today, about 10.7% of all American workers are union members, far below the tally for 1983, when union membership was first accurately tracked and nearly double current figures. Only 6.5% of employees in private industry are in a union.

If you belong to a union, the specifics of your work relationship are probably covered in a collective bargaining agreement. That means nearly everything—work schedules, wages and hours, time off, discipline, safety rules, retirement plans—is spelled out in that contract. If you have a workplace problem, the process available to resolve it is spelled out in your collective bargaining contract, too.

Usually, you are required to discuss your problem first with a designated union representative, who will then take it up with union officials. If your complaint is found to be a reasonable one, the union reps will guide you through a complaint or grievance procedure. If you disagree with the union's assessment of your situation, you can follow the steps provided for appealing the decision.

Some labor unions also operate benefit programs, such as vacation plans, health care insurance, pensions, and programs that provide members with discounts on various types of personal needs, such as eyeglasses and prescription drugs.

Most unions are operated by a paid staff of professional organizers, negotiators, and administrators, with some help from members who volunteer their time. In general, the money to pay unions' staffs and expenses comes from dues paid by their members, which typically total about $50 per member per month. There is no law that specifically regulates the amount of money that unions can charge their members, but it may not be excessive. Courts have provided little guidance in defining this term but have held that a union initiation fee equal to one month's salary would likely be considered excessive.

The laws and court decisions governing labor unions and their relationships with employers are so complex and separate from the rest of workplace law that this chapter can give you only an overview.

If you are already a member of a labor union and want to continue as one, the information provided here can help you double-check on the performance of your union's leaders.

If you are not represented by a union and would like to be, or if you are a member of a union and want out, this chapter will help you become familiar with the basic laws labor unions must follow and alert you to your rights in dealing with unions.

Federal Laws

The federal laws broadly regulating unions —and the copious amendments to those laws—have dramatically changed the look and function of unions over time. The changing laws have also acted as political mirrors, alternately protecting employees from unfair labor practices and protecting employers from unfair union practices as unions' influence in the workplace has ebbed and flowed. Several of the most important federal controls are discussed here.

The National Labor Relations Act

Labor unions secured the legal right to represent employees in their relationships with their employers when the National Labor Relations Act, or NLRA, was passed in 1935. That federal act also created the National Labor Relations Board (NLRB) to police the relationships among employees, their unions, and their employers.

Under the NLRA, an employer may not:

- interfere with or restrain employees who are exercising their rights to organize, bargain collectively, and engage in other protected concerted activities
- interfere with the formation of any labor organization
- encourage or discourage membership in a labor organization by discriminating in hiring, tenure, or employment conditions

- discharge or discriminate against employees who have filed charges or testified under the NLRA, or
- refuse to bargain collectively with the employees' majority representative.

The NLRA requires most employers and unions to negotiate fairly with each other until they agree to a contract that spells out the terms and conditions of employment for the workers who are members of the union. The agency enforces this requirement by using mediators, negotiators, administrative law judges, investigators, and others.

Who Is Covered

With the few exceptions mentioned below, the NLRA applies to all employers involved in interstate commerce.

Who Is Excluded

Certain groups of employees are not covered by the NLRA. They include:

- managers, supervisors, and confidential employees such as company accountants
- farmworkers
- the families of employers
- government workers
- most domestic workers, and
- certain industry groups, such as railroad employees, whose work situations are regulated by other laws.

The NLRA also contains some special exemptions for specific groups of workers within industries that are otherwise covered.

Contact your local NLRB office for more information on whether your job is covered by the NLRA.

The Labor Management Relations Act

In the dozen years following enactment of the NLRA, Congress was progressively bombarded with pleas to rein in the unions' power in the workplace. Both employers and employees contended that they needed protection from union overreaching, such as coercing workers to join by using threats and violence. The public joined in the outcry, complaining about work stoppages that increasingly threatened health, safety, and the food supply.

In 1947, the Labor Management Relations Act, popularly known as the Taft-Hartley Act, was passed. It was aimed at preventing unfair union practices and banned unions from:

- threatening or coercing employees to join a union
- causing or influencing an employer to discriminate against an employee because of membership or nonmembership in a union
- refusing to bargain in good faith with an employer if a majority of employees have designated a union bargaining agent

---

More Workers Now Covered as "Supervisors"

Because supervisors are considered to be part of a company's management rather than its labor force, they cannot join unions and do not enjoy the other rights and protections conferred by the NLRA.

The NLRB issued a decision clarifying which employees are supervisors and which are not. In *Oakwood Healthcare Inc.*, 348 N.L.R.B. 37 (2006), the Board found that employees who have the authority to make work assignments or direct the work of other employees may be supervisors, even if they spend only 10% to 15% of their time on these supervisory duties.

This decision represents a change from previous NLRB decisions, which interpreted the term "supervisor" more narrowly.

In *Oakwood*, the NLRB focused on two supervisory responsibilities: assigning work and directing the work of other employees. It found that an employee who assigns others to particular departments, shifts, or significant tasks is a supervisor, as long as making those assignments requires some independent judgment and discretion and is not simply clerical or routine in nature. An employee who responsibly directs others—that is, who oversees the work of other employees and is held accountable for their performance—also qualifies as a supervisor.

Since the decision, many employees who do not make hiring and firing decisions but exercise some authority over other employees will be classified as supervisors by the NLRB, even if they spend most of their time doing the same work as the employees they supervise.

- inducing or encouraging employees to stop work to force special treatment of union matters, and
- charging excessive fees to employees and employers.

The Labor Management Reporting and Disclosure Act

In a third attempt to right the balance among employees, employers, and unions, Congress passed the Labor Management Reporting and Disclosure Act of 1959. The most important contribution of that law is that it imposes a code of conduct for unions, union officers, employers, and management consultants, holding each to a standard of fair dealing.

Enforcing Your Rights

You can take action against a union and an employer for violations of the NLRA, including unfair labor practices such as threatening workers who join or do not join a union and problems with union elections in the workplace. To begin the process, you must file a charge with a local office of the NLRB. (Get contact information from the agency's website at www.nlrb.gov.)

NLRB staff will investigate your charge to determine whether there has been a legal violation. If it finds merit, it will attempt to settle the matter—or pursue a complaint. If it finds no merit to the claim, you may appeal that decision. However, you will probably need a lawyer's help to do so. (In Chapter 17, see "Hiring a Lawyer.")

Also, there are a number of organizations that may provide free or low-cost help in pursuing union problems and complaints. (See "Where to Get More Help," below, and the appendix for contact information.)

State Right-to-Work Laws

Section 14(b) of the NLRA authorizes each state to pass laws that require all unionized workplaces within their boundaries to be open shops, and nearly half the states have passed such laws. (See the "State Right-to-Work Laws" chart, at the end of this chapter.) In each of these states, you have the right to hold a job without joining a union or paying any money to a union. These are usually called "right-to-work" laws.

One boon for employees in right-to-work states is that the NLRA requires that a union give fair and equal representation to all members of a bargaining unit, regardless of whether they are union members. If you are employed in a right-to-work state and are a member of a bargaining unit represented by a labor union, you can refuse to join the union or to pay any dues. Yet, the union still must represent you, just like your union coworkers. However, you can be required to pay the union's costs for any grievances it brings on your behalf.

If the union representing your bargaining unit fails or refuses to represent you in such situations, you can file an unfair labor practices charge against it with the NLRB.

The Bargaining Unit

The basic union building block under the NLRA is the bargaining unit: a group of employees who perform similar work, share a work area, and could logically be assumed to have shared interests in such issues as pay rates, hours of work, and workplace conditions.

A bargaining unit may be only a part of a larger union, or it may constitute a whole union itself. And a bargaining unit is not always limited to people who work in one building or for one company. For example, the workers in several small, independent sheet metal shops in a specific city will often be members of the same union bargaining unit.

On the other hand, a bargaining unit may include only part of a company. So it is possible—and quite common—for only a small portion of a company's workforce to be unionized, or for various departments in one company to be represented by different unions.

Something that is frequently misunderstood about bargaining units is that they are composed of jobs or job classifications, not of individual workers. For example, if Wilda Samano retires, and her former position as machinist is then filled by Sam Alvarez, the bargaining unit does not change—only the personnel.

Types of Union Work Situations

If you take a job that is covered by a contract between the employer and a labor union, a representative of the union will typically approach you about membership requirements shortly after you are hired.

Unionized work situations generally are either open shop or agency shop. The type of shop that exists within a unionized bargaining unit will be spelled out in the contract between the union representing that unit and the employer. Ask the union representative for a copy of the collective bargaining agreement governing your job before you sign up for union membership.

The Open Shop

Here, a union represents the bargaining unit of which you are a member. However, you are not required to join the union or pay dues to it. Open shops are most commonly found in states that have passed right-to-work laws. (See "State Right-to-Work Laws," above.)

The Agency Shop

You can make your own decision about whether to join the union in an agency shop. But, whether you join or not, you will have to pay the same dues and other fees that union members are required to pay. In return for your dues, the union must represent you if labor problems develop, just as it protects members of a bargaining unit. This type of arrangement is legal in any state that has not passed a right-to-work law. (See "State Right-to-Work Laws," above.)

Union Elections

A union may file a petition with the NLRB when it can show that 30% of employees in the proposed bargaining unit want to be represented by the union. In its petition, the union will include a description of what group of workers it would like to have included in that bargaining unit. The employer usually contests these descriptions and tries to have the size of the bargaining unit trimmed down. Negotiations follow, and, if the union and the employer cannot agree on the exact shape and size of a bargaining unit, the NLRB decides.

An election will then be held, in which all employees in the bargaining unit may vote. If the union receives a majority of the votes cast, it will be certified. The employer will then be required to bargain with the union.

If employees in the bargaining unit no longer want to be represented by a union, they can also petition for a decertification election. At least 30% of the employees in the bargaining unit must show support for the decertification. An election will be held, and unless the majority of the votes are in favor of the union, it will be decertified. If the employees want a different union to represent them, a three-way election will usually be held, giving the employees the choice of the existing union, the new union, or no union.

The NLRB typically will not hold a decertification election:

- within one year of the union's certification by the NLRB, or
- during the first three years of a collective bargaining agreement (except for a 30-day window towards the end of the period).

The Right to Unionize

Sections 7 and 8 of the National Labor Relations Act guarantee employees the right to create, join, and participate in a labor union without being unfairly intimidated or punished by their employers.

Employee Rights

Generally, the courts have ruled that Section 7 of the NLRA gives employees the right to:

- discuss union membership and read and distribute union literature during nonwork time in nonwork areas, such as an employee lounge
- sign a card asking your employer to recognize your union and bargain with it, sign petitions and grievances concerning employment terms and conditions, and ask your coworkers to sign petitions and grievances, and
- display your pro-union sentiments by wearing message-bearing items such as hats, pins, and T-shirts on the job.

Employer Limitations

Most courts have also ruled that Section 8 of the NLRA means that an employer may not:

- grant or promise employees promotions, pay raises, desirable work assignments, or other special favors if they oppose unionizing efforts
- close down a worksite or transfer work or reduce benefits to pressure employees not to support unionization, or
- dismiss, harass, reassign, or otherwise punish or discipline employees if they support unionization. (In Chapter 10, see "Blacklisting" for a related discussion of these laws.)

Religious Objections to Unions

Some employees have religious beliefs that conflict with membership in a labor union. If your religion prohibits you from taking oaths, for example, having to swear allegiance to a labor union might force you to violate your religious beliefs.

In general, the courts have recognized an employee's right to refuse to join a union on religious grounds. However, you can still be required to pay union dues and fees—or to donate their equivalent to a nonreligious charity—if you work in an agency shop in a state that has not passed a right-to-work law. (See "State Right-to-Work Laws," above.)

Deducting Union Dues From Paychecks

One fact on which labor unions and the government agree: It is easier to get money from people who never get to touch that money in the first place. To ease their operations, many union contracts include a dues check-off clause.

Much like income tax withholding, the check-off clause requires your employer to withhold your union dues from your pay and then forward the money to the union. By voting to approve a contract between your union and your employer, you also signify approval of any check-off clause in that contract. So, unions' practice of having employers withhold dues from a paycheck is generally legal.

Where to Get More Help

It is easier to get free legal advice and help with labor union matters than with any other aspect of workplace law.

The place to start is your local office of the National Labor Relations Board (NLRB), which you can find at www.nlrb.gov. If the NLRB considers your union-related problem to be a serious one, it will pay for all the costs of the investigations and hearings required to take your complaint through the legal process.

NLRB Protections for Nonunion Workplaces

Although the NLRB is most often associated with unionized workplaces, it also offers some important protections for employees in nonunionized workplaces. The NLRB prohibits all employers from firing or taking other negative action against employees who engage in "protected concerted activity." This term covers situations where two or more employees get together to try to improve their wages or working conditions. It doesn't necessarily have to be an organized activity. For example, NLRA violations have been found where employers fire employees for discussing their salaries, circulating a petition to improve working conditions, jointly refusing to work under unsafe conditions, and more.

Beginning in 2011, the NLRB began taking an active interest in social media cases, after receiving multiple complaints that employers had fired employees over their posts. To be protected, the employee's social media post must be about the terms of conditions of employment and must involve other employees. For example, a rant by a solo employee about an unfavorable performance review or conflict with a boss probably would not be protected. However, an employee who complains about an employer's tipping policy or a workplace safety issue—and tags several workers to get their input—would likely be protected.

If the NLRB cannot or will not help, you can turn to several other sources. If you consider yourself to be pro-union, contact AFL-CIO headquarters, www.aflcio.org. If you consider yourself to be antiunion, contact the National Right to Work Committee, www.nrtwc.org.

If you are unsure about what your opinion on unions is, call both places. These organizations maintain legal staffs to answer union-related questions. They may even provide you with free legal representation.

State Right-to-Work Laws

Alabama ....Ala. Code §§ 25-7-30 to 25-7-36; Ala Const. art. I, § 36.05

Alaska ....No right-to-work law.

Arizona......................Ariz. Const. art. 25; Ariz. Rev. Stat. §§ 23-1301 to 23-1307

Arkansas.....................Ark. Const. amend. 34, § 1; Ark. Code Ann. §§ 11-3-301 to 11-3-304

California ....No right-to-work law.

Colorado ....No right-to-work law.

Connecticut ....No right-to-work law.

Delaware ....No right-to-work law.

District of
Columbia ....No right-to-work law.

Florida ....Fla. Const. art. 1, § 6; Fla. Stat. Ann. §§ 447.01, 447.03, 447.17

Georgia ....Ga. Code Ann. §§ 34-6-20 to 34-6-28

Hawaii ....No right-to-work law.

Idaho ....Idaho Code §§ 44-2001 to 44-2011

Illinois ....No right-to-work law.

Indiana ....Ind. Code Ann. 22-6-6-8

Iowa ....Iowa Code §§ 731.1 to 731.9

Kansas ....Kan. Const. art. 15, § 12; Kan. Stat. Ann. §§ 44-808(5), 44-831

Kentucky ....Ky. Rev. Stat. Ann. §§ 336.130, 336.132, 336.135, 336.180, 336.990

Louisiana ....La. Rev. Stat. Ann. §§ 23:981 to 23:987 (all workers) and 23:881 to 23:889 (agricultural workers)

Maine ....No right-to-work law.

Maryland ....No right-to-work law.

Massachusetts ....No right-to-work law.

Michigan ....Mich. Comp. Laws §§ 423.1, 423.8, 423.14, 423.17

Minnesota ....No right-to-work law.

Mississippi ....Miss. Const. art. 7, § 198-A; Miss. Code Ann. § 71-1-47

Missouri ....Mo. Ann. Stat. § 290.590

Montana ....No right-to-work law.

Nebraska ....Neb. Const. art. XV, §§ 13 to 15; Neb. Rev. Stat. § 48-217 to 48-219

Nevada ....Nev. Rev. Stat. Ann. §§ 613.230 to 613.300

New Hampshire ......No right-to-work law.

New Jersey ....No right-to-work law.

New Mexico ....No right-to-work law.

New York ....No right-to-work law.

North Carolina ......N.C. Gen. Stat. §§ 95-78 to 95-84

North Dakota ..........N.D. Cent. Code § 34-01-14

Ohio ....No right-to-work law.

Oklahoma ....Okla. Const. Art. 23, § 1A

Oregon ....No right-to-work law.

Pennsylvania ....No right-to-work law.

Rhode Island ....No right-to-work law.

South Carolina ......S.C. Code Ann. §§ 41-7-10 to 41-7-130

South Dakota ..........S.D. Const. art. VI, § 2; S.D. Codified Law Ann. §§ 60-8-3 to 60-8-8

Tennessee ....Tenn. Code Ann. §§ 50-1-201 to 50-1-208

Texas ....Tex. Lab. Code Ann. §§ 101.051 to 101.053

Utah ....Utah Code Ann. §§ 34-34-1 to 34-34-17

Vermont ....No right-to-work law.

Virginia ....Va. Code Ann. §§ 40.1-59 to 40.1-69

Washington ....No right-to-work law.

West Virginia ....W. Va. Code §§ 21-1A-3, 21-5G-1 through 21-5G-7

Wisconsin ....Wis. Stat. Ann. §§ 111.02, 111.04, 111.06, 947.20

Wyoming ....Wyo. Stat. Ann. §§ 127-7-108 to 27-7-115

Immigration Issues

Many immigrants, even those with the documentation required to stay legally in the United States, may incorrectly believe they have no rights under the United States Constitution. However, many of the freedoms guaranteed by the Constitution—to practice religion, to say what you want, to get due process of law, and to live and work free from discrimination, for example—apply regardless of citizenship or immigration status.

Federal Law

The Immigration Reform and Control Act of 1986, also known as IRCA, marked the most comprehensive overhaul of employment-related immigration law since legal controls were passed in the early 1900s.

RESOURCE

Want more information on immigration? For a complete explanation of immigration laws, including step-by-step guidance and forms required to enter and stay in the United States legally, see *U.S. Immigration Made Easy*, by Ilona Bray (Nolo).

Under IRCA, it is illegal for any employer to:

- hire or recruit a worker who the employer knows has not been granted permission by the U.S. Citizenship and Immigration Services (USCIS) to be employed in the United States

- hire any worker who has not completed an INS Form I-9, the *Employment Eligibility Verification Form*, proving the worker's identity and legal right to work in the United States, or
- continue to employ an unauthorized worker.

Documentation Required to Work in the United States

Only legally authorized employees may work in the United States. When you take a new job, you are required to fill out the employee's section of immigration Form I-9 by the end of your first day on the job. You then have three business days to present your new employer with documents that prove:

- that you are who you say you are, and
- that you are legally authorized to work in the United States.

If you use forged, counterfeit, or altered documents to prove your identification or authorization to work, you may be fined and even imprisoned.

When One Document Is Sufficient

USCIS has a list of documents sufficient to prove both identity and eligibility to be employed in the United States. The following are accepted:

- a United States passport or passport card
- an unexpired foreign passport with an I-551 stamp

- an alien registration receipt card or permanent resident card
- an unexpired employment authorization document card, issued by USCIS, that contains a photograph
- for a nonimmigrant alien authorized to work for a particular employer, a foreign passport with Form I-94 or I-94A bearing the same name as the passport and containing an endorsement of the holder's nonimmigrant status
- a passport from Micronesia (FSM) or the Marshall Islands (RMI) with Form I-94 or I-94A indicating nonimmigrant admission under the Compact of Free Association Between the United States and the FSM or RMI, or
- a foreign passport containing a Form I-551 stamp or Form I-551 printed notation.

When Two Documents Are Required

An employee who does not have any of the above must produce two documents: one establishing that he or she is authorized to work in the United States and another verifying identity.

As documents proving employment authorization, USCIS will accept:
- a Social Security card
- a certification of report of birth issued by the Department of State
- an original or certified copy of a birth certificate issued by a state, county, city, or territory of the U.S.

- a Native American tribal document
- a U.S. citizen ID card
- a resident citizen ID card, or
- unexpired employment authorization documents issued by the Department of Homeland Security.

As documents proving identity, USCIS will accept:
- a current U.S. or Canadian driver's license that contains a photograph or description of personal characteristics
- a federal, state, or local identification card with a photograph on it
- a school ID card with a photograph
- a voter's registration card
- a U.S. military card or draft record
- a military dependent's ID card
- a U.S. Coast Guard Merchant Mariner card, or
- a Native American tribal document.

For workers age 18 and younger, USCIS considers a school record or report card, day care or nursery school record, or a hospital record as proof of identity.

Time Limits

New employees have three days to complete the I-9 Form. However, if you require some extra time to pull together the documents proving your identity and authorization—for example, if you need to obtain a certified copy of a birth certificate from another state—your employer can give you an additional 18 business days to produce the required documents. To get an extension of time, you must show proof that you have applied for the documents by producing, for example, a receipt for fees charged for a certified birth certificate.

> ! CAUTION
> **Your employer may copy and keep the forms.** Your new employer is required to note the type of documents you produce and any expiration dates on your Form I-9. Although employers are not required to photocopy such documents, they have the right to do so. If they do, the copies must be kept on file with your Form I-9.

Illegal Discrimination

RCA also makes it illegal for an employer with four or more employees to:

- discriminate in hiring and firing workers—other than unauthorized immigrant workers, of course—because of their national origin
- discriminate in hiring and firing workers because of their citizenship, or
- retaliate against employees for exercising any rights under immigration laws.

To be successful in charging an employer with a violation of IRCA, you must prove that the employer knowingly discriminated against you because of your citizenship or national origin, or that the employer had a pattern of committing the same offense against others.

Enforcing Your Rights

If a prospective or current employer violates your rights under IRCA, you have 180 days from the date of the violation to file a complaint with the Justice Department's Office of the Special Counsel for Unfair Immigration-Related Employment Practices. The most common violation of the antidiscrimination laws protecting immigrants occurs when employers refuse to hire someone because they suspect—incorrectly—that the person is not legally authorized to work in the United States.

The Complaint Process

To begin the complaint process, you can write a letter summarizing the situation to the following address:

Special Counsel
Immigration-Related Unfair Employment Practices
950 Pennsylvania Avenue, NW
Washington, DC 20530

You can also call the special counsel office to discuss your situation with a staff member at 800-255-7688. And you can get basic background information at the website: www.justice.gov/crt/about/osc.

The special counsel has 120 days from the day it receives your complaint to investigate and decide whether it will pursue a charge against the employer before an administrative law judge.

If the special counsel does not bring a charge against the employer within the 120 days or notifies you that it has not found sufficient evidence to support your charges, you have the right to plead your case directly before an administrative law judge. But you must request your hearing within 90 days of the end of the original 120-day period allowed for the special counsel to take action.

Immigration law is a world all its own. You will probably need the help of an attorney with experience in immigration law if you decide to pursue an antidiscrimination complaint after the special counsel has failed to do so. (In Chapter 17, see "Hiring a Lawyer.")

The appendix of this book also contains contact information for a number of groups that may provide advice and legal referrals. Since IRCA specifically outlaws immigration-related discrimination only in hiring and firing decisions, but not in other employment-related actions, such as promotions and wage increases, you may want to file your immigration-related complaint under Title VII of the Civil Rights Act or your state's antidiscrimination laws. (For details on those laws and how to take action under them, see Chapter 7.)

English-Only Rules

The U.S. Census Bureau predicts that by the year 2050, 24% of the population of the United States will be Hispanic—and Asians and Pacific Islanders will make up nearly 10%. Facing this future, American workplaces must consider the legality of rules that limit or prohibit employees from speaking languages other than English on the job.

Supporters of English-only rules claim they are essential so that employers can ensure that workers are obeying company rules and being polite and respectful to coworkers and clients. Opponents denounce the rules as punishing and demeaning to workers who are not fluent in English, and they claim the rules are a thinly veiled method to target and discriminate against immigrant workers. Some also point out that in parts of the country (such as Southern California) that have a workforce rich in immigrants, it is a boon to businesses to train new hires or deal with customers in their native languages.

The Equal Employment Opportunity Commission has found many English-only workplace rules to be wrongful discrimination on the basis of national origin under the Civil Rights Act. (In Chapter 7, see "Title VII of the Civil Rights Act.")

In most situations, employees must be allowed to speak among themselves in their own language while working or during breaks. In fact, EEOC guidelines state that English-only rules are presumed to be illegal, unless there is a clear business necessity for the rule.

The same skepticism applies to workplace screening tests that seem to exclude or disqualify a disproportionate number of applicants of a specific national origin.

Exceptions have been allowed only in cases where there is a clear business necessity, such as for air traffic controllers or for those who must deal with company customers who speak only English. Whenever there is some stricture requiring that employees speak only English on the job, employers must first:

- notify all employees of the rule
- inform all employees of the circumstances under which English is required, and
- explain the consequences of breaking the rule.

In recent legal challenges, courts have upheld some form of English-only rules when they were passed:

- so that supervisors could better manage employees' work, or because customers might object to hearing conversations in a language they could not understand, and
- to promote racial harmony after non-Spanish-speaking employees claimed that hearing Spanish spoken distracted them.

Courts in many of the cases have intimated, however, that employers must exempt employees who do not speak any English from the requirements of English-only rules, or provide at least training in English so that they may learn to speak it. ●

Lawyers and Legal Research

I f you are facing a workplace dispute, there are specialized agencies to advise and assist you. If your problem is a matter of wage and hour law, for example, you can call the Labor Department's investigators directly for assistance. If your problem involves illegal discrimination, you can call the Equal Employment Opportunity Commission and talk over your case with a compliance officer or staff attorney. A number of specialized agencies are noted throughout the book, and a list of additional resources and contact information is contained in the appendix.

With some types of workplace problems, however, you are on your own. If you need help getting your former employer to continue your health care benefits after you have lost your job, for example, no agency is available to help. If you have been denied workers' compensation benefits, you may want to double-check your rights before deciding whether to file an appeal.

In some unsettled legal areas, you may need to decide the best course of action: using an alternative to court such as mediation, going to small claims court, hiring a lawyer to help you through, or doing some of your own legal research. This chapter gives you guidance in using and choosing among your options.

Mediation and Arbitration

Because of how the legal world is portrayed on television and in movies, some people think that a courtroom is the best—and only—place to resolve any legal dispute. In fact, mediation and arbitration can be faster, less expensive, and more satisfying alternatives than going to court. Workplace experts are hailing these less-confrontational methods of solving workplace disputes as the hallmark of forward-thinking companies. And many employers are jumping on the bandwagon by adding clauses to their written employment agreements and employee manuals requiring that workplace disputes be resolved by arbitration or mediation.

Although mediation and arbitration are often lumped together under the general heading of alternative dispute resolution, there are significant differences between the two.

Mediation. Two or more people or groups get a neutral third party—a mediator—to help them communicate. The mediator does not represent either side or impose a decision but helps the disagreeing parties reach a settlement.

Arbitration. Both sides agree on the issue but cannot resolve it themselves. They agree to pick an arbitrator who will come up with a solution. Essentially, the arbitrator acts as an informal judge, but at far less cost and expense than most legal proceedings require.

Mediation and arbitration are sometimes used to help work out the terms of an agreement to end a work relationship, but they are most effective when those involved have a continuing relationship and want to find a mutually acceptable way to work together.

When Mediation Works Best

Mediation offers benefits to many employers and employees, because the resolution to a particular problem is reached quickly and creatively. And, because all involved feel they have a stake in fashioning the agreement, they are more likely to abide by the solution.

Mediation is not the best option for all types of disputes, however, because success depends on both sides being willing to meet in the middle and deal directly with one another. Many workplace experts have found that mediation is particularly effective in resolving these workplace conflicts:

- **Disputes between employees.** Many disputes fester because two people are not able to talk with one another. By setting up a nonjudgmental, nonconfrontational way for them to air their differences, mediation may offer a way for them to change their behavior so they can work together more effectively.
- **Deteriorating performance.** Good employees may stop performing well for any number of reasons. By encouraging judgment-free discussion, mediation can help remove the dynamics of browbeating and defensiveness that often result when a supervisor confronts an employee about a slipping work record.
- **Sexual harassment complaints.** Many such problems involve an initial misperception about what is and is not considered acceptable workplace behavior. They are made worse by an inability to discuss the

differences openly. Mediation can open communication and help ease the hostility that may pollute a work environment.

- **Termination.** While a firing is usually unpleasant for both employers and employees, mediation can help an employee receive a fair hearing of differences when that deck is so often stacked in favor of the company. For the employer, mediation can offer hope for a peaceful parting, free from the threat of future litigation.

 RESOURCE

The appendix lists some good resources for finding professional mediators and arbitrators. The websites for those organizations include some helpful information about understanding the processes involved in alternative dispute resolution.

And for more information about how to choose a mediator, prepare a case, and go through the mediation process, see *Mediate, Don't Litigate: Strategies for Successful Mediation*, by Peter Lovenheim and Lisa Guerin (Nolo).

Small Claims Court

Some disputes over workplace law, such as whether a former employer made unauthorized deductions from your paycheck, usually involve small amounts of money. In many of those cases, you can file your own lawsuit in small claims court to collect the money you are owed.

The hallmark of small claims court is simplicity: It is inexpensive and easy to file a case there, and court procedures are streamlined. You do not need to hire a lawyer to represent you; in some states, lawyers are not even allowed. The small claims hearing is held before a judge, magistrate, commissioner, or volunteer attorney, who will usually decide the case on the spot or within a few days.

The amount you can sue for is limited—typically between $1,500 and $15,000, depending on your state. But these limits increase regularly, so check first with the local court clerk if you decide to use small claims court.

RESOURCE

For more information on using small claims court, see *Everybody's Guide to Small Claims Court,* by Ralph Warner (Nolo).

Class Action Lawsuits

The federal courts sometimes allow lawsuits to be filed jointly by groups of people who have all been injured by the same or similar conduct by an employer. These are called class actions. Because they spread the legal costs among many people who are injured, class actions can make it feasible to sue an employer or former employer where an individual case would be too small for a lawyer to take on. Of course, all those who join in the lawsuit will also share in any judgment.

The legal requirements for pursuing a class action are complex and almost always require a lawyer's help. But keep this option in mind if a number of other workers suffered similar wrongs or injuries to yours.

Your local office of the American Civil Liberties Union (ACLU) should be able to direct you to lawyers who specialize in civil rights class action lawsuits. (See the appendix for contact details of the national headquarters.)

Hiring a Lawyer

If your workplace problem involves a complex or ambiguous area of law—negotiating a complicated settlement, filing a claim of defamation, or a violation of public policy—you will probably need to hire a lawyer for help. Depending on your circumstances and location, a number of places may provide referrals to lawyers with special expertise in workplace law:

- Try local legal clinics. Some may only make referrals to lawyers with appropriate knowledge and experience. And some may have lawyers on staff who will handle your case for a low cost or free of charge. Locate your community's legal aid clinics by looking in the telephone directory under Legal Aid Society or Legal Services, or check with the nearest law school.

- Organizations in your area that serve as advocates for the legal rights of minority groups, such as gay rights coalitions and local chapters of the National Association for the Advancement of Colored People (NAACP), may also make lawyer referrals.
- National organizations that deal with specific types of workplace rights, such as the National Association of Working Women, may know of competent lawyers for referrals.
- Groups of specialized employees may have access to legal help offered by special interest groups. Union workers, for example, can contact the Coalition of Labor Union Women for legal guidance and referrals to experienced attorneys.

See the appendix for listings of organizations that provide legal referrals and for additional information on specialized workplace problems.

RESOURCE

Looking for a lawyer? To find local lawyers, you can also try these excellent and free resources:

- **Nolo's Lawyer Directory.** Nolo has an easy-to-use online directory of lawyers, organized by location and area of expertise. You can find the directory and its comprehensive profiles at www.nolo.com/lawyers.
- **Lawyers.com.** At Lawyers.com, you'll find a user-friendly search tool that allows you to tailor results by area of law and geography. You can also search for attorneys by name.

Attorney profiles prominently display contact information, list topics of expertise, and show ratings—by both clients and other legal professionals.

- **Martindale.com.** Martindale.com offers an advanced search option that allows you to sort not only by practice area and location, but also by criteria like law school. Whether you look for lawyers by name or expertise, you'll find listings with detailed background information, peer and client ratings, and even profile visibility.

Comparison Shopping for a Lawyer

If you take detailed notes on each lawyer mentioned during your research, you should soon have your own small directory of lawyers with employment-related expertise from which to choose.

Be careful that people do not merely give you the names of lawyers they have heard of, or who handled an entirely different kind of case, such as a divorce or a car accident case. Any lawyer can become well known just by renting billboards or buying a lot of advertising time on television. Beware that in many states, lawyers can advertise any area of specialization they choose, even if they have never before handled a case in the area.

Questions to Ask

Keep in mind that individual preferences for a particular lawyer are guided by intangibles such as personality or your comfort level with the person. Here are a few questions you may want to ask a person who gives you a glowing review of a particular employment lawyer:

- Did this lawyer respond to all your telephone calls and other communications promptly?
- Did the lawyer take the time to listen to your explanation and understand your situation fully?
- Were all the bills you received properly itemized and in line with the cost projections you got at the start of your case?
- Did this lawyer personally handle your case, or was it handed off to a younger, less-experienced lawyer in the same firm?
- Did the lawyer deliver what he or she promised?

It may be slightly more difficult to evaluate a lawyer referral you get from an agency or special interest group. Reputable organizations will strike from their referral lists the names of lawyers about whom they have received negative reviews. You can help groups that make referrals keep their information accurate and useful to others if you let them know of both your good and bad experiences with a particular individual.

Deciding on a Lawyer

Once you have a referral to a lawyer—or even better, several referrals—contact each one and see whether he or she meets your needs. Come forearmed with some inside knowledge.

Most lawyers are guided by the principle that time is money. And time and money should also be your guiding concerns in deciding whether to hire a lawyer to help with your workplace claim.

Even the simplest problems can take a long time to be resolved through the legal system. And potential legal problems in the workplace do not often present themselves in straightforward issues. If the case requires a court proceeding, it can take years before a final judgment is reached.

A lawyer's help rarely comes cheap. Legal organizations estimate that workplace rights cases eat up an average of between $8,000 to $30,000 in lawyers' time and other legal costs such as court filings and witness interviews.

Lawyers often take on workplace cases for little or no money up front. They depend on court-ordered fees and often a percentage of your recovery, called a "contingency fee." (See "Paying a Lawyer," below.) This means that a lawyer will be assessing whether your case is likely to pay off so that he or she will be compensated.

Given these circumstances, you will want to be as certain as possible that any lawyer you hire will be doing the utmost to represent you fairly and efficiently, and that you are comfortable with his or her representation.

The Initial Interview

Start by calling for an appointment. Some lawyers will try to screen you over the phone by asking you to discuss the basics of your case. A little of this can be helpful to you both.

You can begin to assess the lawyer's phoneside manner; he or she can begin to assess whether you truly need expert legal advice.

Many lawyers will agree not to charge you for an initial consultation to decide whether to take your case. But be prepared to pay a reasonable fee for legal advice. A charge of between $75 and $250 for a one-hour consultation is typical. Organize the facts in your case well before going to your consultation, and be clear about what you are after, whether it is a financial settlement or reinstatement to your old job. Bring any important documents (such as an employment contract, disciplinary warning, or proposed severance agreement) with you to the meeting. An hour should be more than enough to explain your case and obtain at least a basic opinion on how it might be approached and what it is likely to cost. If you find the right lawyer and can afford the charge, it can be money well spent.

Keep in mind that very few employment law disputes actually end up in a courtroom. Most are settled or resolved in some other way. So you need not be swayed by a lawyer's likely effect on a jury alone. A good lawyer may also offer the valuable advice that you do not have a good case, or may suggest a good strategy for negotiating a settlement.

Paying a Lawyer

Some words to the wise about legal bills: get them in writing.

Most disagreements between lawyers and clients involve fees, so be sure to get all the details involving money in writing, including the per-hour billing rate or the contingency fee arrangement, the frequency of billing, and whether you will be required to deposit money in advance to cover expenses.

Most workplace cases are handled under some form of contingent fee arrangement in which a lawyer agrees to handle a case for a fixed percentage of the amount finally recovered in a lawsuit. If you win the case, the lawyer's fee comes out of the money awarded to you. If you lose, neither you nor the lawyer will get any money.

A lawyer's willingness to take your case on a contingent fee is a hopeful sign of faith in the strength of your claim. A lawyer who is not firmly convinced that your case is a winner is unlikely to take you on as a contingency fee client. Be very wary of a lawyer who wants to take your case on an hourly payment basis. That usually signals that he or she does not think your case is very strong in terms of the money you might be able to recover. It could also mean financial disaster for you, as your legal bills are likely to mount up with no useful results. At the very least, insist that the lawyer write down some specific objectives to be accomplished in your case, and put a cap on how high the fees can climb.

Although there is no set percentage for contingency fees in most types of cases, lawyers often demand about a third if the case is settled before trial and 40% if a case has to be tried. Keep in mind that the terms of a contingency fee agreement may be negotiable. You can try to get your lawyer to agree to a lower percentage—especially if the case is settled quickly—or to absorb some of the court costs.

Sometimes, a lawyer working for you under a contingency agreement will require that you pay all out-of-pocket expenses, such as filing fees charged by the courts and the cost of transcribing depositions: interviews of witnesses and others involved in a lawsuit taken under oath. If this is so, the lawyer will want you to deposit a substantial amount of money—thousands of dollars—with the law firm to cover these expenses. From your standpoint, it is a much better arrangement for the lawyer to advance such costs and get repaid out of your recovery. A commonsense arrangement might involve your advancing a small amount of money for some costs, with the attorney advancing the rest.

In some types of workplace lawsuits, such as Civil Rights Act violations, the court may award you attorneys' fees as part of the final judgment. However, this award may not be large enough to cover the entire amount owed to your attorney under the legal fee contract. Therefore, the contingency fee contract should spell out what happens to a court award of attorneys' fees.

One approach is to have the fees paid to the attorney in their entirety and subtract that amount from the contingency fee on your award. Another common approach is to add the awards for fees and damages and calculate the attorney's contingency fee on the entire amount. Attorneys are apt to angle for this approach in case they disagree with the amount a court awards in legal fees.

Managing Your Lawyer

Most complaints against lawyers have to do with their failure to communicate with their clients. Your lawyer may be the one with the legal expertise, but the rights that are being pursued are yours. You are the most important person involved in your case. You have the right to demand that your lawyer be reasonably available to answer your questions and to keep you posted on your case.

You may need to put some energy into managing your lawyer.

Carefully check every statement. Each statement or bill should list costs that the lawyer has paid or that you are expected to pay. If you question whether a particular bill complies with your written fee agreement, call your lawyer and politely demand that a new, more detailed version be sent before you pay it. Don't feel as though you are being too pushy: The laws in many states actually require thorough detail in lawyers' statements.

Do your homework. Learn as much as you can about the laws and decisions involved in your case. By doing so, you will be able to make informed decisions about your case and may even be able to make a suggestion that will move your case along faster.

Certainly if the other side offers a settlement, you will be in a better position to evaluate whether or not it makes sense to accept it.

Maintain your own file on your case. By having a well-organized file of your own, you will be able to discuss your case with your lawyer intelligently and efficiently, even over the telephone. Being well informed will help keep your lawyer's effectiveness up and your costs down. Be aware that if your lawyer is working on an hourly basis, you will probably be charged for telephone consultations and even emails. But they are likely to be less expensive than office visits.

Firing a Lawyer

If your relationship with a particular lawyer does not seem to be working out for some reason, or if you truly believe your case is not progressing as it should, consider asking another lawyer to take over. Beware, however, that if you are in the midst of a lawsuit, the judge may need to approve the switch. The judge has the discretion to refuse the request if he or she believes change would cause an unreasonable delay or prejudice the other side.

If you are able and anxious to change lawyers, be clear with the first one that you are taking your business elsewhere, and send him or her an immediate written notification of your decision. Otherwise, you could end up receiving bills from each lawyer, both of whom might claim that they handled the lion's share of your case, complicating the matter of who is owed what.

Before you pay anything, be sure that the bill does not amount to more than you agreed to pay. If you have a contingency fee arrangement, it is up to your new lawyer and former lawyer to work out how to split the fee.

Take prompt action against any lawyer whose behavior appears to be deceptive, unethical, or otherwise illegal. A call to your state's bar association should provide you with guidance on what types of lawyer behavior are prohibited and how to file a complaint.

However, unless the lawyer's conduct is plainly dishonest or he or she has abandoned your case, you might not get much satisfaction. However, sometimes the threat of filing a complaint can move your lawyer into action. And, if worse comes to worst, filing a formal complaint will create a document that you will need if you later file a lawsuit against a lawyer for malpractice.

Legal Research

This book gives you a general understanding of the legal principles involved in common workplace disputes. However, in negotiating with your employer, presenting your workplace problem to government investigators, preparing for mediation or arbitration, or working with a lawyer you hire, you may gain additional power and speed the resolution of your dispute by having detailed and specific legal knowledge.

In these situations, you may want to do some legal research of your own. If you have been laid off or fired, you likely have some time on your hands. You may even find it surprisingly therapeutic to get to work doing your own research.

⊘ **CAUTION**

Don't start from scratch. For more general information about specific workplace issues, check the appendix. Many legal and special interest groups publish helpful pamphlets on the legal aspects of workplace issues, such as sexual harassment and age discrimination. Before you do extensive research on your own, take a look at what others have done.

Library Research

The reference sections in most larger public libraries contain a set of local and state laws, as well as a set of the federal statutes. The reference librarian should be able to help you look up any laws that might affect your situation. However, if you want to look up a court case or a ruling by a government agency such as the Equal Employment Opportunity Commission, you will probably have to visit a law library.

In many states, county law libraries are free and open to the public. You can also try the library of the nearest law school, particularly if it's affiliated with a public university funded by tax dollars. Whatever library you choose, you will find that most librarians are not only well versed in legal research techniques, but are also open to helping you through the mazes of legal citations.

Where to Begin

There are several types of research materials concentrating on employment law that you may find useful: secondary sources, such as books and law review articles, and primary sources, such as statutes and cases. These resources serve different purposes.

Secondary sources—general books and scholarly articles—are usually used to get an overview of a particular topic. If you find a good article or chapter on a topic you're interested in, it will give both an explanation of the law and citations to other materials—especially cases—that may prove helpful.

Primary sources—statutes (state and federal laws) and cases (published decisions of state and federal courts)—tell you the current status of the law. Very often, your goals in doing legal research are first to find the statutes that apply to you, and then to find the court cases that interpret the statutes in situations similar to yours. There may be cases with similar facts (for example, a supervisor who persistently asked a female employee to go out with him after she repeatedly said no). Or there may be a court case that raises a similar issue or legal question (for example, whether an employer is legally responsible for paying for an independent contractor's commuting costs). These court decisions may give you some indication of how a government agency or court is likely to decide your case.

The best place to begin your research depends on your situation. If you want some additional general information about a particular workplace issue, or an update on the law since this book was published, you will probably find a recent book or article more than adequate. However, if you want very specific legal information—for example, whether wrongful discharge is a valid legal theory in your state—you will probably need to look at both your state fair employment practice law and any judicial decisions dealing with the issue. The sections that follow describe how to find and use several types of resources to learn about the law that applies to your situation.

 RESOURCE

For more on the specifics of legal research, see *Legal Research: How to Find & Understand the Law,* by Stephen Elias and the Editors of Nolo (Nolo).

Statutes

When people refer to The Law, they are usually talking about statutes: the written laws created by state and federal legislatures.

The Two Research Tracks: Federal and State

Two separate sets of laws control the workplace: federal law and state law. Each has separate statutes, regulations, and court cases, so you must decide which law you are relying on before you start to research.

Title VII of the Civil Rights Act, for example, is a federal law, and the court decisions that interpret it—including those involving the EEOC—are federal cases. However, not all federal decisions carry equal weight. The cases which will be most persuasive in federal court are those from the highest court in that jurisdiction: the United States Supreme Court. On the second level in the hierarchy are the federal courts of appeal. You should look first for cases in the same judicial circuit or geographical region as yours, because these will be more likely to control the outcome of your particular case. And, finally, on the lowest level are the federal district courts; again, look first for cases in your geographical area.

If you are researching your state's laws, you will be looking at state court cases. Most state court systems are similar to the federal system, in that there are three hierarchical levels of courts. The most authoritative cases will be those from your state's highest court —usually called the supreme court—followed by decisions issued by your state appellate court, followed by decisions issued by your state trial court.

Federal statutes are contained in the United States Code. For example, if you are looking for Title VII of Civil Rights Act, 42 U.S.C. § 2000, locate Title 42 of the United States Code and turn to Section 2000.

Finding state statutes is a bit trickier, because states use slightly different systems to number and organize their statutes. Most states use one of the following methods:

- **By topic.** California uses this type of organization. To find Cal. Gov't. Code § 12900, locate the volumes that contain the state's government code and turn to Section 12900.
- **By title.** Vermont, for example, divides its statutes into titles, similar to the federal citation system. To find 21 Vt. Stat. § 495, locate Title 21 of the Vermont Statutes and turn to Section 495.

Inside the back cover of the volume, you will find an unbound supplement called a pocket part. This material updates the information in the main volume, including any amendments or changes to the law that have happened since the main volume was published. It is organized just like the main volume, using the same numerical system. Be sure to check the pocket part every time you use a statute. If you forget this crucial step, you may be relying on law that is no longer valid.

Regulations

In some situations, you may also want to consult the regulations that pertain to a statute. Regulations are the rules created by administrative agencies for carrying out

legislation. If, for example, a statute requires an agency to investigate complaints about workplace safety hazards, there will probably be regulations that give more detail about what form the investigation will take, who will conduct it, and how it will be done.

Federal regulations can be found in the Code of Federal Regulations (CFR). You can find the CFR online at www.gpo.gov.

RESOURCE

Don't forget local laws. Many major cities and some counties also have their own laws on illegal workplace practices, such as discriminating against gay and lesbian workers, and regulations detailing how these laws should be carried out. Do not neglect these in your research. Sometimes a local law will contain the best protections against workplace problems or provide the best remedies. Ask your law librarian how to find and use your city or county code.

Cases

Sometimes, you will find all the information you need in the statutes and regulations. However, laws can be deceptively straightforward, impossibly complex, or somewhere in between. To be sure you get the point, it is wise to also look at court cases that involve the statute and see how the courts apply and interpret it. Courts have been known to take a law with an apparently obvious meaning and turn it on its head.

And, sometimes, you will need to turn to case law because there is no statute that applies to your situation. For example, when you are researching whether a legal theory such as the intentional infliction of emotional distress applies to your situation, you will absolutely need to look at some court decisions, since these issues are decided on a case-by-case basis.

Finding a case interpreting a statute. If you want to track down how a certain statute has been referred to by the courts in a case, your research task will be fairly simple: All you have to do is consult an annotated code. An annotated code is a version of the state or federal statutes that contains summaries of cases that have interpreted various provisions of a statute. There are two sets of federal annotated codes: the United States Code Service and the United States Code Annotated. Most states also have annotated codes. Ask the law librarian where you can find them.

To use an annotated code, look for the numbered section of the statute that is relevant to your situation. If there have been any court cases interpreting that statute, they will be listed after the specific section of the statute, along with a sentence or two describing the case. If the summary of the case leaves you wanting to know more about it, you can track down the case and read it by following the citation given there.

Finding a case using secondary sources. In some situations, you will want to find court decisions on a particular topic without referring to a statute. For example, if you want to find out whether some

uncomfortable situation at work might form the basis of a tort action in your state, you should probably not begin your research with a statute. Common law tort actions were developed almost exclusively by case decisions. Sometimes these torts are also written into code—such as a state criminal statute defining and setting out the punishment for assault—but, more likely, you will have to hunt down a few cases.

One good way to find relevant cases is through secondary sources (discussed below). Quite often, a law review article or book will discuss key cases and give citations for them. If you find a source that analyzes an issue that is important in your case, you will likely get some good leads there.

Treatises

There are hundreds of books—sometimes called treatises—that cover workplace issues. The drawback of most treatises is that nearly all of them are written by and for lawyers, with little effort made to translate legalese into English. Also, these books oftentimes devote many pages to lawyerly concerns, such as how to plead and prove picayune points of law. Still, these volumes will often provide you with helpful background information; they may also lead you to cases that pertain to your situation. When using a legal treatise, be sure to check the back inside cover; most publishers update the books periodically by issuing pocket parts, bound pamphlets noting changes and additions to the text.

How to Read a Case Citation

There are several places where a case may be reported. If it is a case decided by the U.S. Supreme Court, you can find it in either the *United States Reports* (U.S.) or the *Supreme Court Reporter* (S.Ct.). If it is a federal case decided by a court other than the U.S. Supreme Court, it will be in either the Federal Reporter, (F., F.2d, or F.3d), or the Federal Supplement (F. Supp. or F. Supp. 2d).

Most states publish their own official state reports. All published state court decisions are also included in the West Reporter System. West has divided the country into seven regions—and publishes all the decisions of the supreme and appellate state courts in the region together. These reporters are:

A. and A.2d. Atlantic Reporter (First and Second Series), which includes decisions from Connecticut, Delaware, the District of Columbia, Maine, Maryland, New Hampshire, New Jersey, Pennsylvania, Rhode Island, and Vermont.

N.E. and N.E.2d. Northeastern Reporter (First and Second Series), which includes decisions from Illinois, Indiana, Massachusetts, New York,* and Ohio.

N.W. and N.W.2d. Northwestern Reporter (First and Second Series), which includes decisions from Iowa, Michigan, Minnesota, Nebraska, North Dakota, South Dakota, and Wisconsin.

P., P.2d., and P.3d. Pacific Reporter (First, Second, and Third Series), which includes decisions from Alaska, Arizona, California,** Colorado, Hawaii, Idaho, Kansas, Montana, Nevada, New Mexico, Oklahoma, Oregon, Utah, Washington, and Wyoming.

S.E. and S.E.2d. Southeastern Reporter (First and Second Series), which includes decisions from Georgia, North Carolina, South Carolina, Virginia, and West Virginia.

So., So.2d., and So.3d. Southern Reporter (First, Second, and Third Series), which includes decisions from Alabama, Florida, Louisiana, and Mississippi.

S.W. and S.W.2d. Southwestern Reporter (First and Second Series), which includes decisions from Arkansas, Kentucky, Missouri, Tennessee, and Texas.

A case citation will give you the names of the people or companies on each side of a case, the volume of the reporter in which the case can be found, the page number on which it begins, and the year in which the case was decided. For example:

Smith v. Jones Internat'l, 123 N.Y.S.2d 456 (1994)

Smith and Jones are the names of the parties having the legal dispute. The case is reported in Volume 123 of the New York Supplement, Second Series, beginning on page 456; the court issued the decision in 1994.

*All decisions from New York appellate courts are published in a separate volume, New York Supplement (N.Y.S.).

**All California appellate decisions are published in a separate volume, the California Reporter (Cal. Rptr.).

If you are interested in pursuing your legal research through such a treatise, your best bet is to go to a law library and ask the research librarian for some steering on your particular topic.

Law Review Articles

Law reviews are periodicals containing articles written by lawyers, law professors, and law students, usually covering a unique or evolving legal topic. Since workplace law is of great current interest, you will find lots of articles about it. The inside joke about law review articles is that they are made up mostly of footnotes. While annoying to many readers, these footnotes—which contain references or citations to other relevant cases, statutes, and articles—can be gold mines for researchers. Look especially for articles that are published in law reviews from schools in your state, since these will be most likely to discuss your state's law and court decisions.

There are two tools in every law library that can help you find law review articles on topics that interest you: the *Current Law Index* and the *Index to Legal Periodicals*. These volumes are published annually, except for the most recent listings, which are published every month. Both list articles by subject, by author, and by the cases and statutes referred to in the article. If you don't have a case name or a specific statute in mind to guide you, turn to the index and peruse the listings of articles there.

Online Resources

There are currently many websites—maintained by the government, law schools or libraries, law firms, and individuals—that can be useful to employees. They may have just what you are looking for.

 RESOURCE

Check out Nolo.com's employment law section. Under "Employment Law," loads of free information is available for employees interested in finding out more about rights in the workplace. Topics covered include discrimination, fair pay and time off, health and safety, losing or leaving a job, privacy, and more. ●

Resources

The organizations listed here can give you additional information or assistance on specific workplace issues. Some groups offer a wide variety of services, including publications and written materials, telephone counseling and hotlines for advice, support groups or in-person counseling, attorney referrals, and training resources. Some organizations offer only limited services or restrict services to their members or to a limited geographic area, so be sure to ask about possible limitations. Also, ask for an additional, more appropriate referral if the group you contact is not able to help.

Advocacy, Generally

National Workrights Institute
128 Stone Cliff Road
Princeton, NJ 08540
609-683-0313
www.workrights.org
Nonprofit organization providing information and advocacy in workplace rights, with a focus on freedoms of expression and association, privacy, equal treatment, safety and health, and adequate compensation.

Workplace Fairness
8121 Georgia Ave, Suite 600
Silver Spring, MD 20910
240-772-1205
www.workplacefairness.org
Nonprofit organization providing information, education, and assistance to individual workers and their advocates.

Focus is on workplace concerns including hiring, discrimination, wages and hours, working conditions, and termination.

AIDS-HIV

See also organizations listed under Gay and Lesbian.

American Foundation for AIDS Research (AmFAR)
1100 Vermont Ave, NW, Suite 600
Washington, DC 20036
202-331-8600
www.amfar.org
Nonprofit public foundation funds programs for AIDS research, education for AIDS prevention, and public policy development.

Centers for Disease Control and Prevention
National Prevention Information Network
Post Office Box 6003
Rockville, MD 20849
800-232-4636
https://npin.cdc.gov
The CDC National Prevention Information Network (NPIN) provides information about HIV/AIDS, sexually transmitted diseases, and tuberculosis to people and organizations working in prevention, health care, and research and support services.

AIDS United
1101 14th Street NW, Suite 300
Washington, DC 20005
202-408-4848
www.aidsunited.org
A philanthropic and advocacy organization providing funding for education, advocacy,

and research efforts in local communities. Also acts as a clearinghouse for information on HIV and AIDS, youth involvement in prevention, nutrition programming, and return to work efforts.

National Minority AIDS Council
1000 Vermont Ave, NW, Suite 200
Washington, DC 20005
202-858-0021
www.nmac.org
Encourages leadership within minority communities responding to the HIV and AIDS epidemic. Monitors legislation and provides AIDS programs with technical assistance. Distributes information on AIDS, especially information concerning the impact of the disease on minorities.

Civil Rights

American Civil Liberties Union (ACLU)
125 Broad Street, 18th Floor
New York, NY 10004
212-549-2500
www.aclu.org
Advocates individual rights through litigation and public education on a broad range of issues affecting individual freedom, from genetic testing to wrongful discharge. Legal advice and counseling, as well as attorney referrals, provided by state offices.

Electronic Frontier Foundation
815 Eddy Street
San Francisco, CA 94109
415-436-9333
www.eff.org

Grassroots advocacy organization focusing on consumers' digital rights.

Human Rights Watch
350 Fifth Avenue, 34th Floor
New York, NY 10118
212-290-4700
www.hrw.org
International activist group dedicated to preventing discrimination and upholding political freedom.

Disabled Workers

ABLEDATA
103 West Broad Street, Suite 400
Falls Church, VA 22046
800-227-0216
www.abledata.com
A consumer referral service sponsored by the U.S. Department of Education's National Institute on Disability and Rehabilitation Research that maintains a database of more than 36,000 adaptive devices from white canes to voice output programs.

Job Accommodation Network (JAN)
P.O. Box 6080
Morgantown, WV 26506
800-526-7234
TTY: 877-781-9403
http://askjan.org
Provides free consulting services to people with disabilities seeking accommodation information under the Americans with Disabilities Act (ADA) and to employers seeking to accommodate employees with disabilities. Maintains a database of companies

nationwide that have accommodated workers and organizations, support groups, government agencies, and placement agencies that assist the disabled.

National Organization on Disability
77 Water Street, Suite 204
New York, NY 10005
646-505-1191
www.nod.org
Administers the Community Partnership and National Partnership programs, which address educational, employment, social, and transportation needs of people with disabilities. Provides members with information and technical assistance; makes referrals, monitors legislation.

Office on the Americans with Disabilities Act
Civil Rights Division
U.S. Department of Justice
950 Pennsylvania Avenue, NW
Washington, DC 20530
800-514-0301
TTY: 800-514-0383
www.ada.gov
Government agency specialists answer questions about the ADA—except on federal government holidays. Publishes a number of free booklets, including information on how to file a complaint under the ADA. Publications are also available in alternate formats for people with disabilities: Braille, computer disk, audiocassette, and large print.

Social Security Administration
Office of Public Inquiries
1100 West High Rise
6401 Security Boulevard
Baltimore, MD 21235
800-772-1213
TTY: 800-325-0778
www.ssa.gov
Administers and regulates the Social Security Disability Insurance and Supplemental Security Income (SSI) programs.

Discrimination

Equal Employment Opportunity Commission
131 M Street, NE
Washington, DC 20507
800-669-4000
TTY: 800-669-6820
www.eeoc.gov
Government agency that enforces federal laws prohibiting employment discrimination and sexual harassment through investigation, conciliation, litigation, coordination, education, and technical assistance.

National Committee on Pay Equity
555 New Jersey Avenue, NW
Washington, DC 20001
703-920-2010
www.pay-equity.org
Provides information and technical assistance on wage discrimination based on gender and race. Members receive updates and mailings on pay equity activity, a newsletter, discounts on NCPE publications, and access to pay equity networks.

State Agencies That Enforce Laws Prohibiting Discrimination in Employment

Note: Phone numbers listed are for each department's headquarters. Check the website for regional office locations and numbers.

Alabama
EEOC District Office
Birmingham, AL
800-669-4000
www.eeoc.gov/birmingham/index.cfm

Alaska
Commission for Human Rights
Anchorage, AK
907-274-4692
800-478-4692
http://humanrights.alaska.gov

Arizona
Civil Rights Division
Phoenix, AZ
602-542-5263
877-491-5742
www.azag.gov/civil-rights

Arkansas
Equal Employment Opportunity Commission
Little Rock, AR
800-669-4000
www.eeoc.gov/field/littlerock/index.cfm

California
Department of Fair Employment and Housing
DFEH Headquarters
Elk Grove, CA
800-884-1684
www.dfeh.ca.gov

Colorado
Civil Rights Division
Denver, CO
303-894-7855
www.colorado.gov/pacific/dora/civil-rights

Connecticut
Commission on Human Rights and
  Opportunities
Hartford, CT
860-541-3400
www.ct.gov/chro/site

Delaware
Office of Antidiscrimination
Wilmington, DE
302-761-8200
http://dia.delawareworks.com/discrimination

District of Columbia
Office of Human Rights
Washington, DC
202-727-4559
http://ohr.dc.gov

Florida
Commission on Human Relations
Tallahassee, FL
850-488-7082
http://fchr.myflorida.com

Georgia
Atlanta District Office
U.S. Equal Employment Opportunity
  Commission
Atlanta, GA
800-669-4000
http://www.eeoc.gov/field/atlanta

Hawaii
Hawaii Civil Rights Commission
Honolulu, HI
808-586-8636
http://labor.hawaii.gov/hcrc

Idaho
Idaho Commission on Human Rights
Boise, ID
208-334-2873
888-249-7025
http://humanrights.idaho.gov

Illinois
Department of Human Rights
Chicago, IL
312-814-6200
http://www.illinois.gov/dhr

Indiana
Civil Rights Commission
Indianapolis, IN
317-232-2600
800-628-2909
www.in.gov/icrc

Iowa
Iowa Civil Rights Commission
Des Moines, IA
515-281-4121
800-457-4416
https://icrc.iowa.gov

Kansas
Human Rights Commission
Topeka, KS
785-296-3206
www.khrc.net

Kentucky
Human Rights Commission
Louisville, KY
502-595-4024
800-292-5566
www.kchr.ky.gov

Louisiana
Commission on Human Rights
Baton Rouge, LA
225-342-6969
http://gov.louisiana.gov/page/lchr

Maine
Human Rights Commission
Augusta, ME
207-624-6290
www.maine.gov/mhrc

Maryland
Commission on Human Relations
Baltimore, MD
800-637-6247 (in-state only)
410-767-8600
www.mccr.maryland.gov

Massachusetts
Commission Against Discrimination
Boston, MA
617-994-6000
www.mass.gov/orgs/massachusetts-
   commission-against-discrimination

Michigan
Department of Civil Rights
Detroit, MI
313-456-3700
www.michigan.gov/mdcr

Minnesota
Department of Human Rights
St. Paul, MN
651-539-1100
800-657-3704
http://mn.gov/mdhr

Mississippi
Jackson Area Office
U.S. Equal Employment Opportunity
   Commission
Jackson, MS
800-669-4000
www.eeoc.gov/field/jackson

Missouri
Commission on Human Rights
Jefferson City, MO
573-751-3325
877-781-4236
www.labor.mo.gov/mohumanrights

Montana
Human Rights Bureau
Employment Relations Division
Department of Labor and Industry
Helena, MT
800-542-0807
www.erd.dli.mt.gov/human-rights/
   human-rights

Nebraska
Equal Opportunity Commission
Lincoln, NE
402-471-2024
800-642-6112
www.neoc.ne.gov

Nevada
Equal Rights Commission
Las Vegas, NV
702-486-7161
www.detr.state.nv.us/nerc.htm

New Hampshire
Commission for Human Rights
Concord, NH
603-271-2767
www.nh.gov/hrc

New Jersey
Division on Civil Rights
Trenton, NJ
609-292-4605
www.nj.gov/oag/dcr/index.html

New Mexico
Human Rights Division
Santa Fe, NM
505-827-6838
800-566-9471
www.dws.state.nm.us/Human-Rights-
   Information

New York
Division of Human Rights
Bronx, NY
888-392-3644
www.dhr.ny.gov

North Carolina
Raleigh Area Office
U.S. Equal Employment Opportunity
   Commission
Raleigh, NC
800-669-4000
www.eeoc.gov/field/raleigh

North Dakota
Human Rights Division
Department of Labor
Bismarck, ND
701-328-2660
800-582-8032
www.nd.gov/labor/human-rights

Ohio
Civil Rights Commission
Columbus, OH
614-466-2785
888-278-7101
www.crc.ohio.gov

Oklahoma
Oklahoma Human Rights Commission
Stringtown, OK
918-581-2733
888-456-2006
www.okdrs.gov/guide/oklahoma-human-
    rights-commission

Oregon
Civil Rights Division
Bureau of Labor and Industries
Portland, OR
971-673-0764
www.oregon.gov/BOLI/CRD

Pennsylvania
Human Relations Commission
Harrisburg, PA
717-787-9780
www.phrc/pa.gov

Rhode Island
Commission for Human Rights
Providence, RI
401-222-2661
www.richr.state.ri.us/frames.html

South Carolina
Human Affairs Commission
Columbia, SC
803-737-7800
800-521-0725
www.schac.sc.gov

South Dakota
Division of Human Rights
Pierre, SD
605-773-3681
www.dlr.sd.gov/human-rights

Tennessee
Human Rights Commission
Nashville, TN
800-251-3589
www.tn.gov/humanrights

Texas
Commission on Human Rights
Austin, TX
512-463-2642
888-452-4778
www.twc.state.tx/partners/civil-rights-
    discrimination

Utah
Antidiscrimination and Labor Division
Labor Commission
Salt Lake City, UT
801-530-6801
800-222-1238
www.laborcommission.utah.gov/divisions/
    AntidiscriminationAndLabor/index.html

Vermont
Attorney General's Office
Civil Rights Division
Burlington, VT
802-951-6540
www.justice.gov/usao-vt/civil-division

Virginia
Office of the Attorney General
Division of Human Rights
Richmond, VA
804-225-2292
www.oag.state.va.us/programs-initiatives/
    human-rights

Washington
Human Rights Commission
Olympia, WA
800-233-3247
www.hum.wa.gov

West Virginia
Human Rights Commission
Charleston, WV
304-558-2616
www.hrc.wv.gov

Wisconsin
Equal Rights Division
Madison, WI
608-266-6860
http://dwd.wisconsin.gov/er

Wyoming
Department of Employment
Labor Standards
Cheyenne, WY
307-777-7261
www.wyomingworkforce.org/job-seekers-and-
    workers/labor-standards/Pages/default.aspx

Gay and Lesbian

ACLU National Lesbian and Gay Rights Project
See American Civil Liberties Union *under*
Civil Rights.

GLBTQ Advocates & Defenders (GLAD)
18 Tremont Street, Suite 950
Boston, MA 02108
617-426-1350
www.glad.org
Publishes information and provides general
advice on sexual orientation and HIV status.
Provides lawyer referrals.

Human Rights Campaign
1640 Rhode Island Avenue, NW
Washington, DC 20036-3278
800-777-4723
202-628-4160
TTY: 202-216-1572
www.hrc.org

Lobbies Congress, provides campaign support to fair-minded candidates, and works to educate the public on a wide array of topics affecting gay, lesbian, bisexual, and transgender Americans, including relationship recognition, workplace, family, and health issues. The affiliated HRC Foundation engages in research and provides public education and programming.

Lambda Legal Defense and Education Fund
120 Wall Street, 19th Floor
New York, NY 10005
212-809-8585
www.lambdalegal.org
Provides publications, advice, and legal information on gay, lesbian, bisexual, and transgender job discrimination and HIV discrimination issues. Phone-in service for lawyer referrals.

National Center for Lesbian Rights
870 Market Street, Suite 370
San Francisco, CA 94102
415-392-6257
www.nclrights.org
Offers publications, advice, counseling, and lawyer referrals to promote the rights and safety of lesbians and their families.

National Gay and Lesbian Task Force Policy Institute
1325 Massachusetts Avenue, NW, Suite 600
Washington, DC 20005
202-393-5177
www.thetaskforce.org

Political advocacy group for lesbian, gay, bisexual, and transgender individuals. Publishes organizing manual for implementing domestic partnership benefit plans and nondiscrimination policies. Provides referrals for counseling and lawyers.

Immigration

U.S. Citizenship and Immigration Services
800-375-5283
TDD: 800-767-1833
www.uscis.gov
Federal agency responsible for overseeing citizenship, asylum, and employment authorization and enforcing visa and lawful permanent resident applications and procedures.

Labor Departments

U.S. Department of Labor
200 Constitution Avenue, NW
Washington, DC 20210
866-487-2365
TTY: 877-899-5627
www.dol.gov

State Labor Departments

Note: Phone numbers are for department headquarters. Check websites for regional office locations and numbers.

Alabama
Department of Labor
Montgomery, AL
334-242-8055
www.labor.alabama.gov

Alaska
Department of Labor and Workforce
  Development
Juneau, AK
907-465-2700
www.labor.state.ak.us

Arizona
Industrial Commission
Phoenix, AZ
602-542-4661
www.azica.gov

Arkansas
Department of Labor
Little Rock, AR
501-682-4500
www.labor.arkansas.gov

California
Department of Industrial Relations
Oakland, CA
510-622-3273
www.dir.ca.gov/DLSE/dlse.html

Colorado
Department of Labor and Employment
Denver, CO
303-318-8000
www.colorado.gov/CDLE

Connecticut
Labor Department
Wethersfield, CT
860-263-6000
www.ctdol.state.ct.us

Delaware
Department of Labor
Wilmington, DE
302-761-8000
http://dol.delaware.gov

District of Columbia
Department of Employment Services
Washington, DC
202-724-7000
www.does.dc.gov

Florida
Department of Economic Opportunity
Tallahassee, FL
850-245-7105
www.floridajobs.org

Georgia
Department of Labor
Atlanta, GA
404-232-7300
http://dol.georgia.gov

Hawaii
Department of Labor and Industrial Relations
Honolulu, HI
808-586-8844
www.labor.hawaii.gov

Idaho
Department of Labor
Boise, ID
208-332-3570
www.labor.idaho.gov

Illinois
Department of Labor
Chicago, IL
312-793-2800
www.illinois.gov/idol

Indiana
Department of Labor
Indianapolis, IN
317-232-2655
www.in.gov/dol

Iowa
Division of Labor
Des Moines, IA
515-242-5870
www.iowadivisionoflabor.gov

Kansas
Department of Labor
Topeka, KS
785-296-5000
www.dol.ks.gov

Kentucky
Labor Cabinet
Frankfort, KY
502-564-3534
www.labor.ky.gov

Louisiana
Workforce Commission
Baton Rouge, LA
225-342-3111
www.ldol.state.la.us

Maine
Department of Labor
Augusta, ME
207-623-7900
www.state.me.us/labor

Maryland
Division of Labor and Industry
Baltimore, MD
410-767-2241
www.dllr.state.md.us/labor

Massachusetts
Executive Office of Labor and Workforce
    Development
Boston, MA
617-626-7122
www.mass.gov/lwd

Michigan
Department of Licensing and Regulatory
    Affairs
Lansing, MI
517-373-1820
www.michigan.gov/lara

Minnesota
Department of Labor and Industry
St. Paul, MN
651-284-5005
www.dli.mn.gov

Mississippi
Department of Employment Security
Jackson, MS
601-321-6000
www.mdes.ms.gov

Missouri
Department of Labor and Industrial Relations
Jefferson City, MO
573-751-9691
www.labor.mo.gov

Montana
Department of Labor and Industry
Helena, MT
406-444-2840
www.dli.mt.gov

Nebraska
Department of Labor
Lincoln, NE
402-471-9000
www.dol.nebraska.gov

Nevada
Office of the Labor Commissioner
Las Vegas, NV
702-486-2650
www.labor.nv.gov

New Hampshire
Department of Labor
Concord, NH
603-271-3176
www.nh.gov/labor

New Jersey
Department of Labor and Workforce
  Development
Trenton, NJ
609-659-9045
http://lwd.state.nj.us/labor

New Mexico
Department of Workforce Solutions
Albuquerque, NM
505-841-8405
www.dws.state.nm.us

New York
Department of Labor
Albany, NY
518-457-9000
www.labor.ny.gov/home

North Carolina
Department of Labor
Raleigh, NC
800-625-2267
www.nclabor.com

North Dakota
Department of Labor
Bismarck, ND
701-328-2660
www.nd.gov/labor

Ohio
Division of Industrial Compliance
Reynoldsburg, OH
614-644-2223
www.com.ohio.gov/dico

Oklahoma
Department of Labor
Oklahoma City, OK
405-521-6100
www.ok.gov/odol

Oregon
Bureau of Labor and Industries
Portland, OR
971-673-0761
www.oregon.gov/boli

Pennsylvania
Department of Labor and Industry
Harrisburg, PA
717-787-5279
www.dli.pa.gov

Rhode Island
Department of Labor and Training
Cranston, RI
401-462-8000
www.dlt.state.ri.us

South Carolina
Department of Labor, Licensing, and
 Regulation
Columbia, SC
803-896-4300
www.llr.state.sc.us/labor

South Dakota
Department of Labor and Regulation
Pierre, SD
605-773-3101
www.dlr.sd.gov

Tennessee
Department of Labor and Workforce
 Development
Nashville, TN
844-224-5818
www.tn.gov/workforce

Texas
Texas Workforce Commission
Austin, TX
512-463-2222
www.twc.state.tx.us

Utah
Labor Commission
Salt Lake City, UT
801-530-6800
www.laborcommission.utah.gov

Vermont
Department of Labor and Industry
Montpelier, VT
808-828-4000
www.labor.vermont.gov

Virginia
Department of Labor and Industry
Richmond, VA
804-371-2327
www.doli.virginia.gov

Washington
Department of Labor and Industries
Tumwater, WA
360-902-5800
www.lni.wa.gov

West Virginia
Division of Labor
Charleston, WV
304-558-7890
www.wvlabor.com

Wisconsin
Department of Workforce Development
Madison, WI
608-266-3131
www.dwd.wisconsin.gov

Wyoming
Department of Workforce Services
Cheyenne, WY
307-777-7261
www.wyomingworkforce.org

Legal Referrals

National Employment Lawyers Association
2201 Broadway, Suite 310
Oakland, CA 94612
415-296-7629
www.nela.org
National directory of employment law
attorneys.

Mediation and Arbitration

American Arbitration Association
800-778-7879
www.adr.org
National nonprofit organization offering
mediation and arbitration services through
local offices across the country. Also conducts
neutral investigations of workplace disputes.
General information about out-of-court
settlements, negotiation opportunities, rules
and procedures of mediation.

JAMS Resolution Centers
18881 Von Karman Ave, Suite 350
Irvine, CA 92612
949-224-1810
800-352-5267
www.jamsadr.com
International organization providing
mediation and arbitration services, largely
through retired judges.

Mediate.com
P.O. Box 51090
Eugene, OR 97405
541-345-1629
www.mediate.com
National database of mediators searchable by
name, location, or type of practice.

Older Workers

American Association of Retired Persons
601 E Street, NW
Washington, DC 20049
888-687-2277
Spanish: 877-342-2277
TTY: 877-434-7598
www.aarp.org
Nonprofit membership organization of
older Americans open to people age 50
or older. Wide range of publications on
retirement planning, age discrimination, and
employment-related topics, and a "National
Employer Team" listing employers seeking
mature workers. Networking and direct
services available through local chapters.

Retirement Plans and Pensions

See also listings under Older Workers.

Pension Benefit Guaranty Corporation
1200 K Street, NW
Washington, DC 20005
800-400-7242
TTY/TDD: 800-877-8339
www.pbgc.gov

Government agency established to protect pension benefits. Collects premiums from participating companies. Provides insolvent multiemployer pension plans with financial assistance to enable them to pay guaranteed benefits.

Pension Rights Center
1730 M Street, Suite 1000
Washington, DC 20036
202-296-3776
www.pensionrights.org
Nonprofit organization and service network providing pension advice and information.

Safety and Health Issues

American Psychological Association
750 First Street, NE
Washington, DC 20002
202-336-5500
800-374-2721
TDD/TTY: 202-336-6123
www.apa.org
Information on career training, stress and well-being at work, counseling and psychotherapy for work dysfunctions.

Americans for Nonsmokers' Rights
2530 San Pablo Avenue, Suite J
Berkeley, CA 94702
510-841-3032
www.no-smoke.org
Nonprofit advocacy group that campaigns for legislation to assure that nonsmokers can avoid involuntary exposure to secondhand smoke in the workplace, restaurants, public places, and on public transportation.

National Institute for Occupational Safety and Health (NIOSH)
1600 Clifton Road
Atlanta, GA 30329
800-232-4636
TTY: 888-232-6348
www.cdc.gov/niosh
Research institute offering publications on various workplace health and safety issues. Maintains database on indoor air quality, carpal tunnel, workplace homicide, and other current topics. Conducts evaluations of individual worksites. Also makes available training programs, materials, and videos.

National Safety Council
1121 Spring Lake Drive
Itasca, IL 60143
630-285-1121
800-621-7615
www.nsc.org
Conducts research and provides education and information on occupational safety; encourages policies that reduce accidental deaths, injuries, and preventable illnesses; monitors legislation and regulations affecting safety.

Occupational Safety and Health Administration
200 Constitution Avenue, NW
Washington, DC 20210
800-321-6742
TTY: 877-889-5627
www.osha.gov
Federal agency responsible for establishing and overseeing workplace health and safety standards.

Unions

American Federation of Labor and Congress of Industrial Organizations (AFL-CIO)
815 16th Street, NW
Washington, DC 20006
202-637-5000
www.aflcio.org
Voluntary federation of unions on all aspects of union employment. Provides information and assistance for union-related issues at local levels.

American Federation of State, County and Municipal Employees (AFSCME)
1625 L Street, NW
Washington, DC 20036-5687
202-429-1000
TTY: 202-659-0446
www.afscme.org
The largest union for workers in the public service, AFSCME organizes for social and economic justice in the workplace and through political action and legislative advocacy.

Coalition of Labor Union Women (CLUW)
815 16th Street, NW
Washington, DC 20006
202-508-6969
www.cluw.org
National organization with local chapters. Provides education, organizes conferences and workshops, lobbies for legislation, supports strikes and boycotts. Newsletter and written materials. Provides referrals to attorneys and legal rights groups for union workers.

National Right to Work Committee
8001 Braddock Road, Suite 500
Springfield, VA 22160
800-325-7892
www.nrtwc.org
Citizens' lobbying organization supporting right-to-work legislation and opposing compulsory unionism.

Women's Issues

Equal Rights Advocates
1170 Market Street, Suite 700
San Francisco, CA 94102
415-621-0672 (general information)
www.equalrights.org
Nonprofit public interest organization providing legal advice and counseling in both English and Spanish.

9to5, National Association of Working Women
207 E. Buffalo Street, #211
Milwaukee, WI 53202
414-274-0925
www.9to5.org
National grassroots nonprofit membership organization for working women. Provides counseling, information, and referrals for problems on the job—including family leave, pregnancy disability, termination, compensation, and sexual harassment. Publishes legal guides, fact sheets, and videos. Local chapters throughout the country.

National Partnership for Women and Families
1875 Connecticut Avenue, NW, Suite 650
Washington, DC 20009
202-986-2600
www.nationalpartnership.org
A nonprofit, nonpartisan membership organization that uses public education and advocacy to promote fairness in the workplace, quality health care, and policies that help women and men meet the dual demands of work and family.

National Women's Law Center
11 Dupont Circle, NW, Suite 800
Washington, DC 20036
202-588-5180
www.nwlc.org
Works to expand and protect women's legal rights through litigation, advocacy, and public education. Interests include child and family support, health education, employment discrimination, sexual harassment, and income security.

National Organization for Women
1100 H Street, NW, Suite 300
Washington, DC 20005
202-628-8669
TTY: 202-331-9002
www.now.org
A nonprofit advocacy organization that strives to eliminate discrimination and harassment in the workplace. NOW pursues its goals through direct mass actions including marches, rallies, pickets, counter-demonstrations, nonviolent civil disobedience, lobbying, grassroots political organizing, and litigating.

U.S. Department of Labor, Women's Bureau
200 Constitution Avenue, NW, #S-3002
Washington, DC 20210
800-827-5335
202-693-6710
www.dol.gov/wb
Monitors employment issues and promotes employment opportunities for women. Sponsors workshops, job fairs, demonstrations, and pilot projects. Offers technical assistance, conducts research, and provides publications on issues that affect working women.

Work/Life Issues

See also organizations listed under Women's Issues.

A Better Balance
40 Worth Street, 10th Floor
New York, NY 10038
212-430-5982
www.abetterbalance.org
Provides legal support and technical assistance for legislative and voter initiatives around the country aimed at obtaining guaranteed paid sick leave that workers can use for themselves and their families. Also works with state and local officials and the business community to promote flexibility in the workplace, and with local community groups to assess how work/family conflict affects low income workers.

Center for Work/Life Law
University of California
Hastings College of the Law
200 McAllister Street
San Francisco, CA 94102
415-565-4640
Hotline: 415-703-8276
www.worklifelaw.org
Works with employees, employers, attorneys, legislators, unions, journalists, and researchers, providing guidance and technical assistance to help eliminate discrimination based on family responsibilities.

New Ways to Work
555 South Main Street, #3
Sebastopol, CA 95472
707-824-4000
www.newwaystowork.org
Educational and advocacy organization devoted to promoting flexible work arrangements and in training youth for work. Serves as a clearinghouse for information, has an extensive publications list, and offers seminars and training to companies. ●

Index

A

B

Background checks
  obtaining, 127–128
  and privacy rights, 130–132
Bargaining unit of a labor union, 389,
  390–391
Benefits
  for part-time employees, 85, 323
  postemployment, 86–88, 89–101, 323–324
  regular rate of pay vs., 26
BFOQs (bona fide occupational
  qualifications), 228, 236
Birth and FMLA leave, 105
Bisexual employees, 247–248, 425–426
Blacklisting, 292, 330
Blogs and blogging, 145
Bona fide occupational qualifications
  (BFOQs), 228, 236
Bone marrow and organ donation, 111
Bonuses, payroll, 20
Breach of contract, 280, 321–322
Breach of good faith and fair dealing, 281
Breaks and meal periods, 28
Breaks for nursing mothers, 28–29

C

California
  credit discrimination laws, 132
  on English-only rules, 399–400
  Fair Employment and Housing Act, 268
  jury duty laws, 32
  on noncompete agreements, 329
  safety laws, 214
  workers' compensation claims, 354
California Supreme Court, 268
Case law, 412–413, 414

Charge of Discrimination form, EEOC, 227,
  234, 249
Child care benefits or facilities, 114
Child labor restrictions, 24
Child support, wage withholding order for,
  35, 282
Citations, reading, 414
Civic duties, time off for, 31–33
Civil Rights Act (1964), 270, 272
  See also Title VII of the Civil Rights Act
Civil rights resources, 419
Class action lawsuits, 404
Clothing and grooming codes, 148–150
COBRA (Consolidated Omnibus Budget
  Reconciliation Act), 86–88, 324
Collective bargaining agreements, 386
Colorado
  jury duty laws, 32
  medical marijuana laws, 137
"Coming and going" rule, 26
Commissioned employees
  calculating pay rate, 21, 29–30
  and overtime pay laws, 20, 21
  overview, 16, 17–18
Company policies
  on discipline procedures, 288, 289–290
  on discussion of salaries, 232
  dress and grooming codes, 149–150
  on drug testing and rehabilitation, 135
  and email or Internet use, 144–147
  English-only policies, 399–400
  as evidence, 5
  and FMLA leave, 108
  on fringe benefits, 323–324, 327
  on giving reasons for dismissals, 290–291
  on harassment, 267, 274
  and HIV/AIDS, 247

F